GLOBAL STUDIES

INDIA AND SOUTH ASIA

NINTH EDITION

Dr. James H. K. Norton

OTHER BOOKS IN THE GLOBAL STUDIES SERIES

- Africa
- China
- Europe
- Islam and the Muslim World
- Japan and the Pacific Rim
- Latin America
- The Middle East
- Russia, the Baltic and Eurasian Republics,
  and Central/Eastern Europe

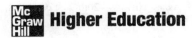 **Higher Education**

Boston   Burr Ridge, IL   Dubuque, IA   New York   San Francisco   St. Louis
Bangkok   Bogotá   Caracas   Kuala Lumpur   Lisbon   London   Madrid   Mexico City
Milan   Montreal   New Delhi   Santiago   Seoul   Singapore   Sydney   Taipei   Toronto

GLOBAL STUDIES: INDIA AND SOUTH ASIA, NINTH EDITION

Published by McGraw-Hill, a business unit of The McGraw-Hill Companies, Inc., 1221 Avenue of the Americas, New York, NY 10020.

Global Studies is published by the **Contemporary Learning Series** group within the McGraw-Hill Higher Education division.

1 2 3 4 5 6 7 8 9 0 QPD/QPD 0 9

ISBN 978-0-07-337986-9
MHID 0-07-337986-7
ISSN 1080-4153

Managing Editor: *Larry Loeppke*
Senior Managing Editor: *Faye Schilling*
Senior Developmental Editor: *Jill Peter*
Editorial Coordinator: *Mary Foust*
Editorial Assistant: *Nancy Meissner*
Production Service Assistant: *Rita Hingtgen*
Permissions Coordinator: *Shirley Lanners*
Senior Marketing Manager: *Julie Keck*
Marketing Communications Specialist: *Mary Klein*
Marketing Coordinator: *Alice Link*
Senior Project Manager: *Jane Mohr*
Design Specialist: *Tara McDermott*
Cover Graphics: *Rick D. Noel*

Compositor: Laserwords
Cover Image: The Hindu Photo Archives

Library in Congress Cataloging-in-Publication Data
Main entry under title: Global Studies: India and South Asia.
      1. India—History—20th-21st centuries. 2. India—Politics and government—1947-.
      3. Asia, Southeaster—20th-21st centuries. 4. Asia—History—20th-21st centuries.
I. Title: India and South Asia. II. Norton, James H. K., *comp.*

www.mhhe.com

INDIA AND SOUTH ASIA

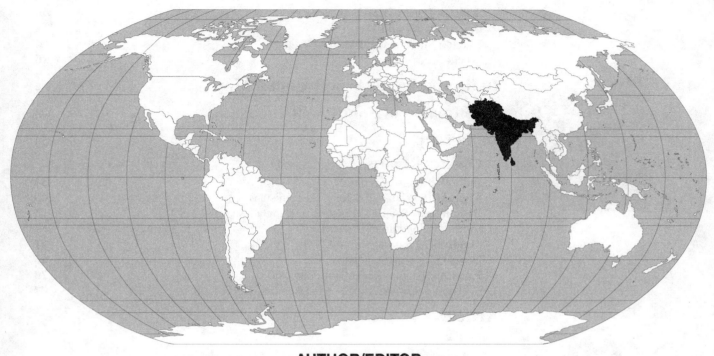

AUTHOR/EDITOR

Dr. James H. K. Norton

The author/editor of *Global Studies: India and South Asia, Ninth Edition,* received a B.S. degree from Yale University, B.A. and M.A. degrees in Sanskrit from Oxford University, and a Ph.D. in Indian philosophy from the University of Madras in India. He taught for 10 years at the College of Wooster, where he was associate professor of religion and chairman of the Department of Indian Studies. While at Wooster, Dr. Norton initiated a junior-year study program for college students in Madurai University, India, now part of the University of Wisconsin College Year in India program. He has also taught at Madurai University, Boston University, and Oberlin College. He is currently farming in Massachusetts, conducting continuing-education courses, and has served for many years on school boards and school advisory councils on Martha's Vineyard. Dr. Norton has spent five years in India, first as a Ford Foundation scholar while doing graduate work at the University of Madras. He has returned as a teacher and as a senior research fellow of the American Institute of Indian Studies. He is a member of the Association for Asian Studies. His articles on Indian philosophy, on comparisons of Eastern and Western thought, and on Martha's Vineyard local history appear in a number of books and journals.

Contents

Using *Global Studies*: India and South Asia

THE GLOBAL STUDIES SERIES

The Global Studies series was created to help readers acquire a basic knowledge and understanding of the regions and countries in the world. Each regional volume provides a foundation of information—geographic, cultural, economic, political, historical, artistic, and religious—that will allow readers to better assess the current and future problems within these countries and regions and to comprehend how events there might affect their own well-being. In short, these volumes present background information necessary to respond to the realities of our global age.

Each of the volumes in the Global Studies series is crafted under the careful direction of an author/editor—an expert in the area under study. The author/editors teach and conduct research and have traveled extensively through the regions about which they are writing.

In this *India and South Asia* edition, the author/editor has written introductory essays on the South Asia region and country reports for each of the countries included.

MAJOR FEATURES OF THE GLOBAL STUDIES SERIES

The Global Studies volumes are organized to provide concise information on the regions and countries within those areas under study. The major sections and features of the books are described here.

Regional Essays

For *Global Studies: India and South Asia,* the author/editor has written an essay, "Five Images of South Asia," focusing on the religious, cultural, sociopolitical, and economic differences and similarities of the countries and peoples in the region. A detailed map accompanies the essay.

Country Reports

Concise reports are written for each of the countries within the region under study. These reports are the heart of each Global Studies volume. *Global Studies: India and South Asia, Ninth Edition,* contains eight country reports, including India.

The country reports are composed of five standard elements. Each report contains a detailed map visually positioning the country among its neighboring states; a summary of statistical information; a current essay providing important historical, geographical, political, cultural, and economic information; a historical timeline, offering a convenient visual survey of a few key historical events; and four "graphic indicators," with summary statements about the country in terms of development, freedom, health/welfare, and achievements.

A Note on the Statistical Reports

The statistical information provided for each country has been drawn from a wide range of sources. (The most frequently referenced are listed on pages viii–ix.) Every effort has been made to provide the most current and accurate information available. However, occasionally the information cited by these sources differs to some extent; and, all too often, the most current information available for some countries is dated. Aside from these difficulties, the statistical summary of each country is generally quite complete and up to date. Care should be taken, however, in using these statistics (or, for that matter, any published statistics) in making hard comparisons among countries. We have also provided comparable statistics for the United States and Canada, which can be found on pages x and xi.

World Press Articles

Within each Global Studies volume is reprinted a number of articles carefully selected by our editorial staff and the author/editor from a broad range of international periodicals and newspapers. The articles have been chosen for currency, interest, and their differing perspectives. There are 21 articles in *Global Studies: India and South Asia, Ninth Edition.*

A brief summary of each article can be found in the table of contents.

Web Sites

An extensive annotated list of selected World Wide Web sites can be found on pages viii–ix in this edition of *Global Studies: India and South Asia.* In addition, the URL addresses for country-specific Web sites are provided on the statistics page of most countries. All of the Web site addresses were correct and operational at press time. Instructors and students alike are urged to refer to those sites often to enhance their understanding of the region and to keep up with current events.

Glossary, Bibliography, Index

At the back of each Global Studies volume, readers will find a glossary of terms and abbreviations, which provides a quick reference to the specialized vocabulary of the area under study and to the standard abbreviations used throughout the volume. Following the glossary is a bibliography, which lists general works, national histories, and current-events publications and periodicals that provide regular coverage on India and South Asia. The index at the end of the volume provides reference to the contents of the volume. Readers seeking specific information and citations should consult this standard index.

Currency and Usefulness

Global Studies: India and South Asia, like the other Global Studies volumes, is intended to provide the most current and useful information available necessary to understand the events that are shaping the cultures of the region today.

This volume is revised on a regular basis. The statistics are updated, regional essays and country reports revised, and world press articles replaced. In order to accomplish this task, we turn to our author/editor, our advisory boards, and—hopefully—to you, the users of this volume. Your comments are more than welcome. If you have an idea that you think will make the next edition more useful, an article or bit of information that will make it more current, or a general comment on its organization, content, or features that you would like to share with us, please send it in for serious consideration.

Selected World Wide Web Sites for India and South Asia

(Some websites continually change their structure and content, so the information listed here may not always be available.)

GENERAL SITES

CNN Online Page
http://www.cnn.com

This is a U.S. 24-hour video news channel. News, updated every few hours, includes text, pictures, and film. Good external links.

C-SPAN ONLINE
http://www.c-span.org

See especially C-SPAN International on the Web for International Programming Highlights and archived C-Span programs.

International Network Information Center at University of Texas
http://inic.utexas.edu

This is a gateway that has pointers to international sites, including South Asia.

Penn Library: Resources by Subject
http://www.library.upenn.edu/resources/subject/subject.html

Rich in links to information about Asian studies, this vast site includes population and demography data.

Political Science RESOURCES
http://www.psr.keele.ac.uk

On this Web site, find a dynamic gateway to sources available via European addresses. A list of country names is available.

ReliefWeb
http://www.reliefweb.int

UN's Department of Humanitarian Affairs clearinghouse for international humanitarian emergencies.

Social Science Information Gateway (SOSIG)
http://sosig.esrc.bris.ac.uk

The project of the Economic and Social Research Council (ESRC) is located here. It catalogs 22 subjects and lists developing countries' URL addresses.

Special Issues
http://specialissues.com

This unusual site is the repository of transcripts of every kind, compiled by Gary Price, from radio and television, of speeches by world government leaders, and the proceedings of groups like the United Nations, NATO, and the World Bank.

United Nations System
http://www.unsystem.org

The UN's system of organizations presents this official Web site. An alphabetical list is available that offers: UNICC—Food and Agriculture Organization.

UN Development Programme (UNDP)
http://www.undp.org

Publications and current information on world poverty, Mission Statement, UN Development Fund for Women, and more can be found here. Be sure to see Poverty Clock.

U.S. Agency for International Development (USAID)
http://www.usaid.gov

The U.S. policy toward assistance to Asian countries is available at this site.

U.S. Central Intelligence Agency Home Page
http://www.cia.gov

This site includes publications of the CIA, such as the World Factbook, Factbook on Intelligence, Handbook of International Economic Statistics, and CIA Maps.

U.S. Department of State Home Page
http://www.state.gov/index.html

Organized alphabetically, this Web site presents: Country Reports, Human Rights, International Organizations, etc.

World Bank Group
http://www.worldbank.org

News (i.e., press releases, summary of new projects, speeches), publications, topics in development, countries and regions are available here. Links to other financial organizations are possible.

World Health Organization (WHO)
http://www.who.ch

Maintained by WHO's headquarters in Geneva, Switzerland, this comprehensive site includes a search engine.

World Trade Organization (WTO)
http://www.wto.org

Topics include a foundation of world trade systems, data on textiles, intellectual property rights, legal frameworks, trade and environmental policies, recent agreements, and others data.

The Economist
http://www.economist.com/asia

The Economist is a weekly international news and business publication offering clear reporting, commentary and analysis on world politics, business, finance, science and technology.

Foreign Affairs
http://www.foreignaffairs.org/asia

Founded in 1921, the Council on Foreign Relations is a non-profit and nonpartisan membership organization dedicated to improving the understanding of U.S. foreign policy and international affairs through the free exchange of ideas.

Human Rights Watch
http://www.hrw.org/asia

Human Rights Watch is dedicated to protecting the human rights of people around the world.

Terrorism Research Center
http://www.terrorism.com

Founded in 1996, the Terrorism Research Center, Inc. (TRC) is an independent institute dedicated to the research of terrorism, information warfare and security, critical infrastructure protection, homeland security, and other issues of low-intensity political violence and gray-area phenomena.

South Asia Terrorism Portal
http://www.satp.org

South Asia Intelligence Review (SAIR) brings regular assessments, data and news briefs on terrorism, insurgencies and sub-conventional warfare, counterterrorism responses and policies, as well as on related economic, political, and social issues, in the South Asian region.

Wikipedia
http://www.wikipedia.org/(Country)

Wikipedia is a multilingual, web-based, free content encyclopedia project. Wikipedia is written collaboratively by volunteers from all around the world.

World Newspapers
http://www.world-newspapers/(Country)

A collection of world newspapers, magazines, and news sites sorted by country and region.

GENERAL INDIA AND SOUTH ASIA SITES

Asia Web Watch
http://www.ciolek.com/Asia-Web-Watch/main-page.html

Here is a register of statistical data that can be accessed alphabetically. Data includes Asian Online Materials Statistics and Appendices about Asian cyberspace.

Asian Arts
http://asianart.com

This online journal for the study and exhibition of the arts of Asia includes exhibitions, articles, and galleries.

Asian Studies WWW Virtual Library

http://coombs.anu.edu.au/WWWVL-AsianStudies.html

Australia National University maintains these sites, which link to many other Web sources, available at each country's location.

Asia-Yahoo

http://www.yahoo.com/Regional/Regions/Asia/

Access a specialized Yahoo search site that permits key-word searches on Asian events, countries, and topics from here.

History of the Indian Sub-Continent

http://www.stockton.edu/~gilmorew/consorti/1aindia.htm

As part of Stockton's World Wide Web Global History Research Institute, the history of the Indian subcontinent has been arranged chronologically at this site. This excellent resource contains maps, pictures, short writings, and scholarly writings.

South Asia Resources

http://www.lib.berkeley.edu/SSEAL/SouthAsia/

From this University of Berkeley Library site there is quick access to online resources in Asian studies as well as to South Asian specialists and other special features.

See individual country report pages for additional Web sites.

The United States

GEOGRAPHY

Area in Square Miles (Kilometers): 3,793,079 (9,826,630) about ½ the size of Russia
Capital (Population): Washington, D.C. (581,530, 2006 est.)
Environmental Concerns: air and water pollution; limited natural fresh water resources; desertification; loss of habitat; waste disposal; acid rain
Geographical Features: vast central plain, mountains in west, hills and low mountains in east; rugged mountains and broad river valleys in Alaska; rugged, volcanic topography in Hawaii
Climate: mostly temperate, but ranging from tropical to arctic

PEOPLE
Population
Total: 303,824,640 (July, 2008 est.)
Annual Growth Rate: 0.883% (2008 est.)
Rural/Urban Population Ratio: 19/81 (WHO 2006)
Major Languages: 82.1% English; 10.7% Spanish; 7.1% other (2000 census)
Ethnic Makeup: 81.7% white; 12.9% black; 4.2% Asian; 1% Amerindian (2003 est.)
Religions: 51.3% Protestant; 23.9% Roman Catholic; 16.1% none or unaffiliated; 8.8% others (2007 est.)

Health
Life Expectancy at Birth: 75.29 years (male); 81.13 years (female) (2008 est.)
Infant Mortality: 6.3/1000 live births (2008 est.)
Per Capita total expenditure on Health: $6,347 (WHO 2005)
HIV/AIDS Rate in Adults: 0.6% (WHO 2005 est.)

Education
Adult Literacy Rate: 99% (2003 est.)
Compulsory (Ages): 7–16; free

COMMUNICATION
Telephones: 172,000,000 (2006)
Cell Phones: 255,000,000 (2007)
Internet Users: 223,000,000 (2008)

TRANSPORTATION
Highways in Miles (Kilometers): (6,430,366 km) (2005)
Railroads in Miles (Kilometers): (226,612 km) (2005)
Usable Airfields: 14,947 (2007)

GOVERNMENT
Type: federal republic
Independence Date: July 4, 1776
Head of State/Government: Barack Obama
Political Parties: Democratic Party; Republican Party; others of relatively minor political significance
Suffrage: 18 years of age; universal

MILITARY
Military Expenditures (% of GDP): $583.283 billion (FY 2008); 4.06% (FY 2006) (SIPRI)
Current Disputes: Wars in Afghanistan and Iraq

ECONOMY
Per Capita Income/GDP: $45,800/$13.84 trillion (2007 est.)
GDP Growth Rate: 2.2% (2007 est.)
Inflation Rate: 2.9% (2007 est.)
Unemployment Rate: 4.6% (2007 est.)
Population Below Poverty Line: 12% (2004 est.)
Natural Resources: many minerals and metals; petroleum; natural gas; timber; arable land.
Agriculture: wheat, corn, other grains, fruits, vegetables, cotton; beef, pork, poultry, dairy products; fish; forest products
Industry: leading industrial power in the world, highly diversified and technologically advanced; petroleum, steel, motor vehicles, aerospace, telecommunications, chemicals, electronics, food processing, consumer goods, lumber, mining
Exports: $1,149 trillion (2007 est.) (primary partners Canada, Mexico, China, Japan, UK)
Imports: $1,965 trillion (2007 est.) (primary partners China, Canada, Mexico, Japan, Germany) (2006)
Human Development Index (ranking): 12 (UNDP 2008)

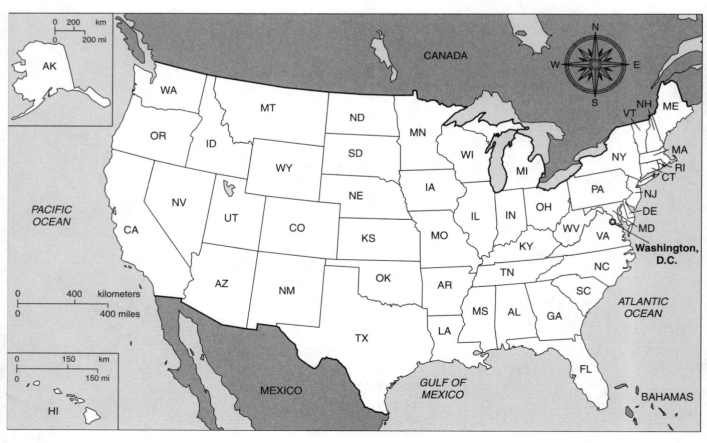

Canada

GEOGRAPHY
Area in Square Miles (Kilometers): 3,854,083 (9,984,670)
Capital (Population): Ottawa (812,129) (2006)
Environmental Concerns: air and water pollution; acid rain; industrial damage to agricultural and forest productivity
Geographical Features: permafrost in the north; mostly plains with mountains in west and lowlands in southeast
Climate: varies from temperate in south to subarctic and arctic in north

PEOPLE
Population
Total: 33,212,696 (July, 2008 est.)
Annual Growth Rate: 0.83% (2008 est.)
Rural/Urban Population Ratio: 20/80 (WHO 2006)
Major Languages: English (Official) 59.3%; French (Official) 23.2%; Other 17.5%
Ethnic Makeup: British Isles origin 28%, French origin 23%, other European 15%, Amerindian 2%, other, mostly Asian, African, Arab 6%, mixed background 26%
Religions: 42.6% Roman Catholic; 23.3% Protestant; 4.4% Other Christian; 1.9% Muslim; 11.8% other; 16% none (2001 Census)

Health
Life Expectancy at Birth: 78.65 years (male); 83.81 (female). (2008 est.)

Infant Mortality: 5.08/1000 live births (2008 est.)
Per Capita expenditure on Health: $3,452 (WHO 2005)
HIV/AIDS Rate in Adults: 0.3% (WHO 2005 est.)

Education
Adult Literacy Rate: 99%
Compulsory (Ages): primary school

COMMUNICATION
Telephones: 21,000,000 main lines (2006)
Cell Phones: 18,749,000 (2006)
Internet Users: 22 million (2005)

TRANSPORTATION
Highways in Miles (Kilometers): (1,042,300 km.)
Railroads in Miles (Kilometers): (48,467 km.)
Usable Airfields: 1,343 (2007)

GOVERNMENT
Type: constitutional monarchy that is also a parliamentary democracy and a federation
Independence Date: July 1, 1867
Head of State/Government: Queen Elizabeth II/Prime Minister Stephen Harper
Political Parties: Conservative Party of Canada, Liberal Party, Green Party, New Democratic Party, Bloc Quebecois.
Suffrage: universal at 18

MILITARY
Military Expenditures (% of GDP): $18,695 million (2008); (1.2%) (2006) (SIPRI)

Current Disputes: with NATO forces in Afghanistan

ECONOMY
Currency (US equivalent): 1.0724 Canadian dollars to $1 US (2007)
Per Capita Income/GDP: $38,400 (2007 est.)/$1.266 trillion (2007 est.)
GDP Growth Rate: 2.7%
Inflation Rate: 2.1% (2007 est.)
Unemployment Rate: 6% (2007 est.)
Population Below Poverty Line: 10.8% (2005)
Labor Force by Occupation: 75% Services, 13% Manufacturing, 6% Construction, 2% Agriculture, 2% other (2006)
Natural Resources: petroleum; natural gas, fish; minerals; cement; forestry products; wildlife; hydropower
Agriculture: wheat, barley, oilseed, tobacco, fruits, vegetables; dairy products; forest products; fish
Industry: transportation equipment, chemicals, processed and unprocessed minerals, food products, wood and paper products, fish products, petroleum and natural gas
Exports: $433.1 billion f.o.b. (2007 est.) (primary partners United States, UK, China) (2006)
Imports: $386.9 billion f.o.b. (2007 est.) (primary partners United States, China, Mexico) (2006)
Human Development Index (ranking): 4 (UNDP 2008)

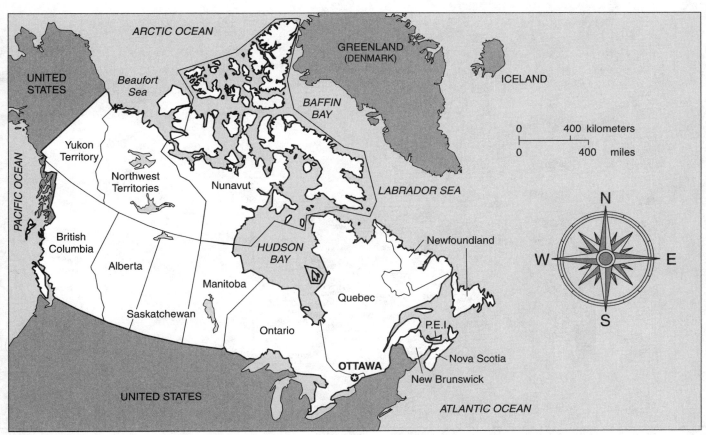

GLOBAL ● STUDIES

This map is provided to give you a graphic picture of where the countries of the world are located, the relationship they have with their region and neighbors, and their positions relative to major trade and power blocs. We have focused on certain areas to illustrate these crowded regions more clearly. The India and South Asia region is shaded for emphasis.

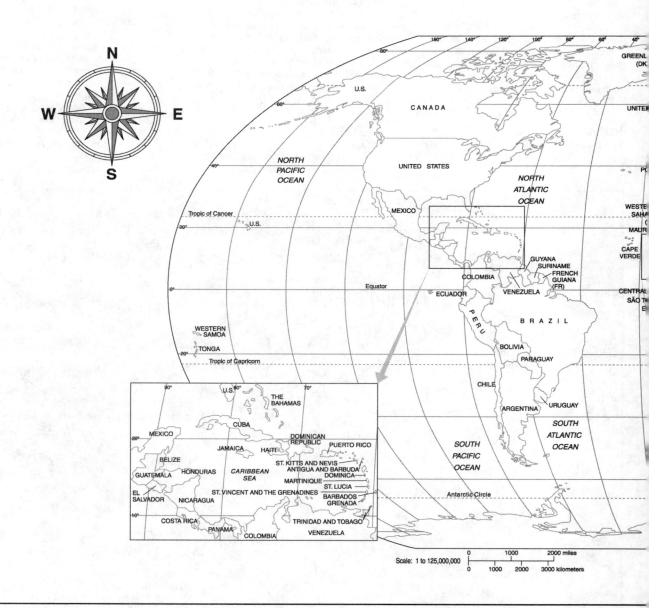

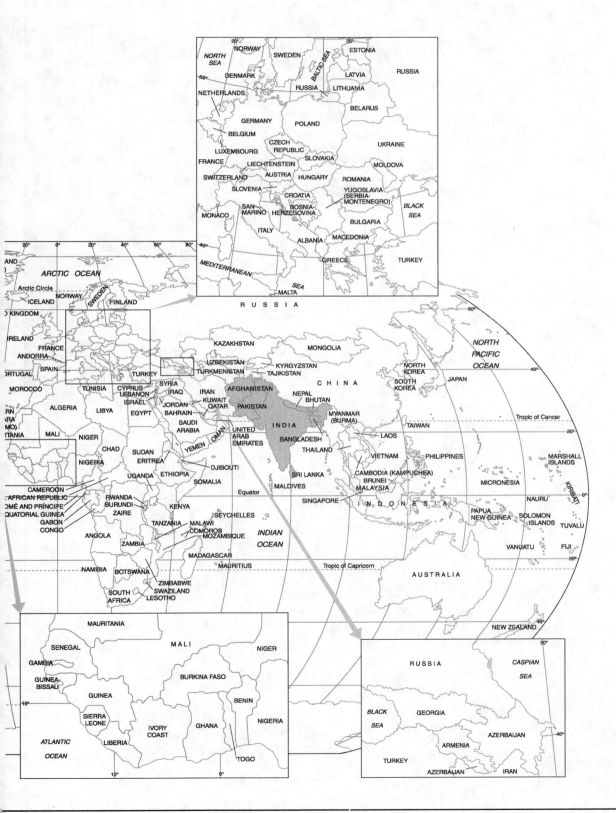

India and South Asia

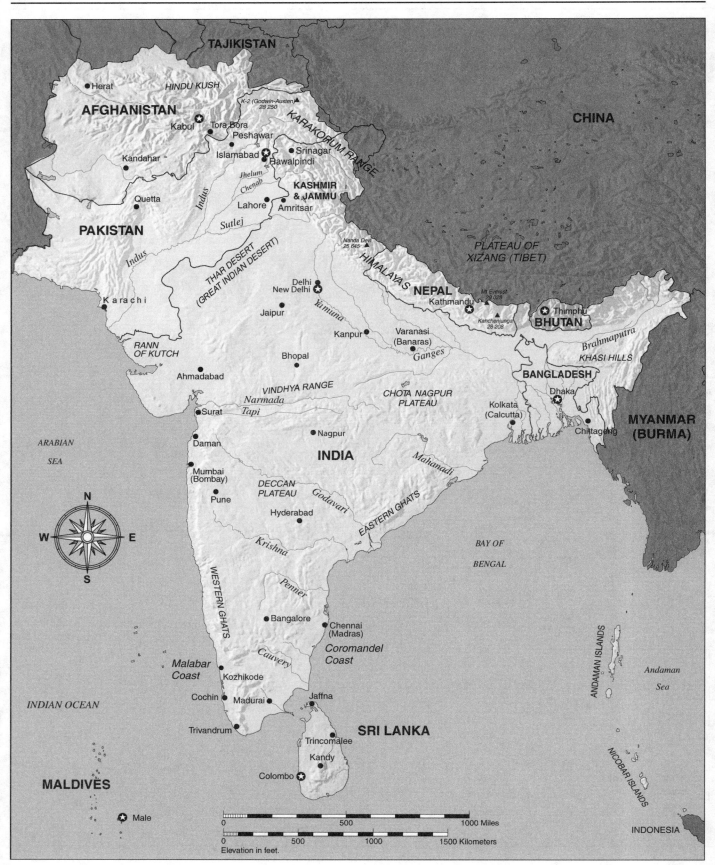

Five Images of South Asia

OUT OF MANY VIEWS, A PORTRAIT

We begin with five images to portray the uniqueness of South Asia. They are not definitive. Every assertion about the subcontinent, it is said, is a contradiction. Rather, they intend to create illuminating foci toward a picture of this immensely varied, fascinating, and increasingly important part of our world.

IMAGE I: SOUTH ASIA, A DISTINCT LAND AND AN ANCIENT CIVILIZATION

A. K. Ramanujan used to tell the story of a Mongolian emperor who had a certain species of nightingale brought to him from Kashmir because he had heard that this bird sang the most beautiful song in the world. But when the bird arrived, it did not sing. It was explained to the enraged conqueror that it sang only when perched on the branch of a chinar tree, and that the chinar tree grows only on the hillsides of Kashmir. Ramanujan concluded this story of what the conqueror needed to do to get his captured nightingale to sing with these words of St.-John Perse:

We know the story of that Mongolian conqueror, taker of a bird in its nest, and of the nest in its tree, who brought back with the bird and nest and song the whole natal tree itself, torn from its place with its multitude of roots, its ball of earth and its border of soil, a remnant of home territory evoking a field, a province, a country, and an empire.

—St.-John Perse, *Birds*
(cited in A. K. Ramanujan, *Poems of Love and War*)

A DISTINCT LAND

South Asia is clearly set apart from the rest of Asia. Geologically speaking, it is a recent addition to the continent. Initially on a separate techtonic plate attached to the east coast of Africa, it broke away about 100 million years ago and drifted slowly east and north across the Indian Ocean. Seventy-two million years later it collided into the southern edge of the Asian continent.

The immense power of this impact pushed the Tibetan plateau more than 3 miles into the air and created a high ridge of snow-clad mountains. The Himalayan range, the highest in the world, is still rising at a rate of about 10 inches per century as a result of that massive collision.

The India tectonic plate is still sliding, pushing down the Burma plate to the east. A sudden springing free of the western edge of the Burma plate caused the devastating earthquake and tsunami that brought such wide-spread death and havoc to Indonesia and the South Asian coastlands on December 26, 2004.

The Himalayas set the subcontinent apart from the rest of Asia to the north. The waters of the Arabian Sea, the Bay of Bengal, and the Indian Ocean enclose its coastal shores to the south. The westerly winds crossing these vast ocean waters and rising over the mountains produce the annual monsoons, seasonal torrents of rain and snow upon which the peoples of South Asia depend for their livelihood.

The subcontinent is divided into four distinct regions by topography and climate. To the north are the frigid south slopes of the Himalayas. All of Bhutan, most of Afghanistan and Nepal, and smaller portions of India and Pakistan fall in this region.

Three wide, alluvial river valleys form the second great plains region across the north-central portion of the subcontinent. The Indus, the Jumna-Ganges, and the Brahmaputra all begin within 100 miles of each other in the Himalayas, but flow in different directions. The Indus flows to the west through Ladakh and Pakistan to the Arabian Sea. The Jumna and Ganges Rivers flow to the south, where they join to flow east across the great northern plain of India. The Brahmaputra flows to the east from its Himalayan source, then south into Bangladesh. There it joins the Ganges and Maghma Rivers to flow through hundreds of tributaries into the Bay of Bengal.

These river systems provide the temperate north-central plains region with a steady, though uneven, flow of melting snow. This region is widely irrigated to nourish the most productive agricultural lands of the subcontinent.

To the south of the northern plains is the highlands region of peninsular India. It rises to a wide plateau, called the Deccan, bordered to the east and west by mountains smaller, but older, than the Himalayas. The central portion of Sri Lanka also rises to highlands, which, together with the Deccan, form the third geographical region of the subcontinent. Because these highlands are not high enough to be snow-covered, farmers in this region are entirely dependent upon the seasonal monsoons for sufficient water to cultivate the land.

From these highlands the land slopes down into the fourth region, the coastal plains and tropical beaches of India, Pakistan, Bangladesh, Sri Lanka, and Maldives. Most of South Asia's largest cities, which developed as trading posts during the seventeenth century and are now great centers of commerce, are in this coastal region.

These four distinct regions, which also include desert and rain forest, contain as wide a range of topography and climate as exists anywhere in the world.

AN ANCIENT CIVILIZATION

Maritime Commerce

The Harappan city culture, the world's earliest known urban civilization, flourished in the Indus River valley, in the northwestern portion of the subcontinent, from 3000 to 1500 B.C. Excavations of their archeological sites and seals reveal that the Harappans produced enough surplus, primarily in cotton and grains, to carry on trade well beyond their own settlements. This commercial activity extended into the developing

What He Said

As a little white snake
with lovely stripes on its young body
troubles the jungle elephant

this slip of a girl
her teeth like sprouts of new rice
her wrists stacked with bangles
troubles me.

Catti Natanar, *Kur* 119
(Translated by A. K. Ramanujan)

Courtesy of James Norton

This small statue of a dancing girl was caste in bronze over 4000 years ago in Mohenjo Daro, the ancient city of the Harappan Civilization in the Indus River Valley. Lost in the sands that buried that city so long ago, her image was captured 2000 years ago by a South Indian poet at the other end of the subcontinent, some 2000 miles away, in this love poem found in the classical Tamil Sangam anthology called the Kuruntokai. Now recovered in the twentieth century from the excavations of the ancient city and in the translations of the classical Sangam poetry, we, too, are tantalized by this tiny, yet enduring image of India.

civilizations in the Fertile Crescent, Africa and Europe to the west, and Southeast Asia and China to the east. It later brought peacocks from the subcontinent to embellish the throne of King Solomon in ancient Israel. It also transported Buddhism to become a major religious faith in East Asia and the rest of the world. And during the Renaissance, it introduced the number zero to change the calculations of mathematics in the Middle East and across Europe.

South Asia remained strategically at the center of commerce through the era of silk trade, to the fiercely competitive activity of European trading companies in the seventeenth and eighteenth centuries, and into the universal scope of information technology in the present day.

Because of the extent and intensity of this trade, it is difficult to trace the origin of many of the concepts and practices which came the other way—brought from other parts of the world to become part of South Asian daily life. We do not know, for example, the origin of the Harappan city builders, whose layout of streets and water use reveal a clear understanding of urban planning. We have no earlier instances of city dwelling to learn how or where these skills were developed. The practice of spiritual discipline called yoga is also of unknown origin, as is the Dravidian culture of south India. Both are old enough to have developed within the Harappan city culture. Attempts have been made to establish links between them. But they could have come from other sources which have been lost, and of which they are the only trace.

Also difficult to unravel is the persistence of so many indigenous cultural threads that have continued to evolve into a wide variety of patterns. So much has been added and nothing ever appears to be thrown away.

Early agrarians on the subcontinent used a large slab and rolling stone, called a saddle-quern, over 6,000 years ago to grind grain into flour. This implement was made obsolete long ago by grinding mills. But it is still used in village kitchens to pulverize condiments to season food and to crush peanuts into peanut butter.

Old practices, many times intermingled with newer things, are still recognizable as significant elements in the heritage of the peoples of South Asia. In the western world of planned obsolescence, such tenacity is hard to imagine. Geeta Mehta, in *Snakes and Ladders,* describes this contrast in a slightly different way: Whereas westerners struggle to recover their past, the problem for the people of India is to discover their present.

The Aryan Migration

In contrast to the more elusive impact of maritime commerce on South Asia, migrations of peoples from other parts of the world are a clearer source of new life and perspective in South Asia. They have come, for the most part, overland, across the Central Asian trade routes between China and the Middle East, down into the northwestern approach to the north-central plains region of the subcontinent.

The Aryan people are the earliest recorded migrants of major impact. Around 1500 B.C., this tribal, martial, and pastoral people from Central Asia drove their horse-drawn chariots and herds of cows into the subcontinent, destroying what remained of the Harappan cities and irrigation channels in their path.

They brought with them an Indo-European language which later evolved into Sanskrit, the classical language of ancient India, and the many contemporary languages that are spoken throughout the northern portion of the subcontinent and on the islands of Sri Lanka and Maldives. They also brought collections of religious songs, which formed the basis of a tenth century B.C. anthology of 1,028 poems called the Rg-Veda, the oldest surviving religious literature in the world. The Veda is still considered *sruti*—that is, inspired; literally, "heard by ancient seers"—the most sacred of all Hindu religious texts. And the Aryans either brought or soon developed a mythic understanding of the world as a sacred reality. This perspective blossomed as Vedic culture during the time of their expansion and settlement across the northern plains of the subcontinent.

During the era of the Aryan settlement, Brahmin priests developed, celebrated, and interpreted an elaborate scheme of sacrifices as expressive of the total sanctity of the world in which they lived. They instituted daily rituals to assure long life, progeny, and prosperity, ceremonies to celebrate the consecration of their leaders and assure them of victory in battle, and disciplines to enhance their sacred powers. They also asserted a dominant role in restructuring Aryan society around their religious activity. One of the later Vedic hymns celebrates the creation of the universe through a cosmic sacrificial offering of primordial man. It sets forward the earliest description of the *varna,* or classical, model of the hierarchical caste system, which divided mankind into four groups. And it placed the priesthood at the top:

> When they divided the Man [in the cosmic sacrifice], into how many parts did they apportion him? What do they call his mouth, his two arms and thighs and feet?
> His mouth became the Brahmin; his arms were made into the Warrior, his thighs the People, and from his feet the Servants were born.
> —Rg-Veda 10.90,11-1 (O'Flaherty translation)

Next to the Brahmins in order of preference on this scale are the Kshatriya, the warriors, or rulers by might. Then came the Vaisya, citizens, with landholding or commercial status. And at the bottom were the Sudra, laborers, and craftspeople.

People were grouped on this scale according to the inherited occupation of their extended family, community, or tribe. The ranking was based on a combination of the ritually purifying-polluting status in a sacrifice of a group's traditional occupation, as determined by the priesthood, and the ability of that social group to maintain social order. Maintaining social order was everyone's responsibility, but it held a specific and elevating prerogative for the priests because they had unique recourse to sacred power, *brahman,* which emanated from their performance of sacrificial rites. This scale clearly envisioned a Brahmin-dominated society.

Subsequent periods in South Asian history and literature do not show general acceptance of this dominant role for the priesthood. In the period between 500 B.C. to A.D. 200, the Sanskrit epics, the Mahabharata and the Ramayana, and early Buddhist literature, give more prominence to the warrior, or princely community, to which the heroes of the epics and the Buddha belonged. Social and world order was not based on the rite of sacrifice, nor was it maintained by the Brahmin priests. It was based, rather, upon princes' strict adherence to their chivalrous obligations, called Dharma.

Rama, the hero of the Ramayana, is portrayed as a prince who is severely righteous in order to assure the peace and well-being

Courtesy of James Norton

The east ornamental gateway (gopuram) of the temple of Meenakshi at the center of the city of Madurai in south India. Meenakshi is an ancient, primordial mother goddess, benefactor and protector of the city, who became incorporated into the Shaivite tradition by being married to Shiva. Their wedding is performed by Lord Vishnu, in the annual Chitirai Festival.

of the people over whom he is called to govern. In that same tradition, Siddharta Gautama, the prince who became the Buddha, the "Enlightened One," taught to his religious community an eight-fold path of righteousness, which he called *dhamma,* the "Way." Heinrich Zimmer, in *Philosophies of India,* describes this path as a "spiritual physician's program of psycho-dietetics" to lead them to realize their Buddha nature and, ultimately, attain the transcendence of *nirvana.*

The high point of Buddhist expansion came upon the conversion of the Mauryan emperor Asoka to the Buddha's Way in the third century B.C. In the eighth year of his reign, Asoka was so deeply moved by the devastation caused by warfare in his defeat of a neighboring kingdom, he decided to reject the use of military force to add to his kingdom. He would rule his realm rather by moral force. His new policy, which he proclaimed on a series of pillars erected throughout his kingdom, was to shun aggression and to seek "safety, control, justice and happiness for all beings." He thus gave a wide legitimacy across the span of his empire in the northern plains region to the Buddhist *dhamma,* upon which his policy was based.

Also during his reign, Asoka sent his son, Mahinda, to bring the teachings of the Buddha to Sri Lanka. Mahinda's arrival in 246 B.C. marks the beginning of the Theravada Buddhist tradition on that island.

Brahmin religious authority continued to spread through the northern plains and peninsular regions of South Asia. But its full cultural impact was not realized until the Gupta imperial dynasty in the fourth century A.D. Sanskrit, the sacred language of the priesthood, had by then become accepted as appropriate for the royal court and all of the intellectual and artistic endeavors that the court supported. The influence of other religious communities, especially Jains and Buddhists, led the Brahmins to become vegetarian in their diet. And a great surge of popular religious lore, long practiced but unrecognized in courtly circles, infused courtly life with new perspectives, enthusiasm, and theistic fervor. The austere righteousness and the intricate, sacrificial purity of the earlier eras were augmented by a sense of divine playfulness spun out in recitations of exemplary cosmic exploits of unnumbered gods and goddesses, of heroes and heroines from a mythic past.

The Gupta Era, from A.D. 300 to 650, was a time of great creative activity, drawing upon and affirming enhanced Sanskritized models devised by the Brahmin priesthood. The poetic works of Kalidasa, the philosophical writings of Shankara, and the artistic creations found at Ajanta, Ellora, and Elephanta all portray the imaginative insight, excitement, and refinement achieved in that eclectic, yet highly disciplined and politically stable, era.

In the centuries following the Gupta era, the Brahmin community gained economic dominance in addition to their intellectual and religious authority. In reward for the Brahmins' courtly and religious services, they received land grants—even entire villages—as gifts from Hindu monarchs. Their increasing prominence in all of these aspects of courtly life established a pattern for social change in those regions of the subcontinent where Hindus predominated. Today, to achieve higher status in the hierarchical caste structure, other communities emulate the patterns of behavior practiced by high-caste Brahmins, a process called Sanskritization.

This label indicates how the pastoral religious traditions of the ancient Aryan cow herders in the central portion of the subcontinent have developed and gained stature and authority during the many centuries since the early Vedic Age.

The Moghul Migration

The second migration to have a major impact on the peoples of South Asia came 3,500 years later, and reveals a different pattern of acceptance. This migration was of militant Turks from Persia, called the Moghuls, who were forced to move into South Asia by the Mongols' triumphant marches across Central Asia.

Babur was the first, when he established a tenuous foothold in 1504 with the capture of the city of Kabul, in what is now Afghanistan. Competition for control of the north-central plains was fierce; and not until the reign of his grandson, Akbar (1556–1605), did Moghul rule begin to establish firm imperial control in that commanding region of the subcontinent.

During his reign, Akbar established an extremely effective administrative network to maintain authority over the realms he conquered. He also maintained a luxurious court, which supported an extensive creativity in art, music, architecture, and literature. Akbar's rule was a magnificent time, driven by his own desire to absorb the best of the wealth of traditions—Persian, Indian, and even European—that he welcomed into his domain.

The fruits of Akbar's attempts to achieve cultural synthesis remain in the arts. The greatest triumph is architectural: the Taj Mahal. Shah Jahan, Akbar's grandson, built this exquisitely beautiful mausoleum in Agra, in memory of his beloved wife, Mumtaz Mahal, who died in 1631. Miniature painting and Hindustani music continue to reveal the integration of art forms introduced under Akbar's imperial patronage. And remnants of his administrative structure adopted by the British colonial government are also evident in village life today.

The Moghuls were not the first Muslims to enter South Asia. Arab traders plying the coastal ports had introduced the new Islamic faith as early as the eighth century. They were followed by itinerant Sufi teachers, who settled in villages throughout the subcontinent. Their commitment to a religious life drew respect and veneration from a number of indigenous peoples receptive to spiritual insight and leadership. The more mystical quality of the faith of these masters converted large numbers to Islam, mostly in the northwest corner of the region, the Punjab, and the northeast, Bengal—areas where Buddhists had previously been the most numerous.

Further conversions took place during the militant rule of the Sultans, who dominated portions of the Gangetic plain for three centuries prior to the arrival of the Moghuls. The mosque, the daily calls to prayer, Muslim festivals, and Islamic law became an authentic part of the social fabric of South Asian life. They were accepted, even though these Muslims were a small religious minority in the central regions of the subcontinent.

The imperial stature, administrative acumen, and grandeur of Moghul rule gave immense institutional status to Islam as a distinct religious faith and political legitimacy to an extensive Muslim community. Even today, Pakistan's aspiration to identify the nation as a modern Islamic Republic builds upon this heritage of that Moghul imperial presence.

But Moghul domination in the political realm did not lead to mass conversions among the much larger Hindu population who resided in the central and southern portions of their empire. Akbar tried to synthesize his refined, imperial Islamic faith within a common South Asian culture. His hope was that all his subjects might share in a single, universalist religion, which he called "Divine Faith," Din-i-Ilahi. Inspired Hindu leaders like Kabir also sought a more inclusive religious perspective among their followers.

Because of the structural integrity and diversity of the many religious communities that fell under the inclusive umbrella of Hinduism, their attempts to unify Islam and Hinduism were not successful. Under British colonial rule during the nineteenth century, the separate religious identities of Hindus and Muslims were affirmed. Their difference as religions became the basis for the division of Bengal in 1905, and the creation of Pakistan separate from India with the departure of the British Raj in 1947.

Religious identity has been at the heart of antagonism and warfare between Pakistan and India since their independence. It is the source of communal riots and terrorism throughout the subcontinent to this day.

The Aryan and Moghul migrations reveal two very different experiences of incorporating foreign peoples into the social fabric of the subcontinent during the long course of its history. But they also identify a single pattern of cultural integration. The early Aryan culture, through continuing interaction and adaptation over a long period of time, came to dominate the social realm—not by political force but by intellectual and religious authority, which set the norms that define the culture. One of those norms is to maintain the integrity of differing linguistic, religious, and ethnic groups who live in the subcontinent by isolating them as discrete cultural units within an abstract, hierarchical framework called the caste system.

The Moghul migration reveals that even extensive political domination, both military and administrative, is not sufficient to create or coerce cultural assimilation in a social environment that accepts cultural pluralism as normal.

Both of these migrations contributed significantly to the development of South Asian civilization. They also demonstrate that the social diversity of language, religion, ethnic community, and social status is deeply rooted in South Asia. As celebrated in the creation hymn (10.90) in the Rg-Veda, social distinctions are a part of cosmic order, and not easily homogenized.

The British Raj

The British colonial Empire brought another significant impact on the evolution of the distinct culture of South Asia. It was not a migration; and, unlike the Moghul experience, it had little impact on the creative arts on the subcontinent. The British Raj was primarily political, imposing colonial rule over the subcontinent from the mid-nineteenth century until the 1940s. Its impact lies largely in the introduction of democracy, industrial development, and technology.

British presence on the subcontinent began in the early 1600s, when the East India Company, with head offices in London, England, established trading centers, first in Indonesia, and then along the coast of India. In these activities, the British entrepreneurs were following a pattern of maritime commerce in this region that goes back to the Harappan cities in the third millennium B.C., during the earliest days of South Asia civilization.

This British commercial interest, which became dominant in South Asia during the eighteenth century, had no intention of establishing any political authority in the subcontinent. The British were there primarily for economic advantage, spending much of their time and effort with local authorities trying to curry favor and exclusive licenses for trade. But as they became more entangled with these authorities, especially as they struggled to diminish competing European interests in the region, they began to bring the peoples of the subcontinent increasingly under their own political control.

In the early 1800s, their greater political involvement stimulated a concern to bring social reform to the subcontinent as well. The character of their reform was most strikingly expressed in a famous "Minute on Education," written by an East India Company Supreme Council member, Thomas Macauly, in 1835.

Macauly urged that the British administrators create a special class of South Asian people who would be "Indian in blood and color, but English in taste, in opinions, in morals, and in intellect." These clerks of the company would be groomed to bring

Royalty-Free/CORBIS (DAS0100)

The greatest period of Muslim influence in South Asia began in the sixteenth century, when the Moghuls dominated the north-central plains. This period was a time of grandeur and elegance. The Taj Mahal is one of the most famous monuments in the world.

the new ideas of individualism, technology, democracy, and nationalism, which were then evolving in Europe and America, to usher South Asia into the modern world.

This energizing—but ethnocentric—reform movement received a resounding jolt in British India in 1857, when an isolated British Indian Army unit rebelled. Eighty-five soldiers were jailed for refusing to use ammunition greased with animal fat. Initially it was a minor incident. But among other things, it revealed a British insensitivity to Hindu religious attitudes toward the use of beef fat (for Hindus, the cow is sacred) and Muslim religious attitudes toward pork (that it is polluting). This minor rebellion became the stimulus for a popular uprising across the entire north-central region of the subcontinent. People took it as an opportunity to express a shared and growing sense of dissatisfaction with the British domination of their land. It grew into the "Great Mutiny" of 1857.

The spontaneity of this revolt contributed to its lack of organization and direction. It was soon subdued by British military might. But its widespread appeal revealed that, for all of the enthusiasm and good will that the British rulers felt toward their South Asian subjects, their intentions—which appeared appropriate in their Western context—were not going to be readily

World Bank 427-IN-12

The crush of peoples and cultures poses significant challenges to democracy in South Asia. Here, afternoon traffic builds near the India Exchange in Calcutta, India.

accepted. The cultural context of South Asia was too substantial, too complex, and too different to be easily reformed.

The reform movement of the early nineteenth century gave way to a more blatant colonial domination of the subcontinent during the second half-century. In 1858, the British Crown assumed direct control of British India. Queen Victoria became the first to bear the title "Empress of India."

The impact of the British Raj is still evident in the setting of the dividing lines that established the boundaries between the nations in Bhutan and Nepal with Tibet by a line drawn along the peaks of the Himalayan mountains—the McMahon Line. British authorities also secured the other borders of these two countries, which were determined before British rule by Gurkha and Tibetan conquests. The Raj used the existing natural and political realities to assert its own governing authority within them.

By contrast, the setting of the borders of Afghanistan did not appear to have recognized indigenous factors. The Durand Line between Afghanistan and Pakistan was first designated by Sir Mortimer Durand, the foreign secretary of the British Indian government in a treaty with Abdur Rahman Khan, the Emir of Kabul, in 1893, to recognize the limit of British administrative control after two unsuccessful Afghan wars. It was further established by a treaty between Czarist Russia and Great Britain in 1907, in response to British colonial interests to contain any Russian aspirations to gain access to the Arabian Sea. As a consequence, Pashto-speaking people, called Pathans, in the northwest corner of the subcontinent were divided.

In 1979, at the time of the Soviet invasion of Afghanistan, about 6 million—more than a third of the total population of

that country—lived on the Afghan side. Another 16 million lived on the other side of the border, constituting the dominant population in the Northwest Frontier Province of Pakistan. A total today of about 40 million people, their separation as dominant minorities between two nationalities remains a significant contention in South Asian politics.

The border determination of greatest impact was the decision by the Raj in 1947 not only to grant independence to a large portion of British India to become a new republic, but also to establish a separate Islamic country, called Pakistan ("Land of the Pure"). At that time, those administrative districts under direct British control with a majority Muslim population were assigned to Pakistan, and those with a Hindu majority to India. The accession of the princely states that were not under direct British control—about 40 percent of the subcontinent—into either India or Pakistan, was to be based on the preference of the ruling maharajas of these states.

There were two large exceptions to this process of accession. The princely state of Hyderabad, in the Deccan, had a Muslim leader and a Hindu majority population. It was absorbed into India when Indian troops rushed into the state to quell riots that came in the wake of the partition of India and Pakistan in 1947. The princely state of Kashmir, on the other hand, had a majority Muslim population and a Hindu maharaja. It was nominally acceded to India by Maharajah Hari Singh in October 1947, as Pakistani forces had begun to enter Kashmir and were fast approaching the city of Srinagar.

The result of this process of border determination was a Pakistan divided into two sections, East and West, on the shoulders of the subcontinent, separated by 1,000 miles of India; and a Kashmir still divided between the unresolved claims of both

India and Pakistan and a United Nations (UN) resolution to encourage the people of Kashmir to have a choice.

Even with the setback experienced in the Mutiny of 1857, Western political ideas of democracy, social reform, and freedom of expression continued to spread through South Asia. The Indian National Congress was formed in 1887 to seek opportunities for South Asians to shape and to participate in a growing body politic. In 1919, Mohandas Gandhi emerged as the leader of this movement. Through the power of his example and his great organizational skills, he was able to build grassroots support for the Congress throughout British India. Enlivened by a spirit of democracy and of political freedom, this movement first paralleled and then superseded British colonial rule.

The British imperial presence also brought to South Asia the concept of a modern nation. An independent, democratically elected government was the goal—certainly for those who were under foreign colonial domination; but also for those who had been under traditional, autocratic rule of hereditary maharajas, tribal leaders, and vestigial imperial domains. Upon achieving independence, South Asian peoples awoke from a long era of unrepresentative leadership. Forceful ideas began to take on relevance: liberty achieved through democracy, prosperity through economic growth, and individual human rights sustained by law. These have become the standards by which the success of a nation's quest for modernization is measured.

The British colonial government set these standards as its expectation of the countries to which it granted independence in the middle of the twentieth century—to India and Pakistan in 1947, and Sri Lanka in 1948. The other smaller nations—Afghanistan, Bhutan, Maldives, and Nepal—which trace the origin of their governments to more autocratic traditions of long standing in the subcontinent, are challenged to hold these same standards to their performance for recognition as modern states. They are all seeking new opportunities for expression, for economic growth, and for taking control of their destiny as politically free peoples among the nations of the world.

The British colonial interaction with South Asia is now over. Yet it continues, like the Aryan and Moghul experiences, to have a discernible impact in the subcontinent. Significant changes are occurring in the political and economic life because of the British Raj, just as the artistic and Islamic influences of the Moghul era are also evident in contemporary South Asia. And the religious and intellectual heritage shaped by the evolution of Aryan culture continues to be profoundly present.

All of these threads—Aryan, Moghul, and British Raj—contribute to a unique and distinctive culture. They are intricately interwoven among themselves and with the many other influences both indigenous and brought by centuries of maritime commerce to form the tapestry of the long, rich, and varied heritage of the peoples who belong to South Asia.

IMAGE 2: A DIVERSE SOCIAL ENVIRONMENT

It is the endurance of this civilization, despite its encounter with a host of other cultures and other political influences, that has led many observers to conclude that the Hindu style is absorptive, synthesizing, or tolerant. What they see is something quite different, namely, Indian civilization's ability to encapsulate other cultures and make it possible for many levels of civilization to live side by side. But encapsulation is neither toleration, absorption, nor synthesis.

—Ainslie T. Embree

The 1.559 billion people in South Asia are more than five times the population of the United States living in half as much space. That is more than a fifth of the total population of the world, and increasing at an alarming pace. The World Bank projects that at the current rate of growth, the population of the subcontinent will exceed 1.8 billion by the year 2025.

Every country in South Asia is seeking to curb this rate, with varying success. Sri Lanka has been the most effective, where the annual growth rate is less than 1 percent. The education of women has been the key to limiting its population growth.

This large population is composed of many different ethnic, religious, linguistic and social groups, displaying a wide variety of beliefs and customs: Sikhs and Buddhists and Jains; Sherpas in the mountains and fishermen and pit weavers along the tropical shores of the coasts; elegant urban aristocrats and naked religious mendicants; tribal peoples and computer engineers; beggars, film stars, and Kathakali dancers; and many more interwoven into the multi-stranded fabric of South Asian life. It is a rich panoply of all sorts and conditions of humanity.

The persistence of caste communities (jatis) in a hierarchical social system that holds them together illustrates the encapsulation of this incredible mix of people that preserves side by side such a multitude of customs and traditions. The caste (jati) into which one is born in India provides a great sense of social cohesion, of belonging, not assumed by individualism in the United States. American students are often troubled that their Indian hosts do not feel comfortable with them until they can identify them as another one of the students at the university. The students are doing their own thing by taking up studies in India, and want to be accepted as individuals. Their hosts feel more accepting of them when they can identify them as belonging to a recognized group.

There are hundreds of thousands of such kinship groups throughout the country, each with its own distinctive characteristics that places it in an encompassing hierarchical order. In a normal village setting, individuals will interact on a daily basis with others from about 20 different jatis. The locally accepted position of their jati in the social hierarchy of the caste system determines the expected norms of their daily interactions, which are careful to respect the distinctive characteristics of each. To the unfamiliar eye, individuals in these jati communities may look the same. In many instances, the distinguishing characteristics must be delineated by very fine strokes to convey the separation that preserves the distinctive character of each. Occupation and affinal relationships are two of the more obvious characteristics that define them.

Jatis are identified by a traditional occupation, from which each derives its name. The name dhobi (washerman) indicates one who belongs to a community of washermen, chamar to a community of shoe makers, or jat to a farmer family. Each jati has a traditional role in which it functions in the economy of the village as a whole, and also in the ceremonies of village festivals, which it has performed for generations. Settlement patterns uncovered in the ancient Harappan cities suggest that the separation of communities by task has been around for a long

Courtesy of James Norton

As with rituals, festivals, innumerable temples, and shrines, daily worship called puja, this man responds to transcendence at a convenient place along the road.

time. Accepting of different groups into a hierarchical rank in the total social fabric is a way for inclusion that preserves for each its own skills and cultural habits. This system of ranking by task is also of longstanding.

Endogamy also preserves the distinctive characteristics of a community by expecting every individual's marriage partner to be selected from their own jati. In a society where young adults are accustomed to have their marriages arranged by their parents, the unique characteristics of the jati are preserved from generation to generation.

With the introduction of democratic forms of government in contemporary South Asia, jati identification has been reaffirmed for those placed in the lower ranks of the caste system in two ways: by reserved electorates and affirmative action.

During the years leading up to India's independence, efforts were made to include a voice for "untouchable," oppressed (Dalit) communities, officially designated as Scheduled Castes by the British Raj census, by reserving a certain number of legislative seats in government for them. Mahatma Gandhi strongly opposed this initiative, asserting that the scourge of untouchability should be removed by social reform, not by instituting it into the structure of government. He was opposed by an articulate leader of the Scheduled Castes, Dr. Bhim Rao Ambedkar, an "untouchable" who had studied jurisprudence at Columbia University, and later became Chairman of the drafting committee that wrote the Constitution of the Republic of India. Gandhi won that battle, by a fast-unto-death in Poona in 1932. But Dr. Ambedkar succeeded in including in India's Constitution adopted in 1950, provision for the reservation of 15 percent of civil service jobs and 7.5 percent of schools for members of Scheduled Castes and Scheduled Tribes. Controversy and public demonstration have continued over the amount and the extent of this affirmative action reservation by the Kalelkar (1953) and Mandal (1979) Commissions. But the identification of its recipients by caste community (jati) identity continues.

The newly formed government of the Republic of Nepal provided for the election of 55 percent of its legislature by proportional representation for women and marginalized and oppressed caste communities to assure full participation in its first national elections on April 10, 2008.

The process of encapsulation as isolating and preserving discrete caste communities is also evident among the many different religious communities and linguistic groups in South Asia into which one is also born. But here the defining characteristics and the structural integrity which has kept them separate, even over long periods of familiarity and interaction, can be done in broader strokes.

MANY RELIGIONS

Hinduism and Islam—one indigenous, the other imported—are by far the largest of the world's religions on the subcontinent. Approximately 62 percent of the population is Hindu and about 31 percent Muslim. Hinduism is the dominant religion in India (80.3 percent of the population) and Nepal (80.6 percent). Islam is dominant in Pakistan (97 percent), Bangladesh (83 percent), Afghanistan (99 percent) and Maldives (100 percent). Buddhism, though started in India, is practiced by only 1.8 percent of the total population of the subcontinent. But it is the predominant religion in Sri Lanka (70 percent) and Bhutan (75 percent). Jains are an even smaller religious community that originated in the subcontinent. They trace their faith to Vardhamana Mahavira, a religious leader who lived in northern India at the same time as the Buddha, in the sixth century B.C. There are also Sikhs, whose religion was founded by Guru Nanak during the sixteenth century, A.D., in the northwestern part of South Asia known as the Punjab. Because religious minorities tend to concentrate in specific regions of the subcontinent, Sikhs, who represent only 1.9 percent of the population of India, are a majority of 62 percent in the State of Punjab.

Other religious communities, originating outside of the subcontinent, include Christians, Jews, and the Parsis, whose Zoroastrian faith had its origin in ancient Persia at the time of the Vedas, more than 3,500 years ago.

All of these religious communities, even when influencing each other, continue to reaffirm the structural integrity of their own faith as separate from the faiths of others. This persistence accounts for the immense variety of Hinduism, which is actually a composite term that includes a multitude of diverse religious groups. Hindus do share some common teachings and perspectives. They all, for example, affirm the transmigration of the soul after death to some other form of life. This belief they share with Buddhists and Jains, which is why many Hindus consider Buddhists and Jains to be within the inclusive umbrella of Hinduism. But the many different communities within Hinduism follow separate religious traditions in an immense variety of ways, each the result of an evolution over a distinct path during many centuries.

The earliest record of the Hindu religious tradition is the Rg-Veda, an anthology of 1,028 poems drawn together from the collections of several families of Vedic priests into its current form around the tenth century B.C. Many of the poems were composed earlier, and presuppose an even earlier history of religious belief and practice. Traditionally the sacred preserve of the Brahmin priesthood, the Veda is not widely known or understood among Hindus today. And the Vedic sacrifices around which the collection of sacred poems was initially created—and upon which the religious authority of the Brahmin priesthood was initially established—are rarely performed.

More characteristic of Hindu life today are the rituals, traditions, and festivals celebrated at the innumerable temples and shrines that dot the countryside, daily worship called puja, and the sanctity of an epic fragment called Bhagavad Gita ("The Song of the Lord"). All of these have been added to the religious practices of the Hindus after the Vedic period (1500 to 500 B.C.).

These later additions reveal that Hinduism has changed significantly since Vedic times. But it has not evolved as a single religious tradition. By incorporating and encompassing many diverse strands at different times in separate ways, it has become a vast array of schools and sects and disciplines, all encompassed within the Hindu fold today.

Among these sects are the Vaishnavites, who worship God as first revealed in the Rg-Veda as Vishnu. They recognize His manifestation in a number of avatars (incarnations) drawn from other and later traditions. These incarnations include Krishna, the Buddha, and Kalki (the "One who is to come"). Shaivites belong to a separate sect that traces the origin of its faith even farther back, to representations of Shiva as Pasupati ("Lord of animals"), found in the artifacts of the Harappan Civilization, and as Nataraj (the "Lord of the Cosmic Dance"). The gods of other regional religious traditions have been incorporated into the Shaivite fold as children of Shiva and his consort Parvati. Ganapati, the elephant-headed god, remover of obstacles, becomes one such deity, who remains the primary focus of worship in the Indian state of Maharashtra.

In addition, Hinduism includes worshipers of Krishna and Ram and of the Goddess in a variety of manifestations: in the Great Tradition as Kali, Durga, or Devi, but also among innumerable regional and local deities who benefit specific villages or protect against certain diseases. Their virtues and powers are enthusiastically celebrated throughout the country in an annual cycle of religious festivals unique to every village.

Courtesy of James Norton

The central back panel on a tenth century Chola Shaivite temple in Tamil Nadu, which portrays Shiva at the center of the verticle image of the lingam, the creative energy of the universe. It expresses the extent of Shiva's transcendence in the images of Brahmá, the god of creation, as an eagle at the top, and Vishnu, the sustainer of the universe, portrayed in his incarnation (avatar) as a boar, when he rescued the earth from the depths of the cosmic flood. Neither can reach to the awesome heights nor the hidden depths of the ultimate power of God.

And there is yoga, a spiritual discipline that does not affirm the existence of any deity. Any description of Hinduism must attempt to contain this complete array of forms and practices, each with its own history, tradition, and authority, for a vast number of religious communities who consider themselves Hindu.

Buddhism also originated in South Asia and evolved as a separate religion since the sixth century B.C. Siddhartha Gautama, the founder of the faith, was born a prince in a remote north Indian kingdom not under the sway of a Brahmin priesthood. He renounced his royal inheritance to seek an ultimate meaning for his life. After many years of diligent search, he received the enlightenment of the "Four-fold Truth." His teaching to his disciples about the pervasive presence of misery (dukha), of its cause and its removal, was the basis on which this religion developed and expanded throughout the subcontinent.

Buddhism was originally the faith of a monastic community, the sangha. It was composed of those who, attracted by the Buddha's example and teaching, abandoned their worldly activities to commit themselves to following his path, or *dhamma,* in communal and meditative isolation. The conversion of the Mauryan emperor Asoka to the Buddha's teaching in the third century B.C. brought about a significant change in the Buddhist tradition. His political authority gave greater currency to the Buddha's *dhamma* throughout the society. He also endowed the community with royal patronage, which encouraged not only its growth but also spawned a creative outburst of Buddhist art, literature, and philosophy. Tributes to this heritage have survived in the exuberant carvings and frescoes in the caves at Ajanta, and in the majestic tranquility of the sculpture of the Buddha teaching at Sarnath. It was this highly expressive and energetic Buddhism that, during the centuries following Asoka, burst forth into two traditions to the far reaches of Asia—the Theravada (teachings of the elders) to Sri Lanka and Southeast Asia, and the Mahayana (vast vessel) to China, Japan, Mongolia, and Tibet.

Buddhism, though indigenous, remained among a dominant Hindu society an encapsulated religious community, even when favored by imperial patronage for several centuries after Asoka. During that time it did manage to introduce vegetarianism as a social virtue to be observed by Brahmins among the Hindus. Unlike Hinduism, it declined dramatically in the north-central region of the subcontinent toward the end of the first millennium, as many were drawn to the teachings of Sufi mystics. Beginning in the eleventh century A.D., that region was subjected to the military attacks and religious zeal of Islamic potentates from Central Asia.

Buddhism survives today in enclaves along the borders of South Asia: in Ladakh, the section of Kashmir closest to China; in Bhutan, also along the Himalayan border, next to Tibet; and in Sri Lanka, off the southeastern coast of peninsular India. It was revived in India among the Mahar community in Maharashtra under the leadership of Dr. Bhim Rao Ambedkar, the chairman of the committee that wrote the Constitution of the Republic of India. During the years leading up to India's independence he protested Hindu discrimination against communities designated as "untouchable," and advocated for the abolition of caste. As a final act of rejection of Hindu caste repression, he converted to Buddhism in 1956.

Christianity was first introduced to the subcontinent, according to legend, by the Apostle Thomas during the first century A.D. It was certainly known to silk traders from Egypt passing through Afghanistan to China during the second century. A small community of Syrian Christians known as the Mar Toma Church migrated to Kerala in the fourth century.

The Portuguese first brought Roman Catholicism to the western coast of India during the 1400s. The English East India Company did not permit Protestant missions to work in the subcontinent until the early 1800s.

Today, these Christian communities add up to less than 3 percent of the total population of South Asia. They have become a significant force in the political life of the subcontinent only in the state of Kerala, at the southwestern edge of the Indian peninsula, where they form nearly one third of the population.

Islam was brought initially to the subcontinent by Arab traders plying the coastal shores of peninsular India soon after the hegira, or flight of Mohammed from Mecca in A.D. 622. Recognition of the integrity of the many encapsulated religions in South Asia became the basis for the wide and rapid spread of

Archeological Survey of India, Government of India

This sculpture, dating from the fifth century A.D., is a majestic portrayal of the heavenly body (*sambhogakaya*) of the Buddha teaching at the deer park in Sarnath, soon after he had attained enlightenment. His earthly body is portrayed on the base by the wheel of dharma among his disciples. The content of his teaching is what remains on earth after his entering nirvana.

the influence of Islamic mystics, called Sufis, during the early years of Islamic influence there. Where Sufi teaching and practice were consistent with the values and experience of the religious communities already there, they were readily venerated and even co-opted. People of many different faiths participated in worship at shrines honoring Sufi saints.

The Islamic faith of the Sultans who began to rule portions of the northern plains of South Asia during the eleventh century, was also recognized, but not so readily accepted. Through their political rule and adherence to the institutions of Islam, Muslims became more defined as a distinct religious community by the pillars of Islamic faith, prayer five times a day, alms giving, pilgrimages to Mecca, and to the application of Shariah, the laws of the faith in civic life.

The predominance of Muslims on the western and eastern ends of the north-central plains region led to the creation of the separate western and eastern arms of the original nation of Pakistan in 1947. Although nearly seven million Muslims migrated from India to Pakistan at the time of independence in 1947, 150 million still reside in India today, forming a significant religious minority (13.4 percent). The population of all Muslims in the subcontinent—close to 491 million—is more than three times the number of Muslims in the Arab world. Only Indonesia, with 205 million, has more Muslims in a single nation.

Most of the Muslims in South Asia belong to the Sunni tradition. In Maldives, one has to be Sunni as a requirement of citizenship. Significant minorities of Shi'ite Muslims live in Afghanistan, Bangladesh, and Pakistan, in which the Islamic faith is the predominant religion of the country, and are subjected to some discrimination. In Pakistan and Bangladesh, Sunnis also challenge the legitimacy of members of the Ahmadhiya sect of Islam.

Communal strife between religions does occur in a variety of forms throughout the subcontinent. The resistance of the people of Kashmir to the imposition of military repression by the government of India in 1982 was expressed in religious terms. It became a battle for the freedom of the Muslim population from what was experienced as an oppressive Hindu India. Armed bands of Islamic militants ambushed, burned, and kidnapped throughout the mountain valleys and in the once placid Vale, all in the name of protecting their religion. The conflict killed many thousands. And thousands of Hindu families fled their homes in fear of this violence.

The invasion of the Sikh Golden Temple in Amritsar in 1984 by the Indian Army to remove a Sikh nationalist leader led to the assassination of Prime Minister Indira Gandhi, followed by the killing of three thousand Sikhs in north India.

The destruction, on December 6, 1992, of the Babri Masjid, a mosque built for the Moghul Emperor Barbur in the sixteenth century in Ayodhya, led to communal rioting across India. More than 1,000 lost their lives in the 10 days of rioting that followed in Mumbai in January, 1993.

Again, in 2002, communal violence broke out in the town of Godhra in Gujarat in response to the death of 58 Hindus, mostly women and children, in the burning of a railway car, while returning from a pilgrimage to Ayodhya. In reprisal, more than 1,200 Muslims in slum dwellings were killed, and many more left homeless. The state government, accused of not acting sufficiently to control the violence, used the event to gain support among the Hindu population for its reelection in December of that year. Recent terrorist bombings in Ahmedabad, Jaipur, and Delhi were carried out by a group of Islamic militants gaining support from the Students Islamic Movement of India (SIMI) radicalized by the Gujurati pogrom. Hindu extremists have been identified as those setting off bombs in the Muslim section of the city of Malegaon, not far from Mumbai, in September, 2006 and 2008.

Religious discrimination has also exacted a toll in South Asia. The comprehensive Sachar Committee Report, released in November 2006, shows that Muslims in India are significantly disadvantaged in education and government jobs.

Experiencing this discrimination also contributed to the disaffection of the Student Islamic Movement of India. Discrimination against Nepali Hindus contributed to their expulsion as refugees from Buddhist Bhutan. And Dalit converts to Christianity in the Indian state of Orissa came under attack when a conservative Hindu community accused them of killing its leader.

Some of the greatest violence based on religious identity in South Asia has not been between religions, but within a single religious community. Muslims, as they have become modern and democratic in independent nations in South Asia, are pulled in opposite directions by two dynamic, opposing reform forces: secularism and fundamentalism.

Jinnah, the founder of Pakistan, a lawyer trained in England, did not consider himself a religious person, nor his country to be theocratic. He rather envisioned a secular, democratic state created to preserve the existence and culture of an Islamic people threatened by a dominating Hindu society in British India. In this he followed the example of Ataturk in Turkey.

This vision continued to be affirmed by Zulfikar Ali Bhutto, founder of the Pakistan People's Party in 1967, and by his daughter, Benazir Bhutto, the first woman to become prime minister of Pakistan in 1988. An enthusiastic majority of moderates, particularly lawyers and entrepreneurs, pushed for the return of democracy to Pakistan in the national elections that overthrew General Musharraf as president in February 2008.

During this same time an Islamic fundamentalist movement gained strength in the Islamic world in an atmosphere of fear and antipathy for Western ways, and of social disruption and disorientation. Old ways were changing, with nothing reassuring to take their place. The fundamentalist Salafiya movements latched onto a clear and assured set of prescriptions of a normative past that then became, for them, a sacred mission to replicate. This Islamist ideology found expression in political parties like the Muttahida Majlis-e-amal (MMA), which required institution of theocratic law (Shariah) enforced by autocratic power (as in the example of Wahabism in Saudi Arabia).

The most far reaching impact of this fundamentalist reform has been in Afghanistan. The Taliban ("religious students") rose in 1993 amongst the Pastho-speaking peoples of southern Afghanistan in protest against the egregious immorality of the Mujahideen ("holy warriors"), who were fighting each other and ravaging the country after the Soviet withdrawal in 1989. Their reforming zeal swept across the country, and by 1999, forces allegiant to it controlled most of the country. They then imposed a harrowing rule of righteous repression, especially upon women, administered by its most conscientious administrative department, of the Promotion of Virtue and Prevention of Vice.

Following the terrorist attacks in the United States on September 11, 2001, and the refusal of the Taliban leadership to extradite or exile Osama bin Laden, United States and coalition forces backed a residual, Tajik-led Northern Alliance force to recapture Kabul and bring about the collapse of the Taliban control of the country.

Hazid Karmai was elected president in national elections held in October, 2004. His support came only from Kabul and Pashto-speaking areas to the south of the city. The weakness of his government, rife with corruption, and the misguided use of force by U.S. and NATO units assigned to protect the country, allowed the Taliban resurgence from sanctuaries in Pakistan with a mission to rid their country of foreign military infidels. The strength of their cause, together with the creation of an indigenous Taliban in Pakistan has produced a reign of terror that threatens the democratically elected governments in both Afghanistan and Pakistan.

Islamist fundamentalism has not gained such support among Muslims in the rest of South Asia. But the vehemence and violence of their mission is dramatically visible in dramatic terrorist acts which occurred on August 17, 2006, when 500 bombs went off simultaneously in 63 of Bangladesh's 64 districts, and more recently, on September 19, 2008, in the bombing of the Marriott Hotel in Islamabad, Pakistan, and on November 26, 2008, in Mumbai, when a heavily armed band of militants attacked the railway station, a Jewish center, and two five star hotels, killing 172 people. All of these acts were done in the name of the Islamist jihad; religious sacrifices to assert their fundamentalist version of their faith.

The differences between and within religions are not always confrontational. Mutual respect is generally accepted in recognizing the integrity of the many religious communities that have been encapsulated. The daily interaction among peoples of different faiths tend to be accommodating and harmonious. But because of the prevalence and immediacy of religion in defining the distinctive character of the many social groups which live side by side throughout South Asia, that identity is readily invoked in conflicts. Even when disputes originate between individuals, they rapidly become characterized by any opposing religious identity of the participants. The same dynamic occurs when people of the many different language groups of the subcontinent confront or threaten one another.

MANY LANGUAGES

Foreign visitors to the growing commercial city of Kolkata (Calcutta) during the late eighteenth century were struck by the immense diversity of languages encountered there. The language of the city marketplace was Portuguese, a vestige of the early domination of East Indian trade by Portugal. The language of government was Persian, also a vestige, of the Moghul imperial past. By contrast, the languages of the courts were Sanskrit and Arabic (depending upon to which tradition of law those pursuing legal redress belonged). None of these languages was the common tongue, or vernacular, of the people who lived in Calcutta. But each had a specific place and context in which it was considered appropriate.

Had the visitors wandered into the streets or into homes, they would have discovered another variety of languages. Different tongues spoken by the common people reflected the places of origin of those who moved to Calcutta to take part in the growing activity and prosperity there. Because most of these people came from the immediately surrounding area, the most prevalent vernacular was Bengali.

Today, the English language has replaced the many foreign languages used in the more formal aspects of contemporary urban life, and Bengali remains the common language of the people. But many other languages are spoken in the streets and homes of the city.

Hundreds of vernaculars are spoken throughout South Asia today. In India alone, thirty-five different languages are spoken by more than a million people. These languages belong to four distinct language families broadly distributed across specific regions of the subcontinent. The major dialects in the northernmost, Himalayan region are Tibeto-Burmese, related to the languages across the northern and eastern borders of the subcontinent. Their presence reveals that those living in the remote valleys of that region had more extensive cultural interaction through the rugged and forbidding mountains and jungles along those borders than with the more settled plains to the south.

The prevalent languages of the northern plains region, Sri Lanka, and Maldives belong to the Indo-European family of languages, distant cousins of Latin, Greek, and the Germanic tongues of the West. The Aryans, migrating cattle herders from Central Asia who wandered into the subcontinent almost 3,500 years ago introduced an earlier form of this language family, called Vedic, to this part of the world.

A totally separate family of languages is spoken among the tribal peoples who still inhabit the remote hill regions of peninsular India. These are generally called Munda languages, and are related to those spoken by the Aboriginal peoples of Australia to the southeast. The Indo-European and tribal families of languages reveal far-reaching interconnections that existed thousands of years ago among peoples who are now widely separated.

Dravidian is yet another language family. Its roots can be traced only to the South Asian subcontinent itself. Today the Dravidian languages are spoken mostly in the south of India and the northern part of Sri Lanka, but they are not confined to the subcontinent. They have been carried to East Africa, Singapore, the Fiji Islands, and the West Indies by immigrants who continue to affirm their South Asian heritage in these many other parts of the world.

Each of the numerous languages that belong to these four families has a specific area in the subcontinent in which it is spoken by the vast majority of the people. It is easy to see where these languages predominate in India and Pakistan, because state borders within these countries have been drawn to enclose specific dominant-language groups. Afghanistan and Sri Lanka are also divided into language-area sections.

The integrity of these languages is retained even beyond the region where they are predominant as minority linguistic pockets in other language areas. Thus, a variety of languages may be found anywhere, especially in cities, where migrants from many parts of the country tend to settle in sections of the city with others who share their native language.

Some of these many languages have developed literary and classical forms of expression, but all are most widely familiar as colloquial dialects, which, like accents, reflect common usage among specific groups of people in particular places. Colloquial dialects would seem to be the form of language most subject to assimilation with other languages that are spoken around it. Because of the diverse social context in which they are spoken, these languages do interact and influence each other. But this interaction has not led to their becoming assimilated into a common tongue. That each continues distinct in its integrity as a separate language is a primary example of encapsulation as a way of describing the social dynamic of the people of South Asia.

UN Photo 153,017/Oddbjom Monsen

These young women of Pushkar, India, are part of the vast cultural mosaic of peoples in South Asia.

The language one learns first in childhood is one's "mother tongue." This way of describing one's native language reveals that, for the people of South Asia, one is born into a language community which is intrinsic to one's identity as a person, even when residing in countries far away from the subcontinent. As is true for an individual's caste community and religion, one is born into them, and they remain inherently descriptive of who one is.

Even though the Muslim population of Pakistan is divided between Sunnis and Shi'ites (77 percent and 20 percent, respectively, of the total population), political identity based on language has played a much more important role than religion. During their early years of independence, the common Muslim faith of the peoples of East and West Pakistan did not override the ethnic and linguistic differences between the Bengali speaking peoples of the east and the Punjabi dominated western wing of the country. That opposition led to the break away and independence of Bangladesh as a separate country in 1971.

Even today, language identity is a vital factor in the distinction between the muhajirs—families who migrated at the time of Pakistan's independence in 1947—and the indigenous peoples of the country. The muhajirs retain and cultivate the use of Urdu, the mother tongue they brought with them from India. They are also primarily an urban community, living mostly in the city of Karachi.

To maintain their identity as a distinct community in the Islamic Republic of Pakistan, about 20 million muhajirs formed a political party, now called the Muttahida Quami Movement (MQM), to represent their interests in the affairs of state. Members in this party have been subjected to severe harassment in Karachi, a city that recorded 1,800 people killed on its streets in 1995, most believed to be politically motivated. The imposition of federal rule and the creation of military courts in the city in November 1998 was understood by the MQM as an effort to destroy the movement as a political force. The leader of the party, Altef Hussain, now resides in self-imposed exile in London.

Sri Lanka is experiencing conflict where linguistic identity reinforces the separation between the regions of a country where different religions are predominant. The majority of Sri Lankans are Buddhists who speak the Sinhalese language. In the northeast region of the country, however, most of the people are Hindu, with significant Muslim enclaves, and are Tamil-speakers. The regional basis of this separation has allowed these communities to coexist for centuries. But the quest to achieve a single national identity since the independence of the country in 1948 has resulted in intense warfare between these two very different communities. Because of the importance of their language differences, these militant groups see the conflict more as cultural—as tigers against lions—rather than as religious.

A map which delineates the predominant language areas throughout the entire subcontinent, like a map of the religious communities described earlier, looks like an intricate patchwork quilt. The pattern of the language quilt, however, is not the same as for religions.

Generally speaking, people belonging to different religions in the same place speak the same language, but those belonging to the same religion speak many languages. Only in the smaller countries of the subcontinent—Bhutan, Maldives, and Sri Lanka—do religious identities and language identities tend to correspond. Only in Maldives, the smallest of the countries of the subcontinent, do these categories coincide with its national boundaries; only there does being a citizen of the country generally mean that one speaks the same language and worships in a common faith.

AN ENCAPSULATED SOCIETY

The difference between urban and rural life in South Asia as defining the identity of a people is important because the total urban population is only 24 percent (vs. 74 percent in the United States). India will soon have the second-largest urban population in the world, but urban dwellers still constitute less than a quarter of the total population of the country. Rural ways and the rural voice still have a significant role, and, as recent national elections in India reveal, a significant voice in determining the priorities and direction of South Asian political life.

There is also a vast disparity between the wealthiest and the poorest of the poor. Recognition of these inequalities has led to the development of SEWA (Self-Employed Women's Association) in India and the Grameen Bank and BRAC (Bangladesh Rehabilitation Assistance Committee) in Bangladesh, institutions that have created effective methods for providing capitalization of assets among the poor. Cooperatives modeled on these programs have been set up throughout the subcontinent, primarily to help women develop self-supporting careers.

Religion, language, urban/rural difference, and wealth/poverty all reveal an immense diversity and variety in the social fabric of South Asia. The violence that often results from their interaction reveals the depth and the extent of these differences as establishing the unique identity of each of the many social groupings into which the nations of South Asia are divided.

Extended kinship groups (jatis), tribes, migrant peoples, religious communities, and even highly mobile urban classes are accepted as they are, as distinct communities within a stratified society. Social pressure toward bonding and conformity within these groups is so strong that they are not expected to assimilate or fit in with the distinguishing characteristics of others. They thus remain an encapsulated yet integral part within the whole fabric of South Asian society.

Although there have been periods of great confrontation, discrimination, and violence, the wide diversity among the many different peoples of South Asia is generally accepted as both inevitable and normal. Like the four-fold layering of humanity set forth in the Vedic hymn celebrating the sacrificial offering of primordial man in the creation of the universe, social diversity is a cosmic reality.

IMAGE 3: THE WORLD AS SYMBOL

The first function [of a symbol] is the representative function. The symbol represents something which is not itself, for which it stands and in the power and meaning of which it participates. . . . And now we come to something which is perhaps the main function of the symbol—namely, the opening up of levels of reality which otherwise are hidden and cannot be grasped in any other way.

Every symbol opens up a level of reality for which non-symbolic speaking is inadequate. The more we try to enter into the meaning of symbols, the more we become aware that it is the function of art to open up levels of reality; in poetry, in visual art, and in music, levels of reality are opened up which can be opened up in no other way.

But in order to do this, something else must be opened up—namely, levels of the soul, levels of our interior reality. And they must correspond to the levels in exterior reality which are opened up by a symbol. So every symbol is two-edged. It opens up reality and it opens up the soul. There are, of course, those people who are not opened up by music or who are not opened up by poetry, or more of them who are not opened up at all by visual arts. The "opening up" is a two sided function—namely reality in deeper levels and the human soul in special levels.

—Paul Tillich, *Theology of Culture*

A Vedic householder, himself a priest, or accompanied by a priest, starts his day before sunrise with a series of rituals. The basic rite, which may be accompanied by acts of purification, is to remove the coals from the household hearth, called the lord of the home hearth, upon which the meals of the house are cooked each day. These coals are moved to another hearth, outside of the house to the east, called the hearth of offering. There, in anticipation of the rising of the sun, the fire is rekindled using special sacrificial grass collected for this ceremony. This act is accompanied by reciting a hymn from the Rg-Veda which celebrates the sacred power revealed in the beauty of the dawn as a moment filled with heightened anticipation. This time of the day is portrayed by a symbol, as a young maiden rising to stir all living creatures into life:

> Daughter of Heaven, she has appeared before us,
> A maiden shining in resplendent raiment,
> Thou sovereign lady of all earthly treasure,
> Auspicious Dawn, shine here today upon us.
>
> Arise! the breath of life again has reached us:
> Darkness has gone away and light is coming.
> She leaves a pathway for the sun to travel.
> We have arrived where men prolong existence.
> —Rg-Veda 1.113, A. A. Macdonell translation

Having invoked this charmed natural presence around the fire of offering in the eastern hearth, the householder awaits the appearance of the sun above the horizon.

This daily ritual, still practiced by some orthodox Brahmins in India today, is a symbolic act which portrays the natural sun, with all of its awesome energy, as representing something beyond itself as a physical reality. It points to a level of transcendent, auspicious power that cannot be grasped in any other way. For the sun is the primary symbol in the householder's life of the cosmic energy which creates order out of chaos and generates prosperity for all mankind. He thus invokes into his household, through the fire of offering, the blessing of that sacred power of the sun as it rises to fill the world with the bounty of its light.

To reaffirm this sacred level of meaning which lies within, but beyond the natural reality of the visible sun, he recites as it appears the words of the Gayatri mantra, one of the most sacred verses of the Veda.

> O face of the True Sun, now hidden by a disc of gold,
> May we know thy Reality, and see thee face to face.

Peoples from ancient times around the world have endowed the sun with symbolic meaning. Because of its awesome height in the sky above the earth, its brightness as a source of light for the entire world, and its consistency of motion as manifesting cosmic order, the sun has stirred man's creative imagination. He sees in it much more than a natural object to be observed in the common understanding as, in the English visionary William Blake's pejorative image, "a round disc of fire somewhat like a Guinea." The consistency and beauty of its moment of arrival, and of the light and blessing which it brings, is simply too awesome, too intense to be experienced objectively. Like his response to the resplendence of the dawn, the Vedic householder enters into that moment passionately and creatively. He celebrates it each morning as a sacred time.

The transcendence revealed in this moment "now hidden by a disc of gold" in the words of the Gayatri mantra, is an ultimate level of reality pointed to by the sun. In Vedic mythology, special recognition was given to a goddess called Aditi. Retaining vestiges of ancient, pre-Aryan mother goddess worship, she is celebrated in the Rg-Veda as the Mother of the solar gods called Adityas, who are revealed in the phases of the sun during the course of a day. The god Varuna, the protector of moral order in the universe, appears at the apex of the day. Martanda, "the death egg," her eighth child, appears at sunset. Her sacred power is also affirmed in her name, which means literally "without limit," "infinite," she who is beyond human understanding. Aditi gives birth out of chaos to cosmic order as manifest in the daily course of the sun. This, for the Vedic priests, was a sacred mystery.

This celebration of the dimension of transcendence at sunrise in the Vedic householder's daily ritual goes back to the religious musings of that robust, cow-herding people called Aryans, who drove their horse-drawn war chariots into the subcontinent from Central Asia more than three thousand years ago. From these early times, Vedic priests saw the world as an experience of sacred celebration rather than as an objective natural reality. Their ritual activity and intellectual pursuits to affirm the world as sacrifice sought to identify that deeper level of reality which gives the experiences and objects of this world the quality of being sacred.

They expressed this level of reality in symbols, as what experiences and objects represent, rather than just the fact of their objective reality. They saw the world as an arena for the refinement of human experience—to realize not just what is, but also what is beyond—to deeper levels of their being.

The pervasive authority of scientific thinking in Western culture encourages the perception of objects as things. They are acknowledged to be as they are observed, and our understanding of the world is built around relationships revealed and confirmed by perceptual data. These relationships are called models, whether they be of things observed directly, such as gravity, or, of abstract patterns, like atomic structure or galaxies. All of these descriptions are based on, and authenticated by, what we perceive as an objective natural world.

We also understand in perceiving an object or experience something more than the facts of its existence. It represents something more as a symbol by pointing to a special meaning or interpretation which it is not itself. If we recognize the pattern of a flag, for example, as belonging to a specific group of people, like a tribe or a country, it is more than a natural object. It stands as a symbol for what defines the identity, allegiance, and destiny of the people it represents. So also, certain events are significant to a people not just because they happened.

The Fourth of July is celebrated to this day, and uniquely, by the American people with stories of the Revolutionary War and other quests for freedom, with fireworks and parades. Also important for the American people is the Exodus experience, an event that happened many centuries ago for the ancient people of Israel when they were freed from slavery in Egypt and found new life in a promised land.

The ancient Vedic priests' celebration of a dimension of transcendence in human experience appears in the poems of an anthology called the Rg-Veda, collected some 3,000 years ago, after their settlement in the subcontinent. As in the poem to Dawn, we can see in them "myth in the making."

They also developed an elaborate system of rituals to reenact, express, and celebrate the cosmos as a sacrificial event. In reciting these poems in this context, they took upon themselves the exclusive task of developing and giving authenticity to this symbolic perception of the world. This role also became the basis for asserting their social priority, as in the Vedic passage that described them as the mouth of primordial Man, whose offering of himself brought about the creation of the universe.

As time went on these scholar-priests began to hold extensive discussions during their sacrifices to explore the meaning of the transcendent reality which their ritual activity, as symbols, represented. Out of this discourse came a collection of narrative works called Upanishads.

In the centuries that followed, the priests further coalesced, elaborated, appended, and refined this appreciation of the sacredness of our world into classical forms. These forms provided the structure for immense intellectual and artistic creativity, which produced many outstanding works of thought and art on different aspects of human experience. Their analytical works, called sastras, were based on careful observation of the natural world around them. But they were not so much descriptions as they were reflections on what this world might be as expressive of a deeper level or order of being.

One of these sastras, called the Laws of Manu, is a remarkable treatise on social structure. It presents an elaborate set of rules of appropriate behavior for a society as though it were divided and ranked into the four *varna*, or classical caste, groupings as set forward in the Rg-Veda: Brahmin (priests), Kshatriya (rulers), Vaisya (citizens), and Sudra (laborers). It also divides one's life into four stages, called ashramas, each one occupying one-quarter of a lifetime: that of being a student, householder, mendicant, and ascetic. The Laws, rather than assuming that a single behavioral norm can apply to all of life, prescribe a distinct set of rules appropriate for each stage. A clear structure was thus imposed upon people's lives that placed upon them specific expectations of how they ought to act in a wide variety of conditions of class and of age. It was a comprehensive and authoritative model for social behavior, not because it described what actually happens, but because it expressed a vision of cosmic social order. It was something to live up to.

Other sastras focus on such topics as statecraft, poetics, philosophy, music, ritual, and the visual arts. These works are remarkable for the depth and precision of analysis that their authors undertook. They reveal that the classical scholar-priests who composed them did not find order or ultimate meaning immediately in the natural world about them. They had too great a sense of the flux and uncertainty in their normal human experience. They sought consistency, rather, in more abstract intellectual patterns, in the refinement rather than the description of what was about them. In art, for example, they suggested that aesthetic value was not in the experience of raw emotion (*bhava*), but in the refinement of that emotion into an aesthetic essence (*rasa*) which generates a sense of awe and beauty. Their attention was thus on what their experience pointed to as symbol rather than what it was as fact.

It was out of this refining analysis that the concept of the number zero emerged—it was in the classical South Asian way of looking at objects that the idea arose that there is something in our number system that is to be counted, even if it is not here.

Of all of the works of analysis during the evolution of the classical tradition, none is greater than the earliest: the description of the structure of language by Panini, the classical grammarian of the Sanskrit language. Every language is a symbol system where particular sounds articulated in a distinct way represent a specific meaning to those who share in understanding that language. Its symbolic character also reveals levels of experience beyond the physical world. Words, sentences, stories, even myths not only express, they also create the significance of what happens to make real for us other dimensions of our experience. Through language, we become part of and celebrate whole new worlds.

Panini probably lived during the fourth century B.C. He analyzed how sounds, as the basic structural units of a language (morphemes), fit together to form words and sentences. Only specific combinations of sounds form words, and specific combinations of words form sentences. When we use them to communicate, words and sentences reveal patterns that are used to relate their meanings. Panini's insight was that these patterns are not established by the meanings of words and sentences, but rather by the structure of language itself.

To analyze the patterns of language, Panini did not focus on the way words and sentences are used in ordinary, colloquial language. He looked at the highly refined, classical form of the Sanskrit language of the priesthood. (The word *sanskrit* means "refined," or "perfected," and identifies the level of abstraction to which the formal use of that language had progressed among the intensively trained scholar-priests during the late Vedic period). In this quest to discover the structure of this highly refined language, Panini identified its abstract form as a profound source of order in human life. Its greatest potential as language was not to describe what is, but, rather, as in Vedic poetry, to point to and affirm what is ultimately real in human experience: to the Reality of the sun, for example, hidden in its appearance.

Panini reduced his study of Sanskrit to eight concise chapters of grammatical rules, wherein each successive rule was an exception to all the rules that preceded it. This impressive intellectual achievement appears even more remarkable in that he achieved this structure without the use of writing; he did it all in his head.

Panini's achievement was matched by other important intellectual quests during the classical period. Elaborations of the concept of cosmic time, time that is not linear, but ceaselessly revolving, are mind-boggling because of the vast span of the cycles proposed. These cycles were described in the Puranic literature, dating from the early years A.D., as extending through four eras, called yugas, of from 432,000 years to 1,728,000 years long. One thousand of these four-era periods add up to a Kalpa, or a day of Brahma. At the end of a 4,320,000,000-year day of Brahma, the created universe comes to an end, or is dormant during Brahma's night, of equal duration, before the cycle begins again.

> Brahma is now in the first kalpa of his fifty-first year. Six Manus of that kalpa have passed away. We are living in the Kaliyuga of the twenty-eighth four-age period (*chaturyuga*) of the seventh *manvantara* of Brahma's fifty-first year. The Kaliyuga began on February 18, 3102 B.C. This would seem to indicate that we have a little less than 426,933 years to go until the Kaliyuga with its twilight comes to an end, and we have to face dissolution!
> —W. Norman Brown, *Man in the Universe*

This concept of time also generated many imaginative images in Sanskrit literature. One is the account of an apsara, a celestial being who lived in the realm of heaven within a different time frame. One heaven day, while at play with her friends in a garden, she fell off of a swing and fainted. While unconscious, she went to earth to be born as a child. She lived to reach adulthood, married and gave birth to children, attended her eldest son's wedding, and saw her grandchildren before she died. She then returned to her apsara friends in the heaven garden. They had anxiously gathered around upon her fall from the swing, and were fanning her. Upon reviving, she told her friends of her earthly experience. They were astounded that so much could have happened to her in so short a span of their time.

Imaginative and creative intellectual effort was also devoted to finding an understanding of self—an answer to the question "Who am I?" And again, the analysis pursued not the question "What am I?" but "Of what is my being a symbol?"

The Upanishads distinguished early on between the self who acts, the agent—"I am the one who does, thinks, feels things"—and the self who observes this agency, called the witness. The active self is the *jiva,* (the living thing), the aspect of self to which the acts of karma, (acts having moral consequences), become attached. Yajnavalkya in the Brhadaranyaka Upanishad was the first to assert that this karma determines into what form of life the *jiva* transmigrates when reincarnated.

Other early scholar-priests, devoted to the study of self, affirmed another dimension of self standing apart from oneself as acting, thinking, feeling, hidden behind the visible self. Because this witness self is detached, observing rather than doing, it transcends the activity in which the *jiva* is involved. This aspect of self is called atma. The atma, because it transcends the natural self, is affirmed as more real, as the ultimate self, of which the natural, active self is a symbol.

> "Bring me a fig," Uddalaka said to his son Shvetaketu.
> > He then asked him to break open and extract a tiny seed out of the fig.
> "Break it open. . . . What do you see there?"
> "Nothing at all, sir."
> "Truly, my son, that subtle essence which you do not see, from that does the great fig tree grow. Believe

me, the whole world has that essence for its Self.
That is the Real. That is who you really are
(*tat tvam asi*)
—Chandogya Upanishad, 6.12.1-3

The Vedanta philosopher Shankara, who lived during the eighth century A.D., ranks with Panini as an intellectual giant among the classical scholars of South Asia. Shankara identified the experience of consciousness in our being as the primary designation of the true self, the atma. It is in witnessing ourselves as being conscious as a symbol that we gain some insight into who we really are, of our ultimately real self.

This way of thinking is not available to those who are literalists, who think that what they see is all that there is to human experience. The classical thinkers of South Asia envisioned and opened up impressive avenues of awareness and expression realized in creative works of art, music, dance, sculpture, and literature. They also discovered and affirmed a transcendent unity in human experience in the world which can be realized through a multitude of symbols. This unity can even be discovered in experiencing the transcendence of our own, isolated, individual selves, should we discover the "ultimate beyond" within.

Such a theme in modern times is expressed by Rabindranath Tagore, artist, educator, in this verse from the *Gitanjali,* for which he received the Nobel Prize in Literature in 1913:

The same stream of life that runs through my veins
night and day runs through the world and dances
in rhythmic measures.

It is the same life that shoots in joy through the dust of
the earth in numberless blades of grass and breaks into
tumultuous waves of leaves and flowers.

It is the same life that is rocked in the ocean-cradle of
birth and death, in ebb and flow.

I feel my limbs are made glorious by the touch of this
world of life. And my pride is from the life-throb of
ages dancing in my blood this moment.

This heritage helps to explain why encapsulation as a social process is such an integral part of the culture of South Asia. The classical scholars understood that languages and religions are cultural constructs. No language or religion is natural in the sense that each has to be what it is, nor that what each language or religion is can be fully explained in natural terms. Different people express their experiences of identical things, even the same event, in very different ways. They even experience them differently.

Thus, attempts to construct a universal language, religion, or nationality have failed because the cultural contexts in which the necessary claims to absolutism are expressed, be it truth or allegiance, are not shared by all peoples. We see things, experience them, and talk about them in different ways, based upon the cultural context in which we are raised.

This understanding of the cultural relativity of language and religion is clearly evident in the pluralistic social context in which the peoples of South Asia live. It does not negate the absolute claims to meaning and truth of the many separate languages and religions around them. Each is recognized to have a functional integrity that distinguishes it from all other languages and religions.

A specific religion evolves as a structural abstraction among a group of people to reflect the uniqueness of their experience of transcendence as a group. Thus the group's religious practices become symbols that point to their identity and integrity for those who acknowledge and worship what is ultimately real for them, together as a community.

Among the Brahmin community, it is not the colloquial or even ritual use of Sanskrit that makes that language sacred. It is rather, the structure of that highly refined language that makes it symbolically expressive of the ultimate meaning of the universe.

A Brahmin teaching states that when God came to create the universe, He did not create objects and then allow Adam, a human being, to invent language by naming what he saw. Instead, He went to the ultimate meaning of what is universally expressed symbolically in the language of the Rg-Veda to find out what He was to create. That level of reality is for the classical tradition more real than the reality of the natural world. Nothing can be literally true in the Veda unless it be ultimately true.

Recognition of structural integrity as characteristic of different languages and religions is the basis for understanding them as symbols. They are not absolutes in themselves but rather point to a transcendent level of reality that is. One can accept the ultimate claim to universality of others for their religious faith to the degree that one understands the ultimacy of that universal reality to which one's own faith is a symbol. It is not a matter of accepting, or even tolerating, another's religion. It is, rather, the challenge of discovering that transcendent level of reality within one's own faith. To people of great faith, the ultimate reality affirmed by all religions is one.

Encapsulation as a social process in South Asia is based on an appreciation for the symbolic way each language and each religion is expressive of what is ultimately true for each social group. It affirms a vital sense of community among those who speak the same mother tongue and join in common religious practices. That is why language and religion play such an important role in the unfolding of democracy as a way of affirming a political identity for the peoples of South Asia.

Sharing a language and a religious faith clearly separates one from all those who do not. Problems arise when one takes this difference as affirming what is exclusive and absolute. Such literalism leads to isolation, antipathy, and violence. It is particularly dangerous in seeking viable national identities among people within geographical boundaries on the basis of religious and language identity.

The classical tradition teaches that the structural integrity of languages and religions is symbolic, and not exclusive nor absolute. When this perspective is understood as opening up oneself to other, deeper levels of reality, the pluralistic social environment of South Asia has not been assimilating nor conforming, but both resilient and accepting of difference.

IMAGE 4: DEMOCRACY IN SOUTH ASIA

"The spirit of democracy is not a mechanical thing to be adjusted by the abolition of forms. It requires a change of the heart."

—Mohandas K. Gandhi

UN Photo 87,040/WT/ARA

Pluralism in South Asia complicates the establishment of a workable political base as minorities strive to find a legitimate place and voice in national life. The religious influence is exemplified by their Sikh teacher addressing some of his followers at the Golden Temple in Amritsar, India. What he tells people is likely to be more relevant to social and political change than what any politician may say.

The nations of South Asia have faced many obstacles in their quest for modern democratic governments.

First of all, the ideology of nationalism based on the will of the people established by adult franchise came from the west through British colonial rule. The formation of such nations evolved over several centuries in western Europe and America among dominant groups of culturally homogeneous people. Those of different cultural backgrounds, those who spoke different languages, and even women, were simply ignored in this process. Because this assumption of a dominant male ethnicity was unchallenged, it was taken for granted that the male citizens' shared sense of identity as a nation would take precedence over any cultural differences among residual minority groups within the nation. All participants in the political process would blend into the culture of the politically dominant.

The assumption that dominant ethnicity determines the distinctive character of a nation could not be easily transposed into the diverse cultural environment of the peoples of South Asia. They are so accustomed to living in what Shashi Tharoor calls "a singular land of the plural," in which no ethnic nor linguistic group is in a majority. They do not understand common citizenship to be something that would demand greater allegiance than the community identities that separate them from all other linguistic, religious, and social groups among whom they live. They were not prepared to think of themselves as having a shared political identity as a nation.

The idea of modern democracy introduced by colonial rule also did not enter a political vacuum. Traditional sources of honor, allegiance, and identity based on patriarchal structures within the family, in the villages, and among petty kingdoms continued to dominate public life. The Great Mutiny of 1857 in British India demonstrated widespread resistance to British colonial attempts to enlighten its South Asian subjects. The British recognized this indigenous authority when they invited the maharajas who fled during the Mutiny to return to administer their former kingdoms. It is also recognized by those who seek to work with the "warlords" in Afghanistan today.

Efforts in the twentieth century to encourage public participation in the political process, to realize a government of the people, reveal the adaptability of village level, caste community, and language area institutions. Established patterns of grass-roots governance continue to be significant factors in implementing and shaping the transition from traditional power structures into democratic forms.

India, Bangladesh, and Nepal have adopted policies that reserve public offices for women. Even there, those women

With the partitioning of India and Pakistan, masses of people migrated because of their religious affiliations. More than 14 million people fled, including these refugees, making it the largest migration in history.

elected to responsible positions still meet strong resistance to their authority from entrenched patriarchal power elites.

Sirimavo Bandaranaike and Chandrika Kumaratunga, who served as prime ministers and presidents in Sri Lanka, Prime Ministers Indira Gandhi in India, Khaleda Zia and Hasina Wajed in Bangladesh, and Benazir Bhutto in Pakistan are all remarkable women who have served their countries with distinction. Yet, each of them has gained prominence in national political life because of the dominant roles of their fathers or husbands. Traditional power structures do not relinquish their authority easily, if at all.

Religion and National Identity

Because language, religion, and nationality affirm self-authenticating corporate identities, political leaders have drawn upon established languages and religions to create national allegiances and encourage participation in the public domain. The traditional affiliations of dominant religious groups are especially convenient for this purpose.

The division of that portion of British India under the colonial government's direct control into India and Pakistan in 1947 deliberately used religious identity to create new nations. It assigned those districts in which the majority of the population was Muslim to Pakistan, and Hindu-majority districts to India.

Muhammad Ali Jinnah, in his appeal for the founding of Pakistan, claimed the uniqueness of their identity to be based on cultural rather than religious difference. More recently, the Bharatiya Janata Party, the ruling party in India from 1999 to 2004, similarly framed its quest for a policy of Hindu nationalism as cultural, as Hindutva (Hindu-ness). They both wanted to avoid the appearance of religious discrimination, even though religious identity was the determining factor.

The use of a religious community's bonding dynamic for political ends changes the relationship it affirms among the people. It reduces religious identity from a symbolic expression of ultimate truth, a *mythos,* to an ideology that is historically concrete, literally true, and both socially and geographically exclusive. At its worst, the political use of religious symbols has led to absolutizing the nation-state itself.

The reduction of religious identity to national identity is pervasive throughout our world today. The fervor created by appealing to people's religious allegiances to promote a political cause or ideology has led to communal rioting, terrorism, and terrible bloodshed. It has left a trail of human misery in the Middle East, Africa, Northern Ireland, the former Yugoslavia, and in South Asia.

The Partition of British India in 1947

The ethnic, linguistic, religious groupings used in Western Europe to build the political identity of nations became especially divisive in South Asia's pluralistic social environment. The creation of the new nations of India and Pakistan out of the British Indian Empire isolated vast numbers of people not included in the dominant religious identity around which the national borders were drawn. Millions of Hindus and Sikhs living in areas of the sub-continent that became Pakistan, and Muslims finding themselves in an independent India, felt threatened as minorities in these newly established nations. Communal violence erupted across the subcontinent.

Children of many faiths and backgrounds who had grown up together, had learned and played together in the same classes in school for years, suddenly, on the day of independence of their country, became enemies. Dazed and mystified, those of minority faiths were whisked away during the night to seek asylum across the border. Many did not make it.

Fourteen million people fled, the largest refugee migration ever experienced in the world. Homeless and threatened in their own lands, they were forced to flee in haste, destitute of any possessions, to cross the new national borders in a quest for survival. As Hindus and Sikhs moved toward India and Muslims toward Pakistan in opposite directions across the border drawn between the two countries, many thousands were abducted and raped, hundreds of thousands senselessly killed.

Kushwant Singh writes of the devastating impact of that violent confrontation on a Sikh village near the border, in his novel *Train to Pakistan:*

Early in September the time schedule in Mano Majra started going wrong. Goods trains had stopped running altogether, so there was no lullaby to lull them to sleep . . . All trains (now crowded with refugees) coming from Delhi stopped and changed their drivers and guards before moving on to Pakistan.

One morning, a train from Pakistan halted at Mano Majra railway station. At first glance it had the look of trains in the days of peace. No one sat on the roof. No one clung between the bogies. No one was balanced on the foot-boards. But somehow it was different. There was something uneasy about it. It had a ghostly quality.

(That evening) the northern horizon, which had turned a bluish gray, showed orange again. The orange turned into copper and then into luminous russet. Red tongues of flame leaped into the black sky. A soft breeze began to blow towards the village. It brought the smell of burning kerosene, then of wood. And then—a faint acrid smell of searing flesh.

The village was stilled in deathly silence. No one asked anyone else what the odour was. They all knew. They had known it all the time. The answer was implicit in the fact that the train had come from Pakistan.

That evening, for the first time in the memory of Mano Majra, Imam Baksh's sonorous cry did not rise to the heavens to proclaim the glory of God.

Those who survived this massive migration did not experience the exhilaration of political freedom. They found themselves bewildered refugees, homeless in the lands of their birth, unwelcome in the lands to which they fled. The Partition of British India led to a human catastrophe that has left an abiding scar on the subcontinent.

The Independence of Bangladesh in 1971

A further consequence of the 1947 partition of British India was the separation in 1971 of East Pakistan to form the independent country of Bangladesh. The ethnic and linguistic identity of the Bengali Muslims, which they share with the people of West Bengal in India, proved stronger than their religious identity as Muslims in a Pakistan dominated by the ethnically and linguistically different, and financially advantaged, Muslim population of West Pakistan.

The Pakistan government, then under the martial rule of General Yahya Khan, sought to preserve its union by military force. It subjected the Bengali freedom fighters movement to an intense military assault from West Pakistan in a desperate attempt to hold the country together. According to a *New York Times* report at that time (June 7, 1971):

People have killed each other because of race, politics, and religion; no community is entirely free of guilt. But the principal agent of death and hatred has been the Pakistani Army. And its killing has been selective. According to reliable reports from inside East Pakistan, the Army's particular targets have been intellectuals and leaders of opinion—doctors, professors, students, writers.

That reign of terror caused over 200,000 deaths. And eight million people fled across the East Pakistan border into the squalor of refugee camps in the neighboring states of India. That number included over 1,500 physicians and 10,000 teachers. The International Rescue Committee reported in 1971:

With the closure of the borders by the Pakistani military, large numbers are continuing to infiltrate through the 1,300-mile border with India through forest and swamps. These groups, with numbers sometimes up to 50,000 in a 24-hour period, have for the most part settled along major routes in India. They are found wherever there is a combination of available ground and minimal water supply . . . The refugee camps may vary in size from small groups to upwards of 50,000. There has been an extraordinary effort on the part of the West Bengal and Indian governments to organize these camps and supply them with at least minimal amounts of food and water.

The refugee diet . . . consists of rice boiled in open clay pots, some powdered milk which is occasionally available, and dall, which is a lentil type of bean used for a thin soup . . . At this point the diet would be classified as barely adequate.

Political turmoil along with annual heavy flooding of its many rivers has sustained the flow of refugees out of the country. It is estimated that anywhere from 7 million to 12 million Bangladeshis are living in India today. Lack of documentation and of will has hampered sporadic attempts to repatriate these refugees to their homeland.

A military coup killed the leader of the freedom movement, Prime Minister Mujibur Rahman, in 1975, just four years after independence. And a second coup killed his successor, General Ziaur Rahman in 1981. Their deaths initiated an intense rivalry between Mujibur Rahman's daughter, Sheikh Hasina, as head of his Awami League, and Begum Khaleda Zia, the widow of General Zia, head of his Bangladesh National Party. As leaders of the country's two largest political parties, their opposition has denied the country political stability for almost twenty-three years.

Islamist militancy and terrorism have grown during this time of political turmoil, particularly on a wave of fundamentalist Islamist fervor throughout the Muslim world following the 9/11 terrorist attacks in the United States. Begum Zia's Bangladesh National Party (BNP) defeated Sheikh Hasina's Awami League government in October, 2001, with the support of the Jamaat-e-Islami. That radical Islamist party had sided with the Pakistani army during the quest for Bangladesh independence in 1971, and has continued to push its agenda for a fundamentalist religious identity for both Bangladesh and Pakistan.

Terrorist incidents rose from sixty in 2004 to ninety in 2005, in which 396 people died. Notable among these incidents were grenade attacks at Awami League political rallies, in Dhaka on August 21, 2004, which killed 22 party members, and in Habiganj on January 27, 2005. The deaths of five Awami League activists there included Shah A. M. S. Kibria, former Finance Minister, Foreign Secretary, and Executive Secretary of the United Nations Economic and Social Commission for Asia and the Pacific. Sheikh Hasina received injuries during those attacks, for which she received treatment in the United States in the summer of 2008.

A dramatic sequel of terrorism happened seven months later. As described by Haroon Habib in *The Hindu,* August 23:

> August 17, 2005, will go down in the annals of Bangladesh history. In an unprecedented act of terror, nearly 500 bombs went off simultaneously in 63 of Bangladesh's 64 districts killing 2 people and injuring at least 200. The targets were government and semi-government establishments, especially the offices of local bodies and court buildings.

The Zia government did little to investigate attacks on its political opposition, and to check the rise of further terrorist acts. Public opinion attributes this reluctance to the need of support from the Islamic fundamentalist parties to retain its tenuous control of power.

Begum Zia's government did make a claim to "successfully combat terrorism in the name of Islam" by high profile arrests in March, 2006, of two terrorist group leaders who had close links with, and the protection of, the Jamaat-e-Islami party, a fundamentalist coalition member in her government. Their capture in anticipation of national elections expected to be held in January 2007, suggested that the ruling Bangladesh National Party acknowledged that popular support for religious extremists, never great, was declining, and their support might become a political liability.

Mob demonstrations leading up to the January election caused its suspension and the imposition of a military-backed caretaker government. During its rule, in an attempt to defuse their political antagonism, both Sheikh Hasina and Begum Zia and some 200 other political leaders from both of their parties were placed in jail on charges of graft and corruption. In a further move toward normalcy, the interim government set December 29, 2008, for national elections for a new government. Under political pressure to assure the participation of both of their parties in these elections, both leaders were released from jail on bail.

With a strong showing in local elections held on August 4, and the triumphant return of Sheikh Hasina from her medical treatment in the United States on November 6, the Awami League did extremely well, winning 230 of 299 seats in the National Legislature in the December 29 national elections. With its commitment to secular government and its more conciliatory stance toward India, the country can look forward to greater control over terrorist activity in its midst.

The Kashmir Crisis

The large number of refugees and continuing incidents of terrorism in South Asia since 1947 reveal the heavy toll in human displacement and suffering caused by religious nationalism in seeking political identity among the culturally diverse peoples of the subcontinent.

When India and Pakistan became independent in 1947, forty percent of British India was under the direct control of independent Maharajas. In recognition of their sovereignty, it was determined that they should decide to which country they should accede, to either India or Pakistan. In most cases, as they were not given any other choice, that was an easy decision. The state of Jammu and Kashmir was unusual in that it had a Muslim majority under the rule of a wavering Hindu Maharaja, Hari Singh. He was already facing an indigenous independence movement closely tied to the Indian National Congress, lead by Sheikh Abdullah, the "Lion of Kashmir."

For Pakistan, Kashmir's accession was an issue of their religious identity as an Islamic state. Because the majority of the population of the state was Muslim, under the rules set by the British Raj for partition, it should be part of Pakistan. India illegally invaded Kashmir in 1947, and has been forcefully occupying that portion of the former princely state that was not liberated by Pakistan in 1948 and by treaty in 1965. Because Pakistan became a separate country to protect the freedom and the cultural integrity of the Islamic peoples in the subcontinent, its support for the freedom of the Kashmiri people from Hindu India's oppression is integral to its identity as an Islamic state. Pakistan has been eager to engage international support to implement 1948 UN resolutions for a plebiscite to let the people of Kashmir decide to which country they want to belong.

For India, it is an issue of the sovereignty of a secular nation. It asserts that Kashmir became an integral part of the country when the Maharajah of Jammu and Kashmir, even under duress, acceded it to India in 1947, according to those terms of the partition of India and Pakistan. Only in the Vale of Kashmir do Muslims outnumber Hindus, who predominate in the Jammu section of the state, as do Buddhists in Ladakh. Because of this diversity of religious groups, India's response is framed in its constitutional commitment to secularism. In Kashmir, as in the nation, the religious identity of any segment of the population should not determine the political status of the whole.

Its claim to sovereignty has been validated, India contends, by elections held for public office in their portion of the state since 1952, although sporadically between 1980 and 2002, and again in 2008. They obviate the need for a UN plebiscite. Such elections, it also points out, have never been held in Pakistan occupied Kashmir, which is ruled by a governor appointed by the central government in Islamabad.

The people of Kashmir are caught in this dispute between India's claim of secular identity and Pakistan's religious nationalism. It led to outright warfare between the two countries, in 1948 and in 1965, when the state was divided along a Line of Control. On either side of this line, both India and Pakistan describe the other's portion as foreign occupied.

The hope of those living in the Vale of Kashmir to preserve their own independent, more accepting, traditional life has been jolted first by heavy handed Indian administration in the name of making them part of India. But even more devastating has been the rise of terrorism as an instrument of opposition to Indian subjection and humiliation of Kashmir's Muslim population. The military occupation and the insurgency in Kashmir have accounted for more than 45,000 deaths there since 1989.

The level of violence also drove some 300,000 Hindu pandits from their ancient homes in the Vale of Kashmir, many as refugees into Jammu. Life in the Vale became for them a living hell.

Salmon Rushdie describes a Pandit's loss of harmony and the peaceful beauty of the sonorous mountains of Kashmir in his novel *Shalimar the Clown*.

[Pandit Pyarelal Kaul] closed his eyes and pictured his Kashmir. He conjured up its crystal lakes, Shishnag, Walur, Nagin, Dal; its trees, the walnut, the poplar, the chinar, the apple, the peach; its mighty peaks, Nanga, Parbat, Rakaposhi, Harmukh. *The pandits Sankritized the Himalayas.* He saw the boats like little fingers tracing lines in the surface of the waters and the flowers too numerous to name, ablaze with bright perfume. He saw the beauty of the golden children, the beauty of the green- and blue-eyed women, the beauty of the green- and blue-eyed men. He stood atop Mount Shankaracharya which the Muslims called Takht-e-Sulaiman and spoke aloud the famous old verse concerning the earthly paradise. *It is this, it is this, it is this.* Spread out below him like a feast he saw gentleness and time and love. He considered getting out his bicycle and setting forth into the valley, bicycling until he fell, on and on into the beauty. *O! Those days of peace when we all were in love and the rain was in our hands wherever we went.* No, he would not ride out into Kashmir, did not want to see her scarred face, the lines of burning oil drums across the roads, the wrecked vehicles, the smoke of explosions, the broken houses, the broken people, the tanks, the anger and fear in every eye. *Everyone carries his address in his pocket so that at least his body will reach home.*

Terrorism as an Instrument of Insurgency in Afghanistan

Terrorist attacks against innocent people in response to competing ideologies and military oppression have been a part of the South Asian landscape for many years. Afghanistan began to experience the severe devastation of warfare and terrorism in 1979, when the Soviet Union sent troops into Afghanistan to suppress those opposed to the Afghan People's Democratic (Communist) Party rule. The military might of the Soviet army forced some 400,000 Afghan Pashtuns to flee into Pakistan, to live in refugee camps among the 16 million Pashtuns who live on the other side of the Durrand Line that divides them between two countries. The Soviet's devastating scorched earth policy over the next decade forced many more across the borders into refugee camps in Pakistan and Iran. By 1989, the number of refugees rose to six million, more than one-third of the country's total population.

Most came across in groups of fifty or one hundred, villages or nomad clans led by maliks, the local tribal chieftains. They brought more than 2 million animals with them—goats, sheep, buffaloes and camels. It was a timeless sight. The men in turbans or woolen or embroidered caps, baggy pants and vests or robes like academic gowns, bandoliers of cartridges across their chests, old rifles or new machine guns on one shoulder. Their sons were dressed the same way, miniatures of their fathers. The animals and the women walked behind. When they stopped, they sometimes took the tents offered by the United Nations or, sometimes, just recreated their katchi villages on the other side of the mountains. Then the men, many of them, went back to kill Russians.

—Richard Reeves, *Passage to Peshawar*

The Pakistan government aided especially those refugees who belonged to conservative religious groups called the mujahideen (holy warriors), who had been engaged in opposing social and political reform in their country even before the Soviet incursion. Finding support for his own military rule by assisting the United States in resisting Soviet expansion into the region, General Zia al-Haq contributed not only advanced military weapons, but also medical assistance, terrorist training, and encouragement to those who fled the devastation of Soviet attacks on their lands. Iran and Saudi Arabia also made significant contributions to the Afghan cause. As a result, the refugee camps became not just places of refuge for those displaced from Afghanistan, but also staging and rehabilitation areas for the mujahideen returning to fight against Soviet occupation in their country.

The success of this insurgency led to the withdrawal of the Soviet army in 1989, and consequently of U.S. support to Afghanistan. Their withdrawal created space for intense internal fighting among rival mujahideen leaders, who were united only to oppose Communist rule in their country. Their warfare for control of Kabul caused immense destruction to the city. Hundreds of thousands fled, reducing by half its prewar population of close to 1 million. Countless others abandoned their blown-out villages.

In 1993, the Taliban, a militant Islamic revolutionary movement, arose amidst the country's political chaos, violence, and corruption with an urgent call for fundamentalist religious reform. With Pakistani and Al Qaeda support, it was able to capture Kabul in 1996, and, by 1999, to dominate some 90 percent of the country. It imposed upon the lands it controlled a welcome sense of peace, together with an extremely oppressive social order based on a religious ideology which asserted strict adherence to Islamic law and rejected democracy as an assault on God's sovereignty over all aspects of human life.

During the years of occupation, internal conflict, and Taliban domination any semblance of civic order and public services simply disappeared. In the solemn words of Barnett R. Rubin, "Afghanistan has been ruled, in whole or in part, at times badly and at times atrociously, but it has not been governed."

Hazardous also were land mines planted through wide, unmapped areas of the country. Reports in the fall of 2002 recorded over 300 land mine injuries a month throughout the country. And then came the intensive bombing by U.S. forces to destroy Al Qaeda and Taliban in response to the terrorist attacks in the United States on 9/11/2001. All of these offered small inducement for the refugees to return to their former homes. Refugee camps, with strong international support, provided some opportunities for education, social reform, health care, and employment not available under Taliban domination in their homelands, especially to women.

By the end of 2001, 12 years after the Soviet withdrawal, 2.2 million refugees were still in Pakistan, 2.4 million in Iran and around 1 million in refugee camps in Afghanistan itself. Two million refugees returned in 2002, overwhelming the meager resources available in Afghanistan. In January 2003, the UN High Commission on Refugees recommended that no more return because of the lack of security, facilities, and humanitarian aid to support them.

In December 2001, a UN-sponsored Bonn Agreement provided for a provisional government, with a U.S. endorsed Pashtun, Hamid Karzai, elected its leader. Steps toward a permanent government began with preparations for a national election for president in October 2004. Karzai won 55 percent of the vote, and became president for a five-year term. Elections for Parliament and 34 provincial assemblies were held in September 2005.

The results of these elections reaffirmed the religiously conservative bases of power among the clan and tribal leaders in the countryside. Their fundamentalist ideology and militant opposition to foreign intervention was revealed in the resurgence of the Taliban among Pashtuns on both sides of the Durand Line, supported by the illicit wealth of opium production. Increasing acts of terrorism, and devastating military battles between the Taliban and U.S. and NATO forces assigned to suppress them are creating havoc and destruction among the civilian population, particularly among the Pashtuns.

Without an effective response to the Taliban's terrorist violence in support of religious fundamentalism and in opposition to foreign military occupation, Afghanistan will remain a battered and impoverished nation. Inefficiency and corruption in government is also slowing meager attempts at reconstruction and rehabilitation among a people too long punished by opposing regional, ethnic, and religious forces within and international competition from outside.

The Changing Face of Terrorism in Pakistan

The encouragement of the mujahideen in response to the Soviet occupation of Afghanistan in 1979, together with General al-Haq's policy of Islamization to gain popular support for his despotic rule, gave impetus to Islamist militancy in Pakistan. And concern to maintain influence in Afghanistan as a policy of "strategic depth" to protect its own safety, led Pakistan to support the expansion of the Taliban as it grew to assert its fundamentalist religious agenda across most of Afghanistan during the 1990s.

The shared religious fervor of the Pashtuns on both sides of the border intensified with the destruction of the twin towers of the World Trade Center in New York on September 11, 2001. The 9/11 attacks confirmed for all Islamist militants the symbolic power of terrorism, even against overwhelming economic and military odds, as it had also overcome the Soviet military occupation in Afghanistan.

Muslims throughout South Asia saw the American "war on terror" in response to 9/11, particularly the invasion of Iraq, as an attack on their faith. Such an assault legitimized the violence of the extremists' jihad (holy war) to protect Islam. Such was evident in the extensive violent protests in Pakistan against a cartoon of Mohammad in a Danish newspaper, which was offensive even to the more numerous but unheard moderate Muslims in the country opposed to violence.

The "war on terror" also presented President Musharraf with a demand to choose whether Pakistan was going to continue to support the Taliban or withdraw it to provide the United States with a base to attack the Taliban and Al Qaeda in Afghanistan. His commitment to join the United States in the "war on terror" contained several ambiguities that continued to complicate this new relationship.

First of all, it did not acknowledge Pakistan's need for its own security to maintain "strategic depth" in Afghanistan by retaining what vestige it could of influence that had, before 9/11, been the charge of Pakistan's military intelligence (ISI). Particularly unsettled by India's increasing diplomatic and rehabilitation activity with the Karzai government in Kabul, the role of ISI in Afghanistan has not been clear.

Pakistan's commitment to the "war on terror" also assumed that General Musharraf, as president, had control over the rugged, mountainous Federally Administered Tribal Areas (FATA) along the border with Afghanistan, into which the Al Qaeda leadership and the Taliban insurgency in Afghanistan escaped during U.S. military engagement in the fall of 2001. Since Pakistan's independence, this area had been loosely administered among autonomous, isolated tribes outside of the jurisdiction of the national government and courts. Fiercely independent, the tribal leaders did not recognize any institution of the government, and particularly the army, as its own.

More complex was Musharraf's assertion that he alone could control the threat of terrorist activity emanating from this area, a conceit that he exploited to garner financial support from the United States to sustain his military government.

A final ambiguity in General Musharraf's commitment of Pakistan to the American "war on terror" was the assumption that use of military force is an effective response to terrorism. Because it is a response to the symptoms of terrorist violence throughout South Asia, military intervention has served more as a stimulant to more violence than a solution to the ideological issues from which it stems.

In reality, rather than suppressing Taliban insurgency in Afghanistan, the "war on terror" created an indigenous Taliban movement in FATA for jihad (holy war) against not only the American "war on terror" but also Pakistan's complicity in it. The Pakistani Taliban soon developed sufficient strength to challenge the tribal leaders in FATA, and to threaten the entire country. Musharraf's attack to remove militant Islamists from the Lal Masjid (Red Mosque) in Islamabad in July, 2007, was a critical step toward his resignation as president on August 18, 2008. By the time of his declaration of a state of emergency on November 3, 2007, he had effectively lost control of everything in the country. The assassination of Benizer Bhutto on December 27, and the results of the parliamentary elections on February 18, 2008, drove home this reality,

The subsequent bombing of the Marriott Hotel in Islamabad on September 20, 2008, was a vivid awakening to Islamist terrorism in the most secure center of the nation. It was becoming a threat to the very survival of Pakistan itself.

The Changing Face of Terrorism in India

Terrorist groups in Pakistan that had taken up the cause of Muslims in Kashmir were also energized by the success of the jihad (holy war) in Afghanistan during the 1980s. Following the withdrawal of the Soviet army from Afghanistan in 1989, India identified large numbers of Islamic militants trained in camps set up by the Lashkar-e-Taiba, Jaish-e-Mohammad, and Hizbul Mujahideen, terrorist organizations with purported contacts with Pakistan's intelligence agency (ISI), to train jihadis to infiltrate into Kashmir to fight with local insurgents and to organize terrorist cells there.

Following 9/11, President General Musharraf of Pakistan sought to use his prominence as a critical ally in the effort to rout Al Qaeda and the Taliban out of Afghanistan to bring his country's claim for Kashmir to the international community for resolution.

Because both India and Pakistan accepted Taliban accountability for terrorism for harboring Al Qaeda terrorists in Afghanistan, India thought that the United States should hold President Musharraf to the same standard for his government's support for those committing terrorist acts in India. After numerous diplomatic encounters to improve relations between the United States and India, the American government applied strong diplomatic pressure on President Musharraf to rein in recognized terrorist groups in Pakistan, and to limit infiltrators and support from them to the insurgency. This he agreed to do in January 2002, and the number of terrorist incidents in Kashmir began to diminish.

Secret negotiations to find a solution to the Kashmir dispute have intensified among private parties and public officials. At the meeting of the Non-Aligned Nations in Havana in September 2006, Prime Minister Manmohan Singh and President Musharraf initiated a framework toward resolving their differences over terrorism and other issues of the Kashmir conflict. Asif Ali Zardari, upon his election as president of Pakistan on September 11, 2008, announced that resolution of this conflict was high on the agenda for his new administration.

But even with this improving environment, terrorist activities in India have not ceased. A series of bomb explosions in a number of cities outside of Kashmir began in 1993, at the same time when Islamist terrorists made their first attempt to blow up the World Trade Center in New York City. Twelve bombs exploded in Bombay, one near the Stock Exchange, killing 287 and wounding 713. On October 29, 2005, an explosion in the Sarojini Nagar Bazaar in New Delhi, killed 62 people, and injured 155 more. A sniper killed an Indian Institute of Technology professor in Bangalore on December 27, 2005. Bombs were set off in a railway station and a Hindu temple in Varanasi on March 7, 2006, killing 21 and wounding 62. More dramatic in this series was another set of bombs set in seven commuter trains leaving Mumbai on July 11, 2006, exploding within a span of 11 minutes, killing 187, and injuring over 700. And even more recently, terrorists carried out a blatant military raid on several high profile hotels, the railway terminal, a hospital, Jewish center, and restaurant in the center of Mumbai's financial district on November 26, 2008. Indian authorities trace these incidents to militant cells, some based in Kashmir, with ties to terrorist groups in Pakistan. Police and covert services have not been adequate to anticipate and avert these devastating attacks.

As in Pakistan, terrorism based on religious ideology is also coming from different indigenous sources. Alleged state government complicity in the mob devastation of the Muslim community in Godhra, Gujurat, following the death of 58 Hindu

pilgrims in a train fire on February 27, 2002, radicalized an indigenous protest movement called the Students Islamic Movement of India (SIMI). An off shoot of this group, calling itself the Indian Mujahideen, claimed responsibility for a series of terrorist bomb attacks in a number of cities, including Jaipur on May 13, Ahmedabad on July 26, and Delhi on September 13, 2008.

A similar form of terrorist act occurred on September 8, 2006, near a mosque in Malegaon, in northern Maharashtra, killing 31 people, and injuring over 200 others. A sequel bombing on September 29, 2008, identified the perpetrators as members of a Hindu extremist group.

These bombings are not the only source of terrorist activity in India. Nor are they all conducted by religious extremists. A violent peasants revolt in the village of Naxalbari, West Bengal started the Naxalite Maoists revolutionary movement in eastern India in 1967. Today, the movement is conducting a terrorist insurgency against the government and civil militias in the mineral rich forests of eastern India, causing havoc, mostly among tribal peoples. A humanitarian doctor, Dr. Binayak Sen, who set up a hospital for the poor in Chhattisgarh, has been imprisoned for alleged links with the Maoists since May 14, 2007. His imprisonment has provided him opportunity to formulate thoughtful, non violent steps toward resolution of this conflict in his October 21, 2008, Letter from the Raipur Jail.

Separatist insurgents in the northeastern states north of Bangladesh have sporadically carried out deadly attacks on the civilian population. On October 30, 2008, three car bombings in Assam killed 77 people. Although there was an initial attempt to place blame for this act on a Bangladesh based Islamist terrorist group (HuJI), evidence of the purchase of the cars used for the bombing identified the National Democratic Front of Bodoland as responsible. The NDFB was formed in 1986 to agitate for a separate state for the Bodo people. Its terrorist activity had been seriously limited by the destruction of its training camps in Bhutan by the Bhutan Royal Army in 2004. This attack also came as a surprise.

With so much terrorist activity going on in India, Prime Minister Manmohan Singh proclaimed at a police academy graduation ceremony on October 27, 2006: "Terrorism is the most dangerous threat today and it has become a hydra-headed monster."

This sentiment was repeated by Maulana Mansoorpuri at a gathering of 6,000 Muslim religious leaders from all over India at the Darul Uloom Deoband in Hyderabad on November 8, 2008 to ratify a fatwa against terrorism. The fatwa asserts emphatically "There is no relation whatsoever between Islam and terrorism. . . . Islam rejects all kinds of unjust violence, breach of peace, bloodshed, murder and plunder and does not allow it in any form."

The use of religious identity for ideological objectives has contributed to much of the terrorist violence in South Asia. Large numbers of civilians have also been killed or become refugees as the result of communal violence in both Sri Lanka and Bhutan, where the overwhelming majority of their populations are Buddhist. That those belonging to religious minorities also speak a different language adds to their separation from the dominant religious majorities in both of these countries. But the source of this violence is more in the quest for national identity than religious ascendancy, in the name of ideology rather than of truth.

The Sri Lankan Experience

Despite its many achievements in democracy, economics, and human development, Sri Lanka has been entangled since 1983 in devastating communal warfare between the government and a militant faction of Tamil-speaking Hindus called the Liberation Tigers for Tamil Eelam (Nation), the LTTE. This dispute has caused over 65,000 deaths and displaced as refugees more than a million people.

Tamil speakers make up about 18 percent of the total population of the country. They live mostly in the northern and eastern part of the island, which has been a Tamil homeland for more than 2,000 years. There they constitute a plurality if not an outright majority in the political districts of that region.

The example of the creation of India and Pakistan would have suggested the division of the island into two countries, based on the majority populations in each of the districts of the British Crown colony, then called Ceylon. But in 1948, it was hoped that the political identity of a unified island nation would take precedence over the religious and linguistic identities of its constituent regions. It was also hoped that such a unifying political identity would prevail over any cultural and linguistic affinity of the Tamil population in northern Sri Lanka with the larger neighboring state of Tamil Nadu, across the Palk Strait in south India.

At the time of independence, there were an additional 800,000 Indian Tamils in Ceylon. They were distinct from the indigenous Tamil community of the north, imported by the British from Tamil-speaking south India during the nineteenth century to work on the coffee, rubber, and tea plantations in the southern hills of the colony. The new Ceylonese government declared these Tamils stateless and pushed for their repatriation to India. In 1964, and again in 1974, the government of India agreed to receive 600,000 "plantation Tamils" back into India. The Ceylonese Tamils saw these deportations as ominous.

Tensions between the Sinhalese majority and Tamil minority increased during a period of uneasy accommodation. In 1956, which marked the 2,500th anniversary of the Buddha's attaining *nirvana,* the newly-elected Sri Lanka Freedom Party passed the "Sinhala Only" act to make the language of the Buddhist majority the one official language of the country. In response to Tamil protests, originally non-violent, communal riots broke out, leading up to 1983, when anti-Tamil riots throughout the country killed over a thousand people. The LTTE, a small, militant separatist group, then rose with a vengeance to defend the linguistic identity and political freedom of the Tamil people. Guerrilla warfare broke out in the predominantly Tamil-speaking areas of the north and east.

The devastation caused by this violent insurgency and the Sinhalese Army response to put it down forced many Tamils to flee the country. By May 1991, some 210,000 refugees were reported to have made it to south India. Another 200,000 sought asylum in Europe. But most displaced by warfare have continued to suffer the ravages of civil conflict in Sri Lanka, dependent upon relief efforts set up within the country itself. They became refugees in their own land.

In 1987, the Sri Lankan government invited India to send a "Peace Keeping Force" to attempt to suppress the LTTE. But

Courtesy of TamilNet

Internal displaced Tamils, who surivived the tsunami in December 2004, are rescued from crossfire between the Sri Lanka army and a Tamil Tiger force in Pettalai along the east coast of Sri Lanka. In this incident, one child died and six are missing.

the deployment of the Indian army was not able to bring the two sides together, and the invitation was withdrawn in 1990.

Between 1983 and 2002, in spite of two brief cease-fires and talks between the LTTE and the Sri Lanka government, warfare increased in intensity and devastation.

With encouragement from the Norwegian government, both sides of the conflict agreed to a cease-fire in 2002, and entered into negotiations toward a political settlement of their dispute. Displaced persons from the northeast region of the country began to return to their homes.

There was little progress in negotiations during a period of military restraint. The LTTE strengthened its forces, abducting children into its military according to UNICEF reports. It also established de-facto administrative control in the north and east region. Because of bickering over control of relief and rehabilitation efforts, even the shared catastrophic impact of the Indian Ocean tsunami in 2004 did not bring the opposing forces any closer together. Military encounters with increasing intensity broke down the cease-fire agreement during 2006. The Sri Lanka army then undertook a costly major offensive against the LTTE, driving its forces during the fall of 2008 into its fortified bases along the northeast coast of the country.

In response to a plea from the government of India over the plight of Tamil civilians endangered by this intensified fighting, President Rajapaksa assured that he was "clear that there are no military solutions to political questions. I am committed to political solution and ending Tamil civilian hardships."

Despair over the restoration in the lives of the Tamil people and a compassionate resolution of their civil conflict is summarized in the plain words of Jagan, recorded by Nirupama Subramanian in *Sri Lanka, Voices from a War Zone:* "We carry a double burden now. We have to fight the Sinhalese racism and the tyranny of the Tigers, both together."

Bhutan: A Nagging Refugee Problem

Even the small country of Bhutan, tucked away in the high Himalayan mountains, has not been immune from an ideological crisis and violence in shaping its path to representative democracy. The shape of the issue appears discouragingly familiar: Can the identity of the nation include as citizens all those living within its borders who belong to distinct ethnic, religious, and linguistic minorities?

The gradual move toward modernization in this mountain kingdom has led to the migration of laborers, some from India, but in greater numbers from Nepal. The Nepali immigrants have settled almost entirely in the more productive southern part of the country, where they live as a distinct minority called Lhotshampas. In 1988 they were estimated to constitute as much as 42 percent of the population of Bhutan.

This migration challenged the traditional way of life of the Bhutanese people. To meet this challenge, made more intense by the awareness that other Buddhist kingdoms in that region—Tibet, Sikkim, and Ladakh—have not survived, the government of Bhutan took a number of actions to create a national identity based upon its Buddhist heritage. These actions included the adoption of Dzongkha as the national language and the mandating of a national dress for formal occasions. These actions were not specifically aimed at the Nepali population. However, they were taken with the clear recollection that it was the agitation of Nepalis living in the neighboring kingdom of Sikkim that led to its absorption into India in 1974.

In 1985, the government passed a Citizenship Act, which allowed citizenship only to those Nepalis who could claim residency before 1958. In 1988, this act was enforced by a census in southern Bhutan, to identify those immigrants who could not claim legal residency. The rigor of this census became a direct assault on the Nepalis. The deportations, social unrest, and terrorist acts which followed led to the flight of many Nepalis from the country. By July, 1993, 85,000 had made their way into refugee camps set up by the United Nations High Commission for Refugees in eastern Nepal.

The governments of Nepal and Bhutan have met 16 times to seek a solution to the plight of these refugees. In 2001, the Bhutan government offered a process for selecting those eligible for repatriation. But its terms were so restrictive that little was accomplished.

There is hope that international pressure can encourage an early and just solution. In September 2008, the United States agreed to admit 4,833 as a first installment of resettling 60,000 of these refugees. Militant factions in Bhutan oppose this resettlement option, convinced that only restoration to full citizenship in Bhutan is an acceptable solution for all refugees now living in deteriorating conditions in the UNHCR camps

in Nepal. They also launched terrorist bombing in Thimpu on January 20, 2008, to protest the exclusiveness of the country's first national elections.

The basic issue remains: how can Lhotshampas be accepted and protected as full citizens in Bhutan's new constitutional monarchy if the nation's identity is defined exclusively by religion and language?

Terrorism in Nepal

Nepal, by contrast, experienced a dramatic change in terrorist activity in 2006. Seventy-seven terrorist incidents occurred in the first three months. Then they suddenly dropped to almost none.

Maoist militants had ravaged the country since 1996, an insurgency against the "feudal autocracy" of the king that has claimed more than 13,000 lives. But in May, 2006, the Maoists decided to abandon armed struggle to remove the oppression of monarchy in Nepal by joining in a cease-fire with a recently empowered Seven Party Alliance. To participate in a democratic republic free of royal interference became for them a more promising way to achieve their revolutionary goals.

Many were skeptical, but the leaders of the Maoists and the Seven Party Alliance agreed on November 21, 2006, to a UN supervised disarmament of both Maoist and Royal Nepali Army forces and a government run by a Council of Ministers, with the king deprived of all power during the interim period.

The immense significance of this Comprehensive Peace Agreement was proclaimed by Girija Prasad Koirala, the leader of the Seven Party Alliance, at the time of signing: "This has given a message to the international community and terrorists all over the world that no conflict can be resolved by guns. It can be done by dialogue."

Further negotiations became necessary to overcome opposition to elections for a national Constituent Assembly from separatist groups, especially among the Madhesi people who live in the southern, Hindi speaking Terai. These discussions led to a dual ballot system to provide proportional representation for women and oppressed and marginalized groups, and constituency level voting for political parties in the Constituent Assembly. Elections were held on April 10, 2008, which provided the Maoist Party with 220 of 601 seats. A coalition of the other major parties led to the election of president Ram Baran Yadav, and the first vice president Parmananda Jha, both of whom are Madhesis. The president, in turn, appointed Pushpa Kamal Dahal, known as Prachanda, the leader of the Maoist insurgency, as prime minister. The Assembly voted (560–4) to depose King Gyanendra on May 28, 2008, to bring a peaceful end to 240 years of monarchy in Nepal.

Strides toward Democracy

Newly elected governments with high voter participation in Nepal, Pakistan, Bangladesh, Bhutan, and the Maldives (which ended 30 years of rule by a benevolent despot without violence in a run-off election for president on October 29, 2008), indicate that the nations of South Asia are making strides toward democracy. But they still face many political and economic challenges. As the diversity among them might suggest, none of them has responded to these challenges in the same way. How each is progressing on its separate path is discussed in each of the country reports that follow.

A common thread among these varied responses has been the attempt to achieve a political solution to adversarial relations among peoples that are based on more traditional and profound expressions of human identity than that of the nation-state. A political solution to human strife was the assumption and the promise in the formation of nations in Western Europe during the eighteenth and nineteenth centuries. But the experience of two world wars in the twentieth century and the continuing presence of terrorist violence and of refugees throughout the world suggest the inadequacy of nationalism based on self-determination as a way to achieve lasting unity and peace.

The independence of nations and freedom of the individual are worthy political goals. But the South Asia experience reveals to us that they are not ends in themselves. Nor can they be imposed.

Alexis de Tocqueville observed in the early years of the nineteenth century that the long-term success of democracy in the United States depends not upon the structure and institutions of the government, but upon the habits of the heart of the American people. Mahatma Gandhi, on the threshold of political independence for the people of India, also realized that democracy was not just a matter of form. It is a matter of the heart and soul of a people.

IMAGE 5: MAHATMA GANDHI

> Generations to come, it may be, will scarce believe that such a one as this ever in flesh and blood walked upon this earth.
>
> —Albert Einstein

The name of Mahatma Gandhi comes up in a number of contexts in looking at the uniqueness of South Asia. His role in shaping the freedom movement on the subcontinent was immense. He identified himself with the common people, adopted their dress and simplicity of life, and traveled from village to village to spread his message of reform. He encouraged everyone to use the spinning wheel and to wear clothes made of the hand-spun cloth called khadi. He called for national boycotts. And he fasted. In these many ways, he managed to get everyone involved in the political process of becoming a new nation.

In this way he was able to restructure the Indian National Congress as the instrument for India's freedom. The power base of this movement had resided in an intellectual elite, who had shaped its policies for achieving independence since 1887. Gandhi, building on a large number of grassroots initiatives, brought the power base to the village level. Under his leadership, removing the oppression of colonial rule was something that was happening to everyone, in every corner of the land.

Of greater international significance is the method of nonviolent protest against social injustice that Gandhi developed during his years in South Africa. He applied this method with confounding consistency in leading the peoples of British India to freedom in 1947. Its effectiveness was partly the result of his ability to discipline people in the deployment of his method. He was also able to command accountability from those who were the oppressors. In this way he established a viable alternative to power politics to achieve historic goals. Gandhi called this method satyagraha, or Soul Force. And he encouraged its use to empower all who are oppressed and powerless to gain the courage, the discipline, and the vision to become free.

In the time since his death in 1948, a number of important events have changed the course of history. The rise of the Solidarity movement in Poland initiated the crumbling of the Soviet Union and its grasp on Central/Eastern Europe. The civil rights movement in the United States, under the leadership of Dr. Martin Luther King, Jr., initiated a national policy on race relations to correct historic injustices to minority students and workers. The election of Nelson Mandela and his African National Congress to political leadership in 1994 brought the end of Apartheid in South Africa. These events released new energy and a vision of hope for positive change in the world. All traced their inspiration for how to disarm oppressive political power with nonviolent public protest to Mohandas Karamchand Gandhi, the man who came to be called the Mahatma.

Early Years

Gandhi was born in Porbandar, a small seaport town on the western coast of the Kathiawar peninsula in western India, on October 2, 1869. His father was a diwan, or prime minister, in the employ of maharajas in that region. Although Mohandas was the youngest, the fourth child of his father's fourth wife, he was expected to continue his father's and grandfather's political careers. He was groomed from an early age for leadership.

Yet Gandhi proved to be an indifferent student. He found mathematics particularly difficult. When he was 13, his parents arranged for his marriage to Kasturbai, a young woman his age. In spite of her gentle and accepting nature, he accounted himself an immature, jealous, and domineering husband. He was later to credit her example as a patient and devoted wife in leading him to see the virtues of a life committed to nonviolence.

Gandhi's mother also had a deep influence on his life. A devout Hindu, she revealed to him by her life of devotion the power of religious faith and fasting. When, at 18, Gandhi went to England to study law, he vowed to her that he would abstain from meat and wine while away. His determination to honor this vow set a pattern of discipline in keeping commitments for the rest of his life.

Gandhi stayed in England for just three years. He proved himself an able enough student to pass the London Matriculation examinations in Latin, French, and chemistry, and, a year later, his law examinations. He was admitted to the Bar on June 10, 1891, enrolled in the High Court on June 11, and sailed for India on June 12.

Shy and sensitive, Gandhi was not able to establish a law practice in Bombay, nor with his brother back in Porbandar. So he leapt at an opportunity with a local firm of Muslim merchants to work on a case in South Africa. The original assignment was for one year. In the course of that year he became so involved in the plight of Indians living in that country that he stayed for more than 20 years—and changed the course of history on two continents.

Margaret Bourke-White, used by permission of Ghandi Serve Foundation GSPEMG1946505013

Mahatma Gandhi spent time every day spinning as an act of self discipline and meditation. He encouraged his followers to do the same and to wear home spun khadi garments as symbolic acts of self reliance expressive of the freedom he sought for his people from British rule. "Be the change you wish to see in the world."

In South Africa

Gandhi's first encounter with discrimination against Indians in South Africa came in 1893, when he was thrown out of a first-class compartment of the train he was taking to Johannesburg. His enraged reaction to this affront convinced him that an appropriate response would be to encourage the diffuse group of Indians living there to work together to protest the many abuses they all experienced as non-whites in that country. He became engrossed in organizing campaigns and demonstrations for Indian rights. Finding this work demanding and effective, he decided to stay on in Africa. He established a law practice in Johannesburg to support his reform efforts and his family, whom he called from India. He also set up a weekly newspaper, *Indian Opinion,* and purchased a farm on which to set up a commune to maintain the paper's publication.

As the South African government imposed more and more restraints on the Indian people living in the country, Gandhi orchestrated a series of nonviolent protest demonstrations that engaged increasing numbers of Indians. His last protest march recruited more than 2,000 men, women, and children, and was joined in sympathy by 50,000 miners and indentured laborers. Such wide participation led the government to reconsider its policy and enact a law in 1914 to prohibit offensive discriminatory practices against all Indians living in South Africa. This movement was so ordered and disciplined by his commitment to nonviolent resistance that Gandhi emerged from this experience a leader of immense stature. He was someone to be reckoned with in South Africa—an achievement that was noticed in England and in India.

The direction of Gandhi's growth in South Africa was, in a significant way, thrust upon him. He could have been treated there with polite respect, done his job, and returned to India unnoticed. Being thrown out of a railway car because of his color and national origin was something Gandhi neither anticipated nor felt he deserved. In responding to this immediate experience of social injustice, he gained a sense of something much greater than just what was happening to him. He discovered a personal mission that he felt compelled to fulfill: to bring together an oppressed people in a quest for social justice.

Being by temperament introspective, deliberate, even fastidious, Gandhi searched within himself for resources to meet this challenge. This quest brought him to affirm intuitively (for he had no formal training in its conceptual intricacies) two precepts drawn from the classical heritage of South Asia. First, and more consciously, Gandhi identified his mission with the ancient concept of dharma, of cosmic moral order. This concept was set forward in the early Sanskrit epics, the Mahabharata and the Ramayana, as the proper behavior for ruling princes—not only as the moral foundation of their authority to rule, but also as the source of the well-being of their subjects.

Gandhi pursued the private aspect of dharma (the moral foundation for leadership) with determination. His autobiography, *The Story of My Experiments with Truth,* written mostly in

1926, is replete with descriptions of his attempts to discipline his personal life around issues of celibacy, vegetarianism, purification, and self-control. He continued this pattern of moral exploration and testing throughout his life, always seeking to be better prepared (by which he meant morally adequate) to undertake the public tasks he felt compelled to perform. Even toward the end of the long struggle for national independence, the primary issue was not whether the British would grant freedom to the people of the subcontinent. His greatest concern was whether he, personally, was morally pure enough to lead the people of India to this goal.

Equally important to Gandhi was the public aspect of dharma—that it was to be realized for everyone's benefit. The cosmic dimension of dharma is realized not in the abstract, nor just in one's personal life, but in the public affairs of humanity. This awareness made his personal experience of discrimination in South Africa a public offense that would be righted only when discrimination would not be practiced against any Indian residing there. Gandhi's awareness of the epic precept of dharma made him sensitive not only to the stringent moral demands of his mission, but also to the magnitude of its objective. He ultimately sought to liberate a people not just from the injustice of colonial rule, but from all oppression, to allow them to become truly free.

The second precept of the classical heritage which Gandhi affirmed by his experience in South Africa was an awareness of a truer, deeper reality of "self" than he normally experienced in the everyday world. He experienced glimpses of a more ultimate reality of being, what in the classical heritage of South Asia was called atma. In his quest for this higher being of self, Gandhi intuited that a vital quality that distinguishes it from the ordinary experience of self is that it is by nature nonviolent:

> Non-violence is not a garment to be put on and off at will. Its seat is in the heart, and it must be an inseparable part of our very being.

It was this deeper, more refined self that was to define the distinctive character of the mission to which he had been called—that only the means could justify the end. Above all else, the means must be nonviolent.

Gandhi's concern for reducing the level of violence in our everyday lives and in the world around us reinforced his moral image of dharma. Joined with an intimation of the atma, nonviolence requires a discipline that identifies and refines our awareness of our true self.

> The acquisition of the spirit of non-violence is a matter of long training in self-denial and appreciation of the hidden forces within ourselves. It changes one's outlook on life . . . It is the greatest force because it is the highest expression of the soul.

Gandhi's living out of these important concepts of dharma and atma identified him on a profound level with the people from India then living in South Africa. He spoke to them out of a context to which they were uniquely prepared to respond as a distinct group of people. It is also significant that his initial steps to leadership took place far from India. Author V. S. Naipaul, recalling his own upbringing as an Indian in Trinidad, describes an important social dimension to Indian life that Gandhi would have only experienced outside of India.

These overseas Indian groups were mixed. They were miniature Indias, with Hindus and Muslims, and people of different castes. They were disadvantaged, without representation, and without a political tradition. They were isolated by language and culture from the people they found themselves among; they were isolated from India itself. In these special circumstances they developed something they never would have known in India: a sense of belonging to an Indian community. This feeling of community could override religion and caste.

Naipaul added that it was essential for Gandhi to have begun his freedom movement for the Indian peoples in South Africa. "It is during his . . . years in South Africa that intimations came to Gandhi of an all-India religious-political mission." Had he begun in India, he would not have known for whom he was seeking independence. In South Africa, Gandhi discovered a destiny for a people to become a free nation. As in the case of his own sense of mission, Gandhi returned to India with the conviction that this free nation could not be born until the people of India had discovered their soul.

Return to India

Gandhi returned to India in 1915, at the age of 45. By then he was recognized as a national hero to a people without a nation. Soon, he was widely acclaimed as the Mahatma, the "Great Souled One."

Gandhi worked toward the removal of British colonial domination in India much as he had worked to overcome discrimination in South Africa: by addressing particular instances of oppression. Initially these did not involve the government. Gandhi first addressed the inequities between English plantation owners and peasants in the eastern province of Bihar, and Indian mill owners and mill workers in the western city, Ahmedabad. Feeling that Indian independence from British colonial rule should not replace one oppression with another, he attacked the subservient role imposed upon women in Indian society. He also took up the plight of "untouchable" communities—what he called "the ulcer of untouchability" in Indian life. Between 1915 and 1948, Gandhi initiated hundreds of nonviolent protest actions against a wide range of social injustices and abuses throughout the country.

One of Gandhi's most important achievements in the independence movement of India was his ability to lead the diverse people of the subcontinent to a shared vision of what it meant to be free. Drawing upon the importance of symbolic thought as developed in the classical heritage of his people, he insisted that people of all stations and walks of life take on the daily discipline of spinning thread for their clothing on a spinning wheel. This action not only freed them from the economic tyranny of dependence upon cloth manufactured in England; more important, spinning encouraged them to be self-reliant even while living under the burden of British colonial rule.

Gandhi's most dramatic act of satyagraha was in 1930, when he led his followers from Ahmedabad on a 200-mile walk to collect salt from the sea, in protest against the salt tax imposed by the British government. What began as a march of 78 men and boys, specially trained to undertake the journey, gathered more and more people as it made its way through the Gujarati countryside. When the column reached Dandi on the shore, the company had grown to thousands. The Oscar-winning film *Gandhi* gives a vivid picture not only of the energetic figure of Gandhi himself leading the march, but also of the dramatic swelling of the crowds who joined behind him to make the salt march a powerful expression of public support. Gandhi compared the march to the Boston Tea Party, which anticipated the war for independence in America. It was the culminating act of a series of nonviolent protests against British rule that led to the beginning of home rule in 1937 and the total withdrawal of British colonial government in 1947.

These examples reveal Gandhi's immense power to draw people into the modern political process by creating powerful symbolic actions. In performing them, people in all reaches of British India began to assert and discover the qualities of freedom among some of the simplest, most immediate elements of their lives: their clothing and food. These simple acts were symbolic in the classical sense in pointing beyond themselves to express what it is to be truly free.

Fasting became another aspect of Gandhi's leadership role during his years in India. He conducted 17 fasts "to the death." The first happened soon after his return from South Africa, as a part of his efforts to resolve the dispute over wages between the mill workers and the mill owners in Ahmedabad in 1918. Like his earlier actions, it was not premeditated, but grew out of the circumstances in which he found himself. The strike that he was urging the workers to sustain was exhausting their resources and their resolve. To encourage them to continue, he decided to subject himself to the same threat of starvation that the prolonged strike was imposing upon them. He could not demand of the striking workers more than he would demand of himself. So he began a fast that would continue until the workers received the wage they were demanding from the mill owners.

Unlike later fasts, this gesture prompted neither wide public awareness nor concern. And Gandhi himself was not entirely comfortable about the coercive elements of his action. But the mill owners were moved by this dramatic placing of himself on the line. After the third day of his fast, they agreed to a compromise in which all parties could feel some gain. Of more lasting significance, Gandhi's action and resolution did not allow the workers to abandon their commitment to improve their lot. He taught them by example to become empowered by their own inner strength.

In 1932, Gandhi began a series of fasts based on his concern for the plight of the "untouchable" communities in India. His initial protest was against the attempt on the part of the British Government to set up separate untouchable electorates in a provisional government in British India, a policy that was supported by Dr. Ambedkar and other leaders of the untouchable communities. Gandhi's objection was that giving the untouchable communities separate political status removed from the Indian community as a whole the need to reform itself by eliminating the scourge of discrimination and oppression based on caste. Dr. Ambedkar saw Gandhi's objection as an attempt to keep untouchables under Hindu oppression. But Gandhi was adamant, and on September 20, he began a fast to raise Hindu consciousness about the evils of caste discrimination and to alter the British proposal. Resolutions against discrimination and intense discussions with the untouchable

leaders immediately ensued. Five days later, a compromise pact was achieved and sent to London, where it was accepted by the Prime Minister. By this fast, Gandhi made a significant impact, for the first time, on a specific British government policy in India. And, as fate would have it, all of this happened while he was imprisoned by the Colonial Government in Yeravda Prison under a century-old regulation which allowed the government to hold him for suspected sedition without sentence or trial.

During the spring of 1933, Gandhi fasted again on behalf of the untouchable communities as an act of purification. He described it as "an uninterrupted twenty-one days' prayer."

Gandhi fasted twice during the final year of his life, in Calcutta from September 1 to 5, 1947; and in New Delhi, beginning on January 13, 1948. In both instances he was responding to the communal rioting between Hindus and Muslims following the partition of British India and the independence of India and Pakistan on August 15, 1947. By this time, as Gandhi entered his 78th year, people throughout the subcontinent were caught up in daily reports on the state of his health during the fasts. And they were stirred to meet his expectations of amity between the two new countries and among the religious communities which resided in both. In January, Gandhi specifically demanded as a condition of ending his fast the reparation to Pakistan of its share of British India's assets retained by the Indian Government. When that was done, the Pakistan foreign minister before the United Nations Security Council directly attributed to Gandhi's fast a "new and tremendous wave of feeling and desire for friendship between the two Dominions."

By his many and creative acts for freedom and by his fasting, Gandhi was able to command enormous authority among the people—all without the benefit of holding any political office. During his many years of leadership in the independence movement, he held only one elective position. He was elected president of the Indian National Congress in 1925. But he held the office for only one year. He stepped down to give a place to Sarojini Naidu, the first woman to be elected to that office.

Being out of political office seemed to increase the impact of his singular, moral basis for authority. It was even more commanding when he took moral positions in direct confrontation with the authority structures of his time. For his opposition to the colonial rule of the British Raj, he spent 2,049 of his politically most active days (more than five years) in jail. His self-affirming authority as a political figure and his commitment to nonviolence as the guiding principle for political action won for Gandhi universal recognition as the conscience of an empire and the "Father of the Republic of India."

Any sense of achievement that Gandhi might have felt because of India's independence in 1947 was negated by the scourge of communal rioting and bloodshed which swept across the subcontinent as the specter of partition of British India into two separate nations loomed. As the time of independence approached, Gandhi did not go to the capital to see the reins of power passed. Instead, he walked from village to village in the Noakhali district of East Bengal, seeking to quench the flames of violence that scorched that land. Gandhi was deeply shaken, doubting his effectiveness to bring the message of nonviolence to the people. But Lord Montbatten, who was in New Delhi as the governor-general of newly independent India, described

Gandhi's effectiveness in a very different way: "In the Punjab we have 55,000 soldiers and large scale rioting is on our hands. In Bengal our forces consist of one man, and there is no rioting."

The Light Endures

Gandhi remained convinced that Muslims and Hindus could live at peace together in a single, secular nation. For Gandhi, truth was not the exclusive possession of any religious community but, rather, what revealed the transcendent unity of all people. This conviction was to cost him his life.

A young Hindu, passionately afraid that Gandhi was threatening Hinduism by being too accommodating to Muslims, assassinated him at his evening prayer meeting on January 30, 1948. That evening, Gandhi's longtime friend and protege, the prime minister of the newly formed government of India, Jawaharlal Nehru, announced his death over the radio:

> Our beloved leader, Bapu, as we call him, the father of our nation is no more . . . The light has gone out, I said, and yet I was wrong. For the light that shone in this country was no ordinary light. The light that has illumined this country for these many years will illumine this country for many more years . . . and the world will see it and it will give solace to innumerable hearts.

In leading the vastly diverse peoples of India to their independence through the first half of the twentieth century, Mahatma Gandhi learned that political power is normally based on oppression and the use of force. But that coercive power leads only to bondage, violence, and suffering. He became convinced that political freedom cannot be achieved by force. It can be realized only in discovering within ourselves a more profound and demanding quality of human identity and relationship, a quality that is characterized by nonviolence. Only when we become genuinely nonviolent in ourselves and in our relationships with others can we become truly ourselves. Nations also must become genuinely nonviolent. Then they, too, will discover an identity as a people which is inclusive of all who live within their borders. Only then can we begin to think about achieving peace among nations.

Eric Ericson, in his perceptive biography, *Gandhi's Truth,* describes this insight as a profound source of hope for the survival of the human race:

> To have faced mankind with nonviolence as the alternative to [such policing activities as the British massacre in Amritsar] marks the Mahatma's deed in 1919. In a period when proud statesmen could speak of a "war to end war"; when the superpolicemen of Versailles could bathe in the glory of a peace that would make "the world safe for democracy"; when the revolutionaries in Russia could entertain the belief that terror could initiate an eventual "withering away of the State"—during that same period, one man in India confronted the world with the strong suggestion that a new political instrument, endowed with a new kind of religious fervor, may yet provide mankind with a choice.

India (Republic of India)

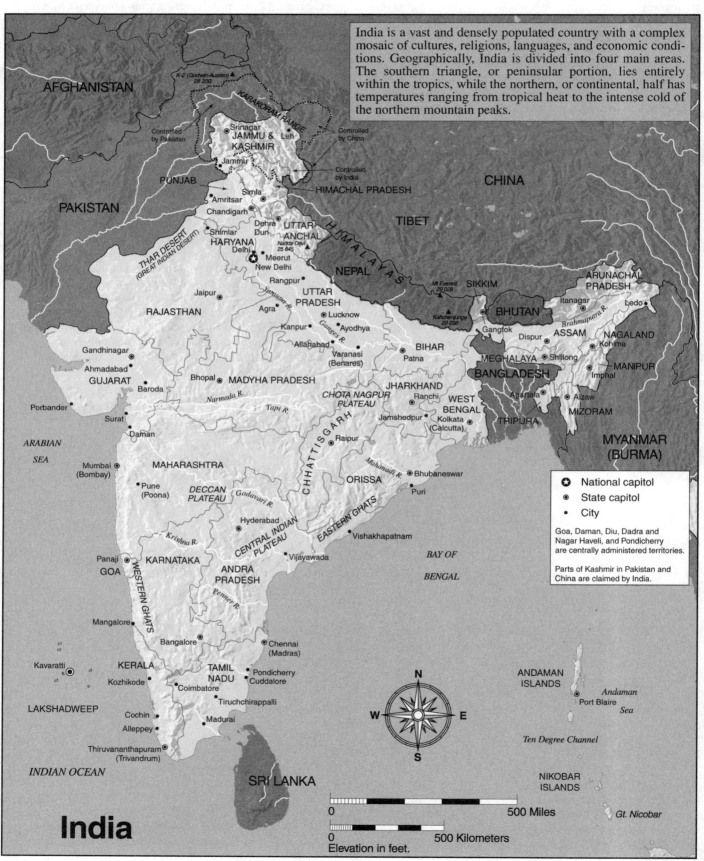

India is a vast and densely populated country with a complex mosaic of cultures, religions, languages, and economic conditions. Geographically, India is divided into four main areas. The southern triangle, or peninsular portion, lies entirely within the tropics, while the northern, or continental, half has temperatures ranging from tropical heat to the intense cold of the northern mountain peaks.

AFGHANISTAN

K-2 (Godwin-Austen)
28 250

KARAKORAM RANGE

Controlled by Pakistan

Srinagar
JAMMU & KASHMIR
Leh
Controlled by China

Jammu

Controlled by India

PUNJAB

CHINA

Simla

HIMACHAL PRADESH

PAKISTAN

Amritsar
Chandigarh

TIBET

Dehra Dun
UTTAR ANCHAL

Shimlar

THAR DESERT
(GREAT INDIAN DESERT)

HARYANA
Delhi
Nanda Devi
25 645

Meerut
New Delhi

HIMALAYAS

NEPAL

Mt Everest
29 028

SIKKIM

Rangpur

Jaipur

Yamuna R.

UTTAR PRADESH

RAJASTHAN

Agra

Lucknow
Kanpur
Ayodhya
Ganges R.
Allahabad
Varanasi
(Benares)

Kahchenjunga
28 208

Gangtok

BHUTAN

Itanagar

ARUNACHAL PRADESH

Ledo

Brahmaputra R.

Dispur
ASSAM

NAGALAND

Kohima

BIHAR
Patna

MEGHALAYA
Shillong

MANIPUR

Gandhinagar

Imphal

Ahmadabad

GUJARAT

Bhopal
MADYHA PRADESH

JHARKHAND

BANGLADESH

Agartala

Baroda

Narmada R.

CHOTA NAGPUR PLATEAU

Ranchi

WEST BENGAL

Aizawl

Porbander

Tapi R.

CHHATTISGARH

Jamshedpur

Kolkata
(Calcutta)

TRIPURA

MIZORAM

Surat

Daman

Raipur

ARABIAN SEA

MYANMAR (BURMA)

Mumbai
(Bombay)

MAHARASHTRA

Pune
(Poona)

DECCAN PLATEAU

Godavari R.

CENTRAL INDIAN PLATEAU

ORISSA

Mahanadi R.

Bhubaneswar

Puri

	National capitol
	State capitol
	City

Goa, Daman, Diu, Dadra and Nagar Haveli, and Pondicherry are centrally administered territories.

Parts of Kashmir in Pakistan and China are claimed by India.

Hyderabad

EASTERN GHATS

Krishna R.

Vishakhapatnam

Panaji

GOA

WESTERN GHATS

KARNATAKA

ANDRA PRADESH

Vijayawada

BAY OF BENGAL

Penner R.

Mangalore

Bangalore

Chennai
(Madras)

KERALA

TAMIL NADU

Pondicherry
Cuddalore

Kavaratti

Kozhikode

Coimbatore

LAKSHADWEEP

Cochin

Tiruchchirappalli

Madurai

Alleppey

Thiruvananthapuram
(Trivandrum)

INDIAN OCEAN

SRI LANKA

ANDAMAN ISLANDS

Port Blaire

Andaman Sea

Ten Degree Channel

NIKOBAR ISLANDS

N
W E
S

0   500 Miles
0   500 Kilometers
Elevation in feet.

Gt. Nicobar

India

India Statistics

GEOGRAPHY

Area in Square Miles (Kilometers):
1,296,010 (3,287.590) (about 1/3 the size of the United States

Capital (Population): New Delhi (17,076,000) (2008 est.)

Environmental Concerns: deforestation; soil erosion; overgrazing; desertification; air and water pollution; lack of potable water; overpopulation

Geographical Features: upland plain (Deccan Plateau) in south, flat to rolling plain along the Ganges, deserts in west, Himalaya Mountains in the north

Climate: varies from tropical monsoon in south to temperate in north, to arctic in the Himalayas

PEOPLE

Population

Total: 1,147,995,904 (July, 2008 est.)

Annual Growth Rate: 1.578% (2008 est.)

Rural/Urban Population Ratio: 71/29 (WHO 2006)

Major Languages: 41% Hindi, 8.1% Bengali, 7.2% Telugu, 7% Marathi, 5.9% Tamil, 5% Urdu, others; 24 languages spoken by 1 million or more persons; 324 distinct languages (Peoples of India 2000)

Ethnic Makeup: 72% Indo-Aryan, 25% Dravidian, 3% Mongoloid and other (2000)

Religions: 80.5% Hindu; 13.4% Muslim; 2.3% Christian; 1.9% Sikh; 1.9% other. (2001 Census)

Health

Life Expectancy at Birth: 66.87 years (male); 71.9 years (female) (2008 est.)

Infant Mortality: 32.31/1000 live births (2008 est.)

Per Capita Total Expenditure on Health: $100 (WHO 2005)

HIV/AIDS Rate in Adults: 0.9% (5.7 million) (WHO 2005 est.)

Education

Adult Literacy Rate: 61% (47.8% female) (2001 census)

Compulsory: in 23 states to age 14

COMMUNICATION

Telephones: 49.75 million main lines (2005)

Cell Phones: 233.62 million (2007)

Internet Users: 60 million (2005)

TRANSPORTATION

Highways in Miles (Kilometers):
1,991,786 (3,851,440 km.) (2002)

Railroads in Miles (Kilometers):
(63,221 km.) (2006)

Usable Airfields: 346 (2007)

GOVERNMENT

Type: federal republic

Independence Date: August 15, 1947

Head of State/Government: President Pratibha Patil / Prime Minister Manmohan Singh

Political parties: Bahujan Samaj Party or BSP; Bharatiya Janata Party or BJP; Biju Janata Dal or BJD; Communist Party of India or CPI; Communist Party of India-Marxist or CPI-M; Dravida Munnetra Kazagham or DMK; Indian National Congress or INC; Janata Dal (United) or JD(U); Jharkhand Mukti Morcha or JMM; Left Front (an alliance of Indian leftist parties); Lok Jan Shakti Party or LJSP; Nationalist Congress Party or NCP; Pattali Makkal Katchi or PMK; Rashtriya Janata Dal or RJD; Samajwadi Party or SP; Shiromani Akali Dal or SAD; Shiv Sena or SS; note—India has dozens of national and regional political parties; only parties or coalitions with four or more seats in the People's Assembly are listed

Suffrage: Universal at 18

MILITARY

Military Expenditures (% of GDP): $26.5 billion (2008) (2.7%) (2006) (SIPRI)

Current Disputes: with Pakistan and insurgents in the state of Jammu Kashmir; with Naxalites in eastern India, independence movements in northeastern India, and terrorist bombings throughout India; border disputes with China; distribution of river waters with Pakistan, Nepal, and Bangladesh

ECONOMY

Currency ($U.S. Equivalent): 41.487 rupees = $1 U.S. (2007)

Per Capita Income/GDP: $2,700 / purchasing power parity $2,989 trillion (2007 est.)

GDP Growth Rate: 9.2% (2007 est.)

Inflation Rate: 6.4% (2007 est.)

Unemployment Rate: 7.2% (2007 est)

Population Below Poverty Line: 25% (2007 est.)

Labor Force by Occupation: 60% agriculture; 12% industry; 28% services; (2003)

Natural Resources: coal (fourth-largest reserves in the world), iron ore, manganese, mica, bauxite, titanium ore, chromite, natural gas, diamonds, petroleum, limestone, arable land

Agricultural: rice, wheat, oilseed, cotton, jute, tea, sugarcane, potatoes, livestock, fish

Industry: textiles, chemicals, food processing, steel, transportation equipment, cement, mining, petroleum, machinery, software

Exports: $150.8 billion f.o.b. (2007 est.) (primary partners United States, UAE, China, United Kingdom) (2006)

Imports: $230.2 billion f.o.b. (2007 est.) (primary partners China, United States, Germany, Singapore) (2006)

Human Development Index (ranking): 128 (UNDP 2008)

India Country Report

India is the largest and most varied of the countries of South Asia. It is the only one to extend through all the subcontinent's geographical regions, from the snowy peaks of the Himalayas, more than 25,000 feet high, to the tropical beaches of the Malabar Coast on the Laccadive Sea. And its population is phenomenally diverse, divided by languages, religions, and cultures, by cities and villages, by extremes of poverty and wealth. It is a land of many contrasts.

India is also crowded, and getting more so every day. On May 11, 2000, the government of India officially recognized the birth of the child that extended its population to one billion. Now 1.148 billion people, about 17 percent of the worlds population, are living on approximately 2.3 percent of its total landmass. Almost four times more people than are living in the United States occupy one-third the amount of space. And their numbers are growing at an annual rate of 1.58 percent.

India reaches farthest to the north among the high peaks of the Karakuram Range in the western Himalayan Mountains, beyond the glacial plateau of Ladakh. There, west of Tibet, India shares a disputed border with China. This boundary extends east through the high ridges of the Himalayas, skirting the mountainous kingdoms of Nepal and Bhutan to the hill country of the northeast frontier. There it encounters another portion of its 2,000-mile contested border with China. It then swings south along the western edge of Myanmar (Burma) and back around Bangladesh to the Bay of Bengal.

Because of the unrelenting arctic cold of the barren glaciers coursing the steep, southern slopes of the Himalayas, much of the northern border area of India is uninhabitable. The average population density is a sparse 70 people per square mile, interspersed in protected gorges and fertile valleys that sustain isolated settlements. Most of the Himalayan peoples tend flocks of sheep, yak, and goats, or work the tea plantations and orchards on the lower foothills. In warmer seasons they form small bands of traders and bearers making arduous, heavy-laden treks through snow-clad passes over the divide into Tibet. The extreme height, isolation, and breathtaking beauty of this region have found expression in distinctive folk traditions of colorful art, music, and dance. Numerous Buddhist monasteries and an occasional Hindu shrine dot the rugged mountain landscape.

DEVELOPMENT

With a growing middle class and economic reforms in 1991, India has a near developed economy. It leads in Intelligence Technology, has a large, young labor force, and a GDP approaching 10% annual growth. But it is lagging in employment growth and infrastructure, and slowing with the global economic recession in 2008. Two thirds of the work force is in agriculture, which produces less than one fourth of the GDP. Almost 30 percent of the population lives in poverty, not sharing in the new wealth.

This remote Himalayan region is the source of a great river system, the Jumna-Ganges. These rivers provide an uneven but unbroken flow of life-sustaining water down the mountain valleys and into the great northern plains, the breadbasket of northern India. The cultivation of grains and rice is the main economic activity on these plains by peoples who live closer and closer together as these rivers, joined at Allahabad, extend to the east toward the Bay of Bengal. The density of the rural population rises to over 2,000 people per square mile in the delta of the Ganges River.

This great central plain is the most arable, irrigated, and populated region of India. Historically, it was the home of its great empires—the Mauryan (320–125 B.C.), Gupta (300–650 A.D.), and Moghul (1508–1857 A.D.) Dynasties. New Delhi, the capitol of India, lies at the upper end of this region, on the Jumna River. Although it became the capitol of British India only in 1911, it is from this site that the Islamic Sultans of the thirteenth century and the Moghul kings in the sixteenth century controlled the plains to the east and the Deccan plateau to the south.

Farther east along the Ganges River are the even more ancient cities of Varanasi and Patna, known before the time of the Buddha in the sixth century B.C. as Kasi and Pataliputra, renowned for their commerce and learning. Much of India's wondrous classical tradition in art, literature, music, and philosophy evolved in this region during the times of imperial dominance and patronage. Even today, the Gangetic plain retains its traditional importance in the political and cultural life of India.*

Rising to the south of the Gangetic plain, in peninsular India, is a wide plateau flanked by two mountain ranges. They are older, smaller, and warmer than the Himalayas, but are also sparsely populated. They have long provided refuge for renegade princes, slopes for coffee and tea plantations, shelter for wild game, and homes for most of India's tribal populations.

As in the central plain, most of the people in the Deccan live in small villages and depend upon agriculture for their subsistence. Because the only sources of water for farming are the unpredictable seasonal rains brought by the southwest monsoon, this region has not had the economic base for the political domination experienced in the Gangetic plain. Only when the great empires of the north have swept south has this region shared in a common history with the rest of the country. Otherwise, separated by geography and language, the Deccan has supported many local kingdoms and developed its own traditions and cultures.

Three of India's larger industrial cities—Hyderabad, Ahmedabad, and Bangalore—are in the Deccan region. Ahmedabad, long known for its textile mills, is today the capitol of India's fastest-growing industrial state. Bangalore has become the center of the nation's high-technology industries—telephones, jet engines, and computers. Hyderabad is also rapidly developing its own high-tech industries and is the base for Microsoft operations in India.

The fourth region of India is the coastal plain, a narrow strip of low-lying, tropical land around the edge of the Indian

*Joshua Hammer, *A Prayer for the Ganges,* Smithsonian, November, 2007.

peninsula. During the monsoon seasons, this plain is filled with luxuriant growth, especially along the southwest Malabar Coast. Its rich harvests of rice and fruits support the highest rural population density in the country—more than 4,000 people per square mile. This region also experienced the devastating impact of recent natural disasters. The official death toll of the Indian Ocean tsunami on December 26, 2004, on the Andaman and Nicobar Islands just north of Sumatra, Indonesia, and the coastlands of Tamil Nadu approached 11,000. That is comparable with the tolls caused by the earthquake in Gujarat in 2001, and by the cyclone in Orissa in 1999.

India's two largest urban centers, the port cities of Mumbai (Bombay) and Kolkata (Calcutta), and its fourth-largest city, Chennai (Madras), are in this coastal region. These cities were built during the expansion of European commerce in the sixteenth and seventeenth centuries and became thriving hubs of commerce under British colonial rule. Today, they are the most important centers for banking, investment capital, and international trade for all of India.

The growth of the population in all of the cities of India is immense. In the metropolitan region of Mumbai (Bombay), India's largest city, the population rose from 9.9 million in 1991 to 16.4 million in 2001, and to 20 million in 2008. By 2015, Mumbai will be the world's second largest city. And India will have the largest urban population in the world.

This increase is due as much to in-migration from the villages with the lure of urban opportunity as to the birth rate and increasing life expectancy of the urban population itself. With this dramatic increase, the pressure on urban lands and services is staggering, the ability to cope near—many would say past—its limit.

This limit was certainly passed by an outburst of urban rioting that erupted in Mumbai for 10 days in January 1993. It began in a climate of communal tension between Hindus and Muslims throughout India following the destruction of a Muslim mosque in Ayodhya in the north-central region of the country on Dec. 6, 1992. Mobs swept through the slums of the city, burning, stabbing, and looting. According to Human Rights Watch, more than 1,000 people were killed and thousands more wounded. Many more fled, homeless, to other parts of the country in the wake of this devastation. Although based on tensions of national scope, the Mumbai riots revealed the latent social unrest and uncontrollable violence that lurk amid the increasing poverty and oppression of a fast-growing urban population.

Even with this staggering urban growth over the next decade, India's cities will

Courtesy of James Norton

Women in Tamil Nadu transplanting young rice plants in paddy supplied by water brought by pipes through the mountains from Periyar Lake in Kerala.

still hold less than 35 percent of its total population. Today, about 71 percent of the population lives in small, agricultural villages, tied to the traditional patterns of a rural countryside. India will be for the foreseeable future a nation of villages.

Control of population growth in India follows a pattern of uneven, but significant change. Nine of the states and Union territories, mostly in the south of India, who govern about 12 percent of the total population, have made remarkable progress in reducing their annual rate of growth in recent years to less than 1.2 percent. Two states, Maharashtra and Punjab, according to the 2006 National Family Health Survey, have achieved a "replacement level" of population, producing an average of two children per family. These states demonstrate that family-planning policies can control population growth. Twelve states, with 55 percent of the population, still have growth rates close to 2 percent. It is their lack of progress toward limiting growth that places the national average at 1.58 percent.

In response to this imbalance, the national government adopted, for the first time, in February, 2000, a 10-year "population policy" encouraging all states to work toward replacement levels of growth. It also proposed not to change the number of representatives from each state in the national legislature for the next 25 years, so that no state would be penalized politically for reducing its proportion of the nation's population.

THE SOCIETY

The differences between the geographic regions of India contribute to, but do not account for, the complex mingling of culture and societies that are found in such wide array within each region. The people are divided in many other ways—by language, religion, and complex social groupings called castes.

Language

The original linguistic survey of British India in 1898 identified 188 languages and 544 dialects. A more recent comprehensive ethnographic study, "Peoples of India," identified 324 distinct languages in the country. Hindi is the most prevalent among the major languages in the northern plains region. Others that belong to the Indo-European family of languages include Bengali, Punjabi, Bihari, and Urdu. Oriya, Marathi, and Gujarati extend beyond the northern plain region into the northern parts of the Deccan and the coastal plains. Tamil, Telugu, Kanarese, and Malayalam are the major languages in the southern part of peninsular India. They belong to a totally different family of languages, called Dravidian.

The Constitution of the Republic of India recognizes 17 Indo-European and Dravidian languages. This list does not include English, which is still the link language, the language of higher education, the professions, and national business and government in most parts of the country. Nor does it include the many tongues spoken by the mountain and tribal peoples who live in the remote parts of the north, east, and peninsular India. These languages belong to very different families of languages which are spoken by Tibetans, Burmese (people of Myanmar), and even by the Aboriginal peoples of Australia.

The government of India recognized the importance of language identity in 1956, soon after the country's independence, when it established new state boundaries. One

was drawn to divide the old British province of Bombay between those who speak the Marathi language and those for whom Gujarati is the mother tongue. This division created the states of Maharashtra and Gujarat. The Presidency of Madras was divided into Tamil Nadu for Tamil speakers, and Andhra Pradesh for those who speak Telegu.

Identification with a particular language is through the family into which one is born, by one's mother, not by one's location. Adjusting the boundaries of the new states to coincide with the predominance of a language group did not change the linguistic identity of those who spoke other mother tongues in that state. Other-language-speakers live as minority groups, many times in enclaves, to preserve the distinctive ethos of their linguistic identities. These different linguistic groups stand out in the cities, where Bengalis and Tamils live in Mumbai (Bombay), for example, and Malayalis and Telugus in Chennai (Madras).

No single language is spoken or understood by more than 40 percent of the people. There have been attempts to establish Hindi, the most prevalent language among the states in the north-central region of India, as the national language. The states of the other regions of the country have resisted this status for any language, particularly one that is not their own. They cannot easily accept having their political identity defined, nor their primary education taught, in any other language than their own mother tongue.

Religion

India is also divided by religions, but in a different pattern. Whereas Hindi is nationally a minority language, Hindus are

80 percent of the total population, and live in every region of the country. Islam is the largest of the minority religions. The practitioners total close to 150 million, slightly less than the total population of Muslims in Pakistan, and more than in Bangladesh. But they are just 13.4 percent of the total population of India. All other religious minorities—Sikhs, Jains, Christians, Buddhists, and others—together make up only 6.6 percent.

The minority religions tend to concentrate in specific regions of the country in large enough numbers to become politically significant. Muslims are an overwhelming majority in Kashmir, and they are a sizable minority in the north-central state of Uttar Pradesh. Sikhs are close to 62 percent of the population of the state of Punjab. And Jains are in sufficient numbers in Gujarat, and Christians in Kerala, along the southwest coast, to have an impact on the cultural, educational, and political aspects of life in those states.

With so many differences, one wonders how India holds together. From the day of its independence as a nation, it has been challenged to find its identity as a multi-ethnic, multi-religious, multi-language country.

Economic Disparity

A four-year-old girl with her legs crippled by polio drags herself to the nearest open drain in Bombay's shantytown Dharavi. She cups the foul-smelling water and pours it on her body. That is her daily morning bath, a ritual repeated by children in thousands of slums across the country.

Some 15 miles south of Dharavi in the expensive neighborhood of Altamount Road, the six-year-old son of a wealthy businessman has a massive birthday bash on the manicured lawns of his father's palatial villa as similar rich children from the neighborhood ride around on camels and ponies supplied for the occasion.

What bonds these two children are the extremes of life that India's 350 million children face every day. By all accounts, the children in the condition that the Dharavi girl finds herself grossly outnumber those who can afford the lifestyle of the boy on Altamount Road.

—Neelish Misra, *India Abroad*
(November 1, 1996)

Another challenge in modern India is the extent and the visibility of poverty. Meager subsistence is the rule for the more than 200 million people in rural areas who live below the poverty line. Because village economy is based upon the production and distribution of food in exchange for craft services or labor—the *jajmani* system—low income means barely above starvation. Seventy-three million people live in urban slums, living on less than $1 a day. In Kolkata (Calcutta), beyond the slum-dwellers, many thousands of homeless sleep on the streets each night.

The scope of India's urban poverty is hard to imagine. V. S. Naipaul gives this vivid description of his visit to the largest slum in Mumbai (Bombay) called Dharavi:

Back-to-back and side-to-side shacks and shelters, a general impression of blackness and grayness and mud, narrow ragged lanes curving out of view; then a side of the main road dug up; then black mud, with men and women and children defecating on the edge of a black lake, swamp and sewage, with hellish oily iridescence . . . [It] was also an industrial area of sorts, with many unauthorized businesses, leather works and chemical works among them which wouldn't have been permitted in a better-regulated city area . . . Petrol and kerosene fumes added to the stench. In this stench, many bare-armed people were at work: gathering or unpacking cloth waste and cardboard waste, working in gray-white dust that banked up on the ground like snow and stifled the sounds of hands and feet, working beside the road itself or in small shanties: large scale rag-picking.*

—*India, A Million Mutinies Now*

The Green Revolution in the late 1950s introduced new, hybrid strains of rice and wheat, and grain production has increased dramatically. Since 1970, India has imported grains only once, in 1987, when lack of monsoon rains diminished the yields enough to create a national shortage. Other times of famine have occurred

---

*"Urban Poverty in India: A flourishing slum," *The Economist,* Dec 19, 2007; "Dharavi, India's largest Slum, eyed by Mumbai Developers," *Los Angles Times* Sept 8, 2008; Matias Echanove and Rahul Srivastava, "Taking the Slum out of 'Slumdog,'" *New York Times,* February 21, 2009.

in different regions when drought, earthquakes, storms, and political unrest have left large numbers of people in both cities and villages with barely enough to eat. Without further reduction in India's birth rate and an increase in urban development, it is hard to imagine how the nation's economic progress will be able to reduce the anguish of poverty and environmental decay for an increasing population. All of the gains now have to be distributed among too many needy people.

Remarkable in this context has been the emergence of a significant middle class, of households that are earning more than necessary for simple survival: food, clothing, and housing. A report to the Millennium Conference held in New Delhi in February, 2000, estimated that 25 percent of the total population in India is affluent and upper middle class, with sufficient income to stimulate a market economy as consumers. This class almost equals the population of the United States. Another 40 percent of the population is identified as lower middle class. They have risen for the most part out of the throes of subsistence and are increasing the level of household incomes at impressive rates. These new incomes created new markets and opportunities for a population long characterized as impoverished, austere, and protected by restrictive economic planning and import controls.

The emergence of the middle class was stimulated by reforms to liberalize India's economy initiated by then Finance Minister Manmohan Singh in 1991. They divested some of the government's public sector industries, reduced government red tape, and decreased restrictions on foreign investment. All of these reforms led to a spurt of an average annual real growth rate in the gross domestic product (GDP) of more than six percent. Impressive growth in the steel, textile, and automotive parts industries culminated in an ambitious plan by Tata Motors to mass produce a $2,500 car. With a growing young labor force to employ in this sector as it expands, (a resource not so available to China) the industrial sector is expected to continue improving.

An even more stimulating part of India's economic development is in its service sector of information technology (IT) and information technology enabled services (ITES), especially since the Y2K crisis. In a more globalized economy, India has taken the lead in software creation, professional-service consulting, and setting up call centers to provide a myriad of financial and support services to companies around the world. Business process outsourcing (BPO) in the IT sector of India's economy grew at an annual rate of 29 percent in 2002, to command 80 percent of the world market, making it the fastest growing industry in India. Exports in the IT sector were worth $36 billion in 2005—one quarter of India's total exports.

This phenomenal growth was built upon a young, educated, two-million strong elite. Although they represent but a small portion of India's labor pool of 464 million, their success and new incomes are producing a ripple effect on the entire economy. They are also producing a new class of "zippies," young adults looking for designer products in high-rise malls around the centers of IT activity in cities across the country.*

Among the number of complex challenges to India's economic development is the global financial crisis that is generating massive recession everywhere. Because India's banks, both nationalized and private, have been under greater regulation, and are less exposed to highly leveraged speculation, the government anticipates a less debilitating impact of this crisis on the Indian economy. Looking to the indigenous base of India's economy, and as national elections approach, it exudes optimism about continuing GDP growth, at least to 7 percent, in spite of the economic slow-down in international markets.

FREEDOM

The world's largest democracy, India has maintained stable parliamentary and local government through free elections and rule of law since the adoption of its constitution in 1950. Terrorist acts by Pakistani and indigenous Jihadis, Naxalites in east central, and separatist groups in northeast India continue to threaten the civilian population.

Even without the challenge of the global crisis, India has development problems of its own. It does not have adequate infrastructure investment to provide necessary transportation and energy for its industrial expansion. Its labor laws, some of which go back to 1947, discourage increasing and seasonal adjustments in employment, and are overly restrictive and protected by political populism. And consumer demand, growing four times faster than the economy, is outstripping the production that generated it. The global recession is, ironically, having an impact on the imbalance in imports and inflationary pressure created by this consumer demand. India will just have to produce more on its own, and has developed the entrepreneurial skills to generate the capital resources to do so.

*Rashmi Bansal, "India's Remix Generation," *Current History,* April 2007.

The agricultural sector has its own set of challenges. It employs two thirds of the labor market, but produces less than a quarter of the GNP. It is growing at only 3 percent, and rural unemployment is increasing, to over 8% in 2005. Globalization and decreasing water supply are increasing stress and indebtedness for farm communities, leading to an increasing number of suicides. Six hundred million people in 600,000 villages across the country are largely untouched by the benefits of the new prosperity. The 73 million who live in urban slums are also excluded by the unequal distribution of new wealth.

Since the election in 2004, the Congress Party's United Progressive Alliance has introduced a number of populist reforms to generate inclusive growth. In a "New Deal for Rural India," it has increased expenditures for debt relief, irrigation, health, and education. Most ambitious is a National Rural Employment Guarantee Scheme, to provide minimum wage for at least 100 days of work to one member of every unemployed household, initially in 200 rural districts. In April 2008, it was extended to all rural districts in the country. The wages are supplied 90 percent by the central government and the work projects are administered by local governments to develop local infrastructure. Although uneven in its implementation, this initiative has provided significant benefit to masses of unskilled, landless workers. Even more important, it has increased family stability and given a sense of empowerment to an impoverished people.**

The economic future of India is tempered by the overwhelming demands of teeming population and extensive poverty in both cities and villages, of environmental degradation, corruption, and strife. But aiming at a balance of productive activities which maintain a continuing growth in GDP and a more equitable distribution of the wealth it creates holds the possibility for India of sustaining a healthy democracy.***

INDIA SINCE INDEPENDENCE

The substantial economic development and control of population growth in India have happened in the context of an even greater affirmation in the lives of the Indian people. With the achievement of independence in 1947, India pulled itself together as a unified, national federation in which every adult citizen has the right to vote.

As a new nation, India had first to establish an independent, sovereign government,

**Jean Dreze, "NREGA: ship without rudder?" *The Hindu,* July 19,2008.
***Sadanand Dhume, "Is India an Ally?" *Commentary,* January, 2008; Tarun Khanna, "China + India, The Power of Two," *Harvard Business Review,* December 2007.

free of colonial domination and holding the allegiance of its vast and diverse population. This task was achieved by the transition of the Indian National Congress, which since 1885 had led the movement for India's political freedom, to the majority political party in a Constituent Assembly set up by the British Raj in 1935. At the time of independence, the Congress Party formed an interim government, with its leader, Jawaharlal Nehru, serving as prime minister. With the adoption of its Constitution on January 26, 1950, the Republic of India became a democratic, secular federation of what is now 28 states and 7 union territories.

The Constitution established a parliamentary bicameral national Legislature: the Lok Sabha (House of the People), with 545 members serving five year terms, and the Rajya Sabha (Council of States), with 12 members appointed by the president and 238 members elected proportionately by the legislative assemblies in each of the states and union territories. Executive leadership is provided by the prime minister, appointed by the president, with the support of a majority of the Lok Sabha. The president is elected to a five year term by a majority of all of the elected and appointed members of the two houses of parliament. The role is severely limited by the Constitution, so that the president serves mostly as a symbolic head of state. But he or she can, upon the advice of the prime minister, suspend both national and state governments. This President's Rule provision has been used in recent times far more frequently than the framers of the Constitution envisioned.

Five uninterrupted years in office was the rule during the early years of the Republic, when the government was firmly under the control of Prime Minister Jawaharlal Nehru. Nehru's charismatic leadership and commitment to democracy brought together many disparate interests into the Congress Party. Since his death in 1964, many of the country's social and regional factions have become more politically savvy in gaining representation for their own interests in the national legislature. The Lok Sabha has thus become more representative of the diversity of the country. But with regional, ethnic, and special interests more dominant, its institutional authority and its ability to achieve a national political agenda have diminished.

The Congress Party began to win less than a majority of seats in the Legislature in the 1970s. Selecting a prime minister became a more complex and tenuous process of forming coalitions than of single party leadership.

By the elections in the spring of 1996, the Bharatiya Janata Party (BJP) became

UN Photo 42,950

In 1950, India adopted its Constitution, thus formally establishing itself as a democratic, secular nation. The first prime minister of this new country was Jawaharlal Nehru (far left), the head of the Congress Party, standing next to Lady Mountbatten.

the first party to compete with the Congress Party on the national level. It won 186 seats, mostly from the north-central plains states. The Congress Party came in a distant second, with 136 seats. The president invited Atal Behari Vajpayee, leader of the BJP, to become prime minister. But he could not garner the support of a 273-seat majority needed to gain the confidence of the Lok Sabha. He resigned even before the newly elected legislature convened.

In the 1998 elections, the BJP again won the most legislative seats, but still fell short of commanding a majority. This time Vajpayee was able to bring together a coalition of 19 parties. The vote to install his government was 274 seats in favor. His victory was achieved only through the last-minute support of a regional party from the state of Andhra Pradesh.

Vajpayee managed to hold this coalition together to remain in office as prime minister for a little more than a year. Then the leader of another coalition party from Tamil Nadu, withdrew her party's support. Without it, Vajpayee lost his majority, and was forced to resign. With no alternative leadership able to achieve a majority, new elections were held in the fall of 1999. The BJP won 183 seats and returned to power in a newly formed coalition of 24 parties, called the National Democratic Alliance. Vajpayee remained in power for almost five full years. Feeling confident of his party's

success based upon their Hindu nationalist platform and economic reforms, he called for elections in April 2004.

Much to everyone's surprise, the BJP was defeated in the polls. The Congress Party eked out a plurality. With a coalition of 15 other parties to form the United Progressive Alliance, and the support of the communist parties, CP-M and CPI, it was able to form a government. On the urging of Sonia Gandhi, leader of the Congress Party, Dr. Manmohan Singh, a Sikh and former finance minister, became prime minister. He immediately set forward a "Common Minimum Programme" to establish a political agenda acceptable to all members of the coalition and the communist parties needed to hold a majority of the Lok Sabha.

Other political parties that represent specific minority interests in the political spectrum have gained strength. The Bahujan Samaj Party (BSP) and the Samajwadi Party (SP), represent Dalits (traditional untouchable communities, 16 percent of the nation's population) and Muslims (13 percent). Though these parties were aligned in opposition to each other, they won increasing numbers of legislative seats in both national and state by-elections. Based on its victories in the 1996 state election, the BSP joined forces with the Bharatiya Janata Party in Uttar Pradesh. Its leader, Mayawati, became the first woman Dalit to hold the office of chief minister of an Indian state.

The Samajwadi Party won the second largest number of votes in the 1998 national elections in Uttar Pradesh, reducing the BJP's dominance in that state and preventing it from winning a majority in the Lok Sabha. The election results suggest that, if the BSP and the SP had joined together, they might have routed the BJP in its greatest stronghold in India. In the 2002 state by-elections, the SP and the BSP won more seats than the ruling BJP, which fell from 158 seats in 1999 to 88. The BJP remained in power in Uttar Pradesh only by joining again with the BSP to form a majority of one in the state Legislative Assembly.

The success of these parties representing the "underclasses" reveals a growing awareness on the part of the disadvantaged communities of how democracy can work to their advantage. Such recognition can only strengthen the role of democratic government to address the needs of all of the people in the nation.

Parliamentary democracy founded in the Constitution of the Republic of India has worked well. Political parties and the ballot box have identified the public will and determined the direction of policy in the Lok Sabha, even for some of the most

secessionist-minded groups in the country. The unexpected defeat of the Bharatiya Janata Party (BJP) in the elections of 2004, and the continuing rise of the Bahujan Samaj Party (BSP) and Samajwadi Party (SP) give dramatic witness to the power of the voice of the people.

The ballot box has also worked to determine the membership and agendas of the similarly structured, though less orderly, legislative assemblies on the state and municipal levels of government.

Elections have become an important part of Indian life. Among the many villages in the country, they are taking on the character of a festival, as reported under the headline "Joy and Order as India's Voting Starts:"

What seemed important was not so much which of the dozens of political parties was up or down, or which local candidate from among the 15,000 running across India was likely to win. What permeated the mood was something as old as independent India itself: the sheer pleasure of taking part in a basic democratic rite, the business of appointing and dismissing governments, that has survived all of the disappointments that Indians have endured in the past half-century. In a troubled land, democracy means there is hope.

—*The New York Times*
(April 18, 1996)

CHALLENGES TO DEMOCRACY

Many factors have contributed to the success of democracy in India. Some will point to the example and the many years of preparation promoted by British colonial rule. Others look to the inspiration of Mahatma Gandhi and his leadership of the Indian National Congress, which brought the independence movement to the people of the subcontinent. Also important has been the Constitution and the vital leadership and vision of Jawaharlal Nehru and the Congress Party in implementing its guarantees. Other factors include the remarkable restraint of the Indian army, the dedicated service of the Indian Administrative Service, and an enlightened press. Yet with all of their important contributions, democracy still faces many challenges in India today.

An unusual challenge came in 1975, unusual because it arose totally in the context of constitutional government itself. And it was quickly met by the power of the ballot box.

In 1975, Prime Minister Indira Gandhi, to protect herself from a legal challenge to her office, asked President Ahmad to declare a "National Emergency," under the "President's Rule" provision in the Constitution. That act suspended for two years the normal function of government and the civil liberties protected by the Constitution. National elections were postponed, opposition leaders were put in prison, and press censorship was imposed. But when national elections were reinstated in 1977, the people of India voted her and the Congress Party out of office. They were not going to have their political freedom eroded. And their's was the final say.

Indira Gandhi had gained prominence as the only child and home provider of Jawaharlal Nehru. She became a widow in 1960, upon the death of her husband Feroze Gandhi, a Parsi journalist, and no relation to the Mahatma. That she became prime minister of India in 1966, and was reappointed in 1980, is itself remarkable because the Indian cultural environment assigns a more subservient role to women, and especially to widows. Her achievement underscores another, more far-reaching challenge to democratic government in India: that the institutions of government, not indigenous to India, function somewhat like a superstructure imposed upon traditional patterns and mores that are both substantial and persistent even as the Indian people become more modern.

HEALTH/WELFARE

 India's commitment to village development and universal education has improved diet, hygiene, medical services, and literacy. Birth control policies are implemented unevenly, and poverty is extensive, especially in urban slums. The National Rural Employment Scheme adopted in 2005 intends to alleviate rural poverty.

Laws, for example, have been enacted to protect women against abuses sanctioned by traditional practices. Dowry has long been expected to be paid by a bride's family to her prospective in-laws as an inducement and condition of marriage. It was outlawed by the Dowry Prohibition Act, enacted in 1961 and strengthened by amendments in the 1980s. The government of India also, in 1993, ratified the International Convention on the Elimination of All Forms of Discrimination Against Women. The practice of dowry nevertheless continues unabated, sanctioning instances of manslaughter or suicide, excused as "dowry death" or "bride-burning," when subsequent dowry demands by the groom's family are not met or issues of incompatibility surface. Dowry demands have increased and spread more widely across India as the society has become more consumer conscious. And the incidence of "accidental" death has increased to 7,000 per year among newlywed women.

With more recent policies to limit population growth and with advanced gender detection technology, India is recording a significant decline in the ratio of girls to boys in the population less than six years old. The national average of sex ratio in the 2001 census was 927 girls to 1000 boys, with many states falling below 800. Government laws in 1994 to prohibit the use of technology for prenatal sex determination have had limited or no impact on the traditional preference for a male heir sustained by the patriarchal structure of the family. Discrimination against women has increased in these and many other ways, even as India adjusts to more modern economic conditions.

Equality for all citizens is another example of an issue affirmed by the Constitution of India, but not fully observed in practice. The framers of the Constitution even included affirmative action provisions to reserve places for those of traditionally untouchable and scheduled castes in education and government. Yet many belonging to lower castes who have benefited by affirmative action in education are not able to get jobs upon graduating from college because of continuing discrimination in the marketplace. This discrimination functions openly in the daily lives of villagers throughout India, and even among Indian nationals who have moved to other, more socially liberal parts of the world.

The Challenge of Caste

Because of its hierarchical structure, the caste system is by definition inequitable, and thus a contradiction to the equality presupposed by democracy. Particularly, those who are of lower rank feel the tremendous weight of its oppression. Those with higher or improving rank are not so troubled by this inherent inequality. One's attitude toward the caste system may depend largely on one's place in the system.

To many the caste system is a rigid structure that divides people into distinct social groups that are ranked in a fixed hierarchy. For others, the system is seen not as separating basically similar people into isolated groups, but rather, as a structure that holds very diverse groups of people together. And its hierarchical structure, rather than fixing people into permanent levels, provides them with some opportunity for social mobility. As with so much about India, the caste system is more complex and more flexible than appears on the surface.

The caste system is based upon a social group for which Westerners do not have a counterpart. In the north of India, the caste community is generally called a jati (a word based on a verbal root meaning "to be born"). It is an extended kinship group whose perimeters extend beyond the natural family. The jati is also endogamous, which means that it provides the pool of acceptable marriage partners. Natural family members are excluded from this pool by generally accepted rules of incest. A jati thus extends the idea of a family to a larger social group made up of extensive cousins and potential in-laws.

Jati is important to an Indian's self-identity. Whereas Westerners tend to think of themselves in society primarily as individuals, in India, one is more apt to think of oneself primarily as belonging to one's jati. It provides a context for all of one's interactions with others, with respect to working, socializing, eating, and especially as regards marriage. In India, where marriages are mostly arranged by parents, the expectation to marry someone of one's own jati is generally the rule.

The jati is further defined by a traditional occupation, passed on from generation to generation, which gives each jati its name. There are many thousands of jati caste communities, throughout India, most of them confined to a single linguistic region. There may be as few as two or three jatis in the remote mountain valleys of the Himalayas. Generally, in the more densely populated areas of India, a villager will interact with about 20 different such caste groups in his normal daily life.

The jati is the social unit that is placed in the hierarchical ranking of the caste system. Here is where the possibility of flexibility, or mobility, arises. That one belongs to a certain jati is fixed by birth. Where that jati is ranked in the hierarchical caste order is not. Its rank is based on some general rules that are accepted by almost everyone. For example, Brahmin jatis of traditional priests are placed at the top of the caste hierarchy. That they are expected to abjure wealth, practice asceticism, and revere learning is a significant feature of this system. It does not hold a high esteem for those who hold political power, are famous, or pursue money and become conspicuous spenders.

The hierarchical ranking of this system demeans in rank jatis that perform menial tasks such as cleaning latrines, sweeping streets, and removing the carcasses of dead animals. People belonging to these jatis are called "untouchables," a designation which reveals the ancient priestly caste's understanding of its own supremacy in rank. Brahmins as a community had to remain ritually pure in order to retain the efficacy and respect for their priestly functions. Those who performed "polluting" functions in the society—those dealing with human waste and animals—had to be avoided for fear of their diminishing the priests' sacred power. They were thus placed lowest on the hierarchical scale and declared "outcastes."

Mahatma Gandhi, in his crusade to remove the scourge of the demeaning term "untouchable," called them Harijans, "children of God," and encouraged members of his religious community to perform the "polluting" functions for themselves. In many parts of India today people in these jatis prefer to be called Dalits (the "oppressed"), and are seeking recognition as equal members of Indian society. Their quest, however, still meets a great deal of resistance throughout the country.

For those jatis that fall between the high-ranked Brahmins and the low-ranked Dalits, though every jati has its own rank, the basis of ranking is not so clear or consistent. Some occupations, such as land cultivators or carpenters, are generally accepted as higher than potters, herders, and washermen. Land or industrial ownership, and thus control over production in a village, called dominance, is an important determinant in caste rank. Social practices, such as ritual observance, dress, vegetarian diet, and with whom one eats, may also determine rank. Different rules apply in different situations. As norms and conditions change, so is the rank of one's jati open to change.

Many examples illustrate this fluidity of ranking. The jati names of several ancient emperors betray an absence of royal blood, or, at least, of earlier royal rank for their caste. Such did not prevent them from becoming kings. A striking, more contemporary example is the Nadar community in south India. It was considered an untouchable community in the nineteenth century, but is now accepted as a merchant caste. K. Kamaraj, a Congress Party member in the Lok Sabha, led the syndicate that first proposed Indira Gandhi to be Congress Party's candidate for prime minister in 1966, following the death of her father. Kamaraj was a Nadar.

Even Mahatma Gandhi's family was not fixed in jati rank. The family name (*gandhi* means "grocer") identifies a bania, merchant, background. Both Gandhi's grandfather and father served as chief ministers for maharajas of small Indian states, a role traditionally reserved for Brahmins. Gandhi was himself thrown out of his jati by

the elders of his community when he went to England to study law. He stepped out of the caste system altogether when he was accepted as a person committed to a religious life, when he became the Mahatma.

The position of any specific jati in the social hierarchy is based primarily on the acceptance of its claim to rank by members of the other jatis with which it interacts. Because mobility is open only to the entire jati, and not to individuals within it, and members of other jatis need to agree, change in rank does not happen quickly. Nevertheless a social dynamic extends through the system that asserts a claim to higher rank and encourages others to accept that claim.

The Caste System and Political Change

Democracy as a form of government does not happen in a social vacuum. In India, the pervasive tenacity of the caste system has contributed a stabilizing context in which democracy has been able to take hold. And its cohesion and flexibility has provided a dynamic within a traditional social context for democracy to work. The right of all adults to vote to determine who will represent them is new to India. In a system that combines diverse peoples, in which every jati has a place, and rules of ascendancy are continually being worked out, the role of the vote in which everyone participates to grant political power emerged as an acceptable way to affirm rank status that already existed within the village hierarchy. The system does not have to change; it simply has to adapt itself to an additional way to assert ascendancy.

Winning of elections by commanding votes has found a place in the traditional caste structure in two important ways. First, because jatis extend through many villages within a linguistic region, they provide cohesive units for regional associations formed to promote political causes important to their jati members as voting blocks in elections. They also function as lobbies in the halls of government between elections. Such blocks have led to the rise of political parties to assert the rights of the Dalits in northern India.

Within a single village, the traditional caste structure adapts to democratic elections by creating voting blocks out of the local authority structures, called factions, already in place in the villages. The power of higher castes in a village faction is based on the control of production and distribution of food that is harvested from village lands. Those who dominate these village resources are quick to convert into votes for their chosen candidates the allegiances created by the dependency of those of

lower jati rank in the village who serve and get food from them. Thus democracy is co-opted to support traditional patterns of social life rather than to reform them.

The slow pace of land reform in India, in contrast to the rapid acceptance of new methods of agriculture that produced an abundance of grain in the Green Revolution, is evidence of this adaptation of democracy to traditional sources of power. New laws have broken up large land estates and reduced absentee landlordism. But politically active, regional landholder jati associations have been able to block legislative action on some of the most difficult village problems: landlessness and under employment, the inequities of wealth and privilege, and landowner-laborer relations. Disputes between landowners and their laborers are still mostly resolved by force, with little interference by the police or protection from the courts.

This amazing, and sometimes horrifying, capacity for persistence and adaptation of India's traditional social institutions is a basis for concern. But they may also provide the multicultural context in which the liberating force of democracy may be achieved without the need for violent revolution.

ACHIEVEMENTS

Through the Green Revolution, India has been self sufficient in grains since 1970. Technology and a growing middle class have attracted increasing direct investment in the economy. The impact of Indian-Americans and popular artists like musician Ravi Shankar reveal the vitality of India's heritage of creativity in language, art, and human relations.

The Challenge of Religious Nationalism

Another persistent challenge to India's democracy as its people have become more politically conscious has been to hold itself together as a nation in the face of many competing and divisive forces for greater religious, linguistic, or ethnic autonomy. Insurgencies and the recent proliferation of terrorist acts throughout South Asia have been pursued in the name of more exclusive political identities.

The writer V. S. Naipaul assumed from his childhood in Trinidad that immigrants from India of many different backgrounds shared a cultural identity as Indians. When he visited India he was surprised to discover that this was not true for the same diversity of people who lived in India itself:

When I got there I found [the idea of being an Indian] had no meaning in India. In the torrent of India, with its hundreds of millions, that continental idea was no comfort at all. People needed to hold on to smaller ideas of who and what they were; they found stability in the smaller groupings of region, clan, caste, family.

—*India: A Million Mutinies Now*

None of these smaller ideas of identity are based on political associations. They are, rather, linguistic, religious, and social, such as caste, into which the people of India are grouped not by events, but by birth.

Because 80 percent of the people of India are Hindu, their religion is readily available to create an exclusive national identity. Their overwhelming number is a source of great concern to those who are in a religious minority: Muslims, Sikhs, Parsis, Buddhists, Jains, Christians, and Jews. The call for the separate nation of Pakistan was in response to this anxiety among the Muslim community in British India. How could a predominantly Hindu society, determined to meet its own objectives in a democracy, not discriminate against, if not actually oppress, people of other religions?

The Indian National Congress, which for 60 years worked constructively and diligently for the independence of India from British rule, was committed to realizing a free India as a secular state. Mahatma Gandhi's vision of a universal religious identity and the democratic idealism of India's leaders in its early years as a republic held to the goal that the government must recognize the presence and the integrity of its many different religious communities. In the words of India's Constitution, "all persons are equally entitled to freedom of conscience and the right freely to profess, practice, and propagate religion." Freedom for all religions prohibits the domination of any religion over any of the others.

The separation between the secular identity of the nation-state and the religious identities of its peoples has not, however, always been clear.

Three specific movements have challenged the commitment to political secularism in India. First is the outright demand by a militant wing of the Sikh community for an independent state, called Khalistan, to be established in the current state of Punjab, in northwest India.

To quell the violence of this nationalist demand in its frequent, random terrorist attacks and kidnappings, the Indian army went into the Golden Temple in Amritsar to rout out of the temple's protective walls a militant Sikh separatist leader who had sought sanctuary there. The outrage felt by

UN Photo 87,052

In India, religious identity often takes precedence over the idea of belonging to a nation. Many religious sects demand political recognition. In 1984, the Indian Army stormed the Golden Temple in Amritsar (pictured above), the sacred shrine of the Sikh community. This action was in response to Sikhs' demand for the establishment of an independent state in Punjab. In retaliation, two of her Sikh bodyguards assassinated Prime Minister Indira Gandhi.

the Sikh community over this assault on the sacred shrine of the entire Sikh community led to the assassination of Prime Minister Indira Gandhi later that year by two Sikh members of her bodyguard. Her death stirred reprisals against Sikhs, killing 3,000 in riots across the north of India.

Continuing violence caused the suspension of the 1991 elections in Punjab. After political order was restored, they were held in February 1992, and a moderate Sikh, Prakash Singh Badal, was elected chief minister of the state. His assassination in August 1995, revealed that tension still existed among Sikhs and with surrounding Hindu communities. Yet, the 1996 and all subsequent elections in Punjab have been conducted with a remarkable reduction of violence.

Indira Gandhi's response to Sikh militancy was secular in intent: to hold India, with all of its religious differences, together as one nation. But religious rather than political identities defined the participants in this confrontation. The drastic consequences were the result of Sikhs and Hindus having greater allegiance to the exclusiveness of their religion than to the inclusiveness of the nation.

The second recent challenge to political secularism in India has been the rise of religious nationalism as a political movement. The man who assassinated Mahatma Gandhi in 1948 did so in the name of Hindu nationalism. He felt that Gandhi's attempts to accommodate the Muslim communities into an independent India were compromising his Hindu faith too much. By this action, he affirmed the greatest fears of those advocating an independent Pakistan: that they

would not receive equal status as a religious minority in the new nation of India. As a consequence of Mahatma Gandhi's example and his death, the quest to achieve a truly secular nation took on great urgency during the early years of India's independence.

As political awareness and participation increased among India's peoples, their religious identity has also been stimulated. One impetus was a television extravaganza. In 1987, a film producer, at the invitation of the national government, created a television series based on the Ramayana, a classical Indian epic.

The original Sanskrit account of the ideal Indian prince, Rama, recognized by Hindus as an incarnation of the Supreme God Vishnu, was composed 2,000 years ago. The story is more popularly known and celebrated among the Hindi-speaking population in a translation of this epic done by a religious poet, Tulsidas, in the sixteenth century A.D. Doordarshan, the national television channel, broadcast the modern television serial, described as "a mixture of soap opera and national mythology," on Sunday mornings in 104 half-hour episodes.

During its broadcast, almost all of India came to a halt. More than 100 million viewers were glued to any television set (some 25 million of them) they could find. The serial was an immense success, both in telling the story and in spreading the virtues of television among millions of new viewers.

The intent of the government and the serial's producers had been to extol India's ancient, albeit Hindu, heritage as a way of encouraging a greater sense of national pride. The serial actually stirred up religious sentiments of both Hindus and the minorities who had reason to fear the arousal of such passion.

The television serial also coincided with the rise of a new political party committed to Hindu nationalism, the Bharatiya Janata Party (BJP). In a country where many have risen to political prominence through the film industry, it is not difficult to ascribe increasing popularity of this new party directly to the broadcast of the Ramayana. Even more did the BJP gain from a sequel television serial. India's other, older and longer epic, the Mahabharata, was presented in 93 hour-long episodes from October 1988 to July 1990. Like the Ramayana, this epic extols the virtues of an ancient Hindu past. And it includes the original recitation of the most revered text of contemporary Hinduism, Bhagavad Gita, "The Song of the Lord."

The Bharatiya Janata Party had won only two seats in Parliament in the elections of 1984. In 1989, its holdings jumped to 89. In the 1991 elections, they won 118 seats, then second only to the Congress Party, which won 225 seats, briefly diminishing that party's hopes for a majority in the Lok Sabha. The BJP won a slim majority that year in the legislative assembly of India's largest state, Uttar Pradesh, a long-time Congress Party stronghold.

In this rise to political prominence, the Bharatiya Janata Party tied its fortunes directly to another incident which is also related to Rama, the hero of the Ramayana, and that also received extensive television viewing attention, but this time as national news. The BJP leadership became actively involved in a campaign to build a temple to Rama on the site of his legendary birthplace in the city of Ayodhya, in eastern Uttar Pradesh. Through a number of public demonstrations, including a chariot procession across northern India, the party was able to rouse a large amount of public support for the building project and for its leadership as a political force. Such a mingling of religion and politics was effective, but potentially dangerous.

What made the building campaign particularly volatile was that the location for the temple to Rama was on the site of the Babri Masjid, a historic, but unused, Muslim house of prayer. This mosque was built in 1528 (purportedly on the site of a temple that had been destroyed) for Babur, the first of the Islamic Moghul Emperors in India. Because the Muslim community was equally eager to preserve the vestiges of its own glorious past in India, the project placed the BJP in direct conflict with the Indian Muslim minority. In hopes of working out a political compromise that would

not stimulate further religious antagonism between Hindus and Muslims, Prime Minister Narasimha Rao placed the dispute over the ownership of this land in the hands of the Supreme Court of India.

The BJP, in control of the Uttar Pradesh government, became impatient with the maneuvering by the prime minister. It supported a rally on Dec. 6, 1992, at the Babri mosque/proposed Rama temple site in Ayodhya. The BJP's aim was to keep national attention on its objective to promote the interests of Hindus, and to urge approval to build the temple. A crowd of over 700,000 people from across the country gathered for the rally in that city of some 70,000 residents. Even though the national government had assigned 15,000 troops there to maintain order, the situation got out of control, and a small group of enthusiasts scaled the Babri mosque and pulled it apart.

The response throughout the country was immediate and devastating. Dormant feelings of anger, fear, frustration, and hatred erupted into communal riots across India. Hundreds of people were killed, and vast numbers of shops and homes destroyed, from Assam to Kashmir to Kerala. The violence quickly spread into neighboring Pakistan and Bangladesh, where Hindu temples and homes were destroyed in reprisal. A tinderbox of communal resentment based on religion had exploded.

These outbursts of communal rioting and the increasing strength of the BJP as a political party both suggested that the Hindu religious identity of the majority of the Indian people was defining their national character more powerfully than the political institutions that were established by the Constitution in 1950. The dawn of Ram Raj, an idyllic age of government led by the power of God, was proclaimed, and the specter of Hindu religious fundamentalism was on the rise.

The BJP continued to increase in political strength. The party's greatest appeal was among an emerging rural middle class throughout north India. This more traditional support suggests that the real power of the BJP was not religious, but rather, the conservative forces of the privileged who dominate India's agrarian society. Even though this political base built on communal sentiment that identifies India as exclusively a Hindu nation, it never got wider support.

To gain a majority in the Lok Sabha, the BJP had to form coalitions with other parties, which caused it to temper some of its extremist Hindu positions. It continued to rewrite India's history in school textbooks and to permit attacks against Christian missionaries and converts. But its assertions of Hindutva (Hinduness) were presented as cultural, not religious. Its main concern

was to be a national political party, not to establish a national religious identity.

The BJP, under the leadership of Prime Minister Vajpayee, in a 24-party coalition called the National Democratic Alliance, stayed in power from 1999 until the elections in 2004 on the national level. But during this time it lost control of legislatures in seven states, retaining its power in only four others. An important exception was in Gujarat, where the BJP survived a challenge in by-elections held in December 2002, in response to communal violence that broke out on February 27, 2002.

That violence began when 58 passengers, mostly women and children, were killed in a train in which they were returning from a pilgrimage to Ayodhya to visit the Ram temple site. The train was allegedly set on fire by a band of Muslim slum dwellers from the town of Godhra, in eastern Gujarat. Attacks in reprisal against Muslim communities in the state led to the destruction of many homes and the death of more than 1,000 people.

Accusations were made that the BJP government in Gujarat did not act to contain the violence against the Muslim population. It was suspended by President's Rule and by-elections were set to be held after a cooling-off period. The party used this episode of communal violence, and a terrorist attack on a Hindu temple in September, to generate political support among the Hindu majority in the state. In the December by-election, the BJP won a commanding majority, 117 out of 182 seats in the state Assembly.

Nationally, however, the violence against Muslims in Gujarat stirred a reaction against Hindu nationalist sentiment. Prime Minister Vajpayee felt called upon to stress the need for a more balanced, secular approach to government. In the elections in the spring of 2004, the BJP won only 138 of the 543 seats in the Lok Sabha.

Their defeat suggested that their religious agenda had played itself out in Indian national politics. Shashi Tharoor expressed a more respectful understanding of the religious integrity of Hinduism than its reduction to political identity when he wrote in response to the communal violence that followed the Ayodhya temple episode:

> It pains me to read in the American newspapers of "Hindu fundamentalism," when Hinduism is a religion without compulsory fundamentals. That devotees of this essentially tolerant faith are desecrating a place of worship and assaulting Muslims in its name is a source of both sorrow and shame. India has survived the Aryans, the Mughuls, the British; it

Press Information Bureau, Government of India/NP16195   Press Information Bureau, Government of India/NP16195

Men and women voting at separate voting stations in Guraz, Jammu and Kashmir on September 16, 2002.

has taken from each—language, art, food, learning—and outlasted them all. The Hinduism that I know understands that faith is a matter of hearts and minds, not bricks and stone.

—*Indian Express*
(January 20, 1993)

The third challenge to political secularism is in the state of Jammu and Kashmir, the one state in India where Muslims are an overall majority. The Congress Party first attempted to suppress an independence movement in Kashmir by successively courting and jailing Sheikh Abdullah, whose initial quest for Kashmiri freedom was from Maharajah Hari Singh before the independence of India in 1947.

After Abdullah's death in 1982, Prime Minister Indira Gandhi, upset by initiatives by his son, Farooq Abdullah, to obtain greater autonomy for Kashmir, appointed a dedicated civil servant, Jagmohan, as governor of the state. He dismissed the state legislature under the "President's Rule" provision in the Constitution, and instituted severely aggressive measures by India's military to enforce his control.

The Muslim separatist movement, energized by this repression, received additional religious fervor and support from militant Muslims, *jihadis,* mostly from Pakistan, who had been fighting in Afghanistan during the 1980s to free that country from Soviet military occupation. Using the weaponry and terrorist tactics learned to overcome the massive strength of the Soviet army, the insurgents attacked the Indian military and many civilians with deadly force. More than 45,000 people were to die in this conflict.

During this time of violence, India's military presence, mismanagement of elections, and human rights abuses continued to erode public support. But the government of India still asserted its claim to sovereignty granted by Maharajah Hari Singh

in 1947, by calling for legislative elections in the fall of 2002 and, again, in 2008. It attempted to encourage the All Parties Hurriyat Conference, a conglomerate of 23 separatist parties in Kashmir, to participate in these elections. The Hurriyat declined, stating that a dialogue between India and Pakistan about their rival claims for Kashmir should occur before any elections that presuppose India's sovereignty over them. Even though many believed that the 2002 elections would not be possible because of the anticipated violence, 44 percent of the electorate voted. They defeated the incumbent National Conference. A coalition of the Peoples Democratic Party, the Congress Party, and the Peoples Democratic Forum, a Communist party, gained a slim majority to form a new government. The new chief minister, Mufti Mohammad Sayeed, head of the PDP, promised to "heal the wounds of militancy" in this terribly ravaged state.

General Musharraf's commitment in January 2002 to stop the infiltration of Pakistani militants into Kashmir led to a considerable reduction of violence in the Valley. And the joint leadership of the PDP and Congress Party was able to restore confidence of the Kashmiri people in their government. A dispute over the use of land by a Hindu religious group in Kashmir during the summer of 2008 led to large demonstrations of young protesters against Indian military occupation in Kashmir and calls by separatist groups to boycott the fall elections. But turnout at the polls, under extensive police protection, was over 60 percent. Omar, Sheikh Abdullah's grandson, and his National Conference were returned to power with a plurality of 28 of 87 seats in the state legislature.

Hope for a resolution of the Kashmir issue is increasing with a more conciliatory attitude of Pakistan's new President Zardari. The Mumbai terrorist attack on November 26, 2008, is making it even more urgent and no less elusive. The Kashmiri remain caught between the conflicting

national ideologies of India's need to affirm its commitment to an inclusive, secular state and Pakistan's claim that it is the only legitimate government for Muslims in the northwestern portion of the subcontinent.*

Although jihadi violence has diminished in Kashmir, Islamist terrorism has increased in other parts of India. A deadly bombing in Mumbai took place in 1993, and again in 2006. Random bombs have also been detonated in a number of other Indian cities. Most devastating, armed militants invaded the financial district of Mumbai, on November 26, 2008, killing 172 in the railway station, a Jewish center, and two of the city's most exclusive hotels. These acts have been traced to terrorist organizations in Pakistan. This support suggests that militant elements in Pakistan remain convinced that the tension created by terrorist attacks throughout the country to destabilize India is the best means to obtain security for Pakistan as well as push their fundamentalist agenda in this volatile region of the world.

Other bomb incidents in Jaipur, Ahmedabad, and Delhi have been traced to indigenous Muslim groups radicalized by the violence against Muslims in Gujarat in 2002. They identify themselves as the Indian Mujahideen. Radical Hindu groups perpetrated terrorist bombings of Muslims in Malegaon, and in Orissa, Hindu extremists torment Christians among the Dalit population there.**

Religious ideology is not the only source of terrorist activity in India. Separatist groups have been selectively bombing in the northeast region of India since 1979, in quest of greater autonomy if not outright independence for the Assamese and Bodo people. And Maoist groups and countering Salwa Judum militias have been spreading violent destruction across the tribal areas of eastern India.*

---

*Steve Coll. "The Backchannel," *The New Yorker,* March 2, 2009.
**Somini Sengupta, "Hindu Threat to Christians: Convert or Flee," *NY Times,* Oct 13, 2008.

Terrorism has become an unsettling force in the quest for economic growth and peaceful democracy in India, and it is taking a heavy toll.

REGIONAL POLITICAL CONCERNS

As India becomes more economically productive, it enters into a global arena with both the United States and China to find more sources of energy. Its economy at the present rate of growth will demand, in twenty years, double what it uses today. India has significant coal reserves, but 90 percent of its oil is imported. That India looks to Iran as a major supplier places it in an adverse relationship with the United States politically as well.

India's quest to be recognized as a nuclear power made nuclear proliferation another major issue in its relations on the world scene. The world was shocked when India tested nuclear bombs in May 1998, and Pakistan followed with tests of its own two weeks later.

Pakistan, because it recognizes India as a continuing threat to its existence, does not feel secure with India's overwhelming nuclear advantage. The rise to power of the Bharatiya Janata Party as a Hindu nationalist party added to Pakistan's apprehensions. It felt compelled to answer India's test.

India did not react to Pakistan's tests. Nor did it respond to Pakistan's nuclear threats during the Kargil incursion in the summer of 1999, which it repulsed with conventional arms. And it did not assert its nuclear capability in its military build-up in 2002 to stop further terrorist acts following the attempt to blow up the Parliament Buildings in New Delhi on December 13, 2001. Both countries recognize the power of the rhetoric of nuclear deterrence, particularly in getting America's attention. But they also avoid any circumstance for the actual use of nuclear weapons. Both realize that nuclear warfare in South Asia would be a catastrophic end for both countries. India's need for nuclear deterrence, ever since 1971, has been to defend itself not from Pakistan, but from other atomic powers, especially China.

Ironically, the American response to India's nuclear tests did not acknowledge that U.S. policy itself contributed to India's need to acquire what its strategic planners call "credible minimum nuclear deterrence." In the absence of binding international disarmament or control over nuclear weapons development, India's security depends upon its developing sufficient second-strike

*Ravi Shankar Prasad, "Where democracy shines through," *The Hindu,* January 14, 2009.

Timeline: PAST

3000–1500 B.C.
Harappan city culture

1500–500 B.C.
Aryan Vedic culture

500 B.C.–A.D. 300
Buddhist civilization

A.D. 200–1000
Classical Hindu civilization

1200–1857
Medival Islamic civilization

1602–1857
British East India Company

1857–1947
The British Raj era

1885
The founding of the Indian National Congress, start of the independence movement

1915
Mohandas Gandhi returns to India from South Africa

1930
Gandhi conducts the Sat March

1935
The Government of India Act provides limited self-government

1947
Independence

1947–1964
The Jawarhalal Nehru era

1950
The Constitution establishes India as a democratic, secular, sovereign nation

1965–1984
The Indira Gandhi era

1975
National emergency was declared and led to the suspension of civil liberties

1984
Operation Blue-star attack on the Golden Temple, Amritsar; the assassination of Indira Gandhi

1984–1991
The Rajiv Gandhi era

1990s
Rajiv Gandhi is assassinated; the Babri Masjd is destroyed and leads to riots nationwide; nuclear tests startle the world; rise to power of the BJP, a Hindu nationalist party

capability to have a credible response to a threat of nuclear attack.

India's one attempt to confront its large Asian neighbor, China, with conventional arms was to settle a border dispute in 1962. This confrontation led to a humiliating rout of India's border forces. Relations with China since have been formal, and inconsequential, due in large part to a lack of interest on China's part. India cannot help feeling that its nuclear capability has been an important protection. And is reluctant to participate in any regional nuclear agreement

PRESENT

2000s
India expands its role in regional and global political and economic organizations

Communal violence in Gujarat leads to state elections

The Kashmir dispute remains intractable and dangerous

2004
Congress Party defeats BJP in national elections

Manmohan Singh becomes Prime Minister

Tsunami devastates Andaman and Nicobar Islands, coast of Tamil Nadu, causing 10,000–20,000 deaths

2006
Terrorism accounted for over 2000 deaths, over half by Kashmiri cells supported by Pakistan based groups in Kashmir and throughout India, notably in Mumbai on July 11, and another 600 by Naxalites in east central India.

2008
Terrorist bombings in Jaipur, Ahmedabad, and New Delhi are traced to indigenous Islamists radicalized by discrimination against Muslims. Armed attack by 10 terrorists on central railway station, a Jewish center, and two 5-star hotels in Mumbai kills 172, strains relations with Pakistan.

2009
National elections for Lok Sabha

that excludes China. Its preference would be to have all the major powers, including the United States, join in an enforceable nuclear disarmament treaty.

India is concerned that U.S. nuclear policy is not committed to a workable timetable to eliminate all nuclear weapons in compliance with the Nuclear Non-Proliferation Treaty, which the United States signed in 1968. It does not have any confidence that the U.S. can restrain, specifically, China's ability to destabilize South Asia by providing nuclear materials to Pakistan. And U.S. policy did not prevent Pakistan from providing nuclear know-how to other countries. In the absence of such assurance, India, for its own security, requires that it retain its nuclear testing option. In spite of immense diplomatic pressure, India, like the United States, has not signed the Comprehensive (Nuclear) Test Ban Treaty.

India has combined its policy of credible deterrence with a unilateral commitment not to make a first-strike use of nuclear arms. It has signed a no-first-strike agreement with China. And Pakistan's President Zardari has offered to join in a similar agreement with India.

The most recent step in India and the United States' dance on nuclear capability came with an agreement for the United States to provide India with nuclear fuel and technology, with certain restrictions on its use and an attempt to restrict any further testing of nuclear weapons by India. It was initiated at a joint meeting of Prime Minister Manmohan Singh and President George W. Bush at the White House on July 18, 2005 and finally accepted by a confidence vote in the Indian Lok Sabha on July 22, 2008, approved by a waiver of the Nuclear Suppliers Group (NSG) on September 6, and ratified by the U.S. Congress on December 8, 2006.

This agreement passed in the Lok Sabha over strong opposition to India's becoming entangled in any subservient relationship with the United States. It passed in Congress partly because the United States does not see India's nuclear arms capability as a threat because of its history of stable, civilian government. Also significant was the influence of the India lobby in the United States, reflecting an increasing population, now some 2 million, of students and professionals who have migrated from India to form the wealthiest ethnic minority in the United States. But the strongest incentive was the hope that a democratic and economically expanding India would become a strategic security partner in future engagement with China. The achievement of this important agreement has not only increased India's nuclear energy potential. It has also recognized India as a legitimate nuclear power.*

_____

*Pavel Podvig, "A Silver Lining to the US-India Nuclear Deal," *Bulletin of the Atomic Scientists,* 21 October 2008.

Because of its overwhelming size, and now with its increasing economic clout, India remains dominant in relation to the other countries of South Asia.

Bhutan's economy is, for example, totally dependent upon Indian investment, and its foreign relations are, by longstanding treaty, handled by the government of India. Though the issue of terrorism in India is most seriously emanating from jihadis trained in Pakistan and infiltrating through Kashmir, Bangladesh, and Nepal, Bhutan acted quickly to India's request to eliminate hideouts and training camps for militant insurgent groups active in Assam and Nagaland in northeastern India. Nepal is also overly dependent upon India for its economic development.

Because of the terrorism issue, relations with Pakistan and Bangladesh have been more contentious. They are both aware that India, by attacking Pakistan in 1971, determined that they are two nations instead of one. Also important, the rivers that represent the major source of water for irrigation in both of these countries, unlike Bhutan and Nepal, originate in and are controlled by their powerful neighbor.

India remains supportive of the Sri Lankan government in its protracted war against the Tamil separatist LTTE, but is wary of the dangers to an increasing number of internally displaced Tamil civilians in the intensifying conflict. India was the first to send naval ships for relief work in Sri Lanka, and to the Maldives and Sumatra, following the tsunami disaster in December, 2004.

India continues to pursue avenues of wider economic and diplomatic cooperation. It maintains an active role in the 113-nation Non-Aligned Movement, which met in Havana, Cuba, in September 2006. It also became a full dialogue partner in the Association of Southeast Asian Nations (ASEAN) in January 1997. This status in ASEAN is shared with the United States, the European Union, Australia, Japan, and South Korea. India's admission overcame the concerns of Southeast Asian leaders that they not be drawn into such South Asian issues as the Kashmir dispute.

India is seeking greater recognition in the world. As its nuclear deal with the United States brought acceptance of it as a nuclear power, it also appreciates the opportunity to contribute to solving the global economic crisis as a developing nation in the G20 deliberations. And it aspires to become a permanent member of an expanded United Nations Security Council.

Even with such substantial gains and aspirations, V. S. Naipaul aptly does not use the word "success" to describe what is happening in India. There is too much poverty, inequality, disparity, conflict, and violence. But he recognizes that much of this condition is the result of an awakening of a new political consciousness in the country. "A million mutinies supported by twenty kinds of group excess, sectarian excess, religious excess, regional excess."

And he finds in this awakening a vision of hope: "the beginnings of self-awareness . . . the beginning of a new way for the millions, part of India's growth, part of its restoration."

Afghanistan (Islamic State of Afghanistan)

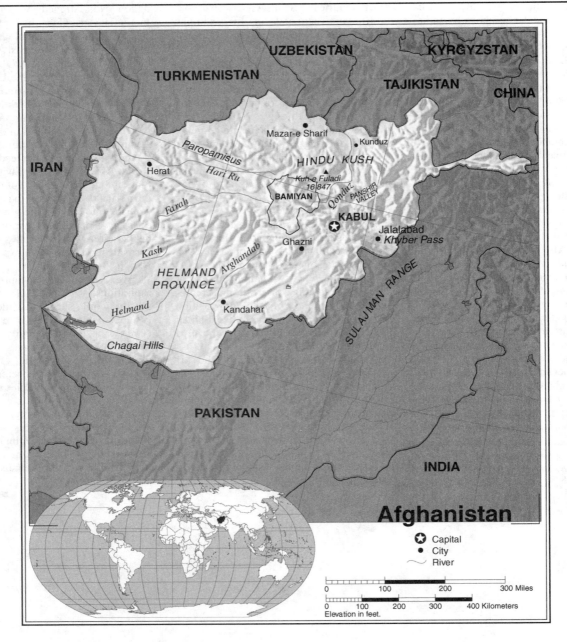

Afghanistan Statistics

GEOGRAPHY

Area in Square Miles (Kilometers):
249,935 sq mi (647,500 sq km) (about
the size of Texas)
Capital (Population): Kabul (2,994,000)
(2005 est.)
Environmental Concerns: limited fresh
water sources; soil degradation;
overgrazing; deforestation;
desertification; air and water pollution

Geographical Features: mostly rugged
mountains; valleys in the north and
southwest
Climate: arid to semiarid; cold winters
and hot summers

PEOPLE
Population

Total: 32,738,376 (July, 2008 est.)
Annual Growth Rate: 2.626% (2008 est.)

Rural/Urban Population Ratio: 77/23
(WHO 2006)
Major Languages: 50% Afghan Persian
or Dari; 35% Pashto; 11% Turkic;
30 minor languages; much
bilingualism
Ethnic Makeup: 42% Pushtun; 27% Tajik;
9% Hazara; 9% Uzbec; 4% Aimak;
3% Turkman; 2% Baloch; 4% other
Religions: 80% Sunni Muslim; 19% Shi'a
Muslim; 1% other

Health

Life Expectancy at Birth: 44.04 years (male); 44.39 years (female) (2008 est.)
Infant Mortality: 154.67/1000 live births (2008 est.)
Per Capita Total Expenditure on Health: $26 (WHO 2005)
HIV/AIDS Rate in Adults: 0.01% (2001 est.) (N/A WHO 2005 est.)

Education

Adult Literacy Rate: 28.1%; (12.6% females) (2000 est.)
Compulsory (Ages): 7–14

COMMUNICATION

Telephones: 280,000 main lines (2005)
Cell Phones: 4.668 million (2007)
Internet Users: 535,000 (2006)

TRANSPORTATION

Highways in Miles (Kilometers): (34,789 km.)
Usable Airfields: 46 (2007)

GOVERNMENT

Type: Islamic Republic
Independence Date: August 19, 1919 (from United Kingdom control)
Head of State/Government: President Hamid Karzai is Chief of State, Head of Government
Political Parties: 43 parties approved by Ministry of Justice
Suffrage: 18 years of age, universal

MILITARY

Military Expenditures (% of GDP): $181 million (2007) (1.5%) (2006) (SIPRI)
Current Disputes: severe internal conflicts with Taliban

ECONOMY

Currency ($ U.S. Equivalent): 46 afghanis = $1 U.S. (2006)
Per Capita Income/GDP: $1,000/$35 billion (2007 est.)
GDP Growth Rate: 12.4% (2007 est.)
Inflation Rate: 13% (2007 est.)
Unemployment Rate: 40% (2005 est.)
Labor Force by Occupation: 80% agriculture; 10% industry; 10% services
Population Below Poverty Line: 53% (2003)
Natural Resources: natural gas; petroleum; coal; copper; talc; barite; sulfur; lead; zinc; iron ore; salt; precious and semiprecious stones
Agriculture: opium poppies; wheat; fruits; nuts; wool; mutton; sheep skins; lambskins
Industry: small-scale production of textiles, soap, furniture, shoes; fertilizer; cement; handwoven carpets; natural gas, coal, copper
Exports: $274 million (not including illicit exports) (primary partners India, Pakistan, United States) (2006)
Imports: $3.823 billion (primary partners Pakistan, United States, India, China, Germany) (2006)
Human Development Index (ranking): N/A (UNDP 2008)

Afghanistan Country Report

Afghanistan is a rugged and mountainous country, nearly the size of Texas. It is divided through its center by the western extension of the high Himalayan mountain range known as the Hindu Kush. The land slopes away from this range in three different directions into jagged foothills and stark river valleys.

DEVELOPMENT

Thirty years of warfare and religious repression have devastated the economy and welfare of the people. Continuing Taliban insurgency, terrorism, and corruption have hindered reconstruction. Poppy cultivation for heroin is the primary source of wealth.

Only 12 percent of this rugged land is arable; and it receives an average rainfall of less than 12 inches a year. Severe drought conditions throughout the country from 1999 to 2006 drastically reduced even that rainfall for agricultural production and decimated the livestock of the Kuchi people, Afghanistan's nomadic herders. Toward the south, the land becomes inhospitable desert, racked by seasonal sandstorms that have been known to bury entire villages. The mountainous terrain in the north has

mineral resources, primarily iron ore and natural gas, which are unexploited but hard to obtain. This part of the country experienced a severe earthquake in February 1998, which destroyed more than 20 villages, killing several thousand people. The country, once celebrated for lush oases and luxuriant gardens of fruit, can nowhere today be characterized as naturally comfortable or abundant, except in the growing of poppies.

The three-way slope of the landscape from the high ridge of the Hindu Kush divides Afghanistan into three distinct ethnic and linguistic regions. Northern Afghans are predominately Uzbeks and Turkmen, who share a strong sense of identity as well as the Turkic language with the peoples who live across their northern border in Turkmenistan, and Uzbekistan—former republics of the Soviet Union.

The Tajik and Hazara peoples, who are 27 and 9 percent of the population respectively, live in the central section on the western slope of the Hindu Kush toward Iran. The Tajik, of ancient Persian origin, are primarily Sunni Muslim. The Hazara are Shi'a Muslims who trace their descent from the invaders of Genghis Khan from Mongolia in the thirteenth century A.D. They share a common language, Dari, which is a dialect of Farsi, the language of Iran (where Shi'a Muslims are predominant).

The Pashtuns (also called Pathans or Pushtuns), are the largest ethnic group, 14 million strong, about 42 percent of the total population. They live on the southeastern slope of the country, and are themselves divided into tribal groups, such as the Durrani and the Ghilzai. The Durrani Pashtuns have been politically the most dominant during the past 300 years.

FREEDOM

National elections for president were held in 2004, and for national legislature in 2005. But public life is still controlled by local and regional clan leaders, war lords, and drug dealers. U.S. and NATO forces are assigned to restore order and security, but the Taliban insurgency continues to grow in strength.

The Pashtuns are mostly Sunni Muslims, but they speak a different language, Pashto. They share this language and ethnic identity with some 26 million Pashtuns, who live across the Durand Line, established as the boundary between them by the British in 1893. The Pakistani Pushtuns provided shelter to more than three million Afghan Pashtun refugees during the Soviet occupation of Afghanistan from 1979 to 1989, and to unnumbered Taliban insurgents since their defeat in 2001. Their common identity also sustains a latent aspiration for a single Pashtun nation. This aspiration is a source of genuine threat to the unity of Pakistan, which has given it urgency to be involved in Afghan affairs.

Emperors briefly united Afghan lands in the twelfth and eighteenth centuries, but neither empire lasted more than a generation. Fiercely independent local chieftains and clan leaders, sometimes called warlords, have been the most powerful political force in the country. They have, for generations, been the bearers of a clan's or tribe's sense of identity, allegiance, and honor.

Afghanistan's traditional wealth was based on its position along the silk route between China and Europe. The petty chiefs extracted from travelers significant bounty in custom fees, commissions for protection, or loot. The prominent role of drug trafficking and arms dealing in Afghan life today draws on this heritage. According to United Nations reports, Afghanistan produces over 90 percent of the world's supply of heroin, worth billions of dollars from 8,200 tons of poppy harvested in 2007, and 7,700 tons in 2008.

MODERN HISTORY

British Indian forces marched into Afghan territory twice during the late nineteenth century, but soon withdrew. In 1893, they left the country in the hands of Abdur Rahman Khan, the Emir of Kabul. During his reign, he hoped to "break down the feudal and tribal system and substitute one grand community under one law and one rule." But the many local chieftains and clan leaders, claiming independent authority, resisted. They did participate in a succession of national councils, called loya jirga, to legitimize royal claims for ceremonial leadership.

In 1953, Sadar (Prince) Mohammed Daoud Khan, then commander of the Afghan army, seized the authority of prime minister to the then Emir of Kabul, Zahir Shah. He instituted many economic and social reforms, leading up to the adoption of a constitutional monarchy with a nationally elected legislative assembly in 1964. His reforming zeal allowed women to remove the chadri (the traditional heavy veil worn in public), and to participate for the first time in that election. Also participating was a newly formed, but already fractious, Communist Party.

Elections were held again in 1969, but this time the religiously and socially conservative clan leaders better understood the electoral process. They gained control of the Assembly in order to preserve their traditional authority, and effectively limited further reform.

Impatient with this resistance, Sadar Daoud overthrew the government in 1973. He sent Zahir Shah into exile and set himself up as military dictator. With both American and Soviet aid, he improved agriculture, by the use of irrigation, and health services, and encouraged an industrial sector to increase the country's wealth. In 1977, he promulgated a new Constitution that outlawed all political parties except his own, including the largely urban and intellectual Communist party. A new assembly then elected Daoud President of the Republic of Afghanistan.

The Soviet Occupation

Resistance to Daoud's nationalist reform program came from both sides of the political spectrum. From the more conservative elements in the countryside, a zealous group of militant clan leaders, armed and trained by Pakistan, arose to harass his government. Strengthened by a rising Islamic-fundamentalist zeal, they called themselves mujahideen—fighters for the faith. But Daoud was more concerned about the growing influence, encouraged by the Soviets, of the leftist, modernizing groups in Kabul. He began to purge suspected Communists from the military and the bureaucracy. Within a year, army officers, threatened by this purge, assassinated him. Nur Mohammed Taraki, leader of the Peoples Democratic (Communist) Party, took over the reins of government.

President Taraki was assassinated in 1979, to be followed by an arch-rival, Hafizullah Amin.

Both leaders had adopted vigorous campaigns to break up the landholdings of the local chieftains and increase literacy among the people. Mujahideen resistance intensified to a point where President Amin sought Soviet aid to protect his government. The Soviet government, fearing that continuing civil strife would diminish its influence and investment, and threaten the security of the adjoining Soviet states to the north, sent 85,000 troops in December 1979. They deposed Amin and his radical faction of the Communist Party, and installed Babrak Karmal to undertake a more moderate approach to socialist reform.

HEALTH/WELFARE

Even with significant foreign aid, because of corruption, warfare, and insurgency, public services are very limited. The traditional repression of women also contributes to the lack of human resource development in health and education.

Forces of resistance in the countryside intensified in their opposition to foreign intervention in addition to the reforms seeking centralization, industrialization, and modernization. In the face of Soviet military repression, more than 3 million Pashtuns crossed the border into Pakistan. The affluent established residences in Peshawar and Quetta. The vast majority moved into hastily constructed refugee camps. Another 2 million fled across the western border into Iran. Having gathered their families into the safety of camps across the border, supplied by Pakistani, Iranian, Saudi, and U.S. military and logistical support, they formed a fighting force of mujahideen to conduct an insurgency in their home country.

This incursion of Soviet military forces in 1979 also intensified the Cold War competition between the United States and the Soviet Union, which transformed Afghanistan into a proxy international battlefield. During the years of occupation, Soviet military strength increased to 120,000 troops. With both sides armed with advanced weaponry, warfare ravaged the countryside. Twelve thousand of 22,000 villages and more than 2,000 schools were destroyed, and 1 million Afghans and 13,000 Soviet soldiers were killed.

The Soviet Withdrawal

In 1986, Dr. Muhammed Najibullah replaced Babrak Karmal as president. In 1988, the leaders of seven mujahideen groups joined in Pakistan to form an interim government in exile. Faced with this resistance, the Soviet Union became unwilling to sustain the losses of an intensifying military stalemate. In 1989, it withdrew its forces, and in 1991, agreed with the United States that both would stop arming the warring factions in Afghanistan.

Lack of cohesion—religious, ethnic, and military—among the mujahideen hampered their attempts to overthrow the Kabul government for three years after the Soviet troops departed. President Najibullah offered to form a joint government with them, but they could only agree that they did not want to share any part of a new government with the Communists.

In March 1992, Najibullah's army overthrew him, and mujahideen forces, under the command of Ahmad Shah Masood, a Tajik from Panshir, overtook the city of Kabul. Their victory was followed by a loya jirga, "national council," to elect Burhanuddin Rabbani, a Tajik, as interim president and draw up a new Constitution. But the rivalry among the mujahideen leaders, particularly between Rabbani and Gulbuddin Hekmatyar, a Ghilzai Pashtun, led to intense fighting in Kabul and a further collapse of civil

UNHCR/16046/A. Hollmann

Millions of refugees who fled to Pakistan and Iran during the Soviet occupation of Afghanistan were reluctant to return to Afghanistan. This was due, in no small part, to the constant fighting among the mujahideen and then to problems with the Taliban. Women and children are particularly vulnerable groups of refugees.

order throughout the country. The periodic assaults and bombings among rival mujahideen parties seeking control of the city reduced much of it to rubble.

In 1993, a group of Pashtun religious students called the Taliban ("seekers of religious knowledge") from the southern city of Kandahar rose up in indignation against the militancy and corruption of the mujahideen. Their reforming fervor spread rapidly among a people weary of uncontrolled violence, fear, and destruction.

ACHIEVEMENTS

 The government continues to seek avenues for peace. Given the continuing devastation and lack of security, the greatest achievement may simply be their survival.

The Taliban became a formidable force, supplied by arms and logistics from Pakistan, manpower from local clan militias, war orphans from Islamic parochial schools called madrasas, religious volunteers (jihadis) from many countries, and financial support and training from Al Qaeda. By the fall of 1996, they controlled the southern two thirds of the country and drove the mujahideen out of Kabul. They established a reign of reactionary religious terror in a city that had aspired for so long to become modern.

Their reforming zeal countenanced many human rights abuses. Most oppressed were women, particularly widows, who were deprived of jobs, humanitarian aid, and education. By 1999, Taliban forces controlled 95 percent of the country. Only a small vestige of the anti-Soviet resistance called the Northern Alliance held out in the northeastern corner of the country.

The Soviet incursion, the deadly fighting among the mujahideen and the rise of the Taliban subjected the Afghan people to the ravages and repression of more than twenty years of war. Many who became refugees during the Soviet occupation, because of the destruction of their homes, the depletion and mining of their fields, and, after October 7, 2001, fear of American bombing, remained in their squalid refugee camps. Women especially hesitated to return, because of fear of repression in their homelands by the fundamentalist fervor of both the mujahideen and Taliban leaders. By the end of 2001, there were still 2.2 million refugees in Pakistan, 2.4 million in Iran and around 1 million in refugee camps in Afghanistan itself.

Restoration

Following the terrorist attacks in the United States on September 11, 2001, an international coalition led by the United States joined forces with the Northern Alliance to destroy Al Qaeda and punish the Taliban for its role in the 9/11 assault on the United States. In a dramatic reversal, Pakistan withdrew its support from the Taliban and it collapsed. Kabul was soon recaptured and Al Qaeda training camps were dismantled.

The coalition victory created a new opportunity for political stability and reconstruction in the country. An impressive list of regional leaders emerged to take part in this effort. Some had joined the mujahideen in opposition to Sardar Daoud's reforms in the 1970s. All had a part in the violent infighting following the Soviet withdrawal, based on their leadership of the many diverse ethnic and tribal groups in the country. Many of them retained their own private militias, and were sustained by foreign aid and a flourishing trade in heroin production. The Tajik leaders of the Northern Alliance were initially the strongest: former president Burhanuddin Rabbani, and Muhammad Fahim and Yunus Qanuni, both successors to Ahmad Shah Masood, military commander of the Northern Alliance, who was assassinated on September 10, 2001.

The United Nations initiated the rebuilding of Afghanistan by gathering representative leadership from across the country in Bonn, Germany, in December 2001. Its intent was to establish institutions of government with authority separate from that of the indigenous leaders. Despite the good intentions, the Afghan government created at Bonn remained on the traditional power base of the so-called warlords.

An international peacekeeping force (ISAF) was also set up to establish security. It began with 8,000 soldiers from over 30 countries. But it had limited reach outside the capital city.

In June 2002, on terms set under United Nations auspices in Bonn, a follow-up council of 1,500 selected leaders convened in Kabul to create a transitional government. It elected as interim president, Hamid Karzai, a Pashtun with strong American support. Because he did not have an indigenous political base, he seemed most suited to hold the office above the taint and fray of traditional clan power struggles and to attract international contributions for rehabilitation.

Steps toward a permanent government began with preparations for national elections for president to be held in October 2004. These included more than 1,600 polling stations set up by the International Organization for Migration in Pakistan for 738,000 refugees still in that country who registered to vote. Eighty percent of them voted. About half of the 500,000 refugees who registered in seven offices in Iran also voted. The IOM achieved the largest refugee participation ever in a national election. Over all, Hamid Karzai received 55.4 percent of the vote.

Karzai's largest support came mostly from Kabul, where the evidence of foreign investment was most visible, particularly in the person of the U.S. ambassador, Zalmay Khalilzad, (known in Kabul as "the Viceroy"). He also had some support from Pashtun regions to the south, where local leaders and the Taliban still retained control. Yunus Qanuni, a Tajik, briefly interior minister and head of intelligence in the interim government, won 16.3 percent of the vote, mostly from his ethnic base in the north-central region of the country. He was subsequently elected Speaker of the Afghan Parliament. Mohammad Mohaqiq, the Hazara leader, received 11 percent from Hazara dominant districts, and 10 percent voted for Rashid Dostum, an Uzbek from the northern region. President Karzai did not appoint any of them to his cabinet.

Parlaimentary elections for the Wolesi Jirga, or lower house, and provincial elections were finally held on September 18, 2005. With the Taliban calling for a boycott, 53 percent of 12 million registered voters cast their ballot. The results included 68 seats, 27 percent, for women. But overall they reinstituted the traditional bases of power in the country. Such did not hold out much promise for institutional independence and reform.*

A survey conducted in 2006 by the Post-Conflict Reconstruction Project of the Center for Strategic and International Studies found the people disappointed in four categories of their public life: security, justice, social well-being, and economic opportunity. That survey concludes:

"Gains have been made in education, communication, government processes, institutional capacity, roads and the private

---

*Carlotta Gall, "In Poverty and Strife, Women Test Limits," *New York Times,* October 6, 2008.

sector. Yet, the big issues from the beginning of the intervention remain: how to manage warlords and continued impunity, how to decrease poppy and drug trafficking, how to stop support for the Taliban, how to deliver electricity and revitalize the judiciary, and how to provide economic development in areas with limited access and infrastructure and serious security constraints."

With the people not convinced of improvement in their lives, and with the Taliban finding safe haven in Pakistan, its insurgency gained in strength. The force used by the American and NATO troops to suppress it, taking an intolerable toll of civilian casualties, made their presence equally burdensome. Increasing recognition that a military solution to this conflict is not possible has led to calls for dialogue with militant Islamist groups not only in Afghanistan, but also in Pakistan, which has its own Taliban terrorist groups. The Saudi government is attempting to initiate talks between President Karzai and Taliban leaders.

Effective counter insurgency will not be easy. Afghanistan has for too long been torn asunder internally by so many levels of conflict: opposition between traditional lifestyles in the countryside and the cosmopolitan urban society in Kabul, and between fundamentalism and reform in Islam played out within longstanding animosities among different ethnic and linguistic groups, and rivalries among tribes, clans, and religious sects.

The country has also to deal with the conflicting interests of neighboring Iran, India, and Pakistan. And major powers have introduced a whole new scale of mass destruction, arms trading, international drug dealing, and terrorist training.

War-ravaged and impoverished for years, the people of Afghanistan need substantial, regionally focused assistance and cooperation to achieve some semblance of sustainable governance and social welfare.

Timeline: PAST

A.D. 1747–1973
Loose tribal federation

1907
The British and Russians establish the boundaries of modern Afghanistan

1973–1978
Military dictatorship

1978–1992
Communist Party rule

1979–1989
Soviet military occupation

1980s
A mujahideen resistance is formed in Pakistan

1990s
Communist government overthrown, Mujahideen leaders compete for control

Taiiban emerges in protest, captures Kabul and dominates most of the country

PRESENT

2000s
Deeming them "un-Islamic," Taliban destroys ancient Bamiyan Buddhist statues. U.S. led coalition in "war against terror" to destroy Al Qaeda joins Northern Alliance to recapture Kabul.

2002
Provisional government set up under UN initiated Bonn Agreement. Hamid Karzai elected interim president.

2004–2005
Presidential and National Assembly elections held. Hamid Karzai elected president.

2005–2009
Taliban insurgency increases against U.S. and NATO forces sent to secure country. Poppy cultivation remains a large percentage of GDP and world heroin market, supports local clan leaders and insurgency.

2009
Election for president

Bangladesh (People's Republic of Bangladesh)

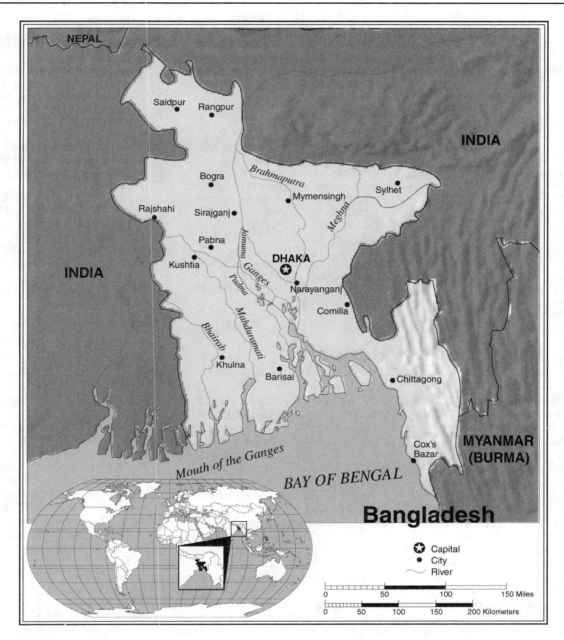

Bangladesh Statistics

GEOGRAPHY

Area in Square Miles (Kilometers):
55,584 (144,000 sq km) (about the size of Wisconsin)
Capital (Population): Dhaka (11,918,442) (2007 est.)
Environmental Concerns: water pollution; soil degradation; deforestation; severe overpopulation
Geographical features: mostly flat alluvial plain; hilly in the southeast

Climate: tropical; monsoon; cool, dry winter, hot, humid summer

PEOPLE

Population

Total: 153,546,896 (July, 2008 est.)
Annual Growth Rate: 2.022% (2008 est.)
Rural/Urban Population Ratio: 75/25 (WHO 2006)
Major Languages: Bangla; English

Ethnic Makeup: 98% Bengali, 2% tribal groups and non Bengali Muslims (1998)
Religions: 83% Muslim, 16% Hindu, 1% other (1998)

Health

Life Expectancy at Birth: 63.14 years (male); 63.28 years (female)
Infant Mortality: 57.45/1000 live births (2007 est.)
Per Capita Total Expenditure on Health: $57 (WHO 2005)

HIV/AIDS Rate in Adults: less than 0.1% (11,000) (WHO 2005 est.)

Education

Adult Literacy Rate: 43.1%; (31.8% female) (2003 est.)
Compulsory (Ages) 6–11; free

COMMUNICATION

Telephones; 1.134 million main lines (2006)
Cell Phones: 34.37 million (2007)
Internet Users: 450,000 (2006)

TRANSPORTATION

Highways in Miles (Kilometers): 128,926 (239,226 km.) (2003)
Railroads in Miles (Kilometers): 1,681 (2,768 km.) (2006)
Usable Airfields: 16 (2007)

GOVERNMENT

Type: parliamentary democracy
Independence Date: December 16, 1971 (from Paskistan)

Chief of State: President Iajuddin Ahmed
Head of Government: Prime Minister Sheikh Hasina Wazed (since January, 2009)
Political Parties: Bangladesh Nationalist Party, Awami League, Islami Oikya Jote, Jamaat-e-Islami, Jatiya Party (Ershad), Jatiya Party (Manzur).
Suffrage: universal at 18

MILITARY

Military Expenditures (% of GDP): $834.9 million (2007) (1%) (2006) (SIPRI)
Current Disputes: boundary disputes with India and Myanmar, illegal trade, migration, violence, transit of terrorists across porous borders

ECONOMY

Currency ($ U.S. Equivalent): 69.893 taka = 1$ U.S. (2007)
Per Capita Income/GDP: $1,300 (2007 est.)/$206.7 billion

GDP Growth Rate: 5.6% (2007 est.)
Inflation Rate: 8.4% (2007 est.)
Unemployment Rate: 1% (2007 est.)
Labor Force by Occupation: 63% agriculture, 26% services, 11% industry (FY 95/96)
Population Below Poverty Line: 45% (2004 est.)
Natural Resources: natural gas; arable land; timber
Agriculture: rice; jute; tea; wheat; sugarcane; potatoes; tobacco; pulses; oilseeds; spices; fruit; beef; milk; poultry
Industry: jute; garments; textiles; food processing; newsprint; cement; light engineering; fertilizer; sugar
Exports: $11.75 billion (2007 est.) (primary partners United States, Germany, United Kingdom, France)
Imports: $16.03 billion (2007 est.) (primary partners China, India, Kuwait, Singapore)
Human Development Index (ranking): 140 (UNDP 2008)

Bangladesh Country Report

Bangladesh, the youngest nation of South Asia, won its independence from Pakistan in 1971. It is also the most densely populated. More than 153 million people, half the population of the United States, live in an area smaller than the state of Wisconsin, at an average rural density of 2,600 per square mile.

Bangladesh is a fertile delta country fed by three major rivers, the Brahmaputra, the Ganges and the Maghma. They expand into 700 rivers to flow in intricate and shifting channels into the Sundarbans—tide country—leading into the Bay of Bengal. The Sundarbans is a land of sandbars and great reefs, many of which are submerged at high tide, with only treetops standing above the water. Its marshy thickets are also the home of crocodiles and the Royal Bengal Tiger.

In the monsoon season, flooding waters frequently overflow the embankments surrounding settlements along these many rivers. The worst flood of the last century, in 1988, paralyzed the central part of the country, killing 800 people and leaving almost 30 million homeless. A single cyclone in May 1991 killed 130,000 people. Devastating flooding occurred again in 1998. In 2004, thirty-nine of the country's 64 districts where overrun with water, leaving 35 million with severe losses estimated

at $7 billion. And in November, 2007, 150 mph Tropical Cyclone Sidr hit the south coast, forcing 1.5 million to flee their homes, destroying crops on 77,450 acres and leaving 1,723 dead. Natural disasters remain a constant threat to all aspects of life in Bangladesh.

It remains one of the poorest countries in the world; 61 percent of the urban population is below the poverty line, according to a recent Asian Development Bank survey, and over half of the total population lives on less than $1 a day. Among the poor are almost 300,000 tribal peoples, along with some 280,000 refugees from Myanmar, isolated among the hills and jungles in the eastern regions of the country. The Lushai, Murung, and Kuki subsist as they have for thousands of years, practicing slash-and-burn agriculture and the rite of bride capture.

DEVELOPMENT

Primarily an agricultural country subject to natural disasters, political instability, and unemployment, Bangladesh has made remarkable progress in human resource development by its many NGOs. Natural gas and textiles have become the greatest producers of wealth.

Independence

The origin of Bangladesh as an independent nation began in 1905, when Lord Curzon, the British viceroy in India, attempted to divide the Colonial Province of Bengal into a predominantly Muslim East Bengal (which then included Assam) and a Hindu West Bengal. In the 1947 partition, when Pakistan became independent, a truncated yet predominantly Muslim province of East Bengal became the eastern wing of Pakistan.

East Pakistan had the larger population, but economic and political power resided in the western wing. Attempts to impose Urdu as the national language of Pakistan, and favoritism toward the western wing in economic development, led to student demonstrations in East Pakistan in 1952.

In 1970, in Pakistan's first popular national elections, the Awami League in East Pakistan, led by Sheikh Mujibur Rahman, won a majority of seats in the national legislature. Because he had long been an advocate for greater Bengali autonomy, the political leaders in West Pakistan refused to accept him as prime minister. In response to this stalemate, President Yahya Khan suspended the Assembly. The people of East Bengal rioted in protest. President Yahya Khan tried to suppress this public outcry by military force.

During eight months of military repression, the Pakistan army killed many hundreds of thousands, and eight million people fled as refugees into India.

In December 1971, India attacked Pakistan in support of the Bengali resistance movement to free the people of East Bengal from Pakistan's military rule. Mujibur Rahman became president, then prime minister of the new nation.

Almost all citizens of Bangladesh share a common Bengali ethnic and language identity, and most are Sunni Muslims. With so much upon which to build a democratic nation—language, religion, culture, and a successful fight for its independence—the country still struggles to achieve political stability.

Although he was a popular leader, Mujibur Rahman did not prove an effective administrator in the face of severe overpopulation, poverty, famine, and natural disasters. His increasingly authoritarian rule led to a military coup in 1975, in which he and most of his family were killed.

FREEDOM

Elections are held on a regular basis and 30 percent of local government offices are reserved for women. Rivalry between the two major parties, corruption, and license for terrorism have led to instability on the national level. Due to public unrest, elections were suspended in January, 2007, and were reinstated in December, 2008.

General Ziaur Rahman, army chief of staff, took over as martial-law administrator with the intent to lead the country back to democracy. He created his own political party, the Bangladesh Nationalist Party (BNP), and encouraged others to participate in national elections to elect 300 members to the national Legislature. (Thirty women members were subsequently to be elected by vote of the Legislature under a constitutional provision that expired in 2001). He also developed an economic policy to increase agricultural production, education, and health care.

Zia restored an independent executive presidency, and won the election in 1978. In the legislative elections in 1979, his BNP won two-thirds of the seats in the national Legislature.

In 1981, dissident military officers assassinated General Zia. The political chaos following his death again led to martial law in

1982, under General Hussain Muhammed Ershad, chief of staff of the army.

Ershad continued General Zia's policies of economic development and social reform. He also instituted a National Security Advisory Council to increase military participation in government. This move caused political unrest that led to his downfall. Although he won the presidential election in 1986, his party won only a very slim and widely questioned majority in the legislative elections that followed.

Two new leaders, each related to Ershad's more charismatic predecessors, came onto the national scene in protest against the 1986 election. Begum Khaleda Zia, the widow of General Zia, became head of the Bangladesh National Party (BNP) after her husband's death. Sheikh Hasina Wajed, the eldest of only two surviving daughters of Mujibur Rahman, led the Awami League (AWL). The rivalry and mistrust between these two has denied the country political stability ever since.

President Ershad first attempted to suppress their protest. Then, in December 1987, he dissolved the Legislature and called for new elections. The BNP and the Awami League both boycotted, and public opinion turned against him. In 1990, he resigned, and Justice Shahabuddin Ahmed of the Supreme Court was appointed acting president.

National elections to restore the government were held in February 1991. Begum Zia was elected president, and her BNP, polling 31 percent of the votes, won 140 seats in the 300-member legislature. The Awami League, although gaining almost the same percentage of the popular vote, came in a distant second, with 84 seats.

A national referendum in September 1991, supported by both the BNP and the Awami League, placed executive power in the hands of the prime minister of the national legislature. Begum Zia then stepped down as president. Because her party did not command a majority of Legislature seats, she accepted the support of the Jamaat-e-Islami, a conservative Islamic party, to win the prime minister's office. Though a small minority, it persuaded Begum Zia's government to condemn a young doctor-turned-author, Dr. Taslima Nasreen, for alleged "blasphemy" in her popular novel, *Lajja*. The government arrested Nasreen for "outrage[ing] the religious feelings" of the people of Bangladesh. Having posted bail, Dr. Nasreen escaped to live in exile in Sweden, Germany, the United States, and ultimately in India. This episode raised international concern, not only for the right of freedom

of expression, but also as an indicator of the political strength of religious fundamentalism in Bangladesh.

HEALTH/WELFARE

In the absence of stable government, many NGOs have evolved to provide extensive disaster relief, job opportunities, education, and environmental protection. The country has made significant gains in literacy, health care, and reduction in birth rate from 3.3 percent to 2 percent since 1971.

The close split of the popular vote between the two leading parties in the 1991 elections led Sheikh Hasina's Awami League to protest the outcome, and call for new elections. In 1994, her party's boycott stymied legislative activity. New elections were held in June 1996. The BNP's standing was reduced to 116 seats, and the Jamaat-e-Islami to three seats. With the support of what remained of General Ershad's party, Sheikh Hasina garnered the votes to become prime minister. This time it became the BNP's turn to boycott the Legislature.

The new Legislature still enacted an important initiative for women in government. This law reserves for them three of the 10 directly elected seats in the 4,298 local councils that form the lowest tier of government in Bangladesh. Elections for these councils started in December 1997, and 14,500 women were elected. This was an important step toward increasing the place of women in a country where traditional religious teachings and social custom have accepted their repression.

Sheikh Hasina's Awami League government was able to complete a full five-year term in control of the national legislature. But her liberalizing initiatives to establish modern secular rule in Bangladesh and build its relationship with India came to a sudden and surprising end in the elections of October 2001. Begum Zia's BNP campaigned on a pro-Islamic and isolationist platform, in alliance with three other conservative parties in order not to split their votes. Their alliance came to power in a landslide victory with 191 seats for the BNP, with 46 percent of the popular vote, and 18 for the Jamaat-e-Islami. The Awami League, with 42 percent of the vote, won only 62 seats. There were many indigenous causes for the rout of the Awami League. But the terrorist attacks in the United States the month before stirred Islamic fundamentalist fervor in Bangladesh, as they did in many places in the Islamic world.

ACHIEVEMENTS

The success of BRAC, Proshika, and the Grameen Bank as NGOs to provide health, education, and financial opportunities for the poor. Professor Yunus, founder of the Grameen Bank, received the Nobel Peace Prize in 2006.

Islamist militancy increased in the country. Sixteen major terrorist incidents led up to grenade attacks on Awami League political rallies in Dhaka on August 21, 2004, and in Habiganj on January 27, 2005. On August 17, 2005, five hundred bombs exploded simultaneously across the country. Rioting broke out in the streets, followed by strikes in protest called by the Awami League. The BNP denied any involvement in any of these incidents. It did arrest two high profile terrorists in March 2006. But it continued to appear restrained in reining in the forces of religious and sectarian violence as it sought continuing Islamic fundamentalist support in the next national election.

The election was set for January 21, 2007, with a caretaker government installed 90 days prior, in October, to assure free and fair voting. The Awami League, now part of a 14 party alliance, immediately protested the composition of the interim government as being pro-BNP and contested some 14 million false names that appeared on the voter rolls. Their alliance carried out a series of crippling transportation strikes throughout the country. As a result, the election was cancelled, and an interim caretaker government, with military support, was installed.

In hopes of overcoming the impasse of their political rivalry, the interim government incarcerated both Khaleda Zia and Sheikh Hasina on charges of graft. In response to public concern about its extending rule, the interim government set new elections for December 29, 2008. With extended negotiations to assure the participation of both parties, voter rolls were corrected, and the two leaders were released on bail.

These elections were won overwhelmingly by the Awami League, taking 230 of 299 seats in the National Legislature. The BNP won 27 and the Jamaat-e-Islami only 2 seats. These results promise a more productive future for the national government under the leadership of Sheikh Hasina.

Outside of government channels, the picture has been more positive. The people have shown outstanding initiative in human development from the ground up to meet the challenges of population growth, rural poverty,

and disaster relief through grassroots, voluntary, non-government organizations (NGOs). The Bangladesh Rehabilitation Assistance Committee (BRAC), with a staff of 108,000, provides health services to more than 100 million people every year, educates 1.5 million children in 52,000 schools, and creates job opportunities for the landless poor. It has become so large that it functions like a parallel state.

Proshika is another large NGO that does environmentally sensitive human development among the extremely poor, with emphasis on organic sustainable farming, planting trees, and installing SONO filters to remove arsenic from well water.

The Grameen Bank, founded by economics Professor Mohammed Yunus, provides small loans to poor people in five-member groups without collateral. It has been successful in creating credit for more than 7.3 million borrowers, 97 percent of whom are women, and recovers more than $5.87 billion a year. The bank also trains its borrowers through its Sixteen Decisions around nutrition, home repair, management skills, and public health. Its effectiveness among the impoverished in Bangladesh has established it as a model for economic empowerment of the poor in more than 43 other countries. Professor Yunus was awarded the Nobel Peace Prize in 2006 for his work to alleviate poverty with the Grameen Bank microcredit initiative.

CHALLENGES

Because of its large and growing population, its limited resources, unemployment, corruption, and a succession of natural disasters, Bangladesh has struggled since its independence to achieve prosperity for its people. Cyclones and floods severely reduce agricultural production, which is barely sufficient to feed Bangladesh's population even in good times.

Many skilled workers found jobs in the Persian Gulf region. In 1998–9, they sent back to Bangladesh $1.71 billion in remittances. But recent unrest there has led to their return to flood the country's already overcrowded job market.

Natural gas is the country's greatest potential resource, with reserves sufficient to provide for its energy needs. But without other natural resources to broaden its industrial base and create new employment, with a decline in the world market for their jute and textiles, the country's largest exports, and with the global economic crisis, a sustained GDP growth of 5.6 percent will be difficult to maintain.

With hopes for continuing international support and a stable, democratically elected

leadership, a resilient and responsive people remain committed to providing education, health care, meaningful employment, and prosperity for all in their nation.

Bhutan (Kingdom of Bhutan)

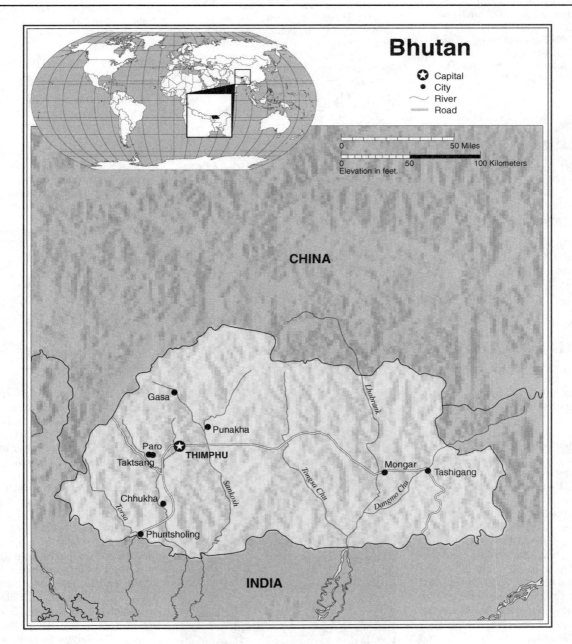

Bhutan Statistics

GEOGRAPHY

Area in Square Miles (Kilometers): 18,147
(47,000 sq km)
Capital (Population): Thimphu (98,676)
(2005)
Environmental Concerns: soil erosion;
limited access to potable water
Geographical Features: mostly
mountainous with some fertile valleys
and savanna

Climate: tropical in southern plains; cool
winters and hot summers in central
valleys; severe winters and cool
summers in the Himalayas

PEOPLE

Population

Total: 682,321 (July, 2008 est.);
Annual Growth Rate: 1.301% (2008 est.)

Rural/Urban Population Ratio: 89/11
(WHO 2006)
Major Languages: Dzongkha;
various Tibetan dialects;
Nepalese dialects
Ethnic Makeup: 50% Bhote; 35% Ethnic
Nepalese; 15% indigenous and migrant
tribes
Religions: 75% Buddhist; 25% Indian-
and Nepalese influenced
Hinduism

Health

Life Expectancy at Birth: 64.75 years (male); 66.35 years (female) (2008 est.)
Infant Mortality: 51.92/1000 live births (2008 est.)
Per Capita Total Expenditure on Health: $85 (WHO 2005)
HIV/AIDS Rate in Adults: less than 0.1% (WHO 2005 est.)

Education

Adult Literacy Rate: 47% (2003 est.)

COMMUNICATION

Telephones: 31,500 main lines (2006)
Cell Phones: 149,400 (2007)
Internet Users: 30,000 (2006)

TRANSPORTATION

Highways in Miles (Kilometers): 2,292 (8,050 km.) (2003)
Useable Airports: 2 (2007)

GOVERNMENT

Type: in transition to constitutional monarchy
Independence Date: December 17, 1907
Chief of State: King Jigme Khesar Namgyel Wangchuk
Head of Government : Prime Minister Jigme Thinley
Political Parties: Bhutan Peace and Prosperity Party, DTP; and People's Democratic Party, PDP
Suffrage: 18 years of age, universal

MILITARY

Military Expenditures (% of GDP): $8.29 million (2005 est.) (1%) (CIA World Factbook)
Current Disputes: internal unrest, refugee issues

ECONOMY

Currency ($ U.S. Equivalent): 41.487 ngultrum = $1 U.S. (2007)

Per Capita Income/GDP: $5,200/ $3,359 billion (2007 est.)
GDP Growth Rate: 22.4% (2007 est.)
Inflation Rate: 4.9% (2007 est.)
Labor Force by Occupation: 63% agriculture, 31% services, 6% industry (2004 est.)
Population below Poverty Line: 31.7% (2003)
Natural Resources: Timber, hydropower, gypsum, calcium carbide
Agriculture: rice, corn, root crops, citrus, foodgrains, dairy products, eggs
Industry: cement, wood products, processed fruits, alcoholic beverages, calcium carbide, tourism
Exports: $350 million (primary partners India, Hong Kong, Thailand) (2006)
Imports: $320 million (primary partners India, Japan, Germany) (2006)
Human Development Index (ranking): 133 (UNDP 2008)

Bhutan Country Report

Bhutan is a small Himalayan country, about the size of Vermont and New Hampshire combined. Its highest point reaches 24,783 feet along the border with Tibet. The land falls through a series of cascading river valleys down the southern slopes toward Assam, on the eastern side of the subcontinent. Its southern border—barely 100 miles away, yet more than 24,000 feet below—touches the edge of the Brahmaputra River plain, through narrow, humid, gorgelike valleys of bamboo jungle.

Most of the 682,321 people in the country (2008 estimate based on the 2005 census) live in the broader, fertile, pine-filled valleys of the central region, from 5,000 to 9,000 feet above sea level. Isolated by its terrain and eager to preserve its Mahayana Buddhist heritage, the country has moved very cautiously into the modern world.

DEVELOPMENT

Ninety-three percent of Bhutan's labor force is in self-sufficient agriculture. Concerned to preserve its Buddhist heritage, it is cautiously developing a tourist industry and, with India's help, expanding its vast hydroelectric potential.

Culturally, religiously, and linguistically, 50 percent of the people of Bhutan are closely related to Tibet. Dzongkha, the most

Courtesy of Richard Ishida/W3C (World Wide Web Consortium). http://rishida.net
The Tiger's Lair (Taktsang) Hermitage.

common language spoken in the northern and western regions, is the official language of the country. Other Tibetan dialects are spoken in the eastern regions, where the people are more closely related by custom to Assam. The remaining 35 percent are Nepali and Hindi-speaking peoples, most

of whom have recently migrated into the country as laborers, and have settled in the southern region closest to India. Several thousand Tibetans fled into Bhutan following the Chinese takeover of their country and subsequent repressions during the 1950s.

The Mahayana Buddhist religion in Bhutan—as distinct from the Theravada Buddhism of Sri Lanka and Southeast Asia—also traces its origin to Tibet: to the Nyingmapa school of the Red Hat sect. Important monasteries, as at Taktsang (the Tiger's Lair), celebrate the teachings of the learned Indian monk Padma Sambhava, who introduced Buddhism into Tibet in the eighth century. He is described as the heroic Guru Rimpoche ("Precious Teacher") coming on a flying tiger to drive the forces of evil out of Druk Yul, "Land of the Thunder Dragon."

A Tibetan lama, Shabdrung Ngawang Namgyal, brought the isolated valley peoples under a single authority in the 1600s. He also established a tradition of religious leadership sustained by identifying the embodiment of his mind reincarnation (Dharma Raja) through successive generations. The religious authority of his Dharma Raja was subsumed during the 1930s under the temporal authority of a dynastic monarchy that was established in 1907 under British colonial rule.

THE MONARCHY

British military forces advanced into Bhutan in 1864 to repel Tibetan and Chinese claims of control over the Himalayan Mountains. In gratitude for his help in their successful attack of Tibet in 1903, the British rewarded Ugyen Wangchuk, then feudal lord (Penlop) of the north-central district of Tongsa, by assisting him to become Druk Gyalpo, the hereditary "Dragon King" of Bhutan, in 1907.

The British continued to oversee the external affairs of the country, but allowed the new king to rule independently in domestic matters. In 1949, with the end of the British Raj, Bhutan extended this agreement "to be guided in regard to its foreign relations" to the government of India. India has allowed Bhutan latitude in establishing international agreements, including support of Bhutan's admission to the United Nations in 1971.

FREEDOM

Three generations of kings have gradually introduced top-down parliamentary reform. The first national elections for a national legislature took place in 2008. In 1985, the National Assembly passed a Citizenship Act, which forced 85,000 Nepalis into refugee camps in Nepal. Attempts at repatriation have been meager. In 2008, the UN High Commission on Refugees initiated a resettlement program that intends to place 60,000 in the United States.

Jigme Dorji Wangchuk, grandson of Ugyen Wangchuk, instituted a number of reforms to bring his country cautiously into the modern era. To encourage more participation in government, in 1952, he established a National Assembly, the Tshoghdu. The Assembly had 151 members, 31 of whom were appointed by the king. The rest were elected by hereditary village headmen in the districts. They also served as local judges in a judicial system in which the king was the chief justice. As king, he also remained the religious head and chief executive of the country.

In 1968, the king granted the Assembly powers to limit his absolute authority. He could no longer veto legislation passed by majority vote of the Assembly. Also, by a two-thirds vote, the Assembly could force the king to abdicate. But in that case, only the next claimant in his hereditary line could succeed him. This provision reproduces on the national level the traditional family expectation that a landholder will pass on his lands to his eldest son as soon as the heir comes of age.

Courtesy of BhutanNewsOnline.com

Former King Jigme Singye Wangchuck with his four wives, Queens Ashi Tshering Yangdon Wangchuck, Ashi Tshering Pem Wangchuck, Ashi Dorji Wangmo Wangchuck, and Ashi Sangay Choden Wangchuck, all sisters.

Jigme Dorji Wangchuck's reforms also included the elimination of serfdom by granting public lands to landless servants. But in order not to disrupt traditional social patterns and create unemployment, he did not break up large private landholdings.

Jigme Singye Wangchuck, then 17 years old, succeeded Jigme Dorji Wangchuk upon his death in 1972. He continued his father's policies of gradual reform. During the summer of 1998, he expanded the powers of the National Assembly by replacing his royal Council of Ministers with a cabinet elected by the Assembly. It was to be "vested with full executive powers to provide efficient and effective governance of our country." The Assembly, with some reluctance, carried out his wishes by electing a cabinet from a list of candidates that he provided.

In 2002, the government began a process to elect its village headmen by popular vote rather than hereditary appointment. In 2005, in his National Day Address, King Jigme Singye Wangchuck announced "that the first national election to elect a government under a system of parliamentary democracy will take place in 2008." At the same time, he announced that he would delegate his kingship to his eldest son, Jigme Khesar Namgyel Wangshuk. The 28-year-old King was crowned by his father at 8:31 A.M. on November 6, 2008, a time designated as most auspicious by royal astrologers. A draft constitution was prepared in 2007, in anticipation of the first national elections, which were held on March 24, 2008. Its provisions require all candidates for the 47 seats in the new National Assembly to have both parents be Bhutnese-born and to hold a graduate degree. Almost 75 percent of the registered voters participated to elect an overwhelming majority of 45 seats to the

Kaptan/Courtesy Bhutan Majestic Travel

His Royal Highness Dasho Jigme Khesar Namgyal Wangchuck, consecrated King of Bhutan on November 6, 2008. He studied at Magdelen College, Oxford University, from which he was awarded M Phil in politics.

Bhutan Peace and Prosperity Party (DPT). Its leader, Jigme Thinley, was elected prime minister on April 9, 2008. The justices of the High Court are still appointed by the king. King Jigme Singye Wangchuck thus led his country toward the beginnings of democracy, while at the same time assuring stability of the government through elite representation.

ECONOMIC DEVELOPMENT

India has been the largest investor in the development of Bhutan's economy. In the face of Chinese threats of invasion over border disputes during the 1950s, the Indian government built a road from Bhutan's southern border to the capital, Thimphu. It took 112 miles of winding roadway to cover a straight-line distance of 45 miles. In 1996, India began a project to extend this roadway into eastern Bhutan.

With India's help, Bhutan has also increased the country's energy potential. The first of six hydroelectric projects, the 336-megawatt Chuka Hydroelectric Project, financed by the Indian government, was completed in 1987, to export electricity to India. The 1,020-megawatt Tala Hydroelectric Project, started in 1997, began production in 2006. India provided 60 percent of the cost and technical assistance for this project. These two, together with the 60-megawatt Kurichhu project (2002) in eastern Bhutan, produce over 40 percent of Bhutan's annual revenue. An even larger joint India project, the Sunkosh 4,060-megawatt project, which would also provide water for irrigation to India, is expected to be completed by 2020.

The importance of this relationship with India was affirmed by Bhutan's response to India's request in 2004 to remove camps set up within its borders by insurgents from

Assam and Nagaland. The Royal Bhutan Army destroyed 30 camps in a swift military operation.

THE CHALLENGE OF MODERNIZATION

Bhutan has extensive forestry reserves that remain virtually unexploited. Twenty percent of the country has been set aside for preservation. The Royal Manas National Park, a 165-square-mile sanctuary established along its southern border, is designed to protect the natural wildlife of South Asia. Many of the species there are endangered.

Tourism in this incredibly beautiful natural environment is being developed on a "low volume and high value" policy to develop its economic potential so as not to undermine the traditional Buddhist life of its people, and to maintain its natural preserve.

The development of the human resources of the country has also taken a measured pace. Canadian Jesuit Father William Mackey has led the development of the nation's educational system to provide 180 schools and a national college. Still, only a small percentage of school-age children attend, and the adult literacy rate is estimated at 47 percent, among the lowest in Asia.

HEALTH/WELFARE

The family and the village have the primary responsibility for the welfare of the people. In the 1950s the king instituted a program for social work for monks living in the state-supported monasteries. The government has also initiated an education program, but the literacy rate remains one of the lowest in South Asia.

Health services are also meager; the expectation is that the family unit will remain the primary source of social welfare. The annual birth rate is a significant 2 percent, but the level of infant mortality is also high. The large number who become Buddhist monks also restrains population growth. The average life expectancy among the Bhutanese people is estimated to be 65.53 years.

Immigration has presented another challenge of modernization to the values of its rich natural and religious heritage. Most of the work force of Bhutan is employed in subsistence farming on the 16 percent of the land that is available for cultivation and pasture. Because this sector is self-sufficient, the country has had to import workers from

Timeline: PAST

A.D. 1616–1930s
Dharma Raja of Tibetan lamas

1907
Tongsa Penlop becomes hereditary king

1910–1947
British control over Bhutan's external affairs

1949
Indian control over Bhutan's external affairs begins

1953
A constitutional monarchy is established; the national Assembly has power to limit authority of king

1972
Jigme Singye Wangchuck becomes king

1980s
The Citizenship Act was enacted to limit citizenship to Nepali migrants. Unrest led to flight and deportation of 85,000 refugees to camps in eastern Nepal.

Building of hydroelectric power and limited tourism begin to contribute to country's economic growth.

1990s
Many Nepali immigrants are denied citizenship; demonstrators protest government policies toward Nepalis

PRESENT

2000s
Gradual government reforms leading to a parliamentary democracy begin.

Attempts to repatriate Nepali refugees from camps in eastern Nepal stall.

2008
National Assembly elections held on March 24; Jigme Khesar Namgyal Wangchuck installed as King.

Initial 5,000 of Nepali refugees resettled under United Nations High Commission on Refugees plan to resettle 60,000 in the United States.

neighboring Nepal and India to provide the labor needed to develop its industry. Their migration has challenged the country's efforts to preserve a national identity out of the exclusive culture of the dominant Buddhist community. To protect this identity, the government passed a law in 1985 to deny citizenship to all who could not claim legal residency before 1958.

A census taken in 1987 to enforce this exclusive nationalistic policy stirred political unrest among the Nepalis living in the southern part of the country, which led to terrorist attacks on schools and other public buildings. Government deportations in response moved eighty-five thousand people out of Bhutan

into refugee camps set up by the United Nations High Commission on Refugees in the eastern part of Nepal.

After thirteen futile attempts to resolve the issue, in 2001, the governments of Bhutan and Nepal agreed to conduct a pilot screening of 12,000 refugees residing in one of the camps in Nepal. The Bhutan representatives divided these refugees into four categories. Only 2.5 percent of them were determined to be bona fide citizens eligible for repatriation to Bhutan. Those assigned to Category II (70 percent) were described as "voluntarily" migrated from Bhutan more than a decade ago. In order to return, they would be required to apply for citizenship. The requirements for readmission include a two-year probationary delay and proof of fluency in the Dzonkha language of northern Bhutan. Screening began in a second refugee camp. But bilateral talks in 2003 failed to resolve issues of screening and of the rights and security of those readmitted.*

In response to the plight of the discouraged and restive 105,000 refugees remaining in seven camps in Nepal, the International Organization for Migration is preparing for the migration of 60,000 of them to resettle in the United States. According to the UN High Commission on Refugees, 5,000 will be resettled in the United States, Australia, and New Zealand in 2008.

Within Bhutan, increasing interaction with western life styles introduced by satellite television and the Internet is also changing attitudes and expectations among the youth. A youth-led Communist Party of Bhutan-Maoists is initiating agitation for a more inclusive government and the return of the Nepali refugees to Bhutan. As a traditional and cautious Bhutan seeks to become more democratic and developed, an enlightened role of the monarchy appears to hold the greatest promise for resolving peacefully the cultural and political tensions created by the modernization of the country.

ACHIEVEMENTS

Twenty percent of the country has been set aside for the preservation of its vast forest and wildlife reserves. In keeping with its Buddhist heritage, it seeks to achieve, as a nation, an increase in Gross Domestic Happiness, rather than GDProductivity.

*Brad Adams, "Letter to Prime Minister of Bhutan regarding discrimination against ethnic Nepalis," *Human Rights Watch*, April 16, 2008.

Maldives (Republic of Maldives)

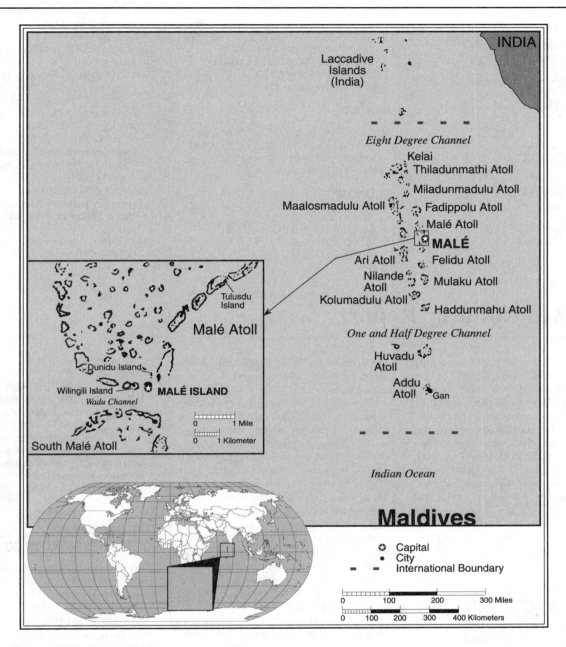

Maldives Statistics

GEOGRAPHY

Area in Square Miles (Kilometers): 115.8
(300) (about 1.7 times the size of
Washington D.C. in land mass, but
stretched as islands over 510 miles of the
Indian Ocean)
Capital (Population): Male (104,403)
(2006) living on 7/10 square mile
island (1.813 sq km)
Environmental Concerns: depletion of
freshwater aquifers; global warming
and sea level rise; coral-reef bleaching

Geographical Features: flat, with white
sandy beaches
Climate: tropical; hot; humid; monsoon

PEOPLE

Population

Total: 379,174 (July, 2008 est.)
Annual Growth Rate: 2.69%
(2008 est.)
Rural/Urban Population Ratio: 70/30
(WHO 2006)

Major Languages: Maldivian Dhivehi;
English is spoken by most government
officials
Ethnic Makeup: South Indians, Sinhalese,
Arabs
Religion: 100% Sunni Muslim

HEALTH

Life Expectancy at Birth: 65.12 years;
(63.73 years male; 66.58 years female)
Infant Mortality: 51.62/1000 live births
(2008 est.)

Per Capita Total Expenditure on Health: $878 (WHO 2005)
HIV/AIDS Rate in Adults: N/A (WHO 2005 est.)

Education

Adult Literacy Rate: 96.3%
Education: 12 years

COMMUNICATION

Telephones: 32,500 main lines (2006)
Cell Phones: 317,800 (2007)
Internet Users: 20,100 (2005)

TRANSPORTATION

Airports: 5
Highways in Miles (Kilometers): (88 km.; 66 km in Malé)

GOVERNMENT

Type: republic

Independence Date: July 26, 1965 (from the United Kingdom)
Head of State/Government: President Mohamed Nasheed
Political Parties: registered in June, 2005: Adhaalath (Justice) Party AP, Dhivehi Rayyithunge Party DRP, Islamic Democracy Party IDP, Maldivian Democratic Party MPD.
Suffrage: universal at 21

MILITARY

Military Expenditures (% of GDP): $45 million (5.5%) (2005 est.) (CIA World Factbook)
Current Disputes: none

ECONOMY

Currency ($ U.S. Equivalent): 12.8 *rufiyaa* = $1 U.S. (2006)
Per Capita Income/GDP: $4,600/$1.588 billion (2007 est.)

GDP Growth Rate: 6.6% (2007 est.)
Inflation Rate: 5% (2007 est.)
Labor Force by Occupation: 60% services, 22% agriculture, 18% industry (2000 est.)
Natural Resource: fish
Agriculture: fish; corn; coconuts; sweet potatoes
Industry: tourism; fish processing; shipping; boat building; coconut processing; garments; woven mats; rope; handicrafts; coral and sand mining
Exports: $167 million f.o.b. (2006 est.) (primary partners Thailand, United Kingdom, Sri Lanka, France, Algeria, Japan) (2006)
Imports: $930 million f.o.b. (2006 est.) (primary partners Singapore, UAE, India, Malaysia, Sri Lanka, Thailand) (2006)
Human Development Index (ranking): 100 (UNDP 2008)

Maldives Country Report

Maldives is a string of 1,192 tiny tropical islands grouped into 26 atolls in the Indian Ocean about 400 miles southwest of India. The island chain stretches 510 miles north to south across the equator. Most of the islands are small, the largest being less than five square miles in area. The highest elevation is only 8 feet above sea level, with many rising barely six feet above the ocean waters. They were easily submerged under the fourteen-foot high Indian Ocean tsunami wave on December 26, 2004, and more frequently by storm swells. They are fragile, remote, but enticingly beautiful.

DEVELOPMENT

Fishing and tourism are the major industries of this nation of islands. Both were severely damaged by the 2004 tsunami. Tourism is recovering rapidly, while fishing boats and housing remain restoration issues.

Most of the islands are covered with lush scrub growth, some have coconut-palm groves, and all are surrounded with coral reefs and clear waters abundant with fish. The mean daily temperature remains at a humid 80° F year-round, especially during the monsoon season from June to August. Because of a shortage of fresh water and arable land on most of the islands, only 200 of them are inhabited. Almost 30 percent of the total population

of 359,008 lives in the capitol city on the island of Male, which is just 7/10 of a square mile.

The earliest inhabitants of Maldives came from south India and Sri Lanka. Remains of shrines indicate the migration of Buddhists around the second century B.C. Divehi, the prevailing language of the islands, is further evidence of early Buddhist settlement. It is derived from Pali, the classical language of Buddhism in India, from which the Sinhalese language of Sri Lanka also comes.

Because the Maldive islands lie across the maritime trade route between Africa and East Asia, Arab traders often stopped there. The arrival of an Islamic Sufi saint in 1153 A.D. led to the conversion of the people to Islam. Since then Divehi is written in Arabic script, with the addition of many Arabic and Urdu words. The Moroccan explorer Ibn Battuta visited Male in the fourteenth century, during his extensive travels through North Africa and Asia. Because of his Islamic scholarship, he was invited to stay on Male as a judge. His accounts give a colorful description of island life at that time. Today, citizenship is restricted to Sunni Muslims, and the country's legal system is based on Shari'a, Islamic law.

Two immense global currents challenge the Maldives today: the revolution of self-determination through democracy and the rise of ocean waters by global warming.

FREEDOM

Rights of citizenship are restricted to Sunni Muslims. Although declared a democratic republic in 1968, it has slowly moved toward legislative reforms and an independent judiciary. Political parties became legal in 2005, the first national election for president was held in October, 2008, and national legislative elections in 2009.

THE BEGINNINGS OF REPRESENTATIVE GOVERNMENT

Strongly united under the authority of a sultan (an Islamic monarch), the Maldivians have remained fiercely independent since the twelfth century. A local leader, Bodu Muhammad Takurufanu, repulsed a brief Portuguese colonial intrusion in 1573. Maldives became a protectorate under the British crown in 1887. Even then, the Maldivian leaders did not permit British interference in local governance.

The British established a military base on the southern island of Gan during World War II and an air base in 1956. But strong anti-foreign sentiment forced the closing of the base in 1976, 14 years before the end of a 30-year lease with the British. The following year, Maldives rejected a Soviet offer to lease the base for $1 million per year.

In 1953, the sultan, Muhammad Amin Didi, declared Maldives a democratic republic, with himself as president. But the power of governance remained with an appointed "Regency Committee." In 1968, Amin Ibrahim Nasir, who had served since 1957 as prime minister in the Committee, instituted a new Constitution with an elected legislature (Majlis). This body selected him as its nominee to become president of the country. The Constitution prohibited political parties to form any opposition.

During his tenure as president, Ibrahim Nasir abolished the post of prime minister and increased his presidency to quasi-sultan status. He won a second five-year term in 1973. He did not seek reelection in 1978, and was succeeded by Maumoon Abdul Gayoom.

President Gayoom was elected for six terms; the only candidate in the national referendum to have his nomination approved by a majority vote of the 42-member Citizen's Majlis. Each time he received more than 90 percent of the popular vote. His 30-year rule came to an end on October 28, 2008, when, under an amended Constitution, he was defeated in a run-off in the country's first multi-party, direct election for president. Mohamed Nasheed, a long time political activist and leader of the Maldivian Democratic Party, became his successor.

HEALTH/WELFARE

The government developed an emergency rescue service able to reach 97 percent of the population widely dispersed among the habitable islands of the country. Its literacy (97.2 percent) is the highest in South Asia.

ECONOMIC DEVELOPMENT

President Gayoom's enlightened economic policies encouraged significant growth in the fishing and tourism industries. Almost half of the country's workforce is employed in fishing, mostly using traditional craft called dhonis. In the 1980s, government funds helped to construct canning and cold-storage facilities, as well as more than 200 modern fishing boats, to expand the catch—and the markets—for this valuable resource.

ACHIEVEMENTS

With substantial international help, the country has made substantive recovery from the tsunami damage. To preserve its fragile environment and its peace-loving character, it is a strong advocate for reducing global warming and making the Indian Ocean a nuclear-free zone.

In 1981, an international airport was constructed on an island near Male to serve with airports on the islands of Hulule and Gan an increasing number of tourists. In 2004, 615,000 came to vacation in 87 resort zones on isolated atolls. With continuing foreign aid, the country sustained an impressive growth rate, around 7 percent from 1995 to 2004, and the second highest per capita income in South Asia.

These industries, together with a reviving coconut crop and a modest shipping fleet, did not balance the import needs of the country, especially for food. The country received more than 20 percent of its revenue as foreign aid, and it continued to accumulate debt.

Then on December 26, 2004, came the devastating tsunami. Although only 108 were drowned, it destroyed 120 fishing vessels and twenty-one of the tourist zones, and left 29,000 homeless. Tourist visitors dropped by 36 percent in 2005. Total damage to the islands was estimated at $470 million, more than 62 percent of its GDP. Impressive international support has helped the country to recover. Tourist centers have been rapidly rebuilt. But it will take years to restore the homes and trades of an impoverished population spread among the inhabited islands.*

Maldives has no institutions of higher learning, and medical facilities are limited. There are only four hospitals. But extended restoration and education programs and an emergency medical rescue service among the outlying islands rank Maldives just below Sri Lanka in the UN Human Resources Development Index. Adult literacy has grown to 97.3 percent. And the government continues to work to improve water supplies and to eliminate water-borne diseases through water purification, desalinization, and other public-health measures.

PUBLIC PROTEST FOR DEMOCRACY

For all of the benefits of economic growth and human services, their fruits were distributed unevenly among the population. In response to this inequality under Gayoom's despotic rule, an increasing cadre of political activists sought greater democracy. The initial government response was suppression. An opposition candidate for president in 1993 was banished from the country for 15 years. Five others, including Mohamed Nasheed, were detained for circulating articles critical of the government. He was designated an Amnesty International Prisoner of Conscience in 1996.

*Raquel Rolnik, "UN Special Rapporteur on Adequate Housing," *UN News Centre*, February 26, 2009.

On September 20, 2003, while Nasheed was in exile in Sri Lanka, Evan Naseem, a political prisoner, was beaten to death in jail. That same year, the Majlis established a Human Rights Commission to look into reports of increasing prison abuses.

In August 2004, Nasheed helped to organize public demonstrations to protest the killing of Naseem, the detention of other political dissidents, and to call for democratic reforms. The government responded by declaring a state of emergency and arrested Nasheed and hundreds of other protesters, including several members of the Majlis advocating for political parties. A year later, on June 3, 2005, the Majlis amended the Constitution to allow political opposition. Three parties, Gayoom's own Dhivehi Rayyithunge Party (MPP), the Islamic Democracy Party (IDP), and Nasheed's Maldivian Democratic Party (MDP) quickly registered. They were later joined by the religiously conservative Adhaalath (Justice) Party (AP).

These steps were not sufficient for a country impatient for political freedom. The Maldivian Democratic Party organized a political rally for November 10, 2006, to push for further constitutional reforms. It was cancelled when the government threatened to punish any who took part.

In response to increasing public pressure, President Gayoom considered further constitutional amendments he hoped could be accepted in a deliberate and orderly manner. His proposal included limited terms for the presidency, a strengthened parliamentary form of government, and an independent Supreme Court. He finally ratified them to establish a new Constitutional order in August, 2008, that anticipated multi-party presidential elections to be held in October.

In the election on October 8, Gayoom won only 41 percent of the vote, to Mohamed Nasheed's 25 percent. Against the combined effort of the opposition parties, he lost to Nasheed's 54 percent tally in the run-off on October 28. As a primary, if reluctant, participant in the turbulent process toward greater democracy, he graciously accepted this end to his 30-year rule.

Multi-party elections for the Majlis for the first time were set for February, 2009.

THE RISE OF THE OCEAN

The islands offered little resistance to the tsunami in 2004. The force of the wave inundated most of the islands, submerging two-thirds of the capital city Male. And it contaminated most of the islands' groves and fresh water supplies.

But increasing population and a developing economy are having a longer-term

Courtesy of Shahee Ilyas

Mali, the capital of Maldives, where more than 100,000 live on the 7/10 square mile island.

impact on the islands' limited resources and fragile environment. The daily use of fresh water is drawing upon the aquifers faster than the annual rainfall replenishes them. And increasing human contamination threatens what water is available.

More critical is salt-water intrusion due to the breakdown of the protective coral reefs and the rise in the level of the ocean due to global warming. To restrain the short-term impact, the government built an expensive, six-foot retaining wall around parts of the island of Male, paid for by the Japanese government, with expensive restoration costs attached. The long-term outlook is overwhelming.

Newly-elected Mohamed Nasheed faces many immediate problems of declining tourism, population growth, high unemployment, and a growing drug culture. Also recognizing the threat of the ocean's rise to the islands' future, he has called for the creation of a sovereign wealth fund, drawn from the country's tourist receipts, to be able, when necessary, to purchase a new homeland for the Maldivian people.

Timeline: PAST

300 B.C.
The earliest evidence of Indian Buddhist civilization

A.D. 1153
Conversion to Islam in Maldives

1153–1968
Maldives is an Islamic sultanate; Bodu Muhammed Takurufanu repulses brief Portuguese intrusion to the islands in 1573

1887–1968
Maldives is a British protectorate

1968
Maldives becomes an independent democratic republic without political parties

1988
An attempted coup is put down by the Indian Army

1990s
The government seeks to improve social services, incurring substantial debt in the process, Maldives agitates for global environmental responsibility

PRESENT

2000s
At the Coral Reef Symposium in October 2000, Maldives' marine environment is cited as heavily damaged by global warming

2004
Public protest for greater democracy leads to declaration of a state of emergency

Tsunami kills 82, causes extensive damage to tourist and fishing industries

2005
Constitution is amended to allow for political parties. Tourist industry quickly restored after tsunami damage. Restoration of fishing fleet and housing remain to be done

2008
Mohamed Nasheed elected in first national democratic elections for president

2009
First election for the Majlis contested by political parties

Nepal (Kingdom of Nepal)

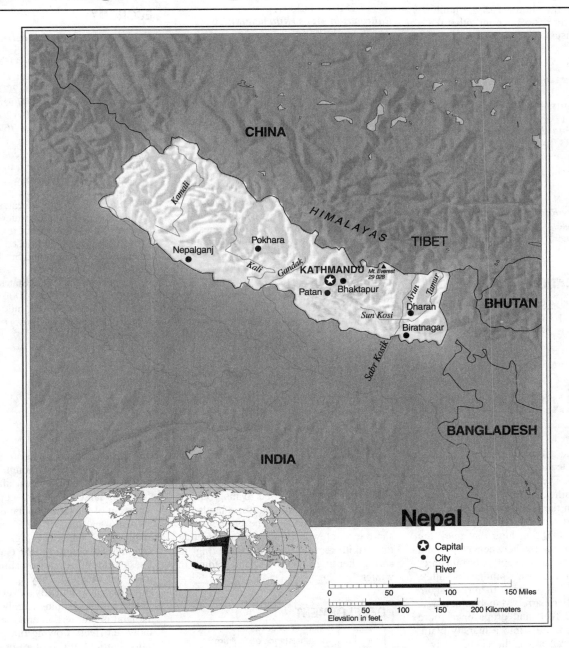

Nepal Statistics

GEOGRAPHY

Area in Square Miles (Kilometers):
56,812 sq. mi. (147,181 sq. km.)
Capital (Population): Kathmandu
(790,597) (2006 est.)
Environmental Concerns: widespread
deforestation, wildlife conservation;
water and air pollution
Geographical Features: Terai, flat river
plain in south; central hills; rugged
Himalaya Mountains in north;
landlocked
Climate: cool summers and severe winters in
the north; subtropical in the south (Terai)

PEOPLE:

Population

Total: 29,519,114 (July, 2008 est.)
Annual Growth Rate: 2.095% (2008 est.)

Rural/Urban Population Ratio: 84/16
(WHO 2006)
Major Languages: 47.8% Nepali;
12.1 Maithali; 7% Bhojpuri; numerous
other languages and dialects; English
link language in government and
business (2001 census)
Ethnic Makeup: 15.5% Chhettri,
12.5% Brahman-Hill, 7% Magar,
6.6% Tharu, 5.5% Tamang,
5.4% Newar, 4.2% Muslim,

3.9% Kami, 3.9% Yadav, 32.7% other
(Gurung, Rai, Lumbu, Sherpa, and
many smaller groups) (2001 census)
Religions: 80.6% Hindu, 10.7% Buddhist,
4.2% Muslim. 3.6% Kirant, other 0.9%
(2001 census)

Health

Life Expectancy at Birth: 61.12 years (male),
60.75 years (female) (2008 est.)
Infant Mortality: 62/1000 live births
(2008 est.)
Per Capita Total Expenditure on Health:
$76 (WHO 2005)
HIV/AIDS Rate in Adults: 0.5%
(2001 est.)

Education

Adult Literacy Rate: 48.6% (34.9% female)
(2001 census)
Education: male 10 years, female 8 years
(2003)

COMMUNICATION

Telephones: 595,800 main lines (2006)
Cell Phones: 1.157 million (2006)
Internet Users: 249,400 (2006)

TRANSPORTATION

Highways in Miles (Kilometers):
(17,280 km.) (2004)
Railroads in Miles (Kilometers): 36
(59 km.) (2006)
Usable Airfields: 47 (2007)

GOVERNMENT

Type: democratic republic
Independence Date: 1768 (unified)
Chief of State: President Ram Barab
Yadav
Head of Government: Prime Minister
Pushpa Kamal Dahal (Prachanda)
Political Parties: Communist Party of
Nepal (Maoist), Communist Party
of Nepal (United Marxist-Leninist),
Nepali Congress Party, Madhesi
Jana Adhikar Forum, Terai Madhesi
Democratic Party/Nepal Sadbhawana
Party, other smaller parties
Suffrage: universal at 18

MILITARY

Military Expenditures (% of GDP):
$132 million (2007) (1.7%) (2006) (SIPRI)

Current Disputes: refugees, control of
Kosi River, illicit drug smuggling

ECONOMY

Currency ($U.S. Equivalent):
72.446 *rupees* = $1 U.S. (2006)
Per Capita Income/GDP: $1,200/
$29.04 billion (2007 est.)
GDP Growth Rate: 2.5% (2007 est.)
Inflation Rate: 6.4% (2007 est.)
Unemployment Rate: 42% (2004 est.)
Labor Force by Occupation: 76% agriculture,
18% services, 6% industry (2004 est.)
Population Below Poverty Line: 31% (2004)
Natural Resources: quartz, timber, water,
scenic beauty, hydropower, lignite,
copper, cobalt, iron ore
Agriculture: rice; corn; wheat; sugarcane;
jute; root crops; milk; water buffalo meat
Industry: tourism; carpets, textiles, small
rice, jute, sugar and oilseed mills;
cigarettes, cement and brick production
Exports: $830 million f.o.b. (2006) (primary
partners India, United States, Germany)
Imports: $2.398 billion (2006) (primary
partners India, China, Indonesia)
Human Development Index (ranking): 142
(UNDP 2008)

Nepal Country Report

Nepal is like a Tantric mandala: colorful and intense, leading to unexpected levels of awareness. The country is breathtaking, like the magnificent Mount Everest's peak, the highest in the world, which dominates a majestic row of 10 Himalayan Mountains over 26,000 feet high that mark the formidable boundary between Nepal and Tibet. The land falls steeply from this arctic height into the lush Kathmandu Valley, some 20,000 feet below. It then rises again over the smaller, barren Mahabharat range, up to 11,000 feet, and drops once more through the foothills into a marshy plain, called the Terai, along the Ganges River, about 900 feet above sea level. Nepal is a land of immense natural contrast, with habitat for a wide variety of species, from the elusive snow leopards in the mountains to elephants, monkeys, tigers, and crocodiles in the Terai.

Nepal is also home to an immense variety of people. Almost 30 million are broadly divided by region, religion, and language into three distinct groups.

The mountainous region to the north is sparsely inhabited, mostly by those of Tibetan descent and language who follow the Lamaist, or Tibetan, Buddhist tradition.

Their dress and many customs are from Tibet. Some, for example, practice polyandrous marriage, wherein the wife of the eldest son is also married to his younger brothers. In such families, their lands are not usually subdivided. The brothers also share in the few seasonal occupations that the frigid terrain allows: cultivating in spring, herding in summer, and trading in winter.

DEVELOPMENT

Most of Nepal's economy relies on subsistence agriculture and diminishing trade between Tibet and India. The successful ascent of Mt. Everest introduced a thriving tourist trade that persisted through the ravages of a militant Maoist insurrection from 1996 to 2006. It remains among the poorest nations in the world.

Even though arable land is scarce and trade has been drastically reduced by the Chinese takeover of Tibet, the people of this region are more prosperous than those living in the more fertile valleys to the south. The alternative to family life presented by the

Buddhist monastic tradition also restrains population growth. Although their small, isolated communities span almost half of the total land area, they constitute only 3 percent of the total population of Nepal.

Almost a third of the population lives in the Terai, the low-lying, southernmost region of the country in the Gangetic plain. These Madeshi are mostly Hindu, although some are Muslim. They speak dialects of Hindi and are ethnically and culturally very close to their Indian neighbors. Because the land is flat, fertile, and nurtured by the snow-fed rivers flowing out of the mountains, agriculture is the primary activity. Although it is a narrow strip of land, only about 20 miles wide, and occupying 17 percent of the country, it produces more than 60 percent of Nepal's gross domestic product (GDP).

Two thirds of the population of Nepal, the Pahari, live in the inter-lying hill region. It is also predominantly agricultural. Arable lands are scarcer than in the Terai and are terraced for farming. Because of the altitude, the growing season is also shorter and the yields lower. At the center of this region is the Kathmandu Valley, a lush alluvial plain 15 miles long and 12 miles wide.

UN photo/Ray Witlin

The festive costume on this child shows the continuation of distinct religious traditions in Nepal.

Nepal's three largest cities: Kathmandu, Patan, and Bhaktapur are in this valley, absorbing more of its land as they continue to expand. Wide arrays of ethnic and cultural identities co-mingle here, interacting with the many surrounding cultures to create a distinctive artistic style and to fuse an overwhelming multiplicity of religious expression. Their Nepali language is based on the Indo-European languages of India, infused with extensive Tibeto-Burman borrowings.

SOCIAL DIVERSITY

Nepali social diversity is partly due to the rugged terrain, which has kept many small groups isolated east to west in the several river valleys that descend down the steep southern slopes of the mountains. Also important, Nepal has long provided extensive trade routes from India north up the river valleys, through the high mountain passes into Tibet, and on into China. Nepali traders along these routes have maintained distinct ethnic identities, whether their primary interaction has been with the Tibetan culture to the north or with the Hindu culture to the south. The success of their mercantile activity with such distinct partners has reinforced the cultural contrasts

between Tibet and India within the central region of Nepal itself.

The hierarchical social structure known as the caste system in India also contributes to Nepal's social diversity. This system, ranking rather than assimilating, maintains the distinctive customs and traditions of different communities. The Nepalese criteria for ranking appear more flexible than in India. The Gurkhas, for example, famous for their military prowess and courage, are recruited from three different Tibeto-Burman language communities from different parts of Nepal. They join together because of the opportunity for military employment that a shared identity as Gurkhas affords. Similarly, several distinct tribal groups in the Terai have claimed a single ethnic identity as Tharus in order to gain strength as a political force not available to them as separate minorities. In contrast, Thaksatae villagers have distanced themselves from other Thakalis, with whom they share ethnic, linguistic, and religious identities, in order to maintain the trading privileges that they have achieved as a distinct community within that group.

POLITICS

Prithvi Narayan Shah, king of the western province of Gorkha forged the unity of present-day Nepal in the eighteenth century A.D. He conquered the surrounding kingdoms and established his dynasty in Kathmandu, the capital of a defeated Newar ruler. His family's reign was circumscribed first by the British East India Company in 1815, and later, in 1845, by the Kathmandu Rana family, which established a powerful and hereditary prime ministry to rule the Shah domain.

In 1950, with the departure of the British Raj from the subcontinent, a national movement, modeled on the independence movement in India and led by the Nepali Congress Party (NCP), overthrew the Rana family. King Tribhuvan Vir Vikram Shah supported the anti-Rana movement and became a national hero. Upon his reinstitution as full monarch in February 1951, he worked to bring constitutional democracy to Nepal. Although his son, Mahendra, who succeeded him in 1955, was less sympathetic, his initiatives still led to national elections in 1959, under a new Constitution that established a Parliament with powers that limited the role of the king. The NCP won a majority in the new Parliament.

A year later, King Mahendra, asserting himself as an absolute monarch, dismissed the NCP government and banned all political parties. In 1962, he introduced a tiered election system, starting on the local level with elections to choose a village council

(panchayat). Members of the local panchayats elected representatives to an 11-member district panchayat, which in turn elected members to the National Panchayat. The National Panchayat elected its own prime minister. But the king reserved the power to appoint all of the Council of Ministers, who ran the government. This structure reinforced the traditional political power of the local landlords throughout the country. The landlords, in turn, reaffirmed the authority of the king.

King Mahendra died in 1972. His son Birendra succeeded him. In 1980, in response to growing public agitation, King Birendra held a referendum to see whether the people wanted to continue the party-banned, tiered election for membership in the National Panchayat or return to a multi-party, national election. The tiered system won by a small margin. Ironically, the majority of those elected to the National Panchayat in 1986 favored limiting the power of the king.

Encouraged by this result, leaders of the banned political parties organized public demonstrations to return to universal suffrage. A growing middle class, disaffected by economic hardship and the bungling, opportunistic leadership of the tier-elected Panchayats, supported this initiative. In response to the popular outcry, King Birendra worked out with the party leaders a new Constitution that limited his absolute sovereign power and established a multi-party, democratically elected, parliamentary government.

National democratic elections—the first since 1959—were held in 1991. The Nepali Congress Party again won a majority. But the leadership could not hold the allegiance of its members, leading to a no-confidence vote in Parliament, its dissolution, and new elections.

FREEDOM

The kingdom of Nepal became a constitutional monarchy in 1959, but parliamentary rule had limited success in meeting the country's many needs. The Maoist insurgency increasingly ravaged and dominated the country until 2006, when it agreed to join in a nationally elected constituent assembly freed of royal interference. National elections were held on April 10, 2008, and the monarchy was abolished on May 28, 2008.

In the 1994 elections, no party won a majority. The Unified Marxist-Leninist Party (UMLP) put together a fragile coalition that lasted for less than a year. The NCP then formed a coalition to gain a majority.

UN photo 140,484/Ray Witlin

The geographic contrast in Nepal is dramatic. The Himalayas are the highest mountains in the world and act as an impressive backdrop for many of the populated areas.

Two years later, this coalition also fell apart. Not wishing to face a new general election, the UMLP gave its support to a monarchist who harked back to the days of King Mahendra, even though his party held only 10 seats in Parliament. Six months later, he was ousted by members of his own party. They formed a new coalition with the NCP. After a stormy six months, Girija Prasad Koirala, a longtime leader in the NCP, became the fifth prime minister in the four years since the 1994 elections.

In the 1999 elections, the Nepali Congress Party won enough seats to form a government of its own under new leadership. But a revolt within the party a year later led to Girija Prasad Koirala becoming prime minister again.

Two crises during this time of political volatility and corruption in Parliament unsettled the country even more.

On July 1, 2001, Crown Prince Dipendra brutally murdered his father. Not permitted by his mother to marry the woman of his choice, the distraught prince dressed in fatigues, grabbed an M-16 rifle, and shot his parents, his younger brother and sister,

and an uncle and two aunts, before taking his own life. This episode shocked the country. The king's brother, Gyanendra, with a temperment ill suited to a country struggling with democracy, was hastily installed as king in his place.

A greater challenge to the government came from a dissident group of militant communist Maoists, strongly opposed to monarchy, corruption, and the oppression of the country's many poor. They drew their revolutionary inspiration from Mao's revolution in China, from the Naxalite movement in India, and the Shining Path, an extremist militant group in Peru. Their

guerrilla agitation started in 1996, with the splintering of the communist parties in Parliament. They began by recruiting support among villagers in the remote and disadvantaged regions in the western part of the country, and demanding "fees" from trekking tourists for "protecting" them. As their movement grew, a reign of terror ensued against those who resisted their cause. Abductions, maiming, and killing, matched in too many instances by abuses by the Royal Nepali Army, increased in intensity and violence throughout the countryside.

A month after the regicide, when a Royal Army unit refused to fight against the Maoist insurgents, Prime Minister Koirala resigned. He was replaced by a rival Congress Party leader, who attempted a truce with the Maoists. But it lasted only a few short months.

In November, 2001, King Gyanendra asserted his royal prerogative by declaring a state of emergency. On October 4, 2002, he dismissed the elected government and took over by royal decree. With foreign aid support, he mobilized the Royal Army of

95,000 to enforce his rule. Then, in hopes of placating the Maoists, he appointed directly a series of prime ministers, none of whom could function because they were opposed by a strong coalition of legislators who objected to the king's dissolution of Parliament. With increasing student activist support, they continued to call for the restoration of parliamentary government.

The conflict brought untold misery to a people already burdened with poverty, high population growth, and illiteracy. The Maoist insurgency cut deeply into tourist revenues and displaced more than 100,000 from their homes. More than 12,000 had been killed. Caught in a deadly battle between monarchy and anarchy, the government, debilitated by continuing political struggles with the king and with itself, was unable to respond.

ACHIEVEMENTS

A cease-fire and election agreement between the Maoist insurgents and the Seven Party Alliance in November, 2006, acknowledged democracy rather than war as the path to peace. Democratic election of a Constituent Assembly in April 2008 to abolish monarchy and create a new constitution is promising for effective governance.

In June 2004, responding to a sense of conflict fatigue on the part of his people, the king tried once again to initiate discussions with the Maoists. But with continuing political infighting in Kathmandu, and with the Maoists now effectively in control of 68 of the 75 districts in the country, they were not interested, particularly not to give any legitimacy to the king, whose rule they saw as evil.

Things began to change dramatically in April, 2006. Mass protests in the streets of Kathmandu forced King Gyanendra to reopen Parliament, under the leadership of a Seven Party Alliance. Even more dramatic, with the king's despotic power diminished, the Maoists realized that the path of violence was no longer an effective way to achieve their revolutionary objectives. They agreed to a cease-fire in May, and entered into negotiations with the Seven Party Alliance to create a representative government that would eliminate the monarchy.

On November 22, 2006, after intense negotiations, and with UN help to neutralize the opposing armies, Pushpa Kamal Dahal, known as Prachanda, the fierce leader of the Maoist insurgency, and the venerable Girija Prasad Koirala, head of the Seven Party Alliance, signed a Comprehensive Peace Agreement that resolved many thorny issues

to establish peace and set up steps toward electing a Constituent Assembly to create a constitution for a new republic. Such an accord between a terrorist group that was used to forcing its own way and an elitist clan of squabbling politicians in Kathmandu was an incredible achievement.

The accord was soon tested by some 24 militant separatist groups among the Madhesi, the native population of the Terai, who had long felt rejected when not neglected by the central government in the valley. The Democratic Madhesi Front (UDMF) led a crippling 16-day strike in the Terai region to press its demands for more representation if it was to participate in the Constituent Assembly elections. To honor its objective of a truly inclusive government, the Seven Party Alliance and Maoist leaders met with the UDMF and agreed to provide proportional representation for the Madhesis, aboriginal people, indigenous nationals, Dalits and backward communities in all government services, and to commit the Constituent Assembly to decide how the autonomous regions of the country would be structured. They further devised a dual voting system that would elect 240 members of the 601 seats in the Assembly directly; 335 members would be elected on a proportional representation of women (50 percent), and marginalized and oppressed communities (31.2 percent Madhesis, 13 percent Dalits); and 26 members would be nominated by the prime minister to assure representation from excluded groups.

The elections were held successfully on April 10, 2008, with the Maoists winning a plurality of 220 seats. At its first meeting on May 28, it voted (560–4) to abolish the monarchy and declare Nepal a democratic republic. On July 21, in a run off election, it voted Ram Baran Yadav president and Parmananda Jha as vice president, both Madhesis from the Terai. In August, President Yadav appointed Prachanda, leader of the Maoist Party, prime minister of the Constituent Assembly.

CHALLENGES

Nepal's industrial potential has long been restrained by trade agreements that tie the country's economy to India's development policies. And its commerce has been severely limited by the difficulty in traversing the trade routes to Tibet. According to the United Nations, 90 percent of the labor force is in agriculture, placing it among the least of the least-developed countries (LDCs). Unemployment is at 47 percent. According to a recent World Bank report, 31 percent of the people live in absolute poverty. The incidence of malnutrition-related retardation and blindness is high. Five thousand girls have been trafficked to

India every year. HIV/AIDS is beginning to take its toll. In education and medical and social services, the country struggles with limited resources and isolation among its diverse population.

Prachanda, whose triumphant, nonviolent journey away from terrorist insurgency to head an inclusive, democratically elected government, must now seek to provide leadership to confront an array of difficult problems. With such overwhelmingly weak economic and human development conditions among such an awesome diversity of peoples in such a rugged, breathtaking landscape, even the effort to grasp such an incredible array of challenges leaves one with a sense of wonder.

Timeline: PAST

A.D. 1742–1814
The Shah dynasty's expansion of the Kingdom of Gorkha

1815
The British East India Company reduces the Gorkha domain to the kingdom of Nepal

1845–1950
Rana family domination of the Shah dynasty

1949
The founding of the Nepal Congress Party

1959–1960
Constitutional monarchy

1960–1991
Absolute monarchy with tiered panchayat election of national legislature

1991
Constitutional monarchy established with a multi-party democratically elected parliament. First national democratic elections held in 32 years

1990s
Fragile governments rule in rapid succession Rise of the Maoist insurgency that increases terror and control of the country

PRESENT

2000–2005
Crown Prince Dipendra murdered King Birendra, succeeded by his brother Gyanendra Country continues to struggle with widespread and severe poverty

2006
Maoists agree to cease-fire, disarmament, and participation in parliamentary government free of royal interference.

2008
Constituent Assembly elections held. By vote of Assembly, monarchy is abolished. Prachanda, leader of the Maoist Party, elected prime minister.

Pakistan (Islamic Republic of Pakistan)

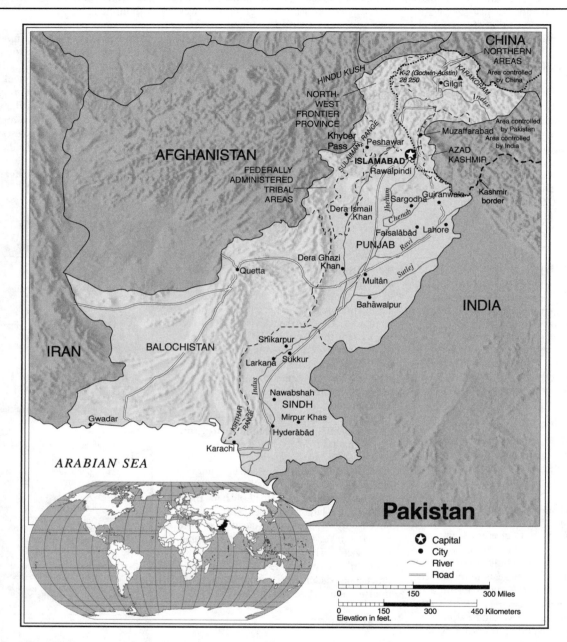

Pakistan Statistics

GEOGRAPHY

Area in Square Miles (Kilometers):
310,403 sq. mi. (803,940 sq. km.)
Capital (Population): Islamabad
(805,235) (1998 census)
Environmental Concerns: water
pollution, deforestation, soil erosion,
desertification, limited water supplies
Geographical Features: Flat Indus
plain in east; mountains in north and
northwest; Balochistan plateau in west

Climate: mostly hot, dry desert, temperate
in northwest, arctic in north

PEOPLE

Population

Total: 172,800,048 (July, 2008 est.)
Annual Growth Rate: 1.999% (2008 est.)
Rural/Urban Population Ratio: 65/35
(WHO 2006)
Major Languages: 48% Punjabi, 12%
Sindhi, 10% Siraiki (a Punjabi variant),

8% Pashtu, 8% Urdu (official), 3%
Balochi, 11% other
Ethnic Makeup: 44.1% Punjabi; 15.4%
Pashtun, 14.1% Sindhi, 14.5% Sariaki;
7.6% Urdu; 3.6% Balochi; 4.7% other
(1998 Census)
Religions: 97% Muslims (77% Sunni,
20% Shia); 3% other

Health

Life Expectancy at Birth: 63.07 years
(male); 65.25 years (female) (2008 est.)

Infant Mortality: 66.94/1000 live births (2008 est.)
Per Capita Total Expenditure on Health: $49 (WHO 2005)
HIV/AIDS Rate in Adults: 0.1% (2001 est.)

Education

Adult Literacy Rate: 49.9% (36% female) (2005 est.)

COMMUNICATION

Telephones: 5.24 million (2006)
Cell Phones: 88.02 million (2006)
Internet Users: 12 million (2006)

TRANSPORTATION

Highways in Miles (Kilometers): (259,758 km.) (2004)
Railroads in Miles (Kilometers): (8,163 km.) (2006)
Usable Airfields: 146 (2007)

GOVERNMENT

Type: federal republic
Independence Date: August 14, 1947
Chief of State: President Asif Ali Zardari

Head of Government: Prime Minister Syed Yousuf Raza Gilani
Political Parties: Awami National Party, ANP, Pakistan Muslim League PML, PML/N (Nawaz Sharif faction), Muttahida Majlis-e-Amal, MMA, Pakistan Peoples Party, PPP, Muttahida Qaumi Movement, MQM, many smaller parties
Suffrage: universal at 18, joint electorates and reserved parliamentary seats for women and non-Muslims

MILITARY

Military Expenditures (% of GDP): $4.517 billion (2007) (3.2%) (2006) (SIPRI)
Current Disputes: Taliban insurgency in Federally Administered Tribal Areas, political unrest in Balochistan; dispute over Kashmir and water sharing problems with India

ECONOMY

Currency ($U.S. Equivalent): Rupees 60.6295 = $1 U.S. (2007)
Per Capita Income/GDP: $2,600/$410 billion (2007 est.)

GDP Growth Rate: 6.4% (2007 est.)
Inflation Rate: 9.2% (2007 est.) rising rapidly in 2008
Unemployment Rate: 7.8% (2007 est.)
Labor Force by Occupation: 42% agriculture, 38% services, 20% industry (2004 est.)
Population Below Poverty Line: 24% (FY 2005–06 est.)
Natural Resources: land, extensive natural gas reserves, limited petroleum, poor quality coal, iron ore, copper, salt, limestone
Agriculture: cotton, wheat, rice, sugarcane, fruits, vegetables, milk, beef, mutton, eggs
Industry: textiles and apparel, food processing, pharmaceuticals, construction materials, paper products, fertilizer, shrimp
Exports: $16.31 billion (2007 est.) (primary partners United States, UAE, Afghanistan, China, United Kingdom) (2006)
Imports: $30.33 billion (2007 est.) (primary partners China, Saudi Arabia, UAE, United States, Kuwait) (2006)
Human Development Index (ranking): 136 (UNDP 2008)

Pakistan Country Report

Pakistan is the second largest nation in South Asia, about one-fourth the size of India, with less than one-seventh of India's population. It lies in the Indus River Valley, between the mountainous border with Afghanistan through which comes the famous Khyber Pass to the northwest, and the Great Indian Desert, and the Rann of Kutch, to the southeast. Long a land of transition between the rugged steppes of Inner Asia and the plains of India, it is today a new nation caught between the heritage of a glorious imperial past and the poetic image of an ideal theocratic future. The name, Pakistan, given by the Muslim poet Muhammed Iqbal in 1930, means "Land of the Pure."

The heritage of the people of Pakistan goes back to the earliest-known urban culture in South Asia. Excavations of the ancient cities of Harappa and Mohenjo-daro, discovered in 1922, reveal an impressive civilization that dates from 3000 to 1500 B.C. Distinctive are its knowledge of hydrology and its use of irrigation to cultivate the valley with the rich waters of the Indus River. Surplus agricultural production led to extensive commerce in cotton and grains throughout the ancient world.

Islam is a religious faith based upon the teachings of the prophet Muhammad revealed in the Koran in Arabia during the seventh century A.D. Arab traders and wandering Sufi mystics were the first to bring the religion into South Asia. The Sufis' spiritual discipline and religious teaching drew large numbers of indigenous peoples to submission to the will of Allah (God) as early as the eighth century. The spread of this vibrant faith and subsequent rule of Islamic sultans and emperors led to the creation of Pakistan as an Islamic Republic in 1947. Today, 97 percent of the 173 million people in the country are Muslim. Of these, 77 percent belong to the Sunni tradition. There are also small minorities of Hindus, Christians, and members of the Ahmadiya Sect of Islam, whose faith is considered heretical by the orthodox.

DEVELOPMENT

Extensive investment in the cotton textile and food processing industries has kept Pakistan's economy growing. But it has not been matched by human resource development. Agriculture still employs half of the labor force, but contributes less to the GDP. Earthquakes in October 2005 and 2008, and a growing indigenous Taliban insurgency impose a devastating impact on human life and development.

Moghuls were militant Turks refined by the elegance of Persia and energized by their Islamic faith. The march of their conquering forces across the northern plains of South Asia to the Bay of Bengal in the sixteenth century marked the period of greatest glory in the heritage of the Pakistani people. Akbar (1556–1605), the greatest of them, is remembered for the opulence and splendor of his court, for the far-reaching administrative control of his empire, and for his elaborate building projects which still stand as massive tribute to his commanding wealth and intellect.

Pakistan became independent at the departure of the British Raj in 1947, created especially for the 7.2 million people (*mohajira*) who migrated from central India to preserve the culture of a staunch Islamic and impressive imperial past. This heritage has been both an asset and an obstacle to its evolution as a modern nation state.

INDEPENDENCE MOVEMENT

The Muslim League was formed in 1906 to represent the interests of the Muslim minority under the British Raj. In the movement for freedom from imperial domination, they became convinced that they would be oppressed, perhaps even eliminated, in an independent India dominated by Hindus. In 1940, the League voted to demand a separate state for the Muslim population of British India.

The British Raj rewarded the persistence of the Muslim League's leader, Muhammad Ali Jinnah, by granting independence in 1947 to two nations instead of one. Its scheme to partition British India created a smaller, more populous East Pakistan, and a dominant West Pakistan, separated by nearly 1,000 miles of India.

This partition was disastrous. The Muslims in British India who most feared Hindu oppression were not those who had the security of living in Muslim majority districts, but those who lived in the Hindu-majority districts in north central India. They felt endangered in their own lands. Hindu and Sikh minorities in districts where the Muslims were in a majority also feared for their lives. This mutual fear caused the migration of 14 million people, Hindus, Sikhs and Muslims moving in opposite directions. Clashes in the border areas, especially in the Punjab, which was split in half between Muslim and Hindu districts, led to the killing of hundreds of thousands of bewildered, anxious people. The consequences of this human catastrophe are still felt among the families that survived.

FREEDOM

Since independence the country has been under martial law longer than democratically elected government. Popular elections were first held in 1971, and then suspended until 1988. National elections in February 2008 reaffirmed Pakistan's commitment to democracy, but the army is still a dominant force in the nation. Women are held to their traditionally subservient role in Islamic society, even after the reform of the Hadood Ordinance in 2006.

QUEST FOR POLITICAL STABILITY

The new Pakistan lacked adequate administrative services to cope with the disruption and bloodshed of the partition. Muhammad Ali Jinnah took upon himself the chief executive duties of governor general in the interim government. In ill health at the time, he died 13 months later.

Liaquat Ali Khan, his successor as prime minister, was assassinated in 1951. The Muslim League, imported from India, lost control of a unifying national agenda to the indigenous sources of provincial power: wealthy landowners and tribal leaders in the five distinct provinces in the country, each divided from the others by ethos and language.

The provincial identities of the people in the new nation accentuated rather than mitigated their differences on the national level. The political solidarity of the Bengali people in the province of East Pakistan was first realized by their opposition to accept Urdu, the language of the *mohajirs,* immigrants from north central India, as the national language of Pakistan. This opposition led to their split from Pakistan to form an independent nation, Bangladesh, in 1971.

Distinct languages in each of the four remaining states in West Pakistan also take precedence over Urdu, which is spoken by 8 percent of the population. In the early years of independence, Urdu speaking immigrants made up 46 percent of the urban population in the country. Today, the Muttahida Quami movement (until recently the Mohajir Quami movement and now divided into two hostile camps), although limited to Karachi for its political base, is the fourth-largest political party in the country.

HEALTH/WELFARE

Emphasis on the military budget has slighted government attention to human resource development in education and social services. The birth rate remains high, and infant mortality at birth is among the highest in South Asia. Adult literacy is low. Among women it is little more than half that of the male population.

Punjabi speakers are more than half of the population. Punjab is the granary of the country, with the most heavily irrigated and productive lands. Industrial development and wealth are also concentrated there. Lahore, its capitol city, was the administrative center for the region under the British Raj. All of these factors contribute to Punjabi domination in the ranks of the army and the civil services.

Sindh is the next-most-important state, sharing with Punjab about 90 percent of the industrial production of the country. Karachi, capital of the state, with a population of over 9 million, is Pakistan's largest city and commercial center, and to date its only seaport. Yet only 12 percent of Pakistanis are Sindhi speakers.

Ten percent of the population lives in the North-West Frontier Provinces, and the Federally Administered Tribal Areas (FATA), which lie along the rugged mountainous border with Afghanistan. The number of Pashtuns, who speak Pashto, increased by the influx of more than 3 million Afghan Pashtuns as refugees during the Soviet occupation of Afghanistan

during the 1980s. Many of them who remain continue to cross the porous Durand Line. Pashtuns, some 40 million strong in this region, do not recognize it as a border between the two countries.

Balochistan, in the arid lands which border Iran and the Arabian Sea, is the largest state (40%) and the richest in natural resources. A seaport is being built with Chinese financing and labor at Gwadar on the coast. Yet the people who speak Balochi are less than 5 percent of Pakistan's population. A separatist movement started in 1973, based on many of the same issues that led to the break away of Bangladesh. It has been suppressed by military force, which killed a respected tribal leader, Nawab Akbar Bugti, in August 2006.

Pakistani Muslims are also significantly divided between a majority who seek a modern Islamic identity, and the more traditional Islamists, who have long felt their commitment to exclusive, coercive theocracy challenged by the quest for modern democracy. With the departure of Soviet forces from Afghanistan in 1989, the jihadis—ones who struggle for the faith—turned to free the Muslims in Kashmir from Indian military occupation. With the intrusion of western values by the defeat of the Taliban in Afghanistan in 2001, their cause took on a new sense of urgency. For the 2003 parliamentary elections, fundamentalist parties formed a coalition called the Muttahida Majlis-e-amal (MMA), representing Balochistan and the North-West Frontier Provinces, bordering Afghanistan. In the National Assembly, it became a significant force in promoting Islamist causes in this region and in the nation as a whole. With its influence greatly reduced in the 2008 elections, terrorism has become an increasing, destructive, alternative path to promote the Islamists' fundamentalist ideology. It is especially attractive among a disillusioned and impoverished youth in a country where those under 24 years old are 47 percent of the total population.

ACHIEVEMENTS

Industrial growth and political stability has been achieved, largely through military domination. Pakistan demonstrated its nuclear capability in tests in 1998.

Another challenge to a stable, democratically elected government in Pakistan is the wide division between the rich and the poor. A 1970 World Bank study found that 80 percent of the capital wealth in Pakistan was concentrated in just 22 families. A subsequent study in 1998 found

42.3 percent of the nation's wealth held by the top 20 percent of the population, with the lowest 10 percent having but 3.7 percent. The disparity between the industrial rich and the slum-dwelling poor in the cities continues to grow.

New wealth and a new class were created in Pakistan during the 1980s by jobs in the Persian Gulf oil fields. More than 2 million young people from all parts of the country sent home more than $4 billion a year, or about 10 percent of the country's gross domestic product. These monies stimulated conspicuous consumer buying, which led to a number of local enterprises using pickup trucks and video equipment. The loss of jobs during the Persian Gulf Wars had a doubly adverse impact on Pakistan's economy, cutting in half the remittances from overseas while increasing the number of unemployed within the country.

Amid all of these challenges to the formation of a single body politic, the Pakistan army has been the strongest force to unite a disparate and disengaged people under the fear of an imminent threat of war with India. Ironically, because of its dominant role to maintain unity and stability, the military has also impeded the growth of democracy in Pakistan. A diplomat recently characterized Pakistan as different from most countries, which, when they become independent, look for an army to protect it. Pakistan is an army looking for a country to defend.

A constitution to establish a national parliamentary government was finally adopted in 1956, affirming the common sovereign identity of the two wings of Pakistan as an Islamic Republic. Yet this and each of the successive attempts to establish democratic rule—in 1971 and in 1988—occurred under the watchful eye of the military, and ended in a takeover: by General Ayub Khan in 1958, by General Yahya Khan in 1969, by General Zia-ul-Haq in 1977, and by General Pervez Musharraf in 1999. In all, the country has been under martial law for 34 of its 62 years as an independent nation.

MARTIAL LAW: 1958–1971

General Mohammad Ayub Khan, commander-in-chief of the Pakistan army, became martial-law administrator in 1958, in hopes of stimulating economic growth among a people "not yet ready for democracy." He replaced the 1956 Constitution with a new Constitution, delegating extensive executive power to a president who would be elected only by those elected to local political offices. They also determined who would be elected to the National Assembly. In 1965, a limited electorate of "Basic Democrats," the 80,000 locally elected council members

whom Ayub Khan accepted as prepared to vote, elected him president.

In the same year he was elected president, war broke out with India over their competing claims for the former princely state of Jammu and Kashmir, most of which India had occupied since 1947. This war ended in military stalemate and a UN-observed ceasefire. An unfavorable peace settlement with India in the Tashkent Agreement of 1966 cost Ayub Khan his popular support.

Growing discontent over military rule during those years spawned two new political leaders, one in each of the wings of Pakistan. Mujibur Rahman, leader of the Awami League in East Pakistan, capitalized on the perception among the Bengalis that they were second-class citizens. His charismatic leadership won immense popular support for greater regional autonomy.

At the same time, Zulfikar Ali Bhutto, a Western-educated diplomat from a large landholding family in the province of Sindh, formed the Pakistan People's Party. Adopting the campaign slogan *Roti, Kapra aur Makon* ("Bread, clothes and shelter"), he mobilized a wide popular following in the western wing of the country toward a policy of democratic socialism. He did not attempt to generate a following of his own in East Pakistan.

President Ayub Khan was not able to contain either the Bhutto or the Rahman initiatives, and, in 1969, was forced to resign. General Yahya Khan, his successor, in a quest to bring order, declared the first popular national elections to be held in Pakistan since its independence, on December 7, 1970. In this election the Awami League won 160 of the 162 seats in the National Assembly assigned to the more populous East Pakistan. Bhutto's Pakistan People's Party won 81 seats of the 132 assigned to West Pakistan.

Bhutto felt that by winning a majority in West Pakistan, he was the rightful leader of the country. When he was not assured that position, he boycotted the new Assembly. In response, President Yahya Khan suspended the legislature, which led to a vehement cry for independence in East Pakistan. Yahya Khan sought to suppress this freedom movement by military force. Millions fled across the border for refuge in India. After several months of unrelenting bloodshed, the Indian government launched a military attack in support of the Bengali rebels. They won independence for a separate Bangladesh on December 17, 1971.

DEMOCRACY: 1971–1977

The freedom of Bangladesh left the Pakistan People's Party with a majority in the National Assembly, and Bhutto became

the president of Pakistan. He led what was left of the country toward a socialist state by nationalizing banking and such major industries as steel, chemicals, and cement. His policy created employment opportunities in an already cumbersome civil-service bureaucracy, but discouraged investment and led to a decline in industrial production.

Bhutto was more successful in restoring parliamentary government. He created a new Constitution—the third in 26 years—that was adopted in 1973. It established a National Assembly of 207 members, all of them elected directly for five-year terms. Bhutto then became prime minister, elected by a majority of the legislature.

Bhutto called for elections in 1977 in hopes of getting endorsement for his leadership and his socialist economic policies. This call spurred an unexpected and virulent opposition of nine parties, which united to form the Pakistan National Alliance (PNA). Bhutto's Pakistan People's Party won the election. But the PNA, which won only 36 of 207 seats in the Assembly, charged that the elections had been rigged and took to the streets in protest. Bhutto called in the army to restore order and sought to negotiate with the PNA to hold new elections. Before any agreement was reached, Mohammad Zia-ul-Haq, chief of staff of the army, seized control of the government.

General Zia-ul-Haq promised to hold elections within 90 days, but then canceled them. He continued to hold out the promise of elections for the following 11 years, during which time he maintained firm military control. Part of that control was to bring charges against Bhutto of complicity in a political murder, which led to Bhutto's trial and execution on April 4, 1979.

MARTIAL LAW: 1977–1988

In the fall of 1979, Zia banned all political parties and imposed censorship on the press. The following year he removed from judicial review any actions of his government and decisions of the military courts. Many of these measures were cloaked in a policy of "Islamization," through which his military regime sought to gain public support by an appeal to traditional laws and teachings of Sunni Islam. Once again, entrenched divisions and political turmoil in the country led to repression more reminiscent of Moghul imperialism than the workings of modern representative government.

Zia's consolidation of power in Pakistan coincided with the collapse of the Shah of Iran, the rise of Saudi Arabia as a power in the Middle East, and the Soviet invasion of Afghanistan. The response of the United States to these developments gave Pakistan a strategic role in protecting western sources of oil and containing Soviet expansion. U.S. support for his repressive military rule not only set back the quest for democracy, but also substantially weakened the authority of the Zia government itself.

DEMOCRACY: 1988–1999

A spirit of democracy did survive, if only partially, in a hasty referendum called by General Zia in 1985 to affirm his policy of Islamization, which elected him executive president for a five-year term. The Constitution of 1973 also survived, though altered by General Zia in an Eighth Amendment, to give the president power to dismiss the prime minister. He then called for legislative elections to be held in November, 1988. Before that date, Zia was killed in a plane crash and the Supreme Court quickly removed the ban on political parties. The elections were held as scheduled.

Bhutto's Pakistan People's Party, led by his daughter, Benazir Bhutto, won a plurality of 93 seats in the 217-member National Assembly, and she was invited to become prime minister. Then just 35 years old, she was the youngest person and the first woman to lead an Islamic nation.

Benazir Bhutto's tenure was based on an uneasy balance within the legislature itself. It was further complicated by competing claims outside the legislature by the other large power brokers in the nation—the army and the president. Even though General Beg, appointed army chief of staff in 1985, advocated restraint from involvement, the army remained a political presence.

In 1989, Benazir Bhutto tried to restore the full authority of the prime minister's office by having the Eighth Amendment of the Constitution repealed, but failed to get the necessary two-thirds vote. In the summer of 1990, her opposition in the National Assembly tried to defeat her, but could not get enough votes. President Ghulam Ishaq Khan then asserted his authority under the Eighth Amendment to dismiss her government with charges of corruption and nepotism.

In the elections which followed her dismissal, Mian Nawaz Sharif, chief minister of Punjab and head of the Islami Jamhorri Ittehad (IJI), or Islamic Democratic Alliance, brought his conservative party together with the communist-leaning Awami National party, dominant in the North-West Frontier Province, and the fundamentalist Jamiat-Ulema-i-Islam party. Their coalition won 105 seats in the 217-member National Assembly by winning 36.86 percent of the

popular vote. Benazir Bhutto's People's Democratic Alliance (PDA) was reduced from 93 to 45 seats, even though it won 36.84 percent of the popular vote. Sharif, a member of a successful industrial family who migrated from Amritsar in East Punjab to Pakistan in 1947, became prime minister.

To fulfill a promise made during the campaign to form a coalition with the fundamentalist Islamic groups, Prime Minister Sharif introduced a law to make the Islamic code of Shari'a the supreme law of Pakistan. At the same time, he asserted that his Shari'a bill would not stand in the path to modernization. The Jamiat-Ulema-i-Islam party withdrew from the ruling coalition, objecting that Sharif's Shari'a bill was too vaguely worded and not being implemented.

Even without their support, Sharif still called upon Islam as a unifying force in holding the country together and in harmony with its neighboring countries to the west. His government enacted blasphemy laws and pushed to amend the Constitution to make the Koran "the supreme law of land." These acts were understood as efforts not only to divert attention from increasing economic woes and other political issues, but also to contain the potentially volatile force of religious fundamentalism as a threat to stability in the country.

Mian Nawaz Sharif also tried to repeal the Eighth Amendment to the Constitution that granted the president the powers of dismissal. President Ghulam Ishaq Khan then invoked it, for a second time, and in April 1993, dismissed the Sharif government, also on charges of corruption and nepotism.

This time, the Supreme Court overruled the president and reinstated the Sharif government. The army chief of staff, General Abdul Waheed, then brokered the resignation of both the prime minister and the president. The National Assembly and state legislatures were then dissolved, and new elections set for October.

In the 1993 elections, Benazir Bhutto's Pakistan People's Party won 86 seats, to 72 for Sharif's party. Her position was strengthened by the election a month later of Farooq Leghari, deputy leader of the PPP, to the office of president.

In her second term as prime minister, Benazir Bhutto pursued policies that destabilized the nation's economy, compromised foreign investment, and drove the inflation rate to 20 percent. In response, she imposed a sales tax that proved very unpopular. An image of rampant corruption in government, together with an attempt to appoint sympathetic judges to the high courts, also eroded her popular support. President

Leghari dismissed her on charges of corruption and nepotism under the Eighth Amendment in November, 1996, and new elections were called for February 3, 1997. To avoid any legal action against her, Benazir Bhutto fled the country.

Even though voter turnout was low, Mian Nawaz Sharif and his Pakistan Muslim League Party won a two-thirds majority in the National Assembly. Benazir Bhutto's opposition party then joined his government to repeal the Eighth Amendment to the Constitution.

Reducing the power of the president did not place any restraint on the third element of political power in Pakistan, the military. Its dominance required the testing of Pakistan's nuclear capability immediately following India's nuclear tests in May 1998, even at the high cost of international disapproval and U.S. economic sanctions. And when Prime Minister Sharif repudiated the military attack into the Kargil District of Kashmir in the summer of 1999, the army chief of staff, General Pervez Musharraf, staged a coup in October. He then brought charges against Sharif for treason and attempted murder. The courts found Sharif guilty, and sentenced him to life in prison, which General Musharraf commuted to a life in exile.

MARTIAL RULE: SINCE 1999

General Musharraf's coup dismissed the parliamentary government elected in 1997. In June 2001, he took over the title of president to establish legitimacy for his martial rule.

Following the terrorist attacks in the United States on 9/11, the United States began military operations in Afghanistan to destroy Osama bin Laden and his Al Qaeda bases there. Pakistan became a necessary ally to provide bases and logistical support. Under strong American pressure, President Musharraf courageously withdrew support for the Taliban, which had been providing this fundamentalist movement with the infrastructure needed to control most of Afghanistan.

By November, 2001, the Al Qaeda had escaped to Pakistan's Federally Administered Tribal Areas (FATA) adjacent to Afghanistan. As the Taliban also began to use this area as sanctuary for its insurrection against the American and NATO forces, Musharraf came under U.S. pressure to seal Pakistan's border with Afghanistan. Eager to maintain U.S. support for his military rule, President Musharraf set up military posts along the border, pursued Al Qaeda fugitives in the country, and disclaimed any continuing support to the Taliban.

Pointing to a significant loss of Pakistani soldiers in attempts to confront Afghan Taliban fighters, in September 2006, he made an agreement with some tribal leaders in Waziristan in FATA not to bring military force into the region if they restricted Taliban cross border activity. This agreement may have reflected the reality of his lack of control in that area. But as the tribal leaders could themselves do little to restrain a resurgent Taliban, his agreement did little to assure the Afghan government and U.S. and NATO forces assigned to fight the Taliban insurgency that Pakistan was an effective ally in this effort. He managed to reassure the American government sufficiently that he alone was capable of restraining terrorism in his country, while at the same time it was recognized that its presence as a threat was essential to his garnering American support for his rule.

Musharraf did not anticipate that his commitment to the "war on terror" would stir up a vigorous and determined, youthful Taliban movement in FATA itself. Pakistani Islamist militants grew in opposition not only to foreign military presence in Afghanistan and deadly U.S. air strikes into Pakistan, but also to the tribal leaders in FATA, and ultimately to the Pakistan army itself for complicity in America's war. This indigenous terrorist movement, growing to a force of 30,000 fighters under the command of Baitullah Mehsud in South Waziristan alone, became sufficiently bold and strong enough to threaten the survival of Pakistan itself.*

President Musharraf managed also to distance his government from any involvement in the proliferation of nuclear technology conducted by A. Q. Khan, the founder of Pakistan's nuclear weapons program. In exchange for a pardon by the president, Mr. Khan took full responsibility for the illicit transfer of nuclear capability to other countries out of his research laboratories without authorization by the government. Musharraf then assured the world that as long as he was in power in Pakistan, its nuclear arsenal would not get into the hands of terrorists, nor into the hands of an anti-American opposition in Pakistan itself.

During the time of this buildup of terrorist activity which Musharraf was supposed to contain, he was also under considerable international pressure to return Pakistan to a democratic form of government. His ambivalent dealings with both Islamist terrorism and with democracy were to become his undoing.

In response to the international call for democracy, General Musharraf set elections for a new national legislature for the fall of 2002. To assure his control in this process, he called for and won a national

referendum on April 30 to extend his presidency for another five years, regardless of the outcome of the legislative elections. He then proposed amendments to the constitution, which included restoring to the president the power to dismiss the prime minister, the cabinet, and even the legislature by decree.

The election results in October did not yield the popular support that Musharraf had sought. A pro-Taliban, anti-American coalition of Islamic fundamentalist parties, called the Muttahida Majlis-e-amal (MMA), won sufficient support in Balochistan and the North-West Frontier Province, closest to Afghanistan, to gain 60 of 342 seats in the National Assembly. Benazir Bhutto's PPP, with her in exile, won 81 seats. Musharraf's own PML(Q) won a plurality of 118 seats. He was not able to form a government for six weeks, until he had enticed enough members away from the PPP to gain majority support. He still did not have enough votes to get the legislature to approve his constitutional amendments. Nevertheless, he closely oversaw the activity of the Assembly under the leadership of his designated prime minister.

Through political maneuvering with the MMA, he got the Assembly to accept his presidency and constitutional changes, with the understanding that he would step down as chief of staff of the army by the end of 2004. Later he tried to remove constitutional constraints to his serving as both president and army chief of staff, but found himself in a confrontation with the Chief Justice of the Supreme Court, whom he suspended for misuse of judicial authority on March 4, 2007. A public protest, led by the country's lawyers, closed down the courts.

Thus began a series of steps to diminish his power, starting with a heavily boycotted election in the national legislature and provincial assemblies to re-elect him president on October 6. When the Supreme Court threatened to question the constitutionality of his election, he declared a state of emergency on November 3. He then placed those judges who did not support the emergency under house arrest. To resolve the issue of his joint tenure, he resigned as army chief of staff on November 28. The state of emergency was lifted on December 15, with parliamentary elections called for January 8, 2008. On December 27, former Prime Minister Benazir Bhutto, who had returned to Pakistan on October 18 in an American brokered deal that intended to have her appointed prime minister by President Musharraf after the elections, was assassinated while campaigning in Rawalpindi. The elections, postponed because of her death until February 18, marked an

enthusiastic return toward democratically elected, parliamentary government.

Benazir Bhutto's PPP and its allies won control of the National Assembly and all of the Provincial Assemblies except Punjab, which was divided among 3 parties. Musharraf's party was resoundingly defeated throughout the country. Under threat of impeachment, he resigned as president on August 18, 2008.

After six months of political positioning, on September 11, 2008, the national and provincial legislatures elected Asif Ali Zardari, Bhutto's husband, president of Pakistan. Nine days later, on the eve of his first address to a plenary session of the National Assembly, a deadly bomb exploded in the nearby Islamabad Marriott Hotel. It was a dramatic reminder of the extent of bold and destructive terrorist acts coming to the very center of the country. In recognition of the serious nature of the threat of terrorism, the prime minister convened a special session of the National Assembly to explore how to deal with it. Though inconclusive, it rejected pursuing a military solution in favor of seeking avenues of dialogue.**

Pakistan's economic health, which improved modestly during the Musharraf years, is now confronted with severe deficiencies enhanced by the world economic crisis. Early attempts by President Zardari to find international support achieved only an IMF loan of $7.6 billion on November 15, 2008, to meet the nation's foreign debt obligations. Longer term solutions to provide both economic health and security from Islamist terrorism continue to challenge Pakistan's fledgling parliamentary government.***

To add to Pakistan's instability, a massive, deadly earthquake shook the mountains of northern Pakistan on October 8, 2005, killing more than 87,000 people. It took army units 3 days to cover 20 miles to get relief to Balakot, at the edge of the epicenter of the 7.6 quake. They found the town flattened, including 200 students crushed in their school building. Volunteers rushed to rescue the survivors before lack of food and medical care, and the onset of the arctic winter months, threatened to add to the quake's toll.

The international community responded generously to the country's call for help, pledging $6.5 billion to meet the rescue and reconstruction costs. And private donations

*Dexter Filkins, "Right at the Edge," *New York Times Magazine,* September 7, 2008.

**Cristina Otten, "The Mumbai massacres and Pakistan's new nightmares," The Hindu, 15/12/2008 URL:http://www.thehindu.com/2008/12/15/ stories/2008121556691100.htm.
***Adrian Levy and Cathy Scott-Clark, "On the Trail of Pakistan's Taliban," *The Guardian,* January 10, 2009.

added another $200 million. Of the more than 600,000 housing units needed by the 3 million made homeless by the quake, a third have yet to be built. A second major (6.5) earthquake in a remote region (NE of Quetta) in Baluchistan on October 29, 2008, destroyed 2,000 homes, adding to the country's relief burden.

INTERNAL CHALLENGES

The failures of America's "war on terror" and weakness of the government in Afghanistan, the rise of an indigenous Taliban terrorist offensive, the global economic crisis, and damaging earthquakes in Pakistan have all contributed to instability and insecurity in Pakistan.

Other challenges have long existed within the governance of Pakistan itself. Sporadic martial rule and a continuing disproportionately high defense budget ($4.517 billion, near 20 percent of the 2007 federal budget), a high rate of population growth (2.1 percent), corruption, the loss of human rights through the imposition of religious blasphemy laws, and, most significantly, the lack of human resources development have long had an impact on the well-being of the country.

Human development factors such as poor working conditions, low wages, especially for women, lack of job security, lack of skill training, and not keeping abreast of fashion trends have contributed to the decline in Pakistan's substantial textile industry. Even with significant investments in production technology and textile machinery and indigenous cotton production, its exports dropped 10 percent in 2006. In tightening world markets Pakistan is not able to compete with Bangladesh, which does not grow cotton.

A lack in human resource development is also evident in the limited—and elitist—opportunity for education in Pakistan. Literacy in the country is now at 49.9 percent, small improvement over the level, according to UNICEF, when Pakistan received its independence in 1947. Half of all secondary level students are educated in private schools, the only place they can get instruction in English, still the language of opportunity in the professions, technology, and trade.

Women are excluded even more from education: Their literacy is little more than half that of the men, (36 percent to 63 percent). Girls represent only a third of the student population. This lack of education opportunity for women reflects the traditional expectation of their subservience and seclusion in Islamic society.

General Zia-ul-Haq affirmed this attitude as national policy when he enacted the Hudood Ordinance in 1979, which places

Timeline: PAST

3000–1500 B.C.
Harappan city culture

A.D. 1526–1857
The Moghul empire

1907
The founding of the Muslim League

1940
The Muslim League adopts the demand for the separate state of Pakistan

1947
The partition of British India; the creation of Pakistan

1948
War with India over Kashmir

1956
The first Constitution establishing Pakistan as an Islamic republic

1958–1969
Military rule of Ayub Khan

1965
War with India over Kashmir

1969–1971
Military rule of Yahya Khan

1970
First national popular elections: Mujibar Rahman's Awami League wins majority of National Assembly; Zulfikar Ali Bhutto's Pakistan People's Party wins West Pakistan majority

1971
War with India, the breakaway of East Pakistan to become Bangladesh, Bhutto becomes president of Pakistan

1973
A Constitution establishing parliamentary democracy is adopted; Bhutto becomes prime minister

1977–1988
Military rule of Zia-ul-Haq; national elections set; helicopter accident kills Zia; Benazir Bhutto becomes prime minister

1990s
Parliamentary democracy is restored, Pakistan tests its nuclear capability in the wake of Indian tests

1999
General Pervez Musharraf, army chief of staff, takes over government.

PRESENT

2000s
Military rule of General Pervez Musharraf Lack of human resource development and growing financial problems threaten the nation's economy.

2001
Pakistan becomes ally of the United States in "war on terror"

2002
Parliamentary elections restored, but President and General Musharraf remains firmly in control of the government.

2005
Deadly earthquake kills 87,000, leaves 3 million homeless in northern part of country.

2006
Nawab Akbar Bugti is killed in military repression of Balochistan insurgency

Government withdraws military from Waziristan tribal areas in agreement for tribal leaders to stop support for Taliban insurgency in Afghanistan.

2007
Lawyers protest President Musharraf's suspension of Supreme Court Chief Justice in March

Benazir Bhutto returns to Pakistan in October to take part in national elections, is assassinated on December 27.

President Musharraf declares national emergency on November 4, lifted December 15

2008
National elections held in February, Bhutto's PPP wins control of National Assembly and all province Assemblies but Punjab.

President Musharraf resigns in August.

Asif Ali Zardari, Bhutto's husband, elected president on September 11.

Islamabad Marriott Hotel damaged by terrorist bomb on September 20.

Pakistan receives $7.6 billion loan from the International Monetary Fund.

Pakistan agrees to bring to justice any Pakistanis responsible for November 26 terrorist attack on Mumbai, India.

particularly poor and illiterate women in danger of being jailed when accused of adultery or if they report being raped. In 2006 General Musharraf introduced a Women's Protection Bill, which attempted to qualify some of the more blatant discrimination against women in the Ordinance. It transfers issues of rape from Islamic law to Pakistan's penal code and makes accusations of adultery more stringent. The bill passed in the National Assembly over the strong objection of the fundamentalist Islamic parties. It was also opposed by human and women's rights groups, who wanted the Ordinance, which they claim has no basis in the Koran,

repealed in its entirety. The admonition of the sixth Five Year Plan proposed during General Zia's reign still hold's true: "In all societies, women's development is a prerequisite for overall national development; indeed no society can ever develop half-liberted and half-shackled."

Pakistan is committed to its survival as a unified, sovereign state, even though threatened by divisive political, social, and religious forces, and by substantive economic and human development challenges. Affirming its integrity as an Islamic republic, its greatest challenge is to become a fully developed modern nation while remaining faithful to the teachings of Islam.

Sri Lanka (Democratic Socialist Republic of Sri Lanka)

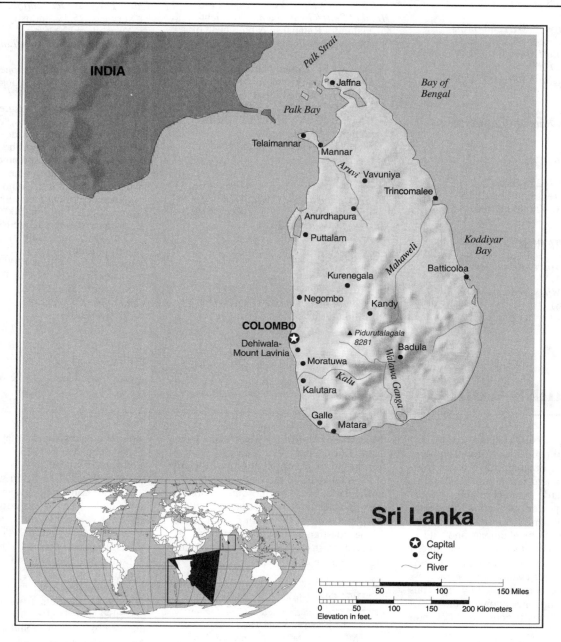

Sri Lanka Statistics

GEOGRAPHY

Area in Square Miles (Kilometers):
(169,930 sq mi) (about the size of West Virginia)

Capital (Population): Colombo (2,436,000 metro area, 656,610 city proper)

Environmental Concerns: deforestation; soil erosion; poaching; coastal degradation; water and air pollution; waste disposal

Geographical Features: mostly plain, mountains in the interior

Climate: tropical monsoons

PEOPLE

Population

Total: 21,128,772 (July, 2008 est.)
Annual Growth Rate: 0.943% (2008 est.)
Rural/Urban Population Ratio: 85/15 (WHO 2006)

Major Languages: 74% Sinhala (Official Language), 18% Tamil, 8% other. English is commonly used in government and is spoken competently by about 10% of the population.

Ethnic Makeup: 73.8% Sinhalese, 7.2% Sri Lankan Moors, 4.6% Indian Tamils, 3.9% Sri Lankan Tamils, 10.5% other (2001 Census provisional data)

Religions: 69.1% Buddhist, 7.6% Muslim, 7.1% Hindu, 6.2% Christian, 10% other (2001 Census provisional data)

Health

Life Expectancy at Birth: 72.95 years
(male), 77.08 years (female)
(2008 est.)
Infant Mortality: 19.01/1000 births
(2008 est.)
Per Capita Total Expenditure on Health:
$189 (WHO 2005)
HIV/AIDS Rate in Adults: 0.1% (2001 est.)

Education

Adult Literacy Rate: 90.7 (2001 census)

COMMUNICATION

Telephones: 2.742 million (2007)
Cell Phones: 7.983 million (2007)
Internet Users: 428,000 (2006)

TRANSPORTATION

Highways in Miles (Kilometers): (97,287
km.) (2003)
Railroads in Miles (Kilometers): (1,449
km.) (2006)
Usable Airfields: 18 (2007)

GOVERNMENT

Type: republic
Independence Date: February 4, 1948
Head of State/Government: President
Mahindra Rajapakse is both head of
state and head of government.
Political Parties: Sri Lanka Freedom
Party SLFP, United National Party
UNP, Janatha Vimukthi Perumuna VJP,
Tamil National Alliance TNA, National
Heritage Party JHU, Ceylon Workers
Congress CWC, Sri Lanka Muslim
Congress SLMC
Suffrage: 18 years of age; universal

MILITARY

Military Expenditures (% of GDP): $804
million (2007) (2.9%) (2006) (SIPRI)
Current Dispute Civil War

ECONOMY

Currency ($U.S. Equivalent):
110.78 *rupees* = $1 U.S. (2007)
Per Capita Income/GDP: $4,100/$81.29
billion (2007 est.)

GDP Growth Rate: 6.3% (2007 est.)
Inflation Rate: 19.7% (2007 est.)
Unemployment Rate: 5.7% (2007 est.)
Labor Force by Occupation: 40.4%
Services, 25.3% Industry, 34.3%
Agriculture (2006 est.)
Population below Poverty Line: 22%
(2002 est.)
Natural Resources: limestone, graphite,
mineral sands, gems, phosphates, clay,
hydropower
Agriculture: rice, sugarcane, grains,
pulses, oilseed, spices, tea, coconuts,
rubber, milk, eggs, hides beef, fish
Industry: processing of rubber, tea,
coconuts, tobacco, and other agricultural
commodities, telecommunications,
insurance, banking; clothing, textiles,
cement, petroleum refining
Exports: $8.139 billion (2007 est.)
(primary partners United States, United
Kingdom, India, Belgium, Germany,
Italy) (2006)
Imports: $10.61 billion (2007 est.)
(primary partners India, China,
Singapore, Iran (2006)
Human Development Index (ranking): 99
(UNDP 2008)

Sri Lanka Country Report

Sri Lanka is a small island nation that hangs like a pendant off the southeast coast of India. Extending 270 miles from north to south, and expanding to 140 miles in width toward its southern end, it occupies just 1.5 percent of the total landmass of the subcontinent. It was once renowned for its pleasant tropical climate and natural beauty. The Indian Ocean tsunami hit Sri Lanka with devastating impact on December 26, 2004. But even more, for the past 25 years, it has been ravaged by civil conflict. The country, once known as the "Pearl of the Orient," has become the "Lebanon of South Asia."

Sri Lanka is divided into two regions: a low-lying dry zone to the north and a mountainous wet zone to the south. At the center of the southern zone are the lush Kandyan Highlands, whose extensive tea and rubber plantations are watered by abundant rainfall, especially during the southwest monsoon season. Ceylonese tea, considered among the finest in the world, has recently been replaced by textiles as the country's leading export.

The northern plains are devoted mostly to rice cultivation for domestic consumption. Irrigation systems, necessary to support agriculture in this region, date from the earliest record of settlers from India, in the fifth century B.C. Marauding forces from south India, which destroyed the city of Anuradhapura in the tenth century A.D., and malaria, borne by mosquitoes bred in the still waters of the irrigation lakes, drove the population of the north-central region to the coastlands. Redevelopment of the blighted north-central region started during the British colonial period.

DEVELOPMENT

Human resource development and land and water reclamation for agriculture and energy have contributed most to Sri Lanka's economic health. In spite of a decline in the world tea market and, even more, the devastation of civil war since 1983 and the 2004 tsunami, the country's largely agricultural economy remains healthy.

In 1968 Sri Lanka undertook the Mahaweli River Project to build five major dams and irrigation works along the 207-mile course of Sri Lanka's longest river, from the central highlands to Koddiyar Bay on the east coast. This development cleared, resettled, and irrigated 900,000 acres. With substantial foreign investment, it was completed in 1983. The project now produces 20 percent of the country's rice and 45 percent of its power generation.

The Sri Lankan people are also divided, north and south. Seventy-four percent of Sri Lanka's population speak Sinhalese, 93 percent of whom are Theravada Buddhists. Eighteen percent of the population is Tamil speaking, two-thirds of whom are Hindu.

The Sinhalese trace their origin to fifth-century B.C. settlers from India. Legend describes their leader, Prince Vijaya, as of the race of the lion, a Sinhal, a symbol of royalty adopted from ancient Persian culture. Sent from north India by his father, he arrived on Sri Lanka on the day of the Buddha's death, in 483 B.C. and established his kingdom in the city of Anuradhapura in the north-central region of the country.

Tradition also traces the origin of Buddhism on the island to Mahinda, the son and emissary of the Indian emperor Asoka, in the third century B.C. This Theravada tradition reveres the teachings of the earliest disciples of the Buddha—the elders (thera)—as contained in the Pali Canon. Itinerant monks from India carried these sacred texts throughout South and

Southeast Asia during the early years of expansion of the Buddhist faith.

Portuguese, who arrived on the south coast of Sri Lanka in the early 1500s, drove many of the Sinhalese people of the south into the mountains. There they established a kingdom around the city of Kandy. Sinhalese Buddhists are divided today between the Kandyans, who live in the Highlands, and the "Low Country" people on the coastlands. The latter are more numerous (60 percent) and more prosperous, living in the more urban, coastal rim of the south.

FREEDOM

Since 1983, the country has been torn apart by civil war between the Sri Lanka government and the militant LTTE, seeking independence for the Tamil speaking minority. This conflict has caused 70,000 deaths, and made many hundreds of thousands homeless as Internally Displaced Persons. International assistance to bring relief was withdrawn during intense fighting in 2008.

The Tamils are also divided into two groups: the Sri Lankan Tamils (70 percent) and the Indian Tamils (30 percent). The Sri Lankan Tamils are found mostly on the north and east coastlands. Almost half of this Tamil community lives in the northernmost district of Jaffna, representing 95 percent of the district population. They share a long history on the island with the Kandyan Sinhalese, with whom they have the most in common culturally and ethnically.

The Indian Tamils were brought to Sri Lanka in the nineteenth century to work as field laborers on plantations set up by the British in the Kandyan Highlands. Their number was greatly reduced during the 1960s and 1970s by their repatriation to India. Those who remained, about 5 percent of the population of Sri Lanka, eventually received status as citizens of Sri Lanka.

Significant Christian and Muslim communities (8 percent and 7 percent), belong to both language groups. The Tamil-speaking Muslims live mostly along the east coast; a minority caught between the northern Tamils and Kandyan Sinhalese.

INDEPENDENCE

The British were the first to unify these peoples under a single government administration, in 1815. They introduced the rudiments of a national government in the port city of Colombo, on the southwest coast, and democratic institutions throughout the country. The first general elections were held in 1931, to select representatives to a National Assembly by universal suffrage under strict colonial control.

On February 4, 1948, Sri Lanka, then called Ceylon, received its independence as a parliamentary dominion in the British Commonwealth. In 1972, the government adopted a new Constitution as an independent republic, with a single legislature of 168 elected members. A further constitutional change, in 1978, endowed the presidency with extensive, independent executive authority. Junius Jayewardene, who had been appointed prime minister in 1978 after a sweeping victory of his United National party (UNP) in 1977, was elected president in separate national elections held in 1982.

His victory occurred at a time of great social unrest in the country. The vigorous pursuit of development, resettlement, and land reform projects had the unanticipated consequence of making many Kandy Sinhalese homeless. Their restlessness was expressed by a militant, Marxist youth group called the People's Liberation Front (JVP), which began devastating attacks on villages throughout the south in 1971. These activities fed into an underlying conflict between the Tamil and Sinhalese populations that broke out into civil war in 1983.

CIVIL WAR

Soon after the independence of Sri Lanka, political leaders from the dominant Sinhalese community began to exploit a popular "Sinhala only" movement to eliminate advantages achieved by the Tamils during the Colonial period. S. W. R. D. Bandaranaike and his Sri Lanka Freedom Party, a coalition of leftist, pro-Sinhala groups, won the elections in 1956. He then introduced a bill to make Sinhalese the only official language of the country. The Tamil leaders responded with a nonviolent demonstration. Their protest incited an unchecked violent response by Sinhala extremists. Bandaranaike's attempt to restrain the anti-Tamil violence, and to find some accommodation for Tamil interests, led to his assassination in 1959 by an extremist Buddhist monk.

HEALTH/WELFARE

The government provides national health care and extensive education, as well as extensive relief and rebuilding for victims of the war and the tsunami. International relief workers and many civilians have been displaced and killed in the crossfire during the wind down of 35 years of civil war.

Adding fuel to the fire, the new constitution, adopted in 1972, eliminated many of the minority protections adopted at the time of independence. In response, Tamil legislators formed a solid political caucus as the Tamil United Front to present their concerns in the national legislature. To diminish the appeal of a growing militancy among their youth, they also sought greater autonomy at the district level, to give them greater freedom and voice in those northern districts where they were in the majority.

The landslide victory of the United National Party in the 1977 elections took away the Tamil United Fronts leverage as a critical voting block at the national level. With the need to resettle some 130,000 families displaced by the new dams in the Mahaweli River Project, the UNP pursued policies that placed more Sinhalese in redefined districts in the northern part of the country. The Tamils then found themselves also losing political power at the district level.

The Tamils loss of political protection during the 1970s fanned the fires of some 36 militant student groups, youthful and eager for social and political change. Among them, the most ruthless and disciplined was the Liberation Tigers of Tamil Eelam (LTTE). It organized and carried out a sustained reign of terror throughout the northern regions of the country. In 1983, the LTTE ambushed a Sri Lankan army unit, inciting anti-Tamil riots in Colombo and across the south. Close to 2,000 Tamils were killed, 100,000 became internally displaced persons (IDP), and 130,000 fled to India as refugees. Civil war had begun.

Unable to control the violence, President Jayewardene invited the government of India in 1987 to send an Indian Peace Keeping Force (IPKF) to Sri Lanka. Faced with the IPKF's ineffectiveness and unpopularity, and with growing violence against the Tamils by the Sinhalese youth group JVP, Jayewardene did not seek reelection in 1988. His United National Party won the elections, and his successor, Ranasinghe Premadasa, asked the Indian Army to withdraw.

The Indian Peace Keeping Force left the LTTE weakened but no less resolved to seek independence for a separate Tamil state at any cost, including through drug trade and suicide bombing. This militant group was implicated in the assassination of President Premadasa on May 1, 1993, by a human time bomb, the same way Rajiv Gandhi, head of India's Congress Party, was killed while campaigning in south India in 1991.

The LTTE asserted its control in the northern Jaffna District by calling for a boycott of the 1994 national legislative

Everyone standing around waiting at a distribution center in Jaffina for scarce food during the summer of 2006, when the Sri Lanka army cut off access to the city. This action caused the collapse of the Norwegian sponsored peace talks with the LTTE in Geneva in October 2006.

elections. Less than 10 percent of the electorate in that district voted. In other parts of Sri Lanka, war-weary voters sought a political rather than military solution to the conflict between the Tamil insurgents and the Sinhalese majority. In hopes for peace, they elected a fragile coalition of leftist parties called the People's Alliance, led by Chandrika Kumaratunga.

Mrs. Kumaratunga was no stranger to politics. She was the daughter of S. W. R. D. Bandaranaike, the popular prime minister, leader of the Sri Lanka Freedom Party in the 1950s. Her mother, Sirimavo Bandaranaike, became leader of the SLFP after his assassination in 1959. She served as the nation's first woman prime minister from 1960 to 1965 and from 1970 to 1977, and as president from 1996 until her retirement in 2000. Mrs. Kumaratunga's husband, a popular film actor, was also active in national politics until his assassination, purportedly by a Sinhala nationalist group, while a presidential candidate in 1988.

Mrs. Kumaratunga initially proposed talks with the LTTE for a cease-fire. When they did not materialize, the Sri Lankan army undertook a major offensive to remove the LTTE from its stronghold in the ravaged city of Jaffna. Her efforts to end the conflict by force did not bring peace.

Although weakened and further isolated from any political base, the LTTE continued to carry out guerrilla attacks in the northeastern coastal region of the country. It recaptured the town of Killinochchi on the vital highway to Jaffna in September 1998 and defeated the Sri Lankan forces in

the Elephant Pass in April 2000. Its reign of terror included the assassination of two Tamil mayors of Jaffna to protest the attempt of a more moderate Tamil United Liberation Front to reestablish civil order there.

ACHIEVEMENTS

 With extensive international help, the country has made substantial recovery from the 2004 tsunami. The Army has effectively defeated the LTTE. The nation looks for restoration and peace from a conflict that has devastated and displaced many of its Tamil minority.

In 2001, the United National Party, campaigning to renew efforts toward peace in the national legislative elections, defeated Kumaratunga's People's Alliance. Prime minister Ranil Wickremesinghe picked up on initiatives for mediation by the Norwegian government to enter into a full cease-fire agreement with the LTTE in February 2002. In July, his government fulfilled a vital precondition of the LTTE to enter into peace talks by withdrawing the ban placed on the LTTE as a terrorist organization. Formal talks with the LTTE then began with Norwegian facilitation in Thailand in September. At a later round of talks in December 2002, the Norwegian mediators offered a proposal called the Oslo Statement to explore an acceptable formula for limited autonomy for the Tamil people within a united sovereign Sri Lanka. It

proved problematic for both parties, and the peace process stalled.

The LTTE did not want to discuss any proposal that presupposed a united, sovereign country. They wanted first to establish an Interim Self Governing Authority for the Tamil-speaking Northern and Eastern Provinces. Once accepted as separate, then they would talk about assurances to make it possible for them to join in a shared governance of the island as a whole.

On the other side, in the national legislative elections held in November 2003, a roused Sinhala nationalist opposition defeated the United National Party. It asserted that Prime Minister Wickremesinghe was making too many concessions in the Norwegian negotiations.

At the end of November 2004, to push its agenda for self rule, the LTTE held "Heroes Week" demonstrations in the northeast region, to commemorate 17,800 Tamils who have died in their 20-year civil war. Alleged security force interference with the demonstrations led to a one-day strike in some northern cities. The ceasefire remained fragile, with UNICEF accusations of child recruitment by the LTTE, and with fighting erupting among factions within the LTTE.

On December 26, 2004, the Indian Ocean tsunami hit the east coast of the country from the tip of Jaffna in the north to the city of Galle in the south. The immense power of its wave killed 30,240 people, and left 833,780 homeless. The survivors of Sri Lanka were overwhelmed by the indiscriminate devastation and heavy toll of the tsunami disaster and then by the incredible outpouring of relief provided by so many from all parts of the world.

Bickering over relief efforts, intensified by the LTTE's dominant control over the northeastern region of the country, quickly dissolved the hope that a shared national calamity might bring the warring sides together.

In the presidential election in November 2005, Mahinda Rajapakse's United Peoples Freedom Alliance was a coalition of Sinhalese nationalist parties that took a hard line for a unitary rather than federalist solution to the civil conflict. The LTTE, which saw more advantage to its cause for self-rule in a hard line opposition in Colombo, enforced a boycott of the election in the region of the island under its control. That stance assured Rajapakse of success at the polls.

The Sri Lanka Monitoring Mission (SLMM) reported in August 2006 an increasing number of major violations in the Cease Fire Agreement in the North and East. United Nation's estimates report more than 3,000 deaths and 225,000 made homeless by terrorist and military action in 2006. And a meeting of both sides in Geneva to resume peace talks in October got nowhere.

To reaffirm his unitary position, President Rajapakse initiated a shared common policy with the United National Party toward firming a strong negotiating position in Norwegian sponsored peace talks. But with the collapse of the cease-fire, he began a major military campaign to eliminate the LTTE from its entrenchment in the Northern and Eastern Provinces, which had been combined during the Indian Army Peacekeeping Force's attempt at reconciliation in 1987. When they were separated by a decision of the Supreme Court in 2006, with the help of a LTTE dissident, Colonel Karuna, the Sri Lanka army forced the LTTE sufficiently out of the Eastern Province to allow provincial elections in May 2008. Chandrakanthan, deputy leader of Karuna's political party (TMVP), was elected Chief Minister of the Provincial Assembly.

Building on this apparent success in the more ethnically diverse Eastern Province, President Rajapakse turned the army's efforts toward the more Tamil dominant Northern Province. The threat of this operation to the lives and relief of the more than 300,000 displaced persons in this area roused great concern and calls for a cease-fire from India.

In response to this concern for the safety of the civilian population during this intensifying military operation, the Rajapakse government assured renewed efforts to pursue a political solution to the conflict and further development efforts in the Tamil dominant regions of the country.

But in 2007, Rajapakse had already created a multi-ethnic panel called the All

Timeline: PAST

500 B.C. Migration of Sinhalese Indians

247 B.C. Mahinda introduces Buddhism

A.D. 1815–1948 British colonial rule

1948 The independence of Ceylon, as a British Commonwealth dominion

1972 A new Constitution establishes Sri Lanka as a democratic republic

1977 The United National Party wins elections by wide margin

1978 The Constitution is modified to establish an independent president

1982–1988 Junius Jayewardene serves as president; anti-Tamil riots break out; Indian Peace Keeping Force

1990s Efforts to achieve a cease-fire between LTTE and Sri Lankan military forces and to negotiate a settlement in the dispute between the Tamil minority and Sinhalese majority fail

PRESENT

2000s Sri Lankan economy hit by civil war and the Indian Ocean Tsunami

2001 The government and LTTE agree to Norway brokered cease-fire and to talks to restore peace.

2004 Indian Ocean Tsunami hits, leaving 30,240 dead and 883,780 homeless.

2006 With death toll of civil war rising to 67,000 since 1983, peace talks between government and LTTE break down.

2008 Sri Lanka army, with help of LTTE dissident, routs LTTE forces out of Eastern Province, and government holds provincial elections, won by dissident's party. Sri Lanka army begins major offensive against LTTE in its strongholds in Northern Province.

Party Representative Committee (APRC) to recommend a form of genuine power sharing which could accommodate minorities that have been sidelined and alienated from the state, while preserving the unity, sovereignty, and territorial integrity of the state. When the panel issued its report, dissension among the 17 members who created it was clearly evident. That the more militant Tamil minorities will accept Rajapakse's unitary proposals as an effective avenue for negotiations for peace does not appear promising.

For even if the army succeeds in routing out the LTTE militarily, the expectation of guerrilla warfare and terrorist attacks, which are continuing in the Eastern Province, holds out little hope to those in the Northern District who have been so ravaged and displaced by these many years of civil war.*

Sri Lanka's experience in seeking an inclusive national identity as a democracy is taking a heavy toll among its people.

*Thomas Fuller, "Sri Lanka War Nears End, but Peace Remains Distant," *New York Times,* February 17, 2009.

India's Democratic Challenge

Ashutosh Varshney

Charting a New Path

India is attempting a transformation few nations in modern history have successfully managed: liberalizing the economy within an established democratic order. It is hard to escape the impression that market interests and democratic principles are uneasily aligned in India today. The two are not inherently contradictory, but there are tensions between them that India's leaders will have to manage carefully.

Students of political economy know that market-based policies meant to increase the efficiency of the aggregate economy frequently generate short-term dislocations and resentment. In a democratic polity, this resentment often translates at the ballot box into a halt or a reversal of pro-market reforms. In the West, such tensions have remained moderate for at least three reasons: universal suffrage came to most Western democracies only after the Industrial Revolution, which meant that the poor got the right to vote only after those societies had become relatively rich; a welfare state has attended to the needs of low-income segments of the population; and the educated and the wealthy have tended to vote more than the poor.

The Indian experience is different on all three counts. India adopted universal suffrage at the time of independence, long before the transition to a modern industrialized economy began. The country does not have an extensive welfare system, although it has made a greater effort to create one of late. And, defying democratic theory, a great participatory upsurge has marked Indian politics, a phenomenon that is only beginning to be understood by scholars and observers: since the early 1990s, India's plebeian orders have participated noticeably more in elections than its upper and middle classes. In fact, the recent wisdom about Indian elections turns standard democratic theory on its head: the lower the caste, income, and education of an Indian, the greater the odds that he will vote. The ruling United Progressive Alliance (UPA), a coalition with the Indian National Congress at its core, counts on the lower social orders as its most important voting bloc.

India's development experience is also likely to be distinct from East Asia's. South Korea and Taiwan embraced universal-franchise democracy only in the late 1980s and the mid-1990s, two decades after their economic upturn began. Other economically successful countries in the region, such as China and Singapore, have yet to become liberal democracies. Periodic

renewals of mass mandates through the ballot box are not necessary in authoritarian countries, but they are in India. Democratic politics partly explains why, for example, privatization has gone so slowly in India compared to in China. In India, workers have unions and political parties to protect their interests. In China, labor leaders who resist job losses due to privatization are tried and jailed for treason and subversion, something entirely inconceivable in India's democracy.

So far, the reform process of the last 15 years has had positive results: by most conventional standards, India's economy is booming. After registering a 6 percent average annual growth rate for nearly a quarter century, the Indian economy has picked up even greater speed. Over the last three years, it has grown at over 8 percent annually, and forecasts for the next few years promise more of the same. Investment as a proportion of GDP has been steadily climbing, exceeding 30 percent lately and raising hopes of an investment boom like that which propelled East Asia's economies. Total foreign direct investment for the current financial year is likely to exceed $10 billion (compared with $100 million in 1990-91) and is rising. Exports are growing at a fast clip, with India's trade-to-GDP ratio more than doubling in 2006 from its 1991 level of 15 percent. The manufacturing sector, like the services sector, is becoming a key engine of the economy, and India's world-class information technology sector continues to grow exponentially, employing less than 0.5 percent of India's labor force but producing about 5 percent of the nation's GDP. Corporate dynamism, rarely associated with India in the past, is fast changing the business map of the country, and India, in turn, is rapidly becoming an important factor in the global strategies of the world's leading international firms.

But how long will the boom last? That depends on India's democratic politics, where economic growth has fed pressures for the redistribution of wealth. Mainstream economic theory about markets and human welfare holds that markets will benefit all in the long run. But long-term perspectives do not come naturally to democratic politicians, who must focus on winning elections in the short term. Accordingly, a low-income democracy such as India must nurture the energies of its entrepreneurs while, in the short run, responding to the reservations and resentments of the masses. How well India's politicians walk this tightrope will determine the outcome of the country's economic transformation.

How It All Began

In Keeping with the prevailing theories in development planning after World War II, in the 1950s India opted for a centrally planned economy with a closed trade regime, heavy state intervention, and an industrial policy that emphasized import substitution. This pro-state and trade-pessimistic development model was characterized by three sets of controls: internal, external, and those relating to the special role of the public sector. The internal regulatory regime heavily employed investment and production controls through an infamous industrial licensing system that regulated aspects of economic activity as varied as plant capacity, output prices, the quantity of capital, the quantity and type of inputs, technology, and the sectors or industries that were required to be reserved for small-scale investors. A host of tariff and quantitative controls were created to protect "infant" domestic producers from external competition. And the public sector was allowed extraordinary authority over the commanding heights of the economy, including the steel, power, telecommunications, and heavy machinery industries.

It was within this thicket of protectionist policies that, in July 1991, reformers in the Congress-led government began to push hard for economic transformation under the looming prospect of a balance-of-payments crisis. Some reforms had already been put in place by Prime Minister Rajiv Gandhi in the mid-1980s, but the big thrust came in 1991-92 as a result of that looming crisis. The finance minister at the time, Manmohan Singh (currently India's prime minister), argued that the macroeconomic stabilization necessary to stave off a crisis was not enough; it had to be reinforced by reforms to make the decision-making and operational environment of firms more market-based. Thus began a series of incremental reforms, which the BJP (Bharatiya Janata Party) continued after it came to power at the head of the National Democratic Alliance (NDA) coalition in 1998.

In some areas of economic policy, progress has been dramatic; in others, little or no progress has been made. India's investment regime has undergone the most extensive reform. The industrial licensing system has been almost completely abolished. Firms are free to make decisions about investment, pricing, and technology. Only three industries—rail transport, military aircraft and ships, and atomic energy generation—are now reserved for the public sector (instead of 18 in the past), and these, too, are beginning to welcome collaboration with private industry on some activities. The rules governing foreign investment have been substantially liberalized. Complete foreign private ownership in a large number of industries, and majority private ownership in most industries, is allowed, excluding airlines, insurance companies, and the major retail trade. And since 1992, foreign institutions have been allowed to buy and sell stocks in Indian firms. Indian companies, in turn, are now free to issue equity in foreign markets.

A great deal of progress has also been made in reforming India's trade and exchange-rate regimes. India now has a flexible exchange-rate system. The average tariff on imports has come down from over 100 percent to just under 25 percent today, and all quota restrictions on trade have been lifted.

Progress has been limited, however, in five areas: fiscal policy, privatization, small-scale industry, agriculture, and labor law. India's fiscal deficits continue to be high. Large agricultural subsidies for inputs, grain, and power are some of the main contributors to these deficits, and almost every attempt at lowering the subsidies has been met by political protests on behalf of farmers. A start toward privatization was made in 2001, but unions and some political parties have vigorously resisted it. To help millions of small producers, many manufactured products continue to be reserved for "small-scale investors" (a status that caps investment at $250,000 per industrial unit), although in 2001, garments, toys, shoes, and auto components were finally removed from the reserved list. No proposal for a complete dereservation of all industries has yet been seriously entertained, hampering the ability of many Indian companies to compete with their counterparts in other developing countries, notably China. And labor laws have not been reformed, meaning that no company operating in India employing more than 100 workers can fire any without government permission—and permission is almost never granted.

What's in It for Me?

Who has really reaped the benefits of the reforms? India has always had a small number of affluent individuals, symbolized by its maharajahs and business tycoons. Now the proportion of the population that is rich has undoubtedly increased, and a substantial middle class has emerged, numbering anywhere between 200 million and 250 million, depending on the measure used. In what is fast becoming an emblem of the rising Indian middle class, six million cell phones are bought every month, making India the fastest-growing market for cell phones in the world. Businesses in the cities are booming, five-star hotels are fully booked, airports are clogged, and flights are regularly oversold.

At the same time, the begging bowls and emaciated faces of malnourished children, historically the most visible signs of mass deprivation on the streets of Indian cities, have not appreciably receded. Poverty has clearly decreased since the reforms began, when roughly a third of the country was below the poverty line, but close to a fourth of the population still lives on less than $1 a day, much to the disappointment of many reformers who had expected a faster decline. The nation's growth on the whole has not been employment-intensive.

Where inequality is concerned, two issues are hotly debated: urban-rural imbalances and the interpersonal income distribution. Over the last ten years, India's economy as a whole may have grown at more than 6 percent per annum, but agriculture, which still supports, fully or in part, around 60 percent of the country's population, has grown at a mere 2.2 percent annually. To be sure, growth rates in agriculture are rarely as high as those in manufacturing and services, but the gap in India has become noticeably large. It is now widely accepted throughout India that urban-rural inequalities have grown since the reforms began.

The statistics on interpersonal income distribution are less conclusive, partly because such data tend to be highly unreliable for developing countries. But opinion polls make it quite clear that a very large proportion of the population believes the reforms have mostly benefited "the rich," which in the public's eye includes the middle class in India. The largest-ever sample drawn for election analysis in India, by the National Election Study (NES) in 2004, showed that those who believed the reforms had benefited only the affluent outnumbered those who thought the reforms had benefited the whole nation; the more one climbs down the social ladder, the greater the former belief. Upper-caste respondents were nearly split on the question, but a wide margin of respondents lower on the socioeconomic scale—especially ex-untouchables, Muslims, and other underprivileged groups—believed the reforms had mainly benefited the rich. The survey results also showed that those who believed the reforms had benefited the whole country voted in large numbers for the BJP-led NDA, whereas those who thought the rich were the only beneficiaries voted disproportionately for Congress and its allies.

These perceptions may not necessarily match reality. It is particularly unclear how the masses interpret the term "reforms." The NES polls focused on only one side of the economic reforms by asking questions such as whether the number of employees in government service should be reduced, whether public-sector businesses should be privatized, and whether foreign companies should be allowed to freely enter the Indian economy. But other questions, reflecting a fuller view, were not asked: Should import tariffs be dropped further so as to allow for the greater availability of cheap consumer goods? Should the rules regulating how banks and post offices function be made easier and more transparent? Should big companies continue to be protected by the government, or should new and smaller companies be allowed to emerge and compete with them? Should the government interfere less in regard to where and at what price to sell grain? Should loss-making government firms be privatized if a substantial proportion of their proceeds could be reserved for public health and education? It is unclear how the masses would respond to a complete picture of reforms and, accordingly, whether the underprivileged segments of society would support deeper reforms.

Whatever better statistics may finally prove, mass perceptions matter in politics. And the overall picture that emerges from current perceptions of the reform process is one of two Indias: an India of booming businesses, growing cities, and a vibrant middle class and an India of struggling agriculture, poor villages, and a large lower class. The rising tide produced by economic liberalization appears to have lifted many boats, but not all. Too large a segment of the population feels ignored by the new economic policies. The current Indian government has thus unsurprisingly made two objectives clear regarding the economy: keep growth strong, but make it more inclusive through public policy. Leaving markets entirely to themselves is not politically feasible in a low-income democracy such as India.

The Democratic Constraint

There are two aspects to the challenge reformers face within India's democratic context: perceptions of the reforms to date and the short-term pain likely to accompany the deeper reforms to come. The economic reforms undertaken thus far have not been those that would directly affect the lives of India's poor masses, and this has fed their resentment against the reforms, which they believe have only benefited the upper and middle classes. The employment effect of the reforms—while significant in skill- and capital-intensive sectors—has not been substantial enough throughout the economy to ameliorate this resentment. Further pro-market reforms—the large-scale privatization of public-sector firms, the implementation of a hire-and-fire employment policy, changes in agricultural policy, radical changes in small-industry sectors, and the drastic reduction of fiscal deficits—will undoubtedly have a direct effect on the lives of the masses, but the long-term benefits of these reforms for India's lower classes are likely to be accompanied by considerable short-term pain. The electoral consequence of this likelihood has meant that Indian politicians have proceeded gingerly on these deep reforms, embracing instead those that directly affect the elite.

It is therefore helpful to think of India's reform politics as following two tracks: what may be termed elite politics and mass politics. This distinction is absolutely crucial in understanding India's reform dynamics. In India, the elite consists mainly of English-speaking upper-caste and urban citizens. Elite politics in India typically takes place in the upper realms of the public sphere: in the interactions between business and government and in the dealings between New Delhi and foreign governments and international financial institutions. Outside government, the upper end of the public sphere includes English-language newspapers and television and the Internet. To the elite, India's economic future has never looked brighter.

But India's mass politics is dancing to a different tune. It is the plebeian social orders that make up this political constituency. Streets and the ballot box are the primary sites of the mass politics, and voting, demonstrations, and riots its major manifestations. Economic reforms are viewed by the poor masses as a revolution primarily for everyone but them. Economists may recommend a more passionate embrace of neoliberalism as a solution to India's poverty, but the poor appear to have plenty of reservations about economic reforms—and they have voting clout in India's democracy.

One can therefore see why elite-oriented reforms (making investment in real estate easier, deregulating the stock market, liberalizing civil aviation) have continued under the current government in India, whereas more radical reforms (changing labor laws, privatizing public enterprises, eliminating agricultural subsidies) have stalled. The latter have run into what might be called a mass-politics constraint. As a result, it is now customary to argue that India has a "strong consensus on weak reforms."

Three factors are typically critical in determining whether any particular policy enters the arena of mass politics: the number of people affected by the policy, how organized those people are, and whether the effect is direct and immediate or indirect and over a long time horizon. The more people affected by a policy choice, the more organized they are, and the more direct the policy's effects, the more likely it is that a policy will generate mass concern.

By this logic, some economic issues are more likely to arouse mass opposition than others. Inflation, for example, quickly becomes a contentious matter in mass politics because it affects most segments of the population. A financial meltdown has a similar effect, because a large number of banks and firms collapse and millions of people lose their jobs. In comparison, stock markets directly concern mainly shareholders, whose numbers are not likely to be large or very organized in a poor country such as India. As a result, short of a financial collapse, stock-market issues rarely, if ever, enter the fray of mass politics in less developed countries. Ethnocommunal conflicts, not economic issues, have until now driven mass politics in India. The consequences of ethnic cleavages and ethnically based policies tend to be obvious to most people, and ethnic groups are either already organized or can organize quickly.

Unlike the economic reforms already implemented, the deeper changes that many economists argue India needs for long-term growth are, by directly affecting the masses—and affecting them negatively to begin with—likely to arouse the passions of the lower class. In India's highly adversarial democracy, political leaders will continue to find it extremely difficult to stake their political fortunes on economic reforms that are expected to cause substantial short-term dislocations and are likely to produce rewards only in the long term. Meanwhile, identity politics—especially caste-based affirmative action and Hindu-Muslim relations—continue to occupy the center of the political stage, consuming substantial political attention and determining electoral fortunes. As a result, what is of great consequence to mainstream economists is of secondary importance to politicians, who prefer predictability in and control over their political universe.

The Sources of Congress' Conduct

Nonetheless, economic reform has been growing in importance in India's electoral politics over the last decade. In a survey of mass political attitudes in India conducted in 1996, only 19 percent of the electorate reported any knowledge of the economic reforms that had been implemented, even though the reforms had been in existence since 1991. In the countryside, where more than 70 percent of Indians then lived, only about 14 percent had heard of the reforms (compared with 32 percent of voters in cities). Nearly 66 percent of college graduates were aware of the dramatic changes in economic policy, compared with only 7 percent of the illiterate poor. (In contrast, close to 75 percent of the electorate—urban and rural, literate and illiterate, rich and poor—reported knowing of the demolition of the mosque in Ayodhya in 1992, and 87 percent took a stand on caste-based affirmative action.) Economic reforms were a non-issue in the 1996 and 1998 parliamentary elections. In the 1999

elections, the biggest reformers either lost or did not campaign on pro-market platforms.

The 2004 parliamentary elections that returned Congress to power, however, hinted at the rising importance of economic reforms to India's mass politics. In dramatic contrast to 1996, when a mere 19 percent of voters even knew of the reforms implemented up to that point, in 2004, according to the NES election survey, over 85 percent expressed clear judgments of them—and the main verdict was that the reforms were primarily elite-serving.

To be sure, economic issues were still not the main reason for the NDA'S election defeat in 2004. Its loss had more to do with regional politics and party alliances. Coalition partners in India tend to be regional parties that are strong only in one or two states (India is made up of 28 states), and national parliamentary elections consequently depend heavily on how regional parties in the large states perform. In two significant states, Andhra Pradesh and Tamil Nadu, the regional allies of the BJP did disastrously. The key issues in these and other states were more regional in nature, rather than related to national or economic issues. The way coalition arithmetic translates to parliamentary seats further undermined the NDA. In a first-past-the-post parliamentary system such as India's, parliamentary seats are not allocated in strict proportionality to ballots won. In the 2004 election, although the BJP-led NDA trailed the Congress-centered UPA by a mere 0.6 percent of the overall popular vote, the latter won a 33-seat advantage (222 seats as opposed to 189 for the NDA).

Nevertheless, the 2004 electoral results suggest that the pressure on politicians to make reforms relevant to the masses is rising, even if it has not yet reached a critical threshold. Resentment of reforms may well prove decisive in the next election, due by 2009. The increasing mass disaffection with the economic reforms helps explain the economic policies of the current government. The 2004 election led Congress' strategists to the conclusion that the party needed to focus its program on the lower and middle echelons of society, which have become the party's main constituency. The Indian government today has some of the ace reformers of post-1991 India, including Prime Minister Singh, Finance Minister Palaniappan Chidambaram, and the economic planning czar, Montek Singh Ahluwalia. But two of its biggest initiatives have been distinctly antimarket: the National Rural Employment Guarantee Act and the extension of affirmative action in higher education. The first measure, passed by Parliament in August 2005, guarantees every unemployed rural household that each year at least one of its members will get 100 days of work. (The scheme, currently in operation in 200 districts, is slated to be extended to the entire country over the next two years.) The second reform reserves 27 percent of the spaces in government-aided institutions of higher education, including the Indian Institutes of Technology and the Indian Institutes of Management, for the "other backward castes."

The UPA is dependent on the left for its parliamentary majority, but this is only part of the story that explains these antimarket measures. More germane is the character of the constituency that now forms the main pillar of Congress' support. Until the mid-1980s, Congress was an umbrella party drawing substantial support from all segments of society, but the BJP and its coalition have since come to represent the socially privileged, the educated, and high-income groups. The upper segments of society constitute no more than 25-30 percent of India's population. Given the kind of support they have given the BJP and its allies over the last ten years, getting them back under the Congress umbrella is not as electorally promising as consolidating gains in the much larger middle and lower segments—especially given the latter's higher rates of voter turnout. It is therefore no surprise that targeted anti-market interventions on behalf of the lower social orders form the centerpiece of Congress' new political strategy.

The BJP, although less constrained than Congress, cannot entirely escape these pressures either. If the BJP is to regain and hold on to power, it will have to resolutely move down the socioeconomic ladder for support, something it has already begun doing. Even a BJP-led government would therefore be expected to push a program of targeted state interventions. Unless the upper segments of Indian society regroup and begin to participate in elections more, they will dwindle as a power in electoral politics, in spite of their control of the press. And until the middle class becomes a majority of the population and starts to participate more vigorously in elections, the plebeian pressures will remain in politics and India's economic reforms will continue to have an ostrich-like character: moving ahead on policies directly affecting the elite but lagging behind on policies that directly, and negatively, hit the masses.

A Tortoise to China's Hare?

Although the mass-politics constraint on India's economic reforms is now beginning to emerge, it need not be a reason for alarm. India's democracy is a short-term constraint but a long-term asset for pro-market reformers. The stability of Indian democracy is not in question. Whichever coalition of parties comes to power, reforms on the whole will continue. Since 1991, four coalitions have ruled India, and none has departed from the path of reforms. The differences have been those of degree and pace, not direction. There is no going back to the old statist economic regime. A middle class with rising incomes that boasts 200 million to 250 million people will continue to attract investor attention. The nation's remarkable human capital at the middle-class level will also draw investors. Moreover, there will continue to be economic reforms largely impervious to the constraints of mass politics: changes to the financial sector, greater rationalization of tax structures, further simplification of investment rules, the liberalization of real estate development, and the modernization of airports.

The mass-politics constraint does mean, however, that reformers in India will have to juggle two separate tasks in the short to medium term: continuing reforms in the elite-oriented sectors and responding to mass needs through further antimarket state interventions. And if market-oriented economic reforms are to be embraced in areas directly relevant to the masses, politicians will have to answer the following questions: How will the privatization of public enterprises, the reform of labor laws, and the lifting of agricultural subsidies benefit the masses? And how long will the benefits take to trickle down? All of these reforms are likely to enhance mass welfare in the long run. Therefore, for democratic politicians, this problem will effectively mean taking measures such as reserving a substantial proportion of the proceeds from privatization for public health and primary education, constructing safety nets for workers as labor laws are reformed, and coming up with a plan for a second green revolution in agriculture in return for drawing down the current huge agricultural subsidies. The last one, in particular, will require both opening up agriculture to market forces and greater public investment in irrigation, agricultural research, and rural infrastructure and education.

But although democratic politics makes life challenging for reformers, it could also turn out to be a huge benefit in the long run. Consider the counterexample of China. It is hard to believe that the single-party state in China will not eventually be challenged from within the existing party structure, by the burgeoning middle class, or by rising peasant and labor unrest. The attendant economic consequences of a political transition or upheaval in China are uncertain. In contrast, democratic India has a viable solution to the problem of political transition: the party, or coalition of parties, that wins elections will run the government. Transition rules are now deeply institutionalized in India, and long-term political stability is a virtual certainty.

The long-term benefits of India's democracy are enhanced by its rule of law and advanced capital markets. Firm-level innovation is normally facilitated by copyright laws and the rewards that capital markets bring to innovative firms. The rule of law continues to evade China, and its capital markets are heavily government-dominated. Who knows what will happen to China's economic progress when, faced with competitive pressure from lower-cost producers, it loses its comparative advantage in labor-intensive mass production. India's innovative firms and skilled labor, on the other hand, are already beginning to make a mark on the international scene—a trend that is likely to continue in the coming years.

Rural Resistance

Tamil Nadu: Workers employed under the National Rural Employment Guarantee Scheme in the State protest against reduced minimum wages.

S. Viswanathan

Thousands of unskilled workers employed in works undertaken by the National Rural Employment Guarantee Scheme (NREGS) across Tamil Nadu are agitated over the erosion of a substantial part of their daily wages. Their apprehensions are based on what labour leaders call "bureaucratic attempts" to deprive the workers of the minimum wage of Rs.80 a day, on a par with the minimum wage fixed for agricultural workers in the State concerned, as suggested by the Centre in the National Rural Employment Guarantee Act, 2005. Using an option provided by the Act, the State government has fixed a minimum wage based on the rates fixed by the Public Works Department, but 60 percent above the PWD rate. In order to quantify the work contributed by each worker, the government has introduced some "unrealistic" work norms, labour leaders opine.

In Villupuram, which is one of the six districts chosen for the implementation of the scheme, protest meetings, demonstrations and road blockades were organised at nine worksites within a span of 15 days in August. At Rettanai village in Tindivanam taluk, when the workers gathered at a site on August 16 to start the day's work, local officials told them that they would be paid only Rs.40 and not Rs.70, which they got on August 14 for the same work. The workers were reportedly told that the wage had been fixed by "the higher officials".

When the agitated workers approached the village panchayat president, M. Kalaichelvan, for clarification, he expressed surprise at the wage revision. Apparently, he was kept in the dark about the decision. (Under the Act, the panchayat chief has a pivotal role in the implementation of the NREGS.) When Kalaichelvan, along with the workers, met the local officials to discuss the matter, the police stormed the village and started beating the workers. When the panchayat president asked the police why the workers were being beaten for seeking a clarification, the policemen caned Kalaichelvan. His brother, a law student, was also beaten up. The police used teargas shells to disperse the crowd and resorted to firing, in which a boy was injured. A number of women and elderly men were among those injured in the police action.

Chief Minister M. Karunanidhi ordered an inquiry by the Revenue Divisional Officer into the incident. He also announced a compensation of Rs.50,000 to the injured boy. Leaders of political parties condemned the police action and demanded a judicial inquiry. N. Varadarajan, State secretary of the Communist Party of India (Marxist), said in a statement that at a meeting of the State Employment Guarantee Council on August 8, P. Mohan, CPI(M) Member of Parliament, had referred to certain irregularities in the implementation of the scheme.

The officials assured him, in the presence of Minister for Rural Development and Local Administration M.K. Stalin that wages would not be fixed arbitrarily and that the minimum daily wage of Rs.80 would be ensured in all the districts. Varadarajan said this assurance was flouted when the daily wage of the Rettanai workers was reduced. He said the officials had also increased the workload by assigning to each 10-member group the quantum of work normally executed by a 17-member team.

Denying charges relating to the payment of wages, Stalin told mediapersons in Madurai a couple of days later that the government paid the beneficiaries more than the minimum wage stipulated by the Centre. He said the wages were paid according to the quantum of work done. If the Centre's formula, on the basis of the PWD wages, was adopted, the daily wage would not be more than Rs.50, he pointed out. The workers' agitation and the brutal police response have thus raised questions about the way the NREGS is being implemented by the State governments.

The scheme, described by Prime Minister Manmohan Singh as the "flagship programme" of his government, is funded mostly by the Centre and implemented by the State governments. It guarantees 100 days of employment in a financial year to any rural household whose adult members are willing to do unskilled manual work and make a demand for it through registration and application. The significance of the scheme has to be seen in the backdrop of the acute agrarian crisis, which is considered to be an offshoot of the neoliberal economic policies pursued by successive governments at the Centre since the early 1990s.

According to National Sample Survey indicators for 2003, the number of rural landless people increased to 33 per cent in 2003 from 22 per cent in 1992. Besides, the rural unemployment rate for the male population shot up from 5.6 per cent in 1993-94 to 8 per cent in 2004-05 and for women it rose to

8.7 per cent from 5.6 per cent during the same period. This and the setback suffered by agriculture compelled the government, economists and political parties to find a solution to the crisis.

Gainful Employment

Following pressure from the Left parties and several constituents of the United Progressive Alliance (UPA), a scheme for gainful employment of the rural poor in order to provide at least partial relief to their sufferings was devised. Thus NREGA emerged as the most prioritised item on the UPA government's agenda when it was formed in 2004. The Act was operationalised in February 2006, putting in place the NREGS. In the first phase, the scheme was taken up in 200 districts in the country. The coverage was extended to 330 districts in the following year and to all rural districts in April 2008.

According to a status report for 2007-08 presented to Parliament, 3.37 crore households in 330 districts were provided employment for 141.62 crore person-days of work (which comes to an average of 42 days during the year). In 2006-07, 2.10 crore households were provided jobs for 90 crore person-days (43.06 days a year on an average). This performance of the NREGS, according to studies, is better than that of the earlier rural employment schemes such as the Jawahar Rozgar Yojana, the Employment Assurance Scheme and the Sampoorna Rozgar Yojana.

The cost of the NREGS is shared between the Centre and the States in the ratio of 90:10. The Centre bears the entire cost of wages for unskilled manual workers and 75 per cent of the cost of materials and wages for skilled and semi-skilled workers. The administrative cost is shared by the Centre and the respective State governments.

Features of NREGS

Apart from guaranteeing a minimum of 100 days of work a year, the NREGS has other significant features. The panchayati raj institutions have a prime role in planning and executing the works undertaken and in arranging for a social audit of the scheme' performance.

Another is the provision for payment of unemployment allowance to an eligible applicant if the (State) government fails to provide employment within a specific period. The State government is required to pay this allowance from its own funds.

A third one is that it has the potential to enhance people's livelihoods on a sustainable basis by creating common permanent assets and protecting and improving existing public resources such as tanks, lakes and land. The scheme's scope for developing rural infrastructure is also considered large. It also gives no room for middlemen and lays stress on manual labour to carry out the works. Trade unionists hope the scheme will become a precursor to the right to employment.

The NREGS gained popularity soon and brought about significant improvement in the quality of life of worker-beneficiaries across the country. This is not to say that there were no complaints about its implementation. There were charges of violation of guidelines, flouting of rules and lack of transparency, among other things.

In fact, the report of the Comptroller and Auditor General (Performance Audit of Implementation of NREGA, 2005), submitted in December 2006, a few months after the implementation of the scheme in the first phase, had some negative findings, mostly concerning diversion or misuse of funds. Economists pointed out that the main focus of the report was on the lack of administrative capacity to run the scheme in a decentralised manner as desired and the need to build this capacity quickly and effectively.

It has to be noted that the report made a specific mention of the shortage of administrative and technical staff in the implementation of the scheme during the first phase of implementation, only with a view to making positive efforts to improve the position while expanding the scheme to more districts (*Frontline,* February 15.)

The potential of the scheme to transform the socio-economic relations among the rural communities is huge and this is evident from the unprecedented public response the scheme has evoked.

In Tamil Nadu, the NREGS was launched on February 2, 2006, in Villupuram, Cuddalore, Dindigul, Nagapattinam, Sivaganga and Thiruvannamalai districts. It was extended the following year to Thanjavur, Thiruvarur, Tirunelveli and Karur districts. In April 2008, in the third and final phase, all the rural districts, numbering 20, were brought under it.

The NREGS now covers 12,618 panchayats in the State. Under the scheme, 56,082 works have been undertaken, of which 11,480 have been completed. Nearly 21 lakh applicants have so far been given jobs and they have created 1,179 lakh person-days. Women account for 82 per cent of the beneficiaries, while Dalits and tribal people constitute 63 per cent.

But for the controversy over the wages, the scheme has, by and large, received wide acclaim, thanks to the huge response from the rural poor, particularly women. Even those who complain of irregularities do not question the need for the scheme or its impact on the lives of its beneficiaries.

According to K. Balakrishnan, general secretary of the Tamil Nadu Vivasayigal Sangam, the crux of the problem in respect of wage fixation and the quantification of the work of each individual in such a massive work is the absence of a foolproof mechanism. "Such a mechanism is necessary, particularly because all the beneficiaries of the scheme are unskilled men and women, whose age ranges from 18 to 80," he told *Frontline.*

There should be transparency in work allocation as well as wage distribution. While making any modification in the wage rates or work norms there should be consultations at different levels, he said, and added that this was perhaps not done at Rettanai village. "There can be no solution to the issue relating to wages at the cost of the spirit behind the Act," Balakrishnan averred.

Water to the People

Bureaucrats and engineers from Tamil Nadu, working with villagers in a landmark experiment, are democratising the access to water. The lessons learnt were shared with an international audience at the Pan-Asian Colloquium on water, organised in collaboration with the IIT in Chennai last month.

ARVIND SIVARAMAKRISHNAN

Villagers have included all communities and castes in the Koodams, public money has been used to renovate tanks and dig new ones . . .

The acronyms come thick and fast—TWAD, IAMWARM—as do names like Change Management Group, and many others. But what really stands out is the attitude of the protagonists, their energy, enthusiasm, commitment, and above all success. They are State-government bureaucrats and agricultural and water engineers. Who? Yes that's right, State bureaucrats and engineers. The water situation across the whole world is extremely serious, not least in India, where groundwater depletion by over-extraction has driven water tables so far down that borewells 500 feet deep are commonplace. The commodification of water and the failure of the State to ensure a reliable supply of clean water to all have had the effect of severely reducing access to water for the poor, which in India means hundreds of millions of people. Furthermore, through many a village, a pipe installed by big landowners takes water to be sold for a variety of uses; the villagers collect what they can from leaks in the pipes. As to the remaining groundwater, this is increasingly contaminated by fertilizer and pesticides, by highly toxic and disease-riddled human faeces, and by medicines in human and animal excreta.

The dominant rhetoric of water supply for two decades and more has been that water is a commodity to be extracted and sold in an unregulated market; at best, States have delegated powers to regulatory bodies, which tend only to follow the techno-managerial practice of buying machinery purportedly to supply water to the public, and on the evidence rarely improve the situation at all. For its part, the private sector has been as techno-managerial as public bodies.

In response, the bureaucrats and engineers of Tamil Nadu have transformed their own practices and the water situation in over 500 villages in the State. The officials concerned have gone for improvement in a big way, listening seriously to villagers for the first time in the latter's' lives, discovering painful things about their own failures and departmental narrowness, and transforming the engagement between millions of people and their State. First, the bureaucrats and engineers transformed themselves under inspirational and far-sighted senior leadership. From Chief Engineers to recent recruits, they went and sat on villagers' floors, listening for the first time to an often humbling story of official failure and indifference. They learnt that in hundreds of villages where water scarcity had been unknown, water itself was now almost unknown. They learnt that meeting their own targets for miles of piping laid often meant nothing in the actual delivery of water, and they learnt that this was the very first time any official had simply sought out villagers and asked them what they thought.

Co-operative Effort

The officials took the Indian Constitution seriously. Under the 73rd Amendment, Gram Panchayats are a part of the structure of the Republic of India, and with each Panchayat representing four or so villages, the bureaucrats, the engineers, and the villagers formed a Koodam, a traditional Tamil forum in which all have equal voices, despite their differences in status and position outside. Following the Koodams, where diversity was respected, differences recognised and consensus decisions were reached, the relevant Gram Panchayats assumed the responsibility for good water practice, drawing upon the advice and knowledge of officials as they needed. The engineers provided enormous amounts of advice and organisational support. For several months at a stretch, many engineers gave their own time, working well into the night after their official working hours.

Many innovations resulted as well. Testing kits are now widely used by children in schools so that water quality can be monitored locally and independently. Other officials were consulted too—in one village, a District Forest Officer permitted access to a reserved forest solely so that drinking water could be drawn thence. One Panchayat member has to walk through snake-infested terrain at all hours to turn on the pump, sometimes crossing a chest-deep torrent as well. He has done this every day for the last three years. On a visit, I too drank the water from the well.

The results are striking. Villagers have included all communities and castes in the Koodams, public money has been used to renovate tanks and dig new ones, check dams—an excellent method of recharge—have been installed in drainage ditches, and above all water is being conserved; areas under sugarcane have fallen by 20 per cent in some cases, rice is grown with far less water using the single-shoot or SRI planting system, and water tables have risen. And costs are substantially down too.

Sustainability must of course be part of the strategy, and here the State is essential; it ensures stability, continuity, and a new form of accountability to citizens, as well as a new form of responsiveness and engagement. Above all, when its citizens engage with the State, it provides incontrovertible public legitimacy grounded in fairness and equity.

The results and the lessons must be shared too. Collaborating with IIT Madras, the TN engineers hosted a Pan-Asian Colloquium on Water from September 25 to 27th. Over the preceding two days, delegates from over 20 countries in Asia, and some from the Americas, visited some of the villages which constitute the Tamil Nadu experiment in the democratisation of access to water. The manifest optimism and passion of the new approach infused the Colloquium; delegates shared details, themes, huge ideas, and thoroughly practical plans, all in a spirit of complete openness, equality, and wonderful friendship. Large private bodies were of course invited, but although the CII sent a representative, they made no contribution to the discussion, and FICCI did not respond to the invitation.

Diminishing Role

Criticism of the private sector's failures was severe but by no means exclusive, though the evidence is overwhelming that the privatisation of water is meant to boost private corporations' profits and not deliver water. Indeed that whole project is starting to stall; following determined public resistance, Uruguay has amended its constitution, recognising the fundamental right to water for all living things; Ecuador is currently amending its constitution to recognise water as a right for inanimate things as well! Mighty water corporations have been thrown out; one such even sued the government of Bolivia—and settled for a nominal sum. Philippine public-service unions have devised their own benchmarking systems to include public access, equity, and fairness among their performance indicators.

For those who attended the Colloquium, the next major event is the World Bank-sponsored World Water Forum in Istanbul in March 2009, and one task would be to democratise that Forum as well. Somehow water, the utter essential for all imaginable life, brings out the most resolute commitment from ordinary people, and is catalysing a form of democratic public engagement which both rejects the private corporation and reshapes the contemporary State. That could only have been done by ordinary people; more power to them and to the public servants who work with them.

HIV in India—The Challenges Ahead

Robert Steinbrook, MD

On April 1, 2007, India will launch a new phase of its National AIDS Control Program (NACP). Its goals include reducing the number of new human immunodeficiency virus (HIV) infections—currently, an estimated 98.5 to 99.5% of India's 1.1 billion people remain uninfected—improving treatment, and providing therapy to more people. The 5-year program, known as NACP-III, has a budget of about $2.6 billion, two thirds of which is earmarked for prevention and one sixth for treatment (with the remainder primarily for management), and represents a substantial increase in the attention to and spending on HIV–AIDS. More than 80% of the funds will come from outside India—from the World Bank and other international organizations, governments, and philanthropies. Most of the funding has already been committed.

When I visited India earlier this year, it was evident that the HIV epidemic was only one of the country's many pressing health problems.[1] India must decide whether to commit more of the resources that are fueling its rapid economic growth—and the growth of its private health care industry—to improvements in public health and basic health care.[2] In 2003, public expenditure on health represented only 1.2% of India's gross domestic product.[3] There are 60 physicians per 100,000 population (as compared with 230 in Britain and 256 in the United States). With regard to HIV, challenges include increasing the number of patients receiving treatment, making additional antiretroviral medications available, improving the monitoring of therapy, training physicians and other health care workers, caring for patients with tuberculosis coinfection . . ., and reducing stigma and discrimination.

Although prevention will account for a smaller percentage of the total NACP resources than at present, it will remain the focus of India's AIDS control strategy. The components of the strategy are similar to those in other South Asian countries and include intensive prevention efforts directed at the high-risk groups of commercial sex workers, injection-drug users, and men who have sex with men, as well as "bridge populations" such as truckers and migrant workers.[4] Avahan (Sanskrit for "a call to action"), the India AIDS initiative of the Bill and Melinda Gates Foundation, addresses gaps in India's national response and aims "to prove that prevention can be done at scale," according to Ashok Alexander, the program's director. The components of India's strategy also include expanded HIV counseling and testing and treatment for sexually transmitted diseases, broad communication of information on prevention, promotion of condom use, an increase in the proportion of blood donation that is voluntary (since payment for donation attracts high-risk donors), improved access to safe blood, and expansion of programs for preventing mother-to-child transmission.

Each year, about 28 million children are born in India. Skilled health care personnel attend less than half of all births; infant mortality is about 55 per 1000 live births. In 2004, only an estimated 4% of all pregnant women received HIV counseling and testing, and only about 2% of HIV-positive pregnant women received antiretroviral prophylaxis, usually consisting of a single peripartum dose of nevirapine. Moreover, HIV-positive pregnant women may benefit from antepartum combination antiretroviral treatment for their own health. Under NACP-III, more pregnant women should receive monitoring of their CD4 cell counts, antiretroviral treatment, regimens designed to prevent HIV transmission (including combinations of antiretroviral drugs), and other services.

In scaling up treatment, India's domestic pharmaceutical industry has a critical role. A paradox is that Indian companies have become major suppliers of low-cost generic antiretroviral medications to low- and middle-income countries in Africa and elsewhere at a time when there are still major unmet needs for HIV treatment in India. Cipla, a company based in Mumbai, manufactures the largest range of HIV drugs and has the largest market share. Cipla exports 18 times as much antiretroviral medication as it sells domestically, according to Amar Lulla, its joint managing director. Retail drug prices are higher in India than in Africa, in part because of taxes. Eventually, enhanced patent protection for pharmaceuticals in India, which took effect in January 2005, may lead to higher prices. So far, however, no relevant patents have been issued.

Initially, "government activities were not [proceeding] at the speed at which the virus was spreading," according to Suniti Solomon, director of Y.R.G. CARE, a nongovernmental treatment, research, and education facility in Chennai. In April 2004, India launched its public-sector antiretroviral treatment program at eight centers. As of January 31, 2007, about 56,500 patients were receiving treatment at 103 centers (see graph); about 62% were men, 32% women, and 6% children. Perhaps 10,000 to 20,000 additional patients were receiving treatment in the private and nongovernmental sectors. The goal is to have 250 public centers open within 5 years, providing free antiretroviral treatment to 300,000 adults and 40,000 children. However, there is no way to know whether this response will be sufficient.

Patients with HIV infection in India can receive care in the private sector that is indistinguishable from that provided in leading treatment centers around the world. All the relevant medications and laboratory tests are available. In fact, HIV medications, like other drugs, are sold over the counter. Some doctors and pharmacists, however, provide treatments that make no sense—Solomon says she knows of instances in which a patient was told to take ineffective regimens, such as one zidovudine tablet twice a day for 21 days. The provision of ineffective regimens and the development of drug resistance are major concerns.

The national program provides laboratory tests, such as CD4 cell counts, and medications at no charge to the patient. At present, five first-line antiretroviral medications are provided: the nucleoside analogues lamivudine, stavudine, and zidovudine and the nonnucleoside reverse-transcriptase inhibitors efavirenz and nevirapine. More expensive first-line medications (i.e., tenofovir and emtricitabine) are not provided, nor are second-line medications and more expensive laboratory tests, such as measurement of plasma HIV RNA levels. The immediate priorities are to start patients on first-line regimens, to achieve high rates of compliance through supervised therapy and intensive counseling, to build infrastructure, and to ensure that people are not "dying for lack of access to drugs that are available and affordable," according to Sujatha Rao, the director general of India's National AIDS Control Organization.

It seems inevitable that the national program will have to cover additional first-line treatments, second-line treatments, and measurement of plasma HIV RNA levels and that its protocols will eventually reflect the updated recommendations of the World Health Organization.[5] Yet the costs of such tests and second-line medications—which, at about $2,000 a year, are about 10 times those of some first-line regimens—remain formidable. According to Rao, a policy of covering additional drugs is "a big responsibility. Once the government says it will provide you with these drugs, it is a commitment forever."

The largest AIDS care center in India is the Government Hospital of Thoracic Medicine, Tambaram Sanatorium, Chennai. Established in 1928 as a 12-bed private tuberculosis sanatorium, it now has extensive outpatient and laboratory facilities as well as 32 inpatient wards, with a total of 776 beds; 8 of the wards are devoted to patients with HIV. Between April 2004 and February 2007, more than 5000 patients began antiretroviral therapy at the hospital. "Every other government and private hospital would just throw the patient out as soon as they found they were HIV-positive," says Soumya Swaminathan, deputy director of the Tuberculosis Research Center in Chennai. "At Tambaram, anyone could walk in at any time. They would be taken care of."

In India, as in much of the world, stigma and discrimination present major barriers to controlling AIDS. In 2005, the HIV–AIDS unit of the Mumbai-based Lawyers Collective, which provides free legal aid, drafted comprehensive antidiscrimination legislation. India's parliament has yet to consider the bill. There are other anti-discrimination efforts, such as a campaign to persuade the courts to overturn, or the parliament to rewrite, Section 377 of the Indian Penal Code, which makes homosexuality illegal and punishable by imprisonment.[1]

Within the next several months, a more accurate estimate of the number of HIV-infected people in India should be released. Although the estimate is eagerly awaited, its effect, if any, on India's resolve is a matter of conjecture. Regardless of the number, the new phase of the AIDS control program is just beginning, and the challenges remain immense.

Notes

1. Steinbrook R. HIV in India—a complex epidemic. *N Engl J Med* 2007;356:1089-93.

2. Luce E. In spite of the gods: the strange rise of modern India. New York: Doubleday, 2007.

3. The 2006 human development report. New York: United Nations Development Programme, 2006. (Accessed February 26, 2007, at http://hdr.undp.org/hdr2006/report.cfm.)

4. Moses S, Blanchard JF, Kang H, et al. AIDS in South Asia: understanding and responding to a heterogenous epidemic. Washington, DC: World Bank, 2006.

5. World Health Organization. Antiretroviral therapy for HIV infection in adults and adolescents: towards universal access: recommendations for a public health approach. 2006 Revision. (Accessed February 26, 2007, at http://www.who.int/hiv/pub/guidelines/en/.)

Dr. Robert Steinbrook (rsteinbrook@attglobal.net) is a national correspondent for the *Journal*.

Shock of Assam

The October 30 serial blasts point to the collusion between local and outside terrorist agencies.

Sushanta Talukdar

A new face of home-grown terror unveiled itself on the streets of Guwahati, Kokrajhar, Barpeta Road and Bongaigaon, all in Lower Assam, on October 30 when nine bombs, including three car bombs, exploded, killing 86 people and leaving 826 injured. The youngest of the blast victims was a five-year-old girl who suffered 80 per cent burns. Her father, who had come to pick her up from school, was killed on the spot.

The terror attacks, carried out with arithmetical precision, was perhaps the worst-ever the country has witnessed. Not surprisingly, Prime Minister Manmohan Singh, United Progressive Alliance (UPA) chairperson Sonia Gandhi, Union Home Minister Shivraj Patil, senior Bharatiya Janata Party (BJP) leader L.K. Advani, Communist Party of India (Marxist) leaders Brinda Karat and Basudev Acharya, and Communist Party of India leader D. Raja rushed to the blasts sites.

After the initial shock and panic, the entire State erupted in protest against the terror strikes. For 11 days, people took to the streets under different banners, both political and non-political, to express their anguish. Bandhs were called by the BJP, the Vishwa Hindu Parishad (VHP), the Bajrang Dal and the All Assam Students Union (AASU).

In Ganeshguri locality, close to the State capital, a mob torched ambulances, police vehicles and other public property to vent their anger against the failure of the security apparatus to prevent the blasts and the loss of lives.

Twelve days after the blasts, the State government claimed that the National Democratic Front of Bodoland (NDFB) and the United Liberation Front of Asom (ULFA) were involved in the explosions. An official release stated that the involvement of some active members of the NDFB and ULFA had come to light during the course of investigation by the Special Investigation Team (SIT). The SIT claimed that it had identified the main culprits. The police have so far arrested eight persons in connection with the serial blasts and related cases. The release further stated that the probable involvement of other agencies and organisations was also under investigation. The State government, however, refrained from naming them, leaving room for speculation about the identity of the agencies and organisations involved.

Chief Minister Tarun Gogoi said that it was unclear if the NDFB as an organisation was involved or only some of its cadre were involved. He maintained that the possibility of "outside forces" providing support to carry out the terror attacks could not be ruled out but added that no force from outside would be able to carry out any major strike without the help of local militant groups. Bangladesh, he said, had become the biggest problem in fighting terrorism in Assam and that Myanmar had become a safe haven for insurgent groups.

Advani, who visited the blasts sites, went on record that the terror attacks had confirmed once again that Bangladeshi soil was used for anti-India activities. He exhorted the Union government to exert pressure, preferably diplomatic, on Bangladesh to ensure that its territory was not used as a base for anti-India activities. Without naming the organisation behind the blasts, the senior BJP leader pointed to newspaper reports based on police sources that the blasts were the handiwork of the Harkat-ul-Jehadi Islami (HUJI) based in Bangladesh, the Lashkar-e-Taiba based in Pakistan and ULFA. He said that although ULFA had denied its involvement he would not exonerate the outfit, going by its past history of targeting innocent Hindi-speaking people. He alleged that ULFA, whose leaders had received shelter in Bangladesh, had transformed itself from an insurgent group into a terrorist outfit.

The Asom Gana Parishad (AGP), the main Opposition party in the State, and the BJP demanded the dismissal of the Gogoi government for its failure to protect lives and for being "soft towards Islamic fundamentalists."

Brinda Karat and D. Raja cautioned against the Sangh Parivar's attempts to communalise the terror attacks. They said terrorists had no religion, language, caste or creed and must be punished.

Police Baffled

The precision with which the terrorists triggered nine synchronised blasts in four districts within half an hour has baffled the Assam Police and security agencies alike. Inspector-General of Police (Special Branch) Khagen Sarma said that while the needle of suspicion pointed to jehadi elements, ULFA might have provided the logistic support to them.

Ballistic experts from the Forensic Sciences Department are under the impression that local outfits lacked the expertise to make such highly sophisticated bombs. It was difficult to gather the huge quantity of explosives used (as much as 80 kg of RDX, or Research Department Explosive), as it was not readily available within the State and the country, they opined.

Forensic investigations revealed that about 25-30 kg of RDX was used in each of the car bombs in Guwahati; ammonium nitrate with plasticisers were used as propellants. Such a huge quantity of explosives was never used in the State in the past—the maximum that was used in a single blast was about 10 kg in the Dhemaji blast by ULFA on August 15, 2004, when 13 people, including 10 children, were killed.

Remnants of a Programmable Time Delay Device, which is often used by ULFA to trigger serial blasts, obtained from the Ganeshguri blast site has led investigators to suspect that ULFA could have provided the logistic support.

The NDFB's name cropped up after the SIT arrested a few Bodo youth in connection with the blasts near the court of the Chief Judicial Magistrate (CJM) and at Fancy Bazaar in Guwahati and at Ganeshguri. Police sources said that the arrested youth had either owned the three cars in which the explosives were kept or provided other forms of logistic support.

On November 10, a day before the State government officially announced the complicity of the NDFB and ULFA in the blasts, contingents of the Assam Police and paramilitary forces were rushed to cordon off the designated camps of the NDFB in Baksa, Udalguri and Kokrajhar. The decision to send the troops to confine the NDFB cadre in the camps came after a meeting of the Strategy Group of the three-tier Unified Command Structure headed by the Chief Minister. Gogoi decided to enforce the ceasefire ground rules strictly.

(The NDFB had entered into a ceasefire agreement with the Centre on May 24, 2005. The extended ceasefire is due to expire on December 31, but if the blasts probe establishes the involvement of the NDFB, New Delhi is likely to call off the ceasefire.)

Cadre of the NDFB, however, refused entry to police officials who wanted to carry out a search inside the camp. The police claimed that 12 blast suspects had taken shelter at the camp.

The NDFB denied its involvement in the blasts and described the allegation as "false and baseless." In a statement issued by its "information and publicity secretary" S. Sanjarang, it stated that "all persons who have been arrested from different places so far on allegations of being involved in the blasts are civilians and they are neither members of the NDFB nor had any relationship with the NDFB."

"The NDFB is working for peace of the entire region and is on the peace process with the Government of India at present to solve the long-cherished political problem of the Boro people through a peaceful negotiation. Our cadre are huddled in the designated camps and are complying with the ceasefire ground

rules at their level best," the statement added. The outfit pointed out the NDFB could not be held responsible simply because "vehicles suspected to be used in the blasts belonged to Boro people."

Meanwhile, ULFA has alleged that the Rashtriya Swayamsewak Sangh was behind the blasts. In an earlier statement, Anjan Barthakur of ULFA's central publicity unit said the blasts were the handiwork of the "Indian occupational force."

The police also arrested Naziruddin Ahmed from Moirabari in Morigaon district. The arrest related to an SMS purportedly sent by a little-known outfit, the Islamic Security Force (Indian Mujahideen), to a television news channel claiming responsibility for the blasts. A senior Home Department official, however, said that the SMS could have been a tactic to confuse the investigators.

Nani Gopal Mahanta, Coordinator, Peace and Conflict Studies, Gauhati University, says that the government has failed on four fronts—anticipation, political strategy, policing, and response to terrorism. Terrorism or insurgency has become part of Assam's polity ever since the emergence of ULFA in 1979.

The Most Bombed Places

The areas where the serial bomb blasts took place in Guwahati are perhaps the most bombed places in South Asia. Nineteen bomb blasts have taken place in Ganeshguri in the past 12 years. The blasts in Tripura and Manipur which occurred a few days before the Assam blasts should have alerted the Gogoi government, he remarked.

In the past 13 years, 788 blasts have rocked the State, while security forces have seized about 5,600 live bombs.

"There is no political strategy to tackle terrorism although it has engulfed the State for more than 29 years. The strategies adopted by the government to tackle terrorism have been rag-tag, piecemeal, divide-and-rule," Mahanta said. He pointed out that the State, which had a population of three crore, had fewer than 60,000 police personnel (the majority of whom are assigned to government offices and VIP security).

This was perhaps one of the lowest police-people ratio in the world, he noted, and said that an insurgency-prone State like Assam should have better disaster management strategies. In this connection, he mentioned the late arrival of ambulances at the blasts sites.

Faced with the accusation of intelligence failure, the Unified Command—the three-tier command structure of the Army, the Assam Police and Central paramilitary forces for counter-insurgency operations—has decided to set up a joint control room at the Assam Police headquarters to ensure quick sharing of hard intelligence. The State Cabinet has decided to set up a research and analysis wing within the Special Branch of the Assam Police for sustained research on the activities of terrorist groups so that primary intelligence can be converted into actionable intelligence.

From *Frontline*, Vol. 25, #24, December 5, 2008. Copyright © 2008 by The Hindu, Kasturi & Sons Ltd. Reprinted by permission.

Why Dr Binayak Sen Must Be Released

APOORVANAND

Dr Binayak Sen seems to have caught the imagination of the mainstream media in India at last. But one has to remember that he has spent a year in a Chhattisgarh jail. An international award by the Global Heath Council named after Jonathan Mann to Dr Sen for his untiring work in the field of people's health and human rights followed by a strong appeal by 22 Nobel Laureates demanding his release seems to have convinced the media that there is something extraordinary about Dr Sen's arrest and that the issue needs to be probed.

Dr Sen, a paediatrician by training, was arrested on May 14 last year by the Chhattisgarh police under the dreaded Chhattisgarh Special Public Security Act and Unlawful Activities Prevention Act, which are in many ways more draconian than the now repealed Prevention of Terrorist Activities Act.

The police claimed it had evidence to prove that Dr Sen was actively helping out Maoists by providing them logistic support. The only piece of evidence they have been able to show till date is the fact that he made 33 visits to Narayan Sanyal, an old, ailing Maoist leader in jail. They were perfectly legal visits and allowed under the jail manual, not something clandestine. Sanyal was suffering from many diseases and required regular medical support.

As a civil right activist and doctor it was not unusual for Dr Sen to come into contact with extremist Maoists, especially since he was in Chhattisgarh, which is reeling under the bloody conflict between the state and the Maoists.

His plea for bail in the Supreme Court was rejected, which did not find it necessary to verify the claims by the state counsel. It agreed with the state that a free Binayak was a threat to the national security in Chhattisgarh.

The state is a dangerous place for civil right activists. It is the most recent destination for rich capitalists eyeing its mineral rich land and want it to be made available. How do you do it unless the tribals are driven out of their lands?

This is a state where governance is traditionally and criminally tilted in favour of moneylenders and the land and forest mafia. And welfare schemes aimed at the poor, especially the tribals, do not trickle down.

In such a scenario there is bound to be an emergence of a movement for justice. It does not necessarily have to be non-violent as the exploitation of the poor, who have been forced to be part of the developmental state, is extremely violent. National prosperity stands in striking contrast to the increasing impoverishment of the tribals.

Chhattisgarh was fertile land for the Maoist movement as the state failed shamefully to make the mechanism of justice work for the poor. Its loyalty to rich, national and multinational companies creates a compelling urge to eliminate anyone coming in the way. A report by an expert group set by the Planning Commission to look at the developmental challenge in extremist affected areas, says, 'there is, however, failure of governance, which has multiple dimensions and is not confined to the inefficiency of the delivery systems only. It is not fortuitous that overwhelmingly large sections of bureaucracy/technocracy constituting the delivery systems come from the landowning dominant castes or middle classes, with their attachment to ownership of property, cultural superiority and a state of mind which rationalises and asserts their existing position of dominance in relation to others. This influences their attitudes, behaviour and performance.'

'Internal displacement caused by irrigation/mining/industrial projects, resulting in landlessness and hunger, is a major cause of distress among the poor, especially the Adivasis. It is well known that 40 per cent of all the people displaced by dams in the last 60 years are forest-dwelling Adivasis? The law and administration provides no succour to displaced people and often treats them with hostility since the displaced people tend to settle down again in some forest region, which is prohibited by law. The Naxalite movement has come to the aid of such victims of enforced migration in the teeth of the law.'

The report further states that the Adivasis displaced from Orissa and Chhattisgarh, settling in the forests of Andhra Pradesh would have been easily evicted by officials but for the presence of the Naxalite movement.

Suffering from continuing land loss and displacement, dwindling livelihood resources, acute malnutrition and pitched against a formidable combine of profit-hungry companies and a callous administration, Adivasis found some solace from the Maoists. The Maoists therefore are not the cause but a result of the miseries of the Adivasis.

Instead of addressing these issues, the state took recourse to a militarist shortcut by helping in creation of an armed campaign called Salwa Judum which vowed to eliminate the Maoists. It employed Adivasis in its ranks, most of the times forcibly. It is not a coincidence that Salwa Judum started days after the signing of contracts between the state and some companies.

Salwa Judum is a law unto itself. Though it is claimed to be a peaceful people's movement in reality it is a State-sponsored peoples' militia which marches into villages, forces people to join or burns their houses, destroys their cattle, livelihood and drives them out. More than 640 villages have been evacuated in this drive. Lakhs of Adivasis have been forcibly removed from their habitations and some 40,000 of them live in Salwa Judum camps set up by the government, living in hellish conditions as another state-sponsored Administrative Reform Committee report found out. The committee was lead by senior Congress leader Veerappa Moily.

The Supreme Court was forced to express its displeasure of Salwa Judum by observing that the government cannot arm people and instigate them to kill others. Defending Salwa Judum was not a state lawyer but counsel for the central government who made an astonishing admission that the state police were unequal to the might of the Maoists. They were employing as special police officers only those who have been at some point, in some way been victimised by the Maoists, he pleaded. It was extraordinary for a state to openly defend an army of revenge.

Dr Sen's consistent opposition to Salwa Judum is the real cause of the state's ire. It was all good and rosy till he confined himself to providing health services to the poor. In fact, the government had invited him to advise on its health programmes. Binayak Sen was a gold medallist from the prestigious Christian Medical College, Vellore, Tamil Nadu. He decided to leave his teaching job at Jawaharlal University in New Delhi to move to Chhattisgarh in 1978 to work with the legendary trade union leader Shankar Guha Niyogi, who built up the formidable Chhattisgarh Mukti Morcha. Niyogi was later killed by the industry mafia. Dr Sen moved around in villages, establishing clinics and providing healthcare to those who were damned by State-run systems.

But as Dr P Zachariah, his teacher at CMC, says, "His interest in civil activism grew out of witnessing malnutrition deaths among children. The lack of governance worried him deeply. Chhattisgarh is a complicated state with a complicated history. The government did not meet the people's needs and it was easy for Naxalites to exploit that. The government found it difficult to deal with militants who operated out of dense forests and took a very repressive stance. In the end, it led to the creation of Salwa Judum."

"The police machinery too was getting large funds to fight the Naxalites. In the dark days that followed, people began to disappear. As a member of the People's Union for Civil Liberties, Binayak couldn't help but get involved. The PUCL was constantly approached by villagers saying that their relatives had disappeared. The police had to be approached, FIRs had to be filed, and Binayak began to help," Dr Zacharaiah said.

Areas of disagreement between Dr Sen and the state government were bound to emerge. He could not have approved of measures like Salwa Judum. His work as the general secretary of the state's PUCL became a pain for the government. He was also staunchly anti-communal and critical of the activities of the Vishwa Hindu Parishad in Adivasi-dominated areas. Otherwise a quiet man, this English-speaking doctor was increasingly becoming a cause of worry for the state government. He was, like other law-abiding activists, a critic of unlawful encounters by the police and thus an impediment to national and multinational companies. He needed to be silenced and removed from the scene.

This was done by the state symmetrically, with an active help from the local media. In April and May last year, the Chhattisgarh police stared a vilification campaign against him when he was away in Kolkata to see his ailing mother. He was declared an absconding Naxalite doctor who had fled to evade arrest. Dr Sen's brother circulated an open letter telling the world that he was not absconding, had gone to visit his mother and the police was in fact indulging in this vilification only to justify his arrest. His fears came true. Dr Sen returned to the state capital Raipur and was immediately arrested under the Chhattisgarh Special Public Security Act and the Unlawful Activities Prevention Act.

These laws do not need actual acts of conspiracy to make you criminal, even a perception that you may, even in future entertain thoughts which would be potentially against the state interest is sufficient reason for arrest.

Appeals by several civil right activists and individuals demanding the repeal of such absurd laws and the release of Dr Sen have been treated with disdain by the Chhattisgarh and central governments.

There is a strong belief in the establishment that all civil right activists are nothing but a respectable cover for extremists of all kinds, including the Maoists. They very conveniently ignore the criticism of Maoist violence by these individuals. What is disturbing is that if this liberal middle space is gone, there would not be a counter voice to violence.

It is only appropriate that the Global Health Council chose Dr Sen for its Jonathan Mann award. His international colleagues cutting across disciplines have asked the state and central governments to create situation for him to be able to receive this award in person which would be given in a public ceremony in the US on May 29. Given the arrogant insensitivity of our state institutions, it is unlikely that the appeals would be heard.

Can we expect our judiciary to help redeem the promise the Constitution makes to the people to safeguard their right to hold opinions and express it even if goes against the official line the state would like all of us to follow?

APOORVANAND is a literary critic and a Reader in Hindi at Delhi University.

Mapping the Indian Mujahideen

India's most feared terrorist group isn't so much an organisation as a movement: a loose coalition of jihadists bound together by ideological affiliation and personal ties.

PRAVEEN SWAMI

Eight days before he was shot dead, top Indian Mujahideen (IM) operative Atif Amin helped to draft the manifesto that the terror group was to issue after the Delhi serial bombings. He insisted on the inclusion of a reference to his heroes.

"We have carried out this attack," read the e-mail sent to newsrooms after the September 13 bombings, "in the memory of two of the most eminent mujahids of India: Sayyid Ahmad, *shaheed,* and Shah Ismail, *shaheed,* (may Allah bestow His Mercy upon them) who had raised the glorious banner of jihad against the disbelievers."

Ahmad and Ismail were killed at Balakote in May 1831, while waging an unsuccessful jihad against Maharaja Ranjit Singh's empire. The two men had set out with 600 followers from Rae Bareilly five years earlier to defend Islam at a time when the Mughal power had, for all practical purposes, given way to British rule.

Like his heroes, Amin found the martyrdom he worshipped: his death was the latest success in a string of nationwide intelligence-led operations targeting the IM. But the arrests of a bewildering succession of its operatives—each proclaimed by police to be "leader", "top commander" and "mastermind"— have done little to further the understanding of just what the group is about or the threat it still poses.

Mapping the IM isn't easy: it is more a social network than structured organisation; a label used by a loose coalition of jihadists bound together by ideological affiliation and personal linkages. In this, it is not unlike the al-Qaeda, whose operatives are drawn from the multiple transnational terror groups allied under the banner of the International Islamic Front for Jihad against Jews and Crusaders.

Who, then, makes up the IM and how do its networks function? India's intelligence services now believe Amin had the overall control of the IM's operations unit: a group of at least two dozen Uttar Pradesh residents, most from the district of Azamgarh. Under Amin's command, the cell's operatives were dispatched nationwide to assemble and plant the explosive

devices used in the bombings which began with attacks on three trial court buildings in the State in November 2007.

Amin and several other core members of the group are thought to have trained with the Harkat ul-Jihad-e-Islami in Bangladesh. In time, they passed on their skills to fresh recruits from Azamgarh, raised by local cleric Abul Bashar Qasmi and Lucknow-based Islamist activist and businessman Shahbaz Husain.

Gangster Riyaz Batkal—a lieutenant of mafioso-turned-jihadist Aftab Ansari—ran a second group which provided funds and logistics support to the IM. Batkal's associate Afzal Usmani, for example, arranged for the theft of the vehicles used as car bombs in Ahmedabad. More important, Batkal's group provided an interface among jihadists in India, the Harkat in Bangladesh, and the Pakistan-based Lashkar-e-Taiba and Jaish-e-Mohammad. Investigators in Maharashtra believe that Batkal's cell provided infrastructure for several past terror operations, including the 2006 serial bombings in Mumbai.

Ansari himself is thought to have been radicalised by the top JeM operative Syed Omar Sheikh—released in the December 1999 Indian Airlines IC-814 hostages-for-terrorists swap in Kandahar and now on death row in Pakistan—when both were in prison together. Ansari then helped to create an organisation of Indian jihadists named after Asif Raza Khan, a gangster killed in a 2001 encounter with the Gujarat police. Among other operations, the Asif Raza Commando Force executed a 2001 terror attack in Kolkata.

Scattered across India

The elements of other IM infrastructure and its top leadership are scattered across India. Qayamuddin Kapadia, leader of the Gujarat-based Students Islamic Movement of India, drew on the banned group's membership for the local guidance and support that Amin and Batkal needed. Bomb components were manufactured at a still unidentified facility near Mangalore. And

Mumbai-based Abdul Subhan Qureshi travelled across India, knitting these multiple terror threads into a single, lethal weave.

Most of those arrested so far are children of the prosperous, but socially conservative, urban middle class. On his Orkut website, Amin identified his camcorder and laptop computer as his most valuable possessions. He also recorded that a copy of the Koran could be found in his bedroom and that he hated music and dating.

Almost all of the Azamgarh cell members studied together in an English-medium school; several went to New Delhi for higher studies in business administration, computers and the media. Parts of the IM manifesto issued after the Delhi bombings, interestingly, were plagiarised from an article by researcher K.K. Shahina for the media critique website, Hoot. The Azamgarh jihadists appear to have been drawn to the IM angered by the horror of the 2002 communal pogrom in Gujarat.

For other IM members, those riots were a lived reality. Among them was Vadodara resident Imran Sheikh, in whose home the bombs used to target Surat are alleged to have been assembled. His mother, Hameeda Bano, was seriously injured in the pogrom. Sheikh's father, Ibrahim Sheikh, had already been made invalid by a chronic cardiac condition, and the loss of Hameeda Bano's income forced him to drop out of school. He began to make a meagre living selling saris in Vadodara's Panigate area.

It was around this time, investigators say, that Kapadia recruited Sheikh. First, he persuaded the sari salesman to abandon the traditionalist religious practices of his parents and join the Jamaat Ahl-e-Hadith, a neo-conservative sect founded by the followers of the Balakote martyrs. Later, in 2005, Kapadia introduced Sheikh to SIMI—and key IM figures like Abdul Subhan Qureshi.

By the time Sheikh was recruited, the IM had begun its war against India—but without the name by which we now know it. In September 2002, just weeks after the Gujarat pogrom, at least 14 young men from Hyderabad set out on secret journeys to terror training camps in Pakistan. Gujarat-based mafioso Rasool Khan Pathan arranged for some to train with the Lashkar, while others were routed to the JeM and the Harkat: a fluid dispersion of assets across organisational lines never seen before the 2002 pogrom.

Within weeks of their return, the new recruits executed their first successful strikes. Asad Yazdani commanded the assassination of the Gujarat pogrom-complicit, the former Home Minister Haren Pandya. Later, Yazdani organised the June 2005 bombing of the Delhi-Patna Shramjeevi Express, the first post-Gujarat terror bombing of real consequence. Yazdani was shot dead by the police in March 2006, just hours after the bombing of the Sankat Mochan temple in Varanasi—an operation the IM claimed as its own in a manifesto released after the November 2007 bombings in Uttar Pradesh.

Yazdani's killing did little, though, to dent the offensive aspirations of the terror networks which now call themselves the IM.

Late in May 2005, the Maharashtra police recovered over 24 kg of Research Department Explosive packed in computer cases which had been shipped across the Indian Ocean to the town of Aurangabad. Investigators later discovered that the explosive was intended for a massive terror campaign targeting Gujarat. Long-time SIMI activist Zabiuddin Ansari, who handled the operation, escaped to Pakistan.

Several similar terror attacks were attempted. In May 2006, the Delhi police shot dead Pakistani Lashkar operative Mohammad Iqbal, the author of another attempted bombing in Gujarat. Feroze Ghaswala, a Mumbai automobile mechanic who joined the jihad after witnessing the 2002 pogrom, and Abdul Chhippa, a computer engineer, were held for their role in the plot. Soon after, India's post-Gujarat jihadists finally succeeded in delivering the vengeance they had long sought: the Mumbai serial bombings of 2006.

Since the Mumbai serial bombings, though, pressure has been mounted on Pakistan to terminate the jihad against India. Indian jihadists based in Pakistan were told they could no longer have the direct operational support of the Harkat or the Lashkar. Explosives like RDX, which could be traced back to Pakistan-based groups, were no longer to be used.

Altered Jihadist Strategies

Last year, evidence of altered jihadist strategies began to emerge. The police learned from a one-time Andhra Pradesh resident Raziuddin Nasir, who was arrested while planning attacks targeting tourists in Goa, that Rasool Khan 'Party' had ordered an escalation of jihadist operations in India. Funds had been collected from Indian supporters of jihad based in West Asia. Later, the interrogation of top SIMI leaders threw up revelations that dozens of men had been recruited to the IM at camps held in Kerala, Karnataka, Gujarat, Maharashtra and Madhya Pradesh through 2007 and early 2008.

No one is certain just who first thought of the name Indian Mujahideen, and under what circumstances. Most of the men who could provide an answer—among them Qureshi and Kapadia—are missing; Amin, of course, is dead.

Where might things go from here? India's police and intelligence services will be focussing on the immediate task: locating and neutralising the IM's surviving leadership before the next big bombing.

But politicians in New Delhi could learn lessons from Sayyid Ahmad's failed jihad. The Balakote jihad was defeated, in part, because of the superior military resources and intelligence assets of Ranjit Singh's armies—and also, historian Ayesha Jalal reminds us, because of the resistance of the Pashtun tribes to Sayyid Ahmad's coercive, shariah-based order. India's politicians must reach out to the young people drawn to the jihad if it is to be defeated, and restore faith in the idea that democracy can indeed deliver justice.

Saving Afghanistan

With the Taliban resurgent, reconstruction faltering, and opium poppy cultivation at an all-time high, Afghanistan is at risk of collapsing into chaos. If Washington wants to save the international effort there, it must increase its commitment to the area and rethink its strategy—especially its approach to Pakistan, which continues to give sanctuary to insurgents on its tribal frontier.

BARNETT R. RUBIN

Taliban Resurgent

Afghanistan has stepped back from a tipping point. At the cost of taking and inflicting more casualties than in any year since the start of Operation Enduring Freedom in 2001 (and four times as many as in 2005), NATO troops turned back a frontal offensive by the Taliban last summer. The insurgents aimed to capture a district west of Kandahar, hoping to take that key city and precipitate a crisis in Kabul, the capital. Despite this setback, however, the Taliban-led insurgency is still active on both sides of the Afghan-Pakistani border, and the frontier region has once again become a refuge for what President George W. Bush once called the main threat to the United States—"terrorist groups of global reach." Insurgents in both Afghanistan and Pakistan have imported suicide bombing, improvised explosive technology, and global communications strategies from Iraq; in the south, attacks have closed 35 percent of the schools. Even with opium production at record levels, slowing economic growth is failing to satisfy the population's most basic needs, and many community leaders accuse the government itself of being the main source of abuse and insecurity. Unless the shaky Afghan government receives both the resources and the leadership required to deliver tangible benefits in areas cleared of insurgents, the international presence in Afghanistan will come to resemble a foreign occupation—an occupation that Afghans will ultimately reject.

For decades—not only since 2001—U.S. policymakers have underestimated the stakes in Afghanistan. They continue to do so today. A mere course correction will not be enough to prevent the country from sliding into chaos. Washington and its international partners must rethink their strategy and significantly increase both the resources they devote to Afghanistan and the effectiveness of those resources' use. Only dramatic action can reverse the perception, common among both Afghans and their neighbors, that Afghanistan is not a high priority for the United States—and that the Taliban are winning as a result.

Washington's appeasement of Pakistan, diversion of resources to Iraq, and perpetual underinvestment in Afghanistan—which gets less aid per capita than any other state with a recent post-conflict rebuilding effort—have fueled that suspicion.

Contrary to the claims of the Bush administration, whose attention after the September 11 attacks quickly wandered off to Iraq and grand visions of transforming the Middle East, the main center of terrorism "of global reach" is in Pakistan. Al Qaeda has succeeded in reestablishing its base by skillfully exploiting the weakness of the state in the Pashtun tribal belt, along the Afghan-Pakistani frontier. In the words of one Western military commander in Afghanistan, "Until we transform the tribal belt, the U.S. is at risk."

Far from achieving that objective in the 2001 Afghan war, the U.S.-led coalition merely pushed the core leadership of al Qaeda and the Taliban out of Afghanistan and into Pakistan, with no strategy for consolidating this apparent tactical advance. The Bush administration failed to provide those Taliban fighters who did not want to defend al Qaeda with a way to return to Afghanistan peacefully, and its policy of illegal detention at Guantánamo Bay and Bagram Air Base, in Afghanistan, made refuge in Pakistan, often with al Qaeda, a more attractive option.

The Taliban, meanwhile, have drawn on fugitives from Afghanistan, newly minted recruits from undisrupted training camps and militant madrasahs, and tribesmen alienated by civilian casualties and government and coalition abuse to reconstitute their command structure, recruitment and funding networks, and logistical bases in Pakistan. On September 19, 2001, Pakistani President Pervez Musharraf told his nation that he had to cooperate with Washington in order to "save Afghanistan and Taliban from being harmed"; accordingly, he has been all too happy to follow the Bush administration's instructions to focus on al Qaeda's top leadership while ignoring the Taliban. Intelligence collected during Western military offensives in mid-2006 confirmed that Pakistan's Inter-Services Intelligence (ISI) was continuing to actively support the Taliban leadership, which is now working out of Quetta, the capital of Baluchistan Province, in western Pakistan. As a result, a cross-border insurgency has effectively exploited Afghanistan's impoverished society and feeble government.

In May of 2006, Amrullah Saleh, the director of Afghanistan's national intelligence agency, completed an assessment of the threat posed by the insurgency. Saleh, who acted as the Northern Alliance's liaison with the CIA during Operation Enduring Freedom, concluded that political progress in Afghanistan had not been matched by an effective strategy of consolidation. "The pyramid of Afghanistan government's legitimacy," he wrote, "should not be brought down due to our inefficiency in knowing the enemy, knowing ourselves and applying resources effectively." U.S. commanders and intelligence officials circulated Saleh's warning to their field commanders and agents in Afghanistan and their superiors in Washington. Sustaining the achievements of the past five years depends on how well they heed that warning.

"Still Ours to Lose"

In the past year, a number of events have raised the stakes in Afghanistan and highlighted the threat to the international effort there. The future of NATO depends on its success in this first deployment outside of Europe. Although it suffered a setback in the south, the Pakistan-based, Taliban-led insurgency has become ever more daring and deadly in the southern and eastern parts of the country, while extending its presence all the way to the outskirts of Kabul. NATO deployed to areas neglected by the coalition, most notably to the southern province of Helmand—and the Taliban responded with increased strength and maneuverability. On September 8, a particularly bold attack on a coalition convoy in the city killed 16 people, including two U.S. soldiers, near the U.S. embassy—the most heavily fortified section of Kabul. Even as NATO has deployed its forces across the country—particularly in the province of Helmand, a Taliban stronghold that produces some 40 percent of the world's opium—the Taliban have shown increasing power and agility.

Meanwhile, the effectiveness of the Taliban's limited institutions and the ruthlessness of their retribution against "collaborators" neutralized much of the Afghan population; only the successful political consolidation of NATO and coalition military victories can start to build confidence that it is safe to support the government. In some areas, there is now a parallel Taliban state, and locals are increasingly turning to Taliban-run courts, which are seen as more effective and fair than the corrupt official system. Suicide bombings, unknown in Afghanistan before their successful use by insurgents in Iraq, have recently sown terror in Kabul and other areas. They have also spread to Pakistan.

On the four trips I made to Afghanistan in 2006 (in January, March-April, July-August, and November), the growing frustration was palpable. In July, one Western diplomat who had been in Afghanistan for three years opened our meeting with an outburst. "I have never been so depressed," he said. "The

insurgency is triumphant." An elder from Kunar Province, in eastern Afghanistan, said that government efforts against the insurgency were weak because "the people don't trust any of the people in government offices." An elder from the northern province of Baghlan echoed that sentiment: "The people have no hope for this government now." A UN official added, "So many people have left the country recently that the government has run out of passports."

"The conditions in Afghanistan are ripe for fundamentalism," a former minister who is now a prominent member of parliament told me. "Our situation was not resolved before Iraq started. Iraq has not been resolved, and now there is fighting in Palestine and Lebanon. Then maybe Iran. . . . We pay the price for all of it." An elder who sheltered President Hamid Karzai when Karzai was working underground against the Taliban described to me how he was arrested by U.S. soldiers: they placed a hood on his head, whisked him away, and then released him with no explanation. "What we have realized," he concluded, "is that the foreigners are not really helping us. We think that the foreigners do not want Afghanistan to be rebuilt."

Yet no one I spoke to advocated giving up. One of the same elders who expressed frustration with the corruption of the government and its distance from the people also said, "We have been with the Taliban and have seen their cruelty. People don't want them back." A fruit trader from Kandahar complained: "The Taliban beat us and ask for food, and then the government beats us for helping the Taliban." But he and his colleagues still called Karzai the country's best leader in 30 years—a modest endorsement, given the competition, but significant nonetheless. "My working assumption," said one Western military leader, "is that the international community needs to double its resources. We can't do it on the margins. We have no hedge against domestic and regional counterforces." After all, he noted, the battle for Afghanistan "is still ours to lose."

The 30-Year War

The recent upsurge in violence is only the latest chapter in Afghanistan's 30-year war. That war started as a Cold War ideological battle, morphed into a regional clash of ethnic factionalism, and then became the center of the broader conflict between the West and a transnational Islamist terrorist network.

It is no surprise that a terrorist network found a base in Afghanistan: just as Lenin might have predicted, it picked the weakest link in the modern state system's rusty chain. Today's Afghanistan formed as a buffer state within the sphere of influence of British India. Because the government, then as now, was unable to extract enough revenue from this barren territory to rule it, its function had more to do with enabling an elite subsidized by aid to control the territory as part of the defense of foreign empires than with providing security and governance to the people of Afghanistan. Hence, the oft-noted paradox of modern Afghanistan: a country that needs decentralized governance to provide services to its scattered and ethnically diverse population has one of the world's most centralized governments. That paradox has left the basic needs of Afghanistan's citizens largely unfulfilled—and thus left them vulnerable to the foreign forces that have long brought their own struggles to the Afghan battleground.

In the eighteenth century, as neighboring empires collapsed, Afghan tribal leaders seized opportunities to build states by conquering richer areas in the region. In 1715, Mirwais Khan Hotak (of the same Kandahari Pashtun tribe as the Taliban leader Mullah Muhammad Omar), overthrew the Shiite governor of Kandahar, then a province of the Iranian Safavid empire; seven years later, his son sacked Isfahan, the Iranian capital at the time. Subsequently, a Turkmen leader, Nader Shah, captured Isfahan and went on to conquer Kabul and Delhi. When Nader Shah was assassinated in 1747, the commander of his bodyguard, Ahmad Khan Abdali (a member of the same Kandahari Pashtun tribe as President Karzai), retreated back to Kandahar, where, according to official histories, he was made king of the Afghans at a tribal jirga. He led the tribes who constituted his army on raids and in the conquest of Kashmir and Punjab.

The expansion of the British and Russian empires cut off the opportunity for conquest and external predation—undermining the fiscal base of the ruler's power and throwing Afghanistan into turmoil for much of the nineteenth century. As the British Empire expanded northwest from the Indian subcontinent toward Central Asia, it first tried to conquer Afghanistan and then, after two Anglo-Afghan wars, settled for making it a buffer against the Russian empire to the north.

The British established a three-tiered border to separate their empire from Russia through a series of treaties with Kabul and Moscow. The first frontier separated the areas of the Indian subcontinent under direct British administration from those areas under Pashtun tribal control (today this line divides those areas administered by the Pakistani state from the Federally Administered Tribal Agencies). The second frontier, the Durand Line, divided the Pashtun tribal areas from the territories under the administration of the emir of Afghanistan (Pakistan and the rest of the international community consider this line to be the international border between Afghanistan and Pakistan, although Afghanistan has never accepted it). The outer frontier, the borders of Afghanistan with Russia, Iran, and China, demarcated the British sphere of influence; the British enabled the emir to subdue and control Afghanistan with subsidies of money and weapons.

In the twentieth century, however, the dissolution of these empires eroded this security arrangement. The Third Anglo-Afghan War, in 1919, concluded with the recognition of Afghanistan's full sovereignty. The country's first sovereign, King Amanullah, tried to build a strong nationalist state. His use of scarce resources for development rather than an army left him vulnerable to revolt, and his effort collapsed after a decade. The British helped another contender, Nader Shah, consolidate a weaker form of rule. Then, in the late 1940s, came the independence and partition of India, which even more dramatically altered the strategic stakes in the region.

Immediately tensions flared between Afghanistan and Pakistan. Afghanistan claimed that Pakistan was a new state, not a successor to British India, and that all past border treaties had lapsed. A loya jirga in Kabul denied that the Durand Line was an international border and called for self-determination of the tribal territories as Pashtunistan. Skirmishes across the Durand Line began with the covert support of both governments. At the same time, Islamabad was aligning itself with the United States in order to balance India—which led Afghanistan, in turn, to rely on aid from Moscow to train and supply its army. Pakistan, as a result, came to regard Afghanistan as part of a New Delhi-Kabul-Moscow axis that fundamentally challenged its security. With U.S. assistance, Pakistan developed a capacity for covert asymmetric jihadi warfare, which it eventually used in both Afghanistan and Kashmir.

For the first decades of the Cold War, Afghanistan pursued a policy of nonalignment. The two superpowers developed informal rules of coexistence, each supporting different institutions and parts of the country; one Afghan leader famously claimed to light his American cigarettes with Soviet matches. But this arrangement ultimately proved hazardous to Afghanistan's health. An April 1978 coup by communist military officers brought to power a radical faction whose harsh policies provoked an insurgency. In December 1979, the Soviet Union sent in its military to bring an alternative communist faction to power, turning an insurgency into a jihad against the invaders. The United States, Pakistan, Saudi Arabia, and others began spending billions of dollars to back the anticommunist Afghan mujahideen and their Arab auxiliaries—laying the foundations for an infrastructure of regional and global jihad.

The civil war seemed to come to an end with the 1988 Geneva accords, which provided for the withdrawal of Soviet troops (while allowing continued Soviet aid to the communist government in Kabul) and the end of foreign military assistance to the mujahideen. But the United States and Pakistan, intent on wiping out Soviet influence in Afghanistan entirely, ignored the stipulation that they stop arming the resistance. The result was a continuation of the conflict and, eventually, state failure.

In the early 1990s, as the Soviet Union dissolved and the United States disengaged, ethnic militias went to war. Drug trafficking boomed, and Arab and other non-Afghan Islamist radicals strengthened their bases. Pakistan, still heavily involved in Afghanistan's internal battles, backed the Taliban, a radical group of mostly Pashtun clerics (the name means "students"). With Islamabad's help, the Taliban established control over most of Afghanistan by 1998, and the anti-Taliban resistance—organized in a "Northern Alliance" of feuding former mujahideen and Soviet-backed militias, most of them from non-Pashtun ethnic groups—was pushed back to a few pockets of territory in the northeast. As their grip over Afghanistan tightened, the Taliban instituted harsh Islamic law and increasingly allied themselves with Osama bin Laden, who came to Afghanistan after being expelled from Sudan in 1996.

After the fall of the Soviet Union, Washington assumed that the collapse of Afghanistan into warring chiefdoms—many of them allied with neighboring states or other external forces—was not worth worrying much about. The Clinton administration began to recognize the growing threat in Afghanistan after the al Qaeda bombings of two U.S. embassies in Africa in 1998. But it never took decisive action, and when the Bush administration took office, it gave priority to other concerns. It took 9/11 to force Washington to recognize that a global terrorist opposition was gathering strength—using human and physical capital that the United States and its allies (especially Saudi Arabia) had supplied, through Pakistan's intelligence services, in pursuit of a Cold War strategic agenda.

Opportunities Lost

When the Bush administration overthrew the Taliban after 9/11, it did so with a "light footprint": using CIA operatives and the Special Forces to coordinate Northern Alliance and other Afghan commanders on the ground and supporting them with U.S. airpower. After a quick military campaign, it backed the UN effort to form a new government and manage the political transition. It also reluctantly agreed to the formation of the International Security Assistance Force (ISAF) to help the new Afghan government provide security and build new military and police forces. In 2003, the ISAF came under NATO command—the first-ever NATO military operation outside of Europe—and gradually expanded its operations from just Kabul to most of Afghanistan's 34 provinces. About 32,000 U.S. and allied forces are currently engaged in security assistance and counterinsurgency under NATO command, while another 8,000 coalition troops are involved in counterterrorist operations. The UN Assistance Mission in Afghanistan coordinates the international community's support for political and economic reconstruction.

In the immediate aftermath of the Taliban's overthrow, the presence of coalition troops served as a deterrent against both overt external subversion and open warfare among the various forces that had been rearmed by Washington. This deterrent created an opportunity to build a functioning state; that state, however, now at the center, rather than the margins, of global and regional conflict, would have had to connect rather than separate its neighboring regions, a much more demanding goal. Accomplishing that goal would have required forming a government with sufficient resources and legitimacy to secure and develop its own territory and with a geopolitical identity unthreatening to its neighbors—especially Pakistan, whose deep penetration of Afghan society and politics enables it to play the role of spoiler whenever it chooses. Such a project would have meant additional troop deployments by the United States and its partners, especially in the border region, and rapid investment in reconstruction. It also would have required political reform and economic development in the tribal areas of Pakistan.

Too little of this happened, and both Afghanistan and its international partners are paying the consequences. Rearming warlords empowered leaders the Afghan people had rejected; enabling the Northern Alliance to seize Kabul put those Pakistan most mistrusted in charge of the security forces. And the White House's opposition to "nation building" led to major delays in Afghanistan's reconstruction.

Effective economic aid is vital to addressing the pervasive poverty that debilitates the government and facilitates the recruitment of unemployed youths into militias or the insurgency. Economically and socially, Afghanistan remains far behind its neighbors. It is the poorest country in the world outside of sub-Saharan Africa, and its government remains weak and ineffective. Last year, it raised domestic revenue of about $13 per capita—hardly enough to buy each of its citizens one case of Coca-Cola from the recently opened bottling plant near Kabul, let alone take on all of the important tasks at hand.

Because Afghanistan has been so poor for so long, real non-drug growth averaged more than 15 percent from 2002 until this year, thanks in large part to the expenditures of foreign forces and aid organizations and the end of a drought. But growth fell to nine percent last year, and the UN and the Afghan government reported in November that growth "is still not sufficient to generate in a relatively short time the large numbers of new jobs necessary to substantially reduce poverty or overcome widespread popular disaffection. The reality is that only limited progress has been achieved in increasing availability of energy, revitalizing agriculture and the rural economy, and attracting new investment."

High unemployment is fueling conflict. As a fruit trader in Kandahar put it to me, "Those Afghans who are fighting, it is all because of unemployment." This will only get worse now that the postwar economic bubble has been punctured. Real estate prices and rents are dropping in Kabul, and occupancy rates are down. Fruit and vegetable sellers report a decline in demand of about 20 percent, and construction companies in Kabul report significant falls in employment and wages. A drought in some parts of the country has also led to displacement and a decline in agricultural employment, for which the record opium poppy crop has only partially compensated.

Moreover, the lack of electricity continues to be a major problem. No major new power projects have been completed, and Kabulis today have less electricity than they did five years ago. While foreigners and wealthy Afghans power air conditioners, hot-water heaters, computers, and satellite televisions with private generators, average Kabulis suffered a summer without fans and face a winter without heaters. Kabul got through the past two winters with generators powered by diesel fuel purchased by the United States; this year the United States made no such allocation.

Rising crime, especially the kidnapping of businessmen for ransom, is also leading to capital flight. Although no reliable statistics are available, people throughout the country, including in Kabul, report that crime is increasing—and complain that the police are the main criminals. Many report that kidnappers and robbers wear police uniforms. On August 24, men driving a new vehicle with tinted windows and police license plates robbed a bank van of $360,000 just blocks away from the Ministry of the Interior.

The corruption and incompetence of the police force (which lacks real training and basic equipment) were highlighted after riots last May, set off by the crash of a U.S. military vehicle. Rioters chanted slogans against the United States and President Karzai and attacked the parliament building, the offices of media outlets and nongovernmental organizations, diplomatic residences, brothels, and hotels and restaurants that purportedly served alcohol. The police, many of whom disappeared, proved incompetent, and the vulnerability of the government to mass violence became clear. Meanwhile, in a sign of growing ethnofactional tensions within the governing elite, Karzai, a Pashtun (the Pashtun are the largest ethnic group in Afghanistan), suspected opposition leaders of fomenting violence by demonstrators, who were largely from Panjshir, the home base of the main Northern Alliance group. (Panjshiri leaders deny the charge.) Karzai responded not by strengthening support for police reform but by appointing commanders of a rival Northern Alliance group to positions in the police force. Karzai argued that he was forced into such an unpalatable balancing act because of the international community's long-standing failure to respond to his requests for adequate resources for the police.

The formation of the Afghan National Army, which now has more than 30,000 troops, has been one of the relative success stories of the past five years, but one reason for its success is that it uses mostly fresh recruits; the 60,000 experienced fighters demobilized from militias have, instead of joining the army, joined the police, private security firms, or organized crime networks—and sometimes all three. One former mujahideen commander, Din Muhammad Jurat, became a general in the Ministry of the Interior and is widely believed—including by his former mujahideen colleagues—to be a major figure in organized crime and responsible for the murder of a cabinet minister in February 2002. (He also works with U.S. Protection and Investigations, a Texas-based firm that provides international agencies and construction projects with security guards, many of whom are former fighters from Jurat's militia and current employees at the Ministry of the Interior.)

Meanwhile, the drug economy is booming. The weakness of the state and the lack of security for licit economic activity has encouraged this boom, and according to the UN Office on Drugs and Crime, opium poppy production in the country reached a record 6,100 metric tons last year, surpassing the 2005 total by 49 percent. This increase belies past claims of progress, made on the basis of a five percent cultivation decrease in 2005. Although the decrease was due almost entirely to the political persuasion of farmers by the government, the United States failed to deliver the alternative livelihoods the farmers expected and continued to pressure the Afghan government to engage in counterproductive crop eradication. The Taliban exploited the eradication policy to gain the support of poppy growers.

Counternarcotics efforts provide leverage for corrupt officials to extract enormous bribes from traffickers. Such corruption has attracted former militia commanders who joined the Ministry of the Interior after being demobilized. Police chief posts in poppy-growing districts are sold to the highest bidder: as much as $100,000 is paid for a six-month appointment to a position with a monthly salary of $60. And while the Taliban have protected small farmers against eradication efforts, not a single high-ranking government official has been prosecuted for drug-related corruption.

Drugs are only part of a massive cross-border smuggling network that has long provided a significant part of the livelihoods of the major ethnic groups on the border, the Pashtun and the Baluch. Al Qaeda, the Taliban, warlords, and corrupt officials of all ethnic groups profit by protecting and preying on this network. The massive illicit economy, which constitutes the tax base for insecurity, is booming, while the licit economy slows.

Sanctuary in Pakistan

Pakistan's military establishment has always approached the various wars in and around Afghanistan as a function of its main institutional and national security interests: first and foremost, balancing India, a country with vastly more people and resources, whose elites, at least in Pakistani eyes, do not fully accept the legitimacy of Pakistan's existence. To defend Pakistan from ethnic fragmentation, Pakistan's governments have tried to neutralize Pashtun and Baluch nationalism, in part by supporting Islamist militias among the Pashtun. Such militias wage asymmetrical warfare on Afghanistan and Kashmir and counter the electoral majorities of opponents of military rule with their street power and violence.

The rushed negotiations between the United States and Pakistan in the immediate aftermath of 9/11 changed Pakistan's behavior but not its interests. Supporting the Taliban was so important to Pakistan that Musharraf even considered going to war with the United States rather than abandon his allies in Afghanistan. Instead, he tried to persuade Washington to allow him to install a "moderate Taliban" government or, failing that, at least to prevent the Northern Alliance, which Pakistanis see as allied with India, from entering Kabul and forming a government. The agreement by Washington to dilute Northern Alliance control with remnants of Afghanistan's royal regime did little to mollify the generals in Islamabad, to say nothing of the majors and colonels who had spent years supporting the Taliban in the border areas. Nonetheless, in order to prevent the United States from allying with India, Islamabad acquiesced in reining in its use of asymmetrical warfare, in return for the safe evacuation of hundreds of Pakistani officers and intelligence agents from Afghanistan, where they had overseen the Taliban's military operations.

The United States tolerated the quiet reconstitution of the Taliban in Pakistan as long as Islamabad granted basing rights to U.S. troops, pursued the hunt for al Qaeda leaders, and shut down A. Q. Khan's nuclear-technology proliferation network. But five years later, the safe haven Pakistan has provided, along with continued support from donors in the Persian Gulf, has allowed the Taliban to broaden and deepen their presence both in the Pakistani border regions and in Afghanistan. Even as Afghan and international forces have defeated insurgents in engagement after engagement, the weakness of the government and the reconstruction effort—and the continued sanctuary provided to Taliban leaders in Pakistan—has prevented real victory.

In his September 21, 2006, testimony before the Senate Foreign Relations Committee, James Jones, a Marine Corps general and the supreme allied commander, Europe, for NATO, confirmed that the main Taliban headquarters remains in Quetta. According to Western military officials in Afghanistan, intelligence provides strong circumstantial evidence that Pakistan's ISI is providing aid to the Taliban leadership shura (council) there.

Another commanders' shura, directing operations in eastern Afghanistan, is based in the Pakistani tribal agencies of North and South Waziristan. It has consolidated its alliance with Pakistani Taliban fighters, as well as with foreign jihadi fighters. In September, Pakistani authorities signed a peace deal with "tribal elders of North Waziristan and local mujahideen, Taliban, and ulama [Islamic clergy]," an implicit endorsement of the notion that the fight against the U.S. and NATO presence in Kabul is a jihad. (During his visit to the United States in September, Musharraf mischaracterized this agreement as only with "an assembly of tribal elders.") According to the agreement, the Taliban agreed not to cross over into Afghanistan and to refrain from the "target killing" of tribal leaders who oppose the group, and the foreign militants are expected to either live peacefully or leave the region. But only two days after the agreement was signed, two anti-Taliban tribal elders were assassinated; U.S. military spokespeople claim that cross-border attacks increased threefold after the deal.

Further north, the veteran Islamist leader Gulbuddin Hekmatyar, a favorite of the ISI since 1973, operates from the northwestern Pakistani city of Peshawar and from the Bajaur and Mohmand tribal agencies, on the border with northeast Afghanistan. This is where a U.S. Predator missile strike killed between 70 and 80 people in a militant madrasah on October 30, and where bin Laden and Ayman al-Zawahiri, al Qaeda's number two leader, are most likely to be found.

The strength and persistence of the insurgency cannot be explained solely by the sanctuary the Taliban enjoy in Pakistan. But few insurgencies with safe havens abroad have ever been defeated. The argument that poverty and underdevelopment, rather than Pakistani support, are responsible for the insurgency does not stand up to scrutiny: northern and western Afghanistan are also plagued by crime and insecurity, and yet there is no coordinated antigovernment violence in those regions.

The Center Can Hold

For several years, Washington has responded to the repeated warnings from Karzai about the Taliban's sanctuary in Pakistan by assuring him that Islamabad is cooperating, that public protests are counterproductive, and that the United States will take care of the problem. But assurances that U.S. forces would soon mop up the "remnants" of the Taliban and al Qaeda have proved false. Nor did the United States offer adequate resources to Karzai to allow him to strengthen the Afghan state and thereby bolster resistance to the Taliban. Karzai's short-term strategy of allying himself with corrupt and abusive power holders at home—a necessary response, he says, to inadequate resources—has further undermined the state-building effort.

Western and Afghan officials differ over the extent to which Pakistan's aid to the Taliban is ordered by or tolerated at the highest levels of the Pakistani military, but they have reached a consensus, in the words of one senior Western military leader, that Pakistani leaders "could disrupt the senior levels of [Taliban] command and control" but have chosen not to. Disrupting command and control—not preventing "infiltration," a tactical challenge to which Pakistan often tries to divert discussion—is the key to an overall victory. That will require serious pressure on Pakistan.

So far, the United States and its allies have failed even to convey a consistent message to Islamabad. U.S. officials should

at least stop issuing denials on behalf of Islamabad, as General John Abizaid, the commander of U.S. forces in the Middle East, did in Kabul on August 27 when he claimed that he "absolutely does not believe" that Pakistan is helping the Taliban. NATO and the coalition members have similarly failed to devise a common course of action, in part out of the fear that doing so could cause Pakistan to reduce its cooperation on counterterrorism. But failing to address Pakistan's support of the Taliban amounts to an acceptance of NATO's failure. The allies must send a strong message to Pakistan: that a lack of forceful action against the Taliban command in Baluchistan constitutes a threat to international peace and security as defined in the UN Charter. Pakistan's leaders, who are eager to show that their government is a full participant in the international community (partly in order to establish parity with India), will seek to avoid such a designation. Washington must also take a stand. Pakistan should not continue to benefit from U.S. military assistance and international aid as long as it fails even to try to dismantle the Taliban's command structure.

On this issue, as on others, Washington should reverse the Bush administration's policy of linking as many local conflicts as possible to the global "war on terror" and instead address each on its own terms. A realistic assessment of Pakistan's role requires not moving Pakistan from the "with us" to the "against us" column in the "war on terror" account books but recognizing that Pakistan's policy derives from the perceptions, interests, and capabilities of its leaders, not from those of the U.S. government. The haven and support the Taliban receive in Pakistan are partly a response to claims Afghanistan has made against Pakistan and are also due to Islamabad's concern about both Indian influence in Afghanistan and Afghan backing for Pashtun and Baluch nationalists operating across the Durand Line.

Accordingly, unified pressure on Pakistan should be accompanied by efforts to address Islamabad's core concerns. The United States and its allies should encourage the Afghan government to open a domestic debate on the sensitive issue of recognition of the Durand Line in return for guarantees of stability and access to secure trade and transport corridors to Pakistani ports. Transforming the border region into an area of cooperation rather than conflict will require reform and development in the tribal territories. And Washington should ask India and Afghanistan to take measures to reassure Pakistan that their bilateral relations will not threaten Islamabad. If, as some sources claim, the Taliban are preparing to drop their maximalist demands and give guarantees against the reestablishment of al Qaeda bases, the Afghan government could discuss their entry into the political system.

Such a shift in U.S. policy toward Pakistan requires a change from supporting President Musharraf to supporting democracy. Pakistan's people have shown in all national elections that support for extremist parties is marginal. The reassertion of the civilian political center, as well as of Pakistan's business class, which is profiting from the reconstruction of Afghanistan, has provided an opportunity to move beyond the United States' history of relying on military rulers. Washington must forge a more stable relationship with a Pakistan that is at peace with its neighbors and with itself.

Back from the Brink

Creating a reasonably effective state in Afghanistan is a long-term project that will require an end to major armed conflict, the promotion of economic development, and the gradual replacement of opium production by other economic activities. Recent crises, however, have exposed internal weaknesses that underscore the need for not only long-term endeavors but short-term transitional measures as well.

The two fatal weak points in Afghanistan's government today are the Ministry of the Interior and the judiciary. Both are deeply corrupt and plagued by a lack of basic skills, equipment, and resources. Without effective and honest administrators, police, and judges, the state can do little to provide internal security—and if the government does not provide security, people will not recognize it as a government.

In 2005, coalition military forces devised a plan for thoroughgoing reform of the Ministry of the Interior. The president and the minister of the interior appoint administrative and police officials throughout the country. Reform cannot succeed unless President Karzai overhauls the ministry's ineffective and corrupt leadership and fully backs the reform. In any case, this plan, already three years behind that of the Ministry of Defense, will show Afghans no results until mid-2007. In September, the government established a mechanism to vet appointees for competence and integrity. Finding competent people willing to risk their lives in a rural district for $60–$70 a month will remain difficult, but if implemented well, this vetting process could help avoid appointments such as those hastily made after the riots last spring.

Government officials have identified the biggest problems in civil administration at the district level. In interviews, elders from more than ten provinces agreed, complaining that the government never consults them. Some ministers have proposed paying elders and ulama in each district to act as the eyes and ears of the government, meet with governors and the president, administer small projects, and influence what is preached in the mosques. They estimate the cost of such a program at about $5 million per year. These leaders could also help recruit the 200 young men from each district who are supposed to serve as auxiliary police. They are to receive basic police training and equipment and serve under a trained police commander. Unlike militias, the auxiliary police are to be paid individually, with professional commanders from outside the district. Elders could be answerable for the auxiliary forces' behavior.

Courts, too, may require some temporary supplementary measures. Community leaders complain forcefully about judicial corruption, which has led many to demand the implementation of Islamic law, or sharia—which they contrast not to secular law but to corruption. One elder from the province of Paktia said, "Islam says that if you find a thief, he has to be punished. If a murderer is arrested, he has to be tried and executed. In our country, if a murderer is put in prison, after six months he bribes the judge and escapes. If a member of parliament is killed . . . his murderer is released after three to four months in prison because of bribery." Enforcement by the government of the decisions of Islamic courts has always constituted a basic pillar of the state's legitimacy in Afghanistan, and the failure to do so is turning religious leaders, who still wield great influence over public opinion, against the government.

The August 5 swearing-in of a new Supreme Court, which administers the judicial system, makes judicial reform possible, but training prosecutors, judges, and defense lawyers will take years. In the meantime, the only capacities for dispute resolution and law enforcement in much of the country consist of village or tribal councils and mullahs who administer a crude interpretation of sharia. During the years required for reform, the only actual alternatives before Afghan society are enforcement of such customary or Islamic law or no law at all. The Afghan government and its international supporters should find ways to incorporate such procedures into the legal system and subject them to judicial or administrative review. Such a program would also put more Islamic leaders—more than 1,200 of whom have been dropped from the government payroll this year—back under government supervision.

Attempts to inject aid into the government have hit a major bottleneck: in 2005 and 2006, the government spent only 44 percent of the money it received for development projects. Meanwhile, according to the Ministry of Finance, donor countries spent about $500 million on poorly designed and uncoordinated technical assistance. The World Bank is devising a program that will enable the government to hire the technical advisers it needs, rather than trying to coordinate advisers sent by donors in accord with their own priorities and domestic constituencies. The United States should support this initiative, along with a major crash program to increase the implementation capacity of the ministries.

As numerous studies have documented over the years, Afghanistan has not received the resources needed to stabilize it. International military commanders, who confront the results of this poverty every day, estimate that Washington must double the resources it devotes to Afghanistan. Major needs include accelerated road building, the purchase of diesel for immediate power production, the expansion of cross-border electricity purchases, investment in water projects to improve the productivity of agriculture, the development of infrastructure for mineral exploitation, and a massive program of skill building for the public and private sectors.

Afghanistan also needs to confront the threat from its drug economy in a way that does not undermine its overall struggle for security and stability. At first, U.S. policy after the fall of the Taliban consisted of aiding all commanders who had fought on the U.S. side, regardless of their involvement in drug trafficking. Then, when the "war on drugs" lobby raised the issue, Washington began pressuring the Afghan government to engage in crop eradication. To Afghans, this policy has looked like a way of rewarding rich drug dealers while punishing poor farmers.

The international drug-control regime does not reduce drug use, but it does, by criminalizing narcotics, produce huge profits for criminals and the armed groups and corrupt officials who protect them. In Afghanistan, this drug policy provides, in effect, huge subsidies to the United States' enemies. As long as the ideological commitment to such a counterproductive policy continues—as it will for the foreseeable future—the second-best option in Afghanistan is to treat narcotics as a security and development issue. The total export value of Afghan opium has been estimated to be 30–50 percent of the legal economy. Such an industry cannot be abolished by law enforcement. But certain measures would help: rural development in both poppy-growing and non-poppy-growing areas, including the construction of roads and cold-storage facilities to make other products marketable; employment creation through the development of new rural industries; and reform of the Ministry of the Interior and other government bodies to root out major figures involved with narcotics, regardless of political or family connections.

This year's record opium poppy crop has increased the pressure from the United States for crop eradication, including through aerial spraying. Crop eradication puts more money in the hands of traffickers and corrupt officials by raising prices and drives farmers toward insurgents and warlords. If Washington wants to succeed in Afghanistan, it must invest in creating livelihoods for the rural poor—the vast majority of Afghans—while attacking the main drug traffickers and the corrupt officials who protect them.

Know Thy Enemy, Know Thyself

Contemptuous of nation building and wary of mission creep, the Bush administration entered Afghanistan determined to strike al Qaeda, unseat the Taliban, and then move on, providing only basic humanitarian aid and support for a new Afghan army. Just as it had in the 1980s, the United States picked Afghan allies based exclusively on their willingness to get rid of U.S. enemies, rather than on their capacity to bring stability and security to the state. The UN-mediated political transition and underfunded reconstruction effort have only partially mitigated the negative consequences of such a shortsighted U.S. policy.

Some in Washington have accused critics of the effort in Afghanistan of expecting too much too soon and focusing on setbacks while ignoring achievements. The glass, they say, is half full, not half empty. But the glass is much less than half full—and it is resting on a wobbly table that growing threats, if unaddressed, may soon overturn.

U.S. policymakers have misjudged Afghanistan, misjudged Pakistan, and, most of all, misjudged their own capacity to carry out major strategic change on the cheap. The Bush administration has sown disorder and strengthened Iran while claiming to create a "new Middle East," but it has failed to transform the region where the global terrorist threat began—and where the global terrorist threat persists. If the United States wants to succeed in the war on terrorism, it must focus its resources and its attention on securing and stabilizing Afghanistan.

BARNETT R. RUBIN is Director of Studies and a Senior Fellow at New York University's Center on International Cooperation and the author of *The Fragmentation of Afghanistan*. He served as an adviser to the Special Representative of the Secretary-General at the UN Talks on Afghanistan in Bonn in 2001.

Beyond the Frame

In Afghanistan, where art is frowned upon, a group of young women use abstract and contemporary lines to explore themes of violence and regeneration. Their paintings will be exhibited in Kolkata from September 19 to 27.

AUNOHITA MOJUMDAR

Yalda Noori is a contemporary artist. Her paintings reveal an engagement with social concerns. Her technique masters a variety of styles. In a haunting painting which she calls "Life passage," a purple sky frames a landscape of cacti plants. Suspended in front is a white translucent bubble with green plants and flowers, almost ephemeral. "I wanted to show the wishes, the dreams of women. They are as fragile as the bubble against the harsh realities of the wishes of other people who do not want women to achieve these dreams." The painting could have been from anywhere. What makes it remarkable is that it was created in Afghanistan by one of a group of young Afghan women who are breaking new ground by exploring intricate themes of violence and regeneration through contemporary art.

An exhibition of their paintings has travelled to India, the first time their paintings are being exhibited in the region outside Afghanistan. The exhibition, organised by the ICCR, will be in Delhi before travelling to Kolkata.

The Taliban ban on most forms of art along with other forms of cultural expression is by now quite well known. Paintings were dragged out of homes, offices and museums and burnt, books with art work were burnt, museum collections were systematically destroyed and film archives were purged to cleanse them of the "unIslamic" depiction of the living, especially human form.

Tradition of Suppression

The damage to Afghan art did not however begin or end with them. The Soviet interpretation of art stifled creativity in the 1980s when the country was under a Soviet-backed regime. The mujahideen who replaced them in power after the fall of the last communist president Najibullah at best tolerated some forms of art and music, with the more conservative elements amongst them disapproving of it entirely.

Even when not directly damaged due to State policies, art suffered during the decades of conflict as people struggled for survival, being forced to pack their belongings and move—again, again and again. Art, a luxury, became one of the first casualties of war.

Since 2001 and the removal of the Taliban there is no political repression of art. However, conservative attitudes remain entrenched in a large section of Afghan society. The long hiatus of the years of war has however meant there was scant opportunity for art or art appreciation to develop. Today the streets of Kabul and the small number of art galleries are dominated by kitsch: imitative paintings of Napoleon on a horse, Western stereotypes of Afghanistan with the mandatory Bactrian camels, *burkhas* and Bamiyan Buddhas. At its best, the art is well executed renditions of realistic or classical paintings. At its worst, it recreates the picture postcards sold as souvenirs.

The development of art is further constrained by the insecurity and difficult economic conditions. Fighting has steadily escalated in large parts of the south and the last three months have seen a doubling of the number of incidents of violence. Bombings, suicide attacks, kidnapping and criminality are quite routine even in the capital city Kabul.

On the economic front, despite $15 million in aid having already been disbursed in the country since 2001, the economic conditions of most Afghans is difficult if not desperate as the gains of aid have been inequitably distributed amongst peoples and regions. Food insecurity has grown and in a situation where 35 per cent of the population cannot meet its minimum dietary needs, art still remains an unaffordable luxury.

Words Won't Do

It is in this milieu that the young women have ventured into the non-traditional area of modern and abstract art, while acknowledging that it does not lend itself to easy interpretations. "Realistic art feels like being within a frame. I find it easier to express myself through contemporary art. When I cannot find words for what I want to say, I paint" says Yalda. Her fellow student at Kabul's new Contemporary Art Centre Afghanistan (CCAA),

21-year-old Nabila Horakhsh agrees. In the painting "Double Standards," on exhibit in the IIC, Horakhsh says she wanted to show the different situation for men and women in Afghan society. "It is up to the viewer to interpret my paintings through their own understanding. Their own feelings of happiness or sadness."

Talking to this reporter in their Centre in Kabul before leaving for India, both Yalda and Nabila expressed their excitement. Friends and family have given them shopping lists which they hope to fulfil but most of all they would like to meet artists. "Will anyone famous come to our exhibition? Where can we meet other students of art? Can we see the fine arts faculty? We want to know what other women painters paint."

Both the young women consider themselves lucky. They have supportive families and the freedom to attend University as well as take classes in the Centre. But they are very much aware that this is not the choice that most women in their society can exercise.

Despite the removal of the Taliban, who were equated with discrimination against women of the worst kind and a new Constitutional guarantee of equality, women in Afghanistan face multiple forms of discrimination with little acceptance of their role in participation in public space. One woman dies in childbirth every 29 minutes, female literacy is 15.8 per cent, 70–80 per cent of the marriages in Afghanistan are forced marriages (including marriage of minor girls) and some aspects of Afghanistan's customary laws allow women to be bartered as restitution for criminal acts, debts and other forms of payment. Even the "modern" law treats women as suspects rather than victims in crimes like rape and other violence, while the judiciary imprisons women who run away from abusive homes, while condoning honour killings by treating them far more leniently than murder. It is a reality that finds expression in a lot of the paintings, but not all the paintings by the young women artists are about women or their dismal situation.

Muqaddasa Yourish's "Primary Colours" is a bold melange of primary colours in geometrical shapes on a canvas slashed through the middle with a knife. "The primacy colours are the building blocks of all colours and here they represent the fundamentals of my country. The cut through them is the injury to my country from the years of fighting," she says.

Ommolbanin Shamsia has been painting for as long as she can remember, as a child and refugee in Iran. But this is the first time that this student of accountancy is taking classes in art. Her painting "Portal" shows a woman standing at the edge of a pool of water. Reflected from the water is not the woman but a young green tree. "This represents woman as life, as regeneration," she says.

The young painters are aware that their paintings are more "difficult," less easy on the eyes and even disturbing. Manezha Hewad, who will also be exhibiting her works in Delhi, says she has "sacrificed beauty for concept as I felt that to be more important."

Most of the students have not studied art before attending this Centre started by the artist and teacher in the Fine Arts Faculty of Kabul University, Mr. Rahraw Omarzad.

Fresh Viewpoints

Omarzad's impetus to start the centre came from his experience in the arts faculty. "By the time the students go through four years of traditional art courses and come to the subject of contemporary art, they have already lost the ability to think out of the box." Omarzad eschewed traditional methods like teaching the students the history of modern art or its techniques. "I just asked them to create art and we discussed each art work in the class. I didn't want them to learn or follow any 'isms' but to learn to think independently."

Omarzad has much to be proud of. A shy man, he is quick to point out that the real stars are the painters and not himself. But underneath his quiet manners is a strong core of belief, a faith that keeps him going even though till date the Centre has not received any core funding, surviving from what it makes from one exhibition to another. The concept of contemporary women's art in Afghanistan is still too unusual for people, whether Afghans or international donors, to invest in.

Growing Discontent

One of the world's largest NGOs has helped millions in Bangladesh, but critics now claim it acts as a parallel state, accountable to no one.

ANNIE KELLY

In the chaotic heart of downtown Dhaka, the 19-story Brac building—home to one of the world's largest NGOs, the Bangladesh Rehabilitation Assistance Committee, an organisation so powerful that it is commonly termed Bangladesh's second government—casts a shadow over one of the city's largest slums. From the top floor, the slum looks like a ramshackle maze of corrugated iron and tarpaulin. But a short boat ride across the river reveals a neighbourhood of neat interlocking streets dotted with open shopfronts, selling everything from firewood to hot cakes, and with centres providing health and education programmes to its 300,000 inhabitants.

Most of the small enterprises here have been funded by Brac micro-finance loans. The slum's school is run by Brac-trained teachers using Brac textbooks. More than 200 Brac-trained health volunteers dispense medical services. Down the road is the Brac University, and a Brac bank sign is just visible across the street.

With an expenditure of £160m, a staff of 108,000 and services that reach more than 110 million people across the country, Brac has grown from a small relief operation into an organisation globally unsurpassed in the scale of the programmes it provides to some of the world's poorest people.

In its 35-year history, it has organised nearly 7 million landless poor into 239,000 village organisations and distributed more than £2bn in micro-finance loans.

Brac's vocational programmes and micro-financing have created in excess of 6m new jobs, its health services reach more than 100 million people every year, and around 1.5 million children are educated in its 52,000 schools. Its belief that climate change and rising sea levels will become the greatest obstacle to raising Bangladesh out of poverty has led to a social forestry programme that planted more than 15m trees in 2007.

"If 25% of Bangladesh is going to be underwater by 2100, then this presents the greatest challenge we have ever faced, and one that I think Brac will play a great role in finding solutions for," says Fazle Hasan Abed, who gave up a promising career in an oil company to help start Brac in 1972 and now, in his role as Brac chairman, is arguably one of the most influential men in Bangladesh.

The NGO's exponential growth is in part to do with the failure of Bangladeshi administrations to provide services for the millions of landless poor, but Brac has also proved to be good at making money. In the 1980s, it saw that the private sector was unwilling to provide support for the growth of small enterprise and stepped in to fill the gap. It now generates around 70% of its own income through a huge array of Brac-branded enterprises.

Following its meteoric rise in Bangladesh, Brac now believes it can replicate its work and influence in other developing countries across the world and solve some of the development dilemmas still left unanswered by northern NGOs.

"As a southern NGO, I think we have a different approach to development," says Brac's executive director, Mahabub Hossain. "We understand poverty because our country is, in many ways, defined by it, and we understand poor people's aspirations and needs. I think that, more than NGOs from the north, we are able to join up the dots."

Hossain says Bangladesh is now a fundamentally different country to what it was pre-Brac. "We are slowly proving it's possible to fight and win the battle with poverty here in Bangladesh," he says.

But Brac's swelling economic clout and increasing monopolisation of Bangladesh's development sector is causing concern in some ranks. There are accusations that Brac is acting like a parallel state, but one that is accountable to no one.

"Brac is an incredibly effective organisation, but it is at the stage where it is basically unchallenged," says Khushi Kabir, one of Brac's first employees and now the head of Nijera Kori, an anti-poverty NGO. "Government dependency on its services has grown to the extent that they almost can't run the country without it."

One area causing concern among NGOs such as Nijera Kori is Brac's environmental record, especially around the promotion of hybrid crop seeds to the millions of farmers taking out Brac micro-finance loans in Bangladesh's rural communities.

Brac moved into hybrid seed production in the 1980s, working first with Chinese seed producers to provide poor farmers with high-yield hybrid rice and maize seeds. Now teams of Brac scientists make their own in two Brac seed production plants. So far, it has cornered much of the hybrid seed market in Bangladesh.

The Bangladesh government has also heavily promoted hybrid seed planting, and aims to boost hybrid seed production from 250,000 hectares in the last planting season to 1m hectares in 2008. Brac and the government are working hand-in-hand to promote the usage of drought-resistant and flood-resistant hybrid seeds developed by international multinationals.

In December, two groups—Nayakrishi Andolon, a movement of 100,000 farmers, and the Ubinig social policy research organisation—accused Brac and the government of being "unethical" and dishonest in their promotion of hybrid crops.

"A group of seed dealers and micro-credit based NGOs are active [in the introduction of hybrid seeds] and are taking advantage of the natural calamities and disadvantaged condition of the farmers. These activities are totally unethical," says Ubinig executive director Farida Akhter, who claims that Brac is complicit in deceiving farmers about true production costs of hybrid seeds and inflating predicted crop yields.

The two groups say Bangladeshi farmers have enough of their own high-yielding varieties of aman and boro rice, which need to be protected and promoted.

"The total agricultural system is now under threat," says Akhter, who blames the promotion of hybrid crops for Bangladesh's increasing mono-crop rice culture. "Due to irrigation for boro rice cultivation through extraction of underground water, the water table has gone down. There are arsenic problems in drinking water, and desertification in the northern region of the country has been intensified."

More damningly, Nayakrishi Andolon and Ubinig also accuse Brac of linking access to micro-finance loans with the purchase of a particular hybrid rice seed, along with fertiliser and pesticide.

It is a claim Brac denies. "Our borrowers always have a choice," says Hossain. "They can either use our seed or not, but the simple fact is you can get twice as much profit from a hybrid rice or maize seed than you can from traditional strains.

"Our population has trebled in the last century, the land is limited, there are more floods, more cyclones, and more of the land we have is getting diverted for urbanisation. There is a huge national food gap. Development is about choices. There is a trade-off in everything we do, and there is an urgent and persistent need for food that we feel we have a responsibility to find solutions for."

Professor Wins $1 Million Prize for Providing Clean Water, One Village at a Time

Tara Laskowski

In the United States, turning on the tap and getting clean drinking water is something most people take for granted. We have the luxury of multimillion-dollar filtration systems and deep wells that pump toxin-free water to our homes.

However, in developing countries such as Bangladesh and West Bengal, India, shallow water wells are the norm for villages. Arsenic, a poisonous element, is naturally occurring in these tube-wells, and in Bangladesh alone, more than 18 million people are daily drinking arsenic-contaminated water.

Arsenic poisoning is a slow, painful process that can cause skin cancer, tumors and ultimately death. Affected people can have difficulty working or even walking, and continued exposure can lead to liver failure, kidney failure and the need for amputation of arms or legs.

For Bangladesh native Abul Hussam, associate professor of chemistry and biochemistry at Mason for more than 20 years, this threat hits close to home. About 10 years ago, his brother, a medical doctor in Bangladesh, started to see the frightening consequences of arsenic poisoning in his village. He asked Hussam to help develop a way of measuring the arsenic levels in wells.

Measuring the Problem

Hussam did his PhD work in analytical chemistry at the University of Pittsburgh. Developing an instrument to measure arsenic levels in drinking water was a perfect match for his interests.

He started with his own family's well in Bangladesh. To his shock, he learned his family had been drinking water with three times the toxicity level of arsenic for more than 20 years, and there was a possibility his own father had died from arsenic poisoning.

"Measurement is absolutely critical—it is my strength and what brought me to this project—but once you know what you have, now the question is, 'What can we do about it?'" says Hussam.

That's when Hussam started looking at ways to build a filter to help provide safe drinking water for his family and neighbors. The challenges required looking at issues such as economy, environment and efficiency. Because Bangladesh is a developing country, the filter had to be inexpensive. Hussam also had to ensure that the materials used were safe for the environment and easy to obtain and reproduce.

After years of research and testing, Hussam and his brothers developed the SONO filter. Simple, inexpensive and made with easily available materials, the filter involves a top bucket, which is filled with locally available coarse river sand and a composite iron matrix (CIM). The sand filters coarse particles and imparts mechanical stability, while the CIM removes inorganic arsenic. The water then flows into a second bucket where it again filters through coarse river sand, then wood charcoal to remove organics, and finally through fine river sand and wet brick chips to remove fine particles and stabilize water flow.

A Distinguished Recognition

When Hussam learned the National Academy of Engineering (NAE) was offering a $1 million Grainger Challenge Award for water filtration systems that removed arsenic from drinking water, he knew his work was perfect for the contest.

After all, the systems had to be affordable, reliable, easy to maintain, socially acceptable and environmentally friendly. They had to meet or exceed the local government guidelines for arsenic removal and require no electricity—everything he had been working on for years.

Last week, he was proven correct. On Feb. 20, Hussam was awarded the Grainger Prize at a gala dinner held in Washington, D.C.

Three prizes were awarded by the NAE, with the support of the Grainger Foundation, from a field of 70 entries. The Silver Award went to the nonprofit Water for People and the Bronze Award was given to the Children's Safe Drinking Water Program at Procter & Gamble Co. Hussam won the Gold Award.

Hussam's $1 million prize will go to George Mason Intellectual Properties Inc., (GMIP) a separate nonprofit corporation established to facilitate the transfer of new discoveries made at George Mason University. GMIP will distribute the majority of the award to a Bangladeshi nonprofit organization that will use the funds to increase its production, quality control and training capacities so more SONO filter units can reach Bangladeshi households more quickly. Most of the remainder will fund Hussam's continuing research in removing toxic cations and anions from drinking water sources. GMIP will keep a small portion of the prize and will pay back the Chemistry Department, which generously funded the tests needed last summer to enable Hussam to enter the contest.

GMIP is also handling potentially still patentable matter in the SONO filter.

Seeing the Difference Firsthand

In 2000, the Hussam family started distributing the SONO filter in Bangladesh. They started with their own village, and donated many of the filters to schools with high arsenic levels in their water.

"At first, the people were not sure if they should listen to us," said Hussam. But after talking to them about the water and showing them the filter—which cost only $35 and lasts at least five years—people started to believe.

"Now, we hear of women who want to use the filtered water to shampoo their hair because it makes it softer," says Hussam. "And people say their tea tastes different and their rice is a different color. It's been very interesting."

Today, there are more than 30,000 of these filters in homes, schools and businesses in Bangladesh. Hussam hopes that with the prize money they can distribute the filter even more widely and help even more people.

He and his brothers have also seen hospital patients improve dramatically from arsenic poisoning by drinking the clean, filtered water.

"The most satisfying aspect of working on this project is seeing people drinking clean water from the SONO filter and feeling better, and for some, the melanosis [poisoning] has been reversed," says Hussam. "It is truly gratifying to see results of our scientific knowledge at work in the field for the betterment of human conditions."

All the King's Men

Bhutan becomes the newest democracy as its unwilling voters elect the Druk Phuensum Tshogpa to power with an overwhelming majority.

S. D. MUNI

South Asia is passing through an election season: Pakistan's February 18 parliamentary elections were followed by Bhutan's National Assembly elections on March 24, and now Nepal is all set to hold its first ever elections to the Constituent Assembly on April 10. All these exercises are a manifestation of the strong upsurge of sentiment for democracy and against the erstwhile autocratic governance in these countries; except that the Bhutanese elections were held in a unique political context. Unlike the situation in Nepal and Pakistan, there was no grassroots upsurge in interest in political change and the establishment of representative institutions. The Bhutanese people were happy to be governed by their traditional monarchy, whose criteria for development were defined within the parameters of the "Gross National Happiness" felt and enjoyed, not only materially but also "spiritually", by the people.

Bhutan's call for democracy was a top-down sermon by the King himself, Jigme Singhye Wangchuk, much against the unwillingness of and initial resistance by the people. While, in his neighbourhood, the Nepal King was hell-bent on going to any length to cling to power and the military regimes in Pakistan and Myanmar were most unwilling to abandon autocracy, the King of Bhutan decided in 2005 to institute democracy by handing over executive power to elected representatives. He got a new Constitution drafted accordingly, and went around his country discussing the draft Constitution and pleading with his people to learn to rule themselves through their elected representatives. The new Constitution makes it mandatory for future Kings of Bhutan to retire at the age of 65. The King can also be removed by a two-thirds vote in Parliament. King Jigme Singhye Wangchuk himself abdicated in favour of his son Jigme Khesar Namgyal Wangchuk, who is in his twenties, in 2006. Political parties were reintroduced in April 2007 by lifting a 50-year-old ban on them and elections to the Lower House of Parliament were scheduled for March 2008.

The Bhutan elections are unique not only because they were ordered by the King but also because, unlike in other South Asian countries, educational qualification was made an important factor. Under the newly framed election laws, no one can contest parliamentary elections without having a graduate degree.

Bhutan has a small graduate community of just 3,000 persons. This is also indicative of the fact that in a country where the rate of literacy is still around 42 per cent, the graduate community may mostly come from the upper and elite sections of society.

Elections were also constrained as the contesting parties were screened before they were given permission to participate. The Druk People's Unity Party (DPUP) was disqualified after scrutiny for what was described as lack of "credible leadership". It was alleged that more than 75 per cent of the party members were school dropouts. The elimination of the third party from the race reduced the two-stage electoral process into a direct contest. The Election Commission also disqualified a candidate of the People's Democratic Party (PDP) who tried to play up the problem of Bhutanis of Nepali origin. This was done to send out a firm message that there was no room in Bhutan for communal and sectarian politics. It was a clear decision to keep the Nepali issue out of the political process.

The new electoral laws also bar a person from contesting if any of his/her parents was a migrant Bhutanese. The parents of contestants have to be Bhutan-born. The electoral process was also kept free of religious issues. Monks were not allowed to vote. No wonder, there were no sensitive or contentious issues. In fact, there was not much to distinguish between the two major contenders, the PDP and the Druk Phuensum Tshogpa (DPT), or the Bhutan Peace Party. While the DPT promised a compact government, equal and just treatment to all citizens and a high standard for political conduct, the PDP tried to lure voters by offering a salary rise and promising infrastructure development, including the construction of an airport in eastern Bhutan.

It was a keenly contested election. As many as 74.4 per cent of the more than 318,000 registered voters cast their votes. Even the King appealed to voters to exercise the franchise. People walked long distances to cast their votes. Some expatriate Bhutanese also returned home to participate in the elections. The Election Commission gave one lakh Bhutanese rupees, in addition to essential election material, to each candidate towards poll expenses. A candidate could also spend one lakh Bhutanese rupees of his/her own to boost his/her electoral prospects. The Commission also organised a television debate between the leaders of the contending parties. The DPT levelled corruption charges against the PDP, saying that the latter was bribing voters, but these were stoutly countered by the PDP.

The election results upset all calculations. Analysts in Bhutan and India had expected a close fight, with a difference of not more than five to 10 seats between the winner and the loser. Even the DPT, which emerged victorious with an overwhelming majority, had not expected to win more than 30 of the 47 seats it contested. It won 45 seats. The PDP, which was routed, has asked for a re-poll or at least a serious investigation into the factors that caused such a landslide in favour of the DPT. This heavily lopsided outcome has been attributed to various factors.

Some observers have blamed the faulty mechanism or improper use of the voting machines. Others have given credit to the campaigning style of the DPT and the impressive articulation by its leader, Jigme Y. Thinley, in the debate as well as during the campaign. The DPT had five senior Ministers in its ranks and there was an impression that the party had the blessings of the King, although the PDP had a leadership related to the royal family. The active participation of senior civil servants in the DPT's electioneering confirmed this impression. Since the election was seen as a gift from the King, voters chose the party that was seen as the King's party.

Bhutan's top-down experiment in democracy, therefore, starts with an extremely weak opposition. The two elected PDP members have threatened to resign if the causes of their party's defeat are not investigated sincerely. In order to compensate for the weak opposition, the DPT leader and the Prime Minister-elect has promised accountable, corruption-free and transparent governance down to the constituency level. He assured the people that he would do everything to "establish firm foundations for a great democracy" under constitutional monarchy. "We are all subjects of one King. And in this small country, we are all a family," he remarked.

Ethnic Issues

While the international community has welcomed the democratic initiative of Bhutan, some criticism has come in for the neglect of Nepali refugees from Bhutan who have been languishing for years in Nepal and India. More than a 100,000 of the refugees were not included in the voters' list and were not allowed to participate in the elections. Extremist elements, including members of the Bhutan Communist Party, which is closely affiliated to the Communist Party of Nepal (Maoists), have infiltrated this section. They tried to disrupt the electoral process by exploding bombs in various parts of Bhutan since January and on the eve of the elections. The extremists are against the third-party solution of the refugee problem wherein the refugees are being absorbed in the United States and some European countries.

The ethnic issue, although kept carefully out of the electoral process, will need to be addressed seriously by the new democratic establishment. Nine Nepali-speaking candidates belonging to the DPT have been elected to Parliament, but this number is too small compared with the size of the ethnic Nepali population in Bhutan even after the disbursement of the Nepal-based refugees.

The new government will also confront a foreign policy challenge in the form of an assertive and sensitive China, in the context of the renewed Tibet issue and the impressive development of infrastructure in the Himalayas, with roads reaching the Bhutanese borders. The boundary question has yet to be settled between Bhutan and China. As for India, a stable, democratising, friendly and confident Bhutan is the best security asset in the turbulent Himalayas.

The writer is a Senior Visiting Fellow, Institute of South Asian Studies, Singapore.

New Home for Bhutan's Refugees

Nestled between India and China, the tiny Himalayan kingdom of Bhutan seems an unlikely starting point for large-scale ethnic displacement. But since the early 90s more than 100,000 members of the Nepalese-speaking Bhutanese population have been living in refugee camps in eastern Nepal, evicted from Bhutan for their pro-democratic activities. This year almost 5,000 Bhutanese refugees will leave their camps for resettlement in the US, according to a report by the UNHCR. Kishor Pradhan, who has been in exile since 1990, hopes to become one of them.

KISHOR PRADHAN

It was in 1986, while I was in high school, that I first felt discriminated against because of my ethnicity. I was a Lhotshampa, which meant I was from the south of the country and spoke Nepalese. My other ethnic Nepalese friends and I wanted to celebrate Dashain, the biggest Hindu festival, so we bunked class. When the school principal berated us for our behaviour we apologised to him—little did I know that far greater repression was yet to come.

After finishing school I went to college in eastern Bhutan. At that time it was the only higher education institute in the nation. I wanted to take science but couldn't because I had only scored 59%. So I studied commerce.

After Zangley Dukpa (now minister of health) became the college principal, the atmosphere became tense. He introduced stringent rules that were intended to repress my minority Nepali-speaking community. He closed down our Nepali Literary Association, which organised recitals of Nepali poems. We were required to wear the national dress (called Gho, a knee-length robe tightened at the waist by a belt) instead of our ethnic Daura Suruwal, a long double-breasted garment flowing below the waist, worn with trousers.

Then in 1989 Principal Dukpa issued an order that prohibited Lhotshampa students from celebrating Dashain. We saw this as discrimination and decided to celebrate anyway. A debate ensued and the security forces were summoned. Our photos were taken, and later the security forces came to our hostel and arrested my classmates.

When I heard that Lhotshampa people were being arrested and tortured, I left for my home in southern Bhutan. When I got there I found that the area had already become a hotbed of peaceful pro-democratic protest. Soon I was told that the security forces were searching for me, and in February 1990 I left for India. I walked for two hours to Kulkule and from there I rode a bus to Jayagaon in West Bengal, India. In Jayagaon I met a lot of Bhutanese refugees. As the crackdown continued in Bhutan, the number of refugees grew.

In the Indian border town of Garganda, refugees were being relocated to temporary camps. Various refugee forums were established there. I joined a group of like-minded refugee youths and in 1990 we formed the People's Forum for Human Rights. Some of the refugee leaders went to eastern Nepal looking for a place to shelter the refugees. Nepal, which doesn't share a border with Bhutan, was generous and provided us with land on the bank of the Mai River in the south of the country. I shuttled between India and Nepal, transporting the refugees—mostly children, elderly people and women.

We were able to draw the attention of non-profit organisations and donor agencies. Caritas Nepal, Oxfam and Lutheran World Service were the first to help us. Then, towards the end of 1991, the UN High Commissioner for Refugees (UNHCR) started to manage the camps. To this day, my fellow countrymen still live in these seven sprawling camps.

I was registered in one of the camps, but my desire to learn and explore kept leading me to the outside world. I won a scholarship to a college in Kathmandu, the capital city of Nepal. It felt like my dream had come true when I was accepted to study science. After two years I won another scholarship to study for a bachelor's degree in Calcutta, India.

In 1999, I married my long-time sweetheart, who was also a refugee. We left for Kathmandu, where I taught accounting in a number of schools. I wanted to teach because I didn't like depending on the rations provided by the World Food Programme.

Life was good in Kathmandu, but the homelessness, lack of identity and the bitter past always came back to haunt me. Again, I and a few other professional Lhotshampas banded together to form an organisation—this time it was the Bhutanese Refugee Youth Forum.

In 2005 we were invited to attend a UN conference in New York, so I and one other member of our forum flew to the US. While we were there we met others from Bhutan who had sought refuge in America. They advised us to seek asylum. It sounded convincing. After all, the 15 rounds of talks between Nepal and Bhutan had failed to bring any hope to the 100,000-plus refugees languishing in camps in Nepal.

A year after I applied for asylum I was interviewed by the US Department of Homeland Security. But I have not been given asylum and no one has contacted me to tell my why. I have done several odd jobs while I've been here. For the past couple of years I have been working in New York, in software quality assurance. But every year I have to renew my employment authorisation card and life is still in limbo.

I am happy that the US has offered to resettle 70,000 Bhutanese refugees. Many of them are still trickling into the cities and communities of the US. I just hope that I will be granted the right to stay here—and I hope my wife and nine-year-old daughter will be able to join me. I hope that eventually we will have a place to call home.

KISHOR PRADHAN was speaking to Deepak Adhikari.

Maldives: Silent Revolution

B. MURALIDHAR REDDY

Winds of change are sweeping South Asia. After the people's revolution in Nepal put an end to monarchy and ushered in a republic, it was the turn of the Maldives to bring about a new era of democracy.

In the country's first ever multiparty elections held on October 8, President Maumoon Abdul Gayoom, 71, won 40 per cent of the popular vote and polled the highest number of votes among the candidates. The Constitution mandated a minimum of 50 per cent votes, and a run-off became necessary between him and Mohamed Nasheed, 41, who came second. Nasheed, whom Gayoom had imprisoned a decade ago, became the combined candidate of the entire opposition, and in the run-off on October 28, he beat Gayoom by a 10 per cent margin.

The old order giving way to the new is perhaps just the beginning of a series of changes in the Republic of Maldives, a collection of nearly 2,000 islands and many lagoons nestled in coral atolls southeast of India. The President-elect is committed to holding the country's first multiparty parliamentary elections in February 2009.

Though Gayoom is responsible for putting the Maldives on the world map as a tourist destination, his regime was marked by charges of nepotism and corruption. Dubbed Robert Mugabe by the opposition for his autocratic ways, he banned political parties and stifled dissent even as he periodically renewed his own mandate through elections with only one name on the ballot. Pressure from within and outside finally forced him to draw up a "road map to democratic reforms", a key component of which was a multiparty democracy.

Born on May 17, 1967, President-elect Nasheed was educated in Sri Lanka and in the United Kingdom, where he got a bachelor's degree in maritime studies from Liverpool John Moores University. He was 11 years old when Gayoom first came to power in 1978. He began his career as a journalist and incurred the wrath of the government with his strong criticism. Slapped with 27 charges, he was jailed or banished to a remote atoll for a total of six years. Amnesty International named him a "prisoner of conscience" in 1996.

Though popularly known by his nickname Anni, many in his Maldivian Democratic Party (MDP) refer to Nasheed as "Nelson Mandela". He was first elected to Parliament in 1999 but lost his seat in 2001 after being prosecuted for "theft". He formed the MDP while in exile in Sri Lanka in 2003, a year that saw riots in the capital Male over the killing of a youth and a crackdown by the authorities.

In 2004, Nasheed was at the centre of pro-democracy protests that were sparked off after he went to commemorate the anniversary of the riots and to press for more reforms. He was arrested, and the government declared a state of emergency, which prompted the European Union to threaten sanctions against the Maldives.

Nasheed said his government would hold snap elections halfway through his five-year term—a sign, he claimed, of his commitment to a healthy democracy. Under election laws, he must assume office by November 11. That will formally end the 30 years of rule by Gayoom, who did not allow political parties until 2005.

Nasheed will have to do a tightrope walk to balance the interests of the diverse groups that backed his candidature. He will also have to live up to the expectations generated by the campaign slogan of "change".

Nasheed said his main task would be to sell off state trading enterprises, cut down the size of the Cabinet and turn the $62-million presidential palace, which Gayoom built, into the first university of the Maldives. He maintained that he was inheriting a virtually bankrupt nation and would immediately seek international aid of $300 million to stabilise an economy dependent on fisheries and tourism.

Despite being jailed by the Gayoom administration, he said he believed the elder politician might still be able to play a role. Gayoom was born in 1937. He attended Al Azhar University in Cairo, Egypt, and earned degrees in law, education, and Islamic studies. After working as a lecturer in Nigeria, he returned to the Maldives in 1971 and held a number of ministerial and diplomatic posts, including that of the Deputy Ambassador to Sri Lanka and the Ambassador to the United Nations. In 1978, he was elected President following the resignation of Emir Ibrahim Nasir. He was re-elected for the fifth consecutive term in 1998.

Gayoom was the target of coup attempts in 1980, 1983 and 1988. The one in 1988, carried out by mercenary soldiers, was crushed with the help of 1,600 Indian paratroopers. He will be best remembered abroad for his battle against climate change, which he said threatened to wipe the tiny coral islands off the face of the earth. Although he made the Maldives the richest South Asian nation with a per capita income of over $2,200, about 40 per cent of its 300,000 people live on less than a dollar a day.

From *Frontline*, Vol. 25, #23, November 21, 2008. Copyright © 2008 by The Hindu, Kasturi & Sons Ltd. Reprinted by permission.

Fragile Peacemaking Underway as Nepal Ushers in Democracy, Seeks Talks with U.S.

After a decade-long civil war that left about 13,000 people dead ended in 2006, Nepal has reached a milestone in its peace process even though it is being guided by the same man who led the insurgency.

Veronica Zaragovia

Pushpa Kamal Dahal, who goes by the name Prachanda, or "the fierce one" in Nepali, was elected prime minister Aug. 15 after Nepal's constituent assembly ended the Himalayan nation's 239-year-old monarchy and declared the impoverished country a republic.

The assembly has two years to draft a constitution that speaks to the needs of Nepal's multi-ethnic population of more than 29.5 million.

Prachanda made his first trip to the United States for a meeting of the U.N. General Assembly in late September. During a speech on the sidelines of the New York meeting, he said his government would maintain democracy and not nationalize the economy.

"There is serious confusion and misunderstanding about our overall position in terms of economic development," he told the Asia Society think tank, according to Reuters. "We are not fighting against the capitalistic mode of production."

He said his government was committed to the peace process and to democracy, while trying to raise living standards in his impoverished country.

"We are in a democratic phase and we are going to apply the democratic form of government—it is quite clear," said Prachanda, who reportedly faced some tough questions from audience members skeptical of the leadership plans of the former guerrilla leader.

In April, Nepal held an election in which the Maoist-derived Communist Party of Nepal, led by Prachanda, won the largest number of votes and took 220 seats in the 601-member assembly. This election marked the first time Nepal had a mixed electoral system through representation and direct vote.

The Maoist party's victory came as a surprise because of its underground status during the decade-long civil war, during which it didn't participate in the political process and was widely labeled as a guerilla movement.

The Maoists formed a coalition with the CPN-UML, or the Unified Marxist-Leninists, and the Madhesi Janadhikar Forum, which represents the Terai region bordering India. The CPN-UML party took 103 seats and the Madhesi Janadhikar Forum got 52. Members of the CPN-UML didn't attend an Aug. 22 ceremony because of a dispute over the country's deputy prime minister, Bloomberg News reported.

Prachanda named Ram Bahadur, an ex-rebel commander, as minister of defense of his coalition cabinet—giving the Communist Party of Nepal (Maoist) control of the army that Prachanda fought during the civil war.

Prachanda's party is on U.S. terrorism blacklists and he was a wanted guerrilla until the 2006 peace deal that led to his party's election victory this year. The U.S. is reported to have once provided weapons and training to the deposed king's army to wipe out Prachanda and his Maoist guerrillas.

Despite the sanctions, Prachanda was granted permission to visit New York where he attended a gala dinner hosted by President Bush and spoke kindly of the U.S.

"As this is my first visit to the United States of America, I would like to extend my sincere admiration to the spirit of the American dream," he said, likening events in Nepal to the American Revolution.

Prachanda told the Agence France-Presse that he did not broach the embarrassing subject of removing his group from the terrorism blacklists when meeting Mr. Bush, but said he was candid at a later meeting with senior U.S. officials.

"I asked them, 'Tell me why the U.S. leadership has not changed their position and if there is some problem, we are ready to discuss,'" Prachanda said. "Because we came so far in this process and if the U.S. leadership really wants this democracy . . . you should have to rethink about your position as soon as possible. It will be better for both U.S. and Nepal.'"

The embattled nation is fraught with economic challenges, ranking among the world's 50 least-developed nations, according to a United Nations report. Most families survive as subsistence farmers with 24 percent of the population living on less than $1 per day, according to the U.N. World Food Programme. As many as 2.5 million people need food aid because of natural disasters, drought and rising prices.

The economic situation in Nepal spurs many citizens to seek opportunities in other countries.

"Nepal is a poor country, so there's a lot of migration to the Middle East, Malaysia, South Korea and the challenge is to provide jobs, health care, education and a livelihood," said Sanjeev Sherchan, assistant director for South and Central Asia policy programs at the Asia Society in New York.

"Right now, the youth goes to the Middle East, and it's not that they earn so much, but that opportunity doesn't even exist in Nepal, which has an agricultural industry."

The political instability and the decade-long Maoist insurgency also affected the education system. Schools often close down due to frequent strikes and demonstrations, and many Nepalese students seek to further their education in India, the United States and the United Kingdom, said Anup Kaphle, a fellow at the Atlantic Media Company in Washington, D.C.

"It's very important that the new government at least make an attempt to create new opportunities so that the massive brain drain stops immediately," Kaphle continued. "It's important for the country as well as young people to work together in the building of the new republic."

Tourism, once a dominant industry, fell sharply due to the civil war.

"Once the euphoria settles down, the people will have expectations," Sherchan said. "People just want a functioning government that will start the process of drafting a constitution that will address their needs."

Despite the changing tides in the country, Sherchan said Nepal's political situation isn't yet stable.

The president and vice president are from the south of Nepal, which has long cultivated ties to India. Vice President Parmananda Jha took his oath in July in Hindi rather than Nepali, which launched a violent reaction in a country that has long felt overshadowed by its southern neighbor.

A bomb was thrown at his house on Aug. 17, wounding one soldier, according to Al-Jazeera. Although some critics called for his resignation and others demanded that he take the oath again in Nepali, protests subsided after Jha apologized.

Nepalese have long felt India dominates their country, and Jha's action inflamed that sentiment.

"Looking from a small country's lens to India—this is a constant feeling that India is meddling," Sherchan said.

India borders Nepal on three sides and because it is landlocked, Nepal depends on access to Calcutta's port for trade. The border between them is very porous, and no visa or passport is necessary. Additionally, Hindi is the language that unites Nepal's ethnic groups in the south.

Some imports come from China, Nepal's northern neighbor, but the mountainous terrain between them makes India the bigger trade and tourism partner.

"For Nepal to be under India's shadow is not a choice, it's more of a necessity," said Kaphle. "And while Nepalese often feel frustrated that India interferes too much in Nepal's politics, we have to understand that as a landlocked country, we really do not have any choice."

Despite the political upheaval, Nepal's people appear to be giving the new party a chance.

"They had seen the same parties come and go," said Sherchan of the Asia Society. "A coalition government would last nine months, 14 months—there were so many changes and even the king was active in changing prime ministers. The aspirations were not met of ordinary Nepalese."

Even when the coalition would change, the same politicians and senior leaders would remain.

"The Maoists want to include younger faces, people from different ethnic groups, backward classes, women—they gave a sense of inclusiveness which is not the case of previous years," Sherchan said.

Date with Democracy

Interview with Bhojraj Pokharel, Chief Election Commissioner, who is conducting an election that is unique in many ways.

Siddharth Varadarajan

From the absolute monarchy that King Gyanendra was trying to foist on his reluctant "subjects" to the inclusive democracy envisaged by the country's radical new election system, Nepal has come a long way. On April 10, its citizens will elect a Constituent Assembly whose primary task will be to write a new Constitution and oversee governance until the next elections.

If the idea of a Constituent Assembly formed through universal adult franchise is a rarity in the world and unique to South Asia, the system of election is the first one to be designed explicitly to ensure the equitable representation of women and all oppressed and marginalised groups in society.

The Constituent Assembly will have 601 seats, 335 of which will be elected through proportional representation (PR) and 240 through first-past-the-post (FPTP) constituency-level contests. The Prime Minister will nominate an additional 26 members so as to ensure representation to any group that may have been left out, as well as to include jurists, academics and others whose presence might help the process of drafting the Constitution.

The Maoists, whose 10-year-long 'people's war' played a big role in fatally weakening the monarchy, had originally demanded an election system that would be on the basis of proportional representation. But in the face of stiff opposition from the Nepali Congress (N.C.) and the Communist Party of Nepal (Unified Marxist-Leninist) or CPN (UML), the former rebels settled for a mixed system in which only half the seats would be chosen through proportional representation. This forced compromise triggered a protest by the traditionally disenfranchised Madhesis of the Terai region demanding complete proportional representation. In a final compromise, the share of the first-past-the-post seats was cut to 40 per cent.

What makes the election system unique is not just the dual voting system, in which every elector will be given two ballot papers, one to choose the FPTP candidate and the other the party. More revolutionary is the elaborate system of reservation prescribed for the proportional representation list by the election law. In each party's proportional representation list, 50 per cent of the candidates have to be women, 13 per cent

must be Dalits, 31.2 per cent must be Madhesis, 37.8 per cent must be from indigenous/oppressed communities and 4 per cent must be from backward areas. The share of women has to be 50 per cent overall as well as within each group for which reservation is prescribed.

The task of managing the election lies squarely on the shoulders of Bhojraj Pokharel, the widely respected retired civil servant who is the country's Chief Election Commissioner. In an interview at his office in Kathmandu in March, Pokharel spoke about the preparations, the problem of security, and the significance and methodology of the polling process.

Excerpts:

The election is barely days away. How are your preparations going?

Today, we are in the final stages of preparation. All polling stations have been finalised, the required logistics are at the district headquarters and are moving down, and returning officers are in their place. These are the final steps of any election preparation. Total focus is on the booth level, micro-level issues. Side by side, the accreditation of observers, both national and international, is on.

It is said this will be the most observed election in South Asia.

At the national level, 148 agencies have been accreditated. Depending on their capacity, the number of observers they field could be anywhere from two-digit to even five-digit numbers. At the international level, March 20 was the last date for accreditation and 14 or 15 organisations have been registered. All told, we are expecting the total number of international observers to be around 600, while the national observers will be very high, at around 75,000.

What is the role of the United Nations in the elections?

The U.N. role is twofold. First, it [the U.N. Mission in Nepal, or UNMIN] is providing technical assistance to the commission both at the central level and at the regional and district levels. The second is its role in monitoring. Since UNMIN is a partner of the Election Commission, the U.N.

Secretary General has named five independent international figures who will report to him directly on the conduct of the elections.

As the date for the elections draws closer, there are increasing fears about security. Newspapers are full of reports of clashes and abductions. How worried are you about the security situation? Do you think this may compromise the elections?

People should remember that this election is part of the conflict-management and peace-building process here. Post-conflict situations are difficult everywhere, and Nepal is no exception. So we cannot expect 100 per cent normalcy in the country. But if we compare the situation now with that during the preceding weeks and months, one can say the security situation is going in a positive direction. The government has used its total capacity to maintain law and order.

At the same time, the situation is such that even if everything is OK today, nobody knows what will happen tomorrow. So the challenge for Nepal is to maintain the level of security already achieved and focus on troubled areas. In the southern part of Nepal, some armed groups are operating and threatening candidates and voters. Neutralisation of that threat is important to us. Otherwise, in this part of the world elections are difficult even in normal times.

One of the most fascinating aspects of the election is the system of group representation you have built into the proportional representation system. How was this system devised?

At the institutional level, we are a technical agency, and whatever the legislature's thinking is on the design of the elections, we follow. We cannot cross the constitutional limit. However, if you look at the decade-long conflict in Nepal, its main cause was non-inclusion, or exclusion, of people, in addition to economic causes.

During the peace process, our leaders thought the time had come when those sections of the population that did not get attention and justice for centuries—women, Dalits, Janajatis, Madhesis, and so on—should have their share. So the guiding principle came from the Constitution [formulated by the outgoing Parliament].

We have a mixed voting system—a combination of first-past-the-post and proportional representation—and the strategic objectives come from the Constitution itself. So for the FPTP list, it was said that parties should pay heed to inclusion. But for the PR list, there was a specific formula laid down. We prepared the first draft of the election system in consultation with the parties. The present commission played a key role in formulating these drafts but direct credit has to go to Parliament and its leaders. We were the technical agency but the overall spirit of what our leaders wanted was to make the system inclusive.

Many of the parties are said to have had a tough time nominating the required number of women as well as Dalits and others. In India, some of the political parties have played the principle of reservation for women against that of reservation for Dalits and backward castes, to the detriment of women, but Nepal has hit upon a unique system.

The election legislation is very complicated and its management is not easy. To choose candidates in normal times is difficult for most parties, so now you can imagine how difficult this election is for them. It was difficult for most parties even to produce their lists of names.

Once you talk about having x per cent and if a party is contesting a small number of seats, this small number also has to be apportioned on the principle of inclusion. So you can see how difficult things were. But even if implementation is difficult, the spirit has ensured representation.

The parties are required by law to send 50 per cent women; for example, 13 per cent Dalits, and 50 per cent must be women from that group. The essence of our electoral policy is to give proper representation to oppressed groups on the basis of their share in the population. And half of them must be women, as must half of all MPs elected by PR.

With such a complex system, how confident are you that the electorate will understand fully how things work? Is there adequate information being provided?

True, there is a lot of information involved, but who needs what level of information is critical. Voters should know why they are participating, how they can participate and use their voting right.

However, in our social context, even if we try and push, we cannot explain the whole process to everyone. So our voters' education programme is designed to give the minimum package of information that can be digested and used so that the ballot is not invalidated.

We are using radio and TV, and male and female volunteer-schoolteachers are making door-to-door visits with election kits. Today, 95,000 volunteers are in the field and our aim is to visit all households in the country.

There have been allegations that some parties, especially the Maoists, have fielded "dummy candidates" in order to be able to use more vehicles and have more sympathetic observers in polling stations. What is the truth of the matter?

Officially, we have not received any complaint of any party fielding dummy candidates. Every citizen has the right to stand. How can we question their intention?

There have also been allegations of misuse of state machinery by Ministers.

Generally, in our part of the world, governments in power have a tendency to use public property [for their campaigns]. This is the general trend we have observed in the past. And we are watching.

The N.C. and the UML say the state media are biased against them because the Information Minister is a Maoist. And

the Maoists say the private media are biased against them. How do you deal with such charges?

We receive complaints that the state media are biased and we have asked them to be neutral. We also convened a meeting of the private media and asked them to report in a balanced manner. But reporters say: There are 54 political parties. Some have bigger programmes than others. How can we treat all of them in the same way? These are some of the difficulties editors and reporters mentioned. For the Election Commission, of course, all parties are equal.

How quickly will the results of the elections be known? There are apprehensions about what might happen if there is a long delay, especially between the announcement of the results of the FPTP vote—which tends to favour well-established parties—and of the PR seats.

Managing the election and the post-election situation is equally important to us. Once the ballot boxes are collected in the district headquarters, our policy is to count both the FPTP and PR ballots simultaneously wherever this is physically possible. But there could be space limitations in some places. If it is not possible to count both ballots together, our policy is to first count the FPTP ballots, announce the results, and then count the PR ballots.

So there will be a gap between the announcement of the FPTP and PR results. In fact, it will probably take eight to 10 days to give the full results of the FPTP seats. Of course, in the majority of districts, the PR ballots will also have been counted. And our policy will be for the counting centres to announce result updates every two hours, including PR.

But the PR results will have to be centrally tabulated here to decide which parties will have how many of the 335 PR seats. And to identify the winning candidates on the PR side will again take time. Parties will have seven days to finalise their list and we will have to again verify that they have met the legally prescribed percentages in terms of women, Madhesis, and so on. So, even if we know the party distribution, the identity of the winning candidates on the PR side will take time.

Maoists Lose Religion Battle in Nepal

SUDESHNA SARKAR

Nepal's former Maoist guerrillas, who had fought successfully against the state army in the past and brought about the end of the Shah dynasty, were forced to bite the dust before the powerful Newar community of Kathmandu valley and pledge not to interfere with traditional religious festivals.

The once armed Maoist party, which also abolished Hinduism as the state religion and transformed the Himalayan kingdom into a secular republic, had to Sunday backtrack on an ambitious budget that sought to usher in an economic revolution and cut down on religious allocations allotted by the Hindu governments in the past.

Maoist deputy chief and Finance Minister Baburam Bhattarai's Nepali Rs.236 billion ($3.7 billion) budget tabled in the interim parliament Friday had sought to implement austerity measures by stopping the allocations earlier made for religious festivals, most of which ended with animal sacrifices.

Unfortunately for the new Maoist government, the new budget came at a time the Newars—a community who were the original inhabitants of Kathmandu and still dominate Nepal's business and industrial sector—were celebrating their annual Indrajatra festival that honours the rain god and is attended by the head of state.

The slashing of funds for the festival triggered a two-day uproar that saw chaos in pockets of the capital with hundreds of baton-wielding protesters forcing shops to down shutters and transport to vanish.

"The protests will continue till we get a public apology from the finance minister," said Ananda Shrestha, a 30-year-old Newar who took part in the protests in the posh Durbar Marg area of the capital. "We regard the curtailment of the budget an attack on our culture and religion."

The dispute gathered heat with Newar MPs from the opposition Nepali Congress party as well as other non-Newar lawmakers from other parties flaying the move in the interim parliament Sunday.

Newars, who had voted for Maoist chief Pushpa Kamal Dahal Prachanda in the April election, warned that the mistake could cost the party dear in the next election. "If the elections were held today, even the prime minister would be likely to be defeated," said Adarsha Tuladhar, a member of the outraged community.

Veteran columnist Shyam K.C. Monday asked the government to begin austerity measures at home—with the ministers.

"The PM, just over a month after assuming office, has gone on three foreign outings, none of which were really necessary," K.C. wrote in his weekly column in the Kathmandu Post daily. "Does anyone know how much it cost the country to send the PM on his journeys even as parts of the country burn?"

In the beginning, the government tried to suppress the protests by deploying riot police. However, after the situation started going out of control, the finance minister was forced to open negotiations with the protesters which ended in a five-point agreement late Sunday night.

The blockade of key roads in the capital was lifted Monday after the Maoist-led government agreed to restore the slashed allocations, pay for the medical treatment of the protesters hurt in clashes with security forces and form a commission to study the socio-religious traditions prevalent for centuries and recommend within a month what to do about them.

The protests indicate Nepal still remains deeply religious and other plans of the Maoists, especially ambitious ones like scrapping the Kumari or living goddess system, are now likely to be quietly abandoned.

Pakistan Democracy: An Interview with Husain Haqqani

Pakistan's new democracy tackles complex domestic and foreign policy problems, sharing goals with the US and India.

Nayan Chanda

Nayan Chanda: Ambassador Husain Haqqani of Pakistan to the United States, Welcome to Yale. Husain Haqqani has been a very, very well known figure in Pakistan. He has worked for three prime ministers, and he has been at the Carnegie Endowment for International Peace and at Boston University, and now he's the ambassador.

Let me ask you first, having served three prime ministers, and with all the experience you have, how do you see the sixth experiment with democracy in Pakistan? How has it started off? How do you see the prospect—is the sixth time lucky?

Husain Haqqani: Well, Nayan, I think that the reason why Pakistan has not been able to build a democracy in the past is because of the invasions of its civil military elites. And I think this time around the international factors, the local factors, and even the perception of the elites in Pakistan is very different. If you go back in history, you will notice that Pakistan's first military coup was within 10 years of independence, primarily because the civil military elite felt that the complications of working out a democracy were not worth it, that nation-building could be more easily done under an authoritarian regime. That delusion lasted for quite a while, but it ended and we had our first elected civilian government in the 70's. After that, General [Mohammad] Zia ul-Haq entered the process, and his argument was that Pakistan needed to be an ideological state.

Now both of those arguments, that nation-building is better under authoritarianism, and that Pakistan is better off as an ideological state defined by a small group of theocrats or theocratically inclined elites, have both been proven to be mistakes. The third attempt at military intervention—serious attempt—was under General Musharraf, and he represented the notion that Pakistan can be better run by a technocratic elite. And we have seen that dream in tatters as well now. I see no argument in favor of authoritarianism left in Pakistan. Yes, there are some people who still say that we have to be an

ideological state, that we can be much better accomplished under a benevolent dictator, yes, there are a few people who still say that maybe the government should be run by technocrats and not by politicians. But there is great consensus in Pakistan that to forge a Pakistani national identity, all Pakistani provinces, all Pakistani ethnic groups, need to feel that they are part of Pakistan, and the only way they will feel a part of Pakistan is through an elected democratic process. Second, the technocrats also sometimes get purely technocratic decisions right, but they are unable to bring the nation together. And lastly, when it comes to the external factors, when General Zia ul-Haq became Pakistan's president in a military uniform, many countries in the world had military governments. When Musharraf became Pakistan's ruler, he was one of two or three.

So now the international momentum is also against military dominated governments. I think all those factors have come together, but most important is the fact that this time the restoration of democracy has come at a very high price. We lost Benazir Bhutto who was much beloved, and in her assassination—it's very interesting,that Gallup did polling after that and showed that there has never been such unanimity in Pakistan in public opinion on grief. When her father was assassinated, some people didn't mind it. When General Zia-ul-Haq died, Pakistani society was divided between those who were fond of him and those who hated him. In Benazir Bhutto's assassination, it was as if a national dream had been killed. And most political leaders in Pakistan are reconciled to the fact that, yes, we will disagree with one another, but we will never help another military coup. So I think this time, there are many factors that will strengthen Pakistan's evolution as a democracy.

Chanda: Yes, I think the question really is whether the army is reconciled to the loss of its authority that they exercised through Musharraf, and also their plans to sell the land it owns to build its general headquarters. The question is, does the army have the right to sell the state land to build its own headquarters? That is one small example of the army acting as a state within a state.

Haqqani: Look, let us go to the more fundamental question. Pakistan needs a military. But what Pakistan needs is for its military to work under civilian authority, constitutional authority. I think that the new army chief and most of his close commanders all realize that the army's professionalism suffered immensely with the army being drawn into politics. Will this transition be instantaneous? No, it won't. But the army has been brought into many things and it will take some time to get out of them. But the important things that have already started happening: The Army Chief General Ashfaq Parvez Kayani has already withdrawn all those serving military officers who were filling up civilian positions in government—a big change. The interservices intelligence has shut down its political wing—a major thing, because that was the instrument of intervention in politics. The army didn't play any role in trying to influence the outcome of the February 18th elections, or of the political process subsequent to that. Because they didn't do anything to influence the choice of prime minister, they did nothing to influence the choice of president, and the electoral processes had been taking on their own dynamic. And I think that the things that you're talking about—about the military's having welfare schemes with economic dimensions, etc., I think we will be able to rationalize those over time as well.

Chanda: The other question that has been raised is that General Musharraf is gone, but it looks like the current government is pursuing the same policies, whether it's the question of the war on terror or the question of privatizing state organizations and even raising the price of utilities as has been pressed on by the nation's financial institutions. In all of these policies, the Asif Ali Zardari government seems to be pursuing Musharraf's policies. Is there any change?

Haqqani: That [Asif] Ali Zardari government represents what is essentially a national consensus on issues such as privatization. Whether Nawaz Sharif was in power, whether General Musharraf was in power, or the new elected government, even the previous PPP government led by Benazir Bhutto—none of them could do without privatization, for the simple reason that Pakistan has just too many state-owned enterprises that are not sufficiently efficient, and it is much easier for them to be sold off and their value recovered for the benefit of Pakistan's economy. So privatization falls in that category. Similarly, the question of raising prices of utilities—again, basically, it's a question of market prices. Oil prices have gone up. The government has to pay for the oil to buy it from the Gulf. And that oil is then sold to the utilities, and after all that has to be recovered . . . So that is also another category: It is not Musharraf's policy, it's the global market's policy. The only thing that is left is the war on terror, and here, the big difference. Musharraf says we are fighting the war on terror because America told us to do so. This government says that we have to fight terrorism because terrorism is a

threat to Pakistan. I think that while the conduct of the war is going on, the fact of the matter is that the war's aims have changed very seriously. The aim of General Musharraf was to please the United States. The aim of the elected government is to work with the United States and other allies to ensure Pakistan's own safety and security, and to make sure that Pakistan is not seen as or becomes a safe haven or a base for extremist groups all over the world. So I think that the change of the objective actually makes the policy very different.

Chanda: There is a very significant change in the US approach to Pakistan, with the July signing of President Bush's secret national security directive in which he authorized the military to intervene in Pakistan without prior notification, and the result of which was the first attack on Pakistani territory on September 3rd. This is a change that follows the departure of Musharraf. The question is, is the new policy designed to put pressure on the civilian government, or is it just because the US elections are approaching and you needed to do something against terrorism in a more demonstrative way? What was the purpose?

Haqqani: First, if the directive was signed, as you said, in July, then Musharraf was still there, so it wasn't post-Musharraf. And I don't know if the directive has been signed. If it is a secret directive, the US government, I'm sure, can keep secrets even though they don't seem to keep them from the New York Times. But, let me just say that the operation that the US forces conducted on September 3 was a mistake. It achieved no war aim, they did not get any terrorists or militants, they did not manage to kill Al Qaeda leaders or the Taliban, and it only served to enrage the Pakistani public. Since then, we have engaged with US officials. We understand political complications, we come from political backgrounds ourselves, President Zardari is a politician, he understands politics. The two parties are engaged in an election campaign—the November elections are coming and people are asking, what happened, did we succeed in getting Osama bin Laden, and if not, why not? So therefore, in the context of the campaign, it makes sense for some people, but there's another dimension to it also. There are American troops in Afghanistan and they are in harm's way and they are attacked. And when they are attacked and they ask their Afghan counterparts, why are we under attack, what's happening, and they are told that some of these Taliban and these Al Qaeda people are coming from Pakistan, then they feel all the more reason to want to do something about it. But all wars require intelligent actions, not just actions. And the intelligent thing to do is to let Pakistan take care of the Pakistani side of the border because if it escalates, if American troops get inducted, they will have another theater of war without necessarily having any war aims being fulfilled. We have spoken to the Americans about this. They now understand that if Pakistan is willing to step up to the plate—which it is, Pakistan wants to step up action on its side of the border. We have paid a dear price, even in the past, even under Musharraf: Hundreds of Pakistanis were killed—Pakistani soldiers were killed. But the problem was that these soldiers were sent in to battle the Taliban without adequate counter-insurgency training. The elected government has asked the United States to help us get that counter-insurgency training. We have asked the US to provide us the equipment that is needed for this kind of warfare, You see, Pakistani soldiers have been trained to fight a different kind of war on a different border. This is different terrain, so we need different types of trained soldiers. The mistake under Musharraf was that the training was not there, the equipment was not there, and the soldiers were sent in large numbers. We sacrificed many lives in the process. Now, we are going to have an intelligent war. Now, I don't know if you've noticed, in the last two to three weeks, in Bajul, Pakistan has conducted a very methodical operation. From the . . .

Chanda: In the Northwest frontier . . .

Haqqani: "From the Northwest frontier, bordering Afghanistan, bordering the Kunar province, air power has been deployed. And, because it has been a methodical operation, several hundred militants and Taliban have been killed, and they are feeling the pressure, which is why they are attacking Pakistani cities again. We will have to bear that fear, and we will have to do something about protecting our cities against the suicide bombers as well. But, as President Zardari and Prime Minister [Yousuf Raza] Gilani repeatedly say: "This is Pakistan's war. We have to save Pakistan from becoming a Taliban home. The Taliban's vision is not our vision. The Taliban don't want young women to ever receive an education. The have been blowing up schools in Pakistan. And more Pakistanis have been killed by suicide bombers than Americans have been killed, so we don't look at this as an American war that we have to fight to please America. We are fighting for our own nation, for our own future, and I think as long as the Americans understand that, and not withstanding any specific directive or not, the American forces will stay on the Afghan side of the border, and Afghanistan, Pakistan, the US and NATO will work cooperatively to make sure that terrorists are denied the opportunity to organize and raise attacks on both sides of the Pakistan-Afghan border.

Chanda: You have mentioned in some other occasions that President Musharraf carried the policy of "running with the hare, hunting with the hound," in terms of dealing with terrorism. Why was that? Why did he have this two-faced policy on terrorism?

Haqqani: Well, I think it wasn't a two-faced policy in his perspective, what he was doing was . . . First of all you must understand that before 9/11 he didn't see terrorism as a menace in itself which is very different from Benazir Bhutto and Mr. Zardari, who have always seen terrorism as a threat because they don't intellectually agree with it. General Musharraf thought this is just sub-conventional warfare and it gives some leverage in regional politics. So that was the point of view. And after 9/11, it was very difficult for him to make the major change. He made medium- to short-term changes. He understood that you have to forsake the Taliban, and that you have to curtail the operational militant groups on the other side as well. But having said that, from day one, I don't know if you can recall, there are many interviews of his, there was a time when he used to argue that the Taliban and Al-Qaeda need to be treated differently. Then he started saying Afghan Taliban and Pakistani Taliban need to be. He just never made the transition from thinking of these people as elements of a regional strategic problem, a regional strategic design, to thinking that they are a problem. And I think that now . . .

Chanda: So they were pawns that he could play?

Haqqani: He thought that they were pawns that he could play. Even after attempts on his life, he only thought about "okay, the groups that are responsible for trying kill me, we need to go after them. He didn't understand that what needs to be eliminated is the whole idea that somehow blowing yourself up for a cause is a good thing, because very frankly, irrespective of the objective, terrorism is a nuisance, and a problem, and a threat. It is all of those things, and it's a menace. Terrorism needs to be eliminated because it is a threat, not because "Terrorist A" is okay, but "Terrorist B" is good. There are no "good" terrorists and "bad" terrorists. And I think the Pakistani military leadership and the Pakistani civilian leadership that have been elected in February of this year understand that.

Chanda: There have been considerable improvements, at least in appearance, in relations between Pakistan and Afghanistan. President [Hamid] Karzai and President Zardari seem to get along well. Now, has there been any progress on the investigation that General Kayani said he was launching on the allegation, by the United States and by India, that ISI was involved in the bombing of the Indian embassy in Kabul?

Haqqani: I think that we are working on finding out the bombing of the Indian Embassy in Kabul. We will have more details at some point in the future, but as of now we do understand that there was no conscious decision on the part of any Pakistani organization to be part of it. This was a terrorist act, and if those terrorists are in any part of Pakistan including the travel areas, the Pakistani government will definitely act against them. The important thing is that President Zardari has articulated a vision. His vision is one of close ties with Afghanistan and friendship with India. While we have disagreements with India, while we have the outstanding disputes of Jammu and Kashmir, we would still want to normalize relations with them because, again, it is more important to move forward and to have less pressures on Pakistan from the external side. And India and Pakistan together can have many economic benefits for each other. Afghanistan and Pakistan together can definitely strengthen each other as nations. And we have historic relations. Let us be honest: India and Pakistan have 5,000 years of common history, and 60 years of partition. Afghanistan and Pakistan have hundreds of years of common history. So there's no reason why we should be stuck in adversarial mode and not find commonalities on which we can work together. That said, we will occasionally disagree. President Karzai and President Zardari will also disagree. Prime Minister Manmohan Singh and President Zardari will disagree. But there has to be a fundamental difference in approaching each other as permanent enemies or looking upon each other as neighbors who can deal with issues on an issue-by-issue basis.

Chanda: On Kashmir. What's the position of President Zardari and Prime Minister Gilani as to move forward again on Kashmir, which has been . . . ?

Haqqani: Well, I think India and Pakistan both have to find creative solutions to the Kashmir problem. There are strong emotions in Pakistan on the Kashmir issue. I'm sure there are strong views in India on the Kashmir issue. And then the people of Kashmir, they have a position and their point of view needs to be heard. They need to be part of the solution. The important thing is that the bilateral engagement of India and Pakistan should not be stopped because we are not making progress on the issue of Jammu and Kashmir. But the issue of Jammu and Kashmir should not be ignored, so we have to find ways of engaging, and at the same time finding solutions to this dispute that has bedeviled relationships between our two countries. The difference is that there are people in Pakistan who have argued that if we cannot have a solution to Kashmir, we needn't have forward movement with India. I think that we can continue to engage and, at the same time, look for a solution. I, personally, do not have a solution to offer right now.

Chanda: But, in terms of engaging, what are the areas you think Pakistan and India could engage? And, the impact of their engagement, would it be positive on other issues?

Haqqani: Let me just say that we need to have a very sensible approach to resolving the Siachen Glacier dispute. Both sides lose more people to frostbite in those glaciers than in actual fighting. So it's in the interest of both sides to try and find a solution to that. The solution is almost there—it's a question of signing it and moving on. The Sir Creek issue, that's also something that can be resolved.

Chanda: This is on the border, near Sind?

Haqqani: Basically, it's a demarcation issue. My point is: Reduce the portfolio of disputes. Third, move forward on bilateral trade. Open up trade more. People-to-people contacts. We need to expand to range of contacts between the two people. Whenever Indians and Pakistanis meet, whether its over a curry or over a cricket match, or over a Masala movie, they always manage to be able to talk to each other in a much more friendly way than they can when they are just dealing with politics. So I think that people-to-people contacts need to be expanded. In terms of trade, we must understand that once the Indian markets open for Pakistani products, Pakistan gets access to a 1 billion strong market. And so there are opportunities for Pakistan. There are synergies between our two countries. Above all, Pakistan is the energy corridor for India. If there is an Iran-India pipeline, it will have to go through Pakistan. If there's a Turkmenistan-India pipeline it will have to go through Afghanistan and Pakistan. If there's a pipeline from the Gulf, it will have to go through Pakistan. So, all of those things are the basis from which we can hopefully open up our relationship and have less issues of hostility and more basis for cooperation.

Chanda: Final question, coming back to the United States. The presidential debate was yesterday. A lot of focus on foreign affairs was devoted to your country. How do you think that these two presidential candidates, their vision of Pakistan and how to deal with the problem, how do you see that?

Haqqani: I think that it would not be appropriate of me to insert myself into the American political debate, but let me say one thing: As ambassador, I am personally engaged with both campaigns. The advisors that Senator Obama and Senator McCain have, both of them have listened to our point of view. We have listened to theirs. Pakistan is important for the next president, whoever he may be. Pakistan is important for the United States. While we are not completely happy with the tone of the conversation about Pakistan these days, it's important that for the first time Pakistan is receiving the attention that it deserves. Now you and I have known each other for many years. Pakistan has always been seen in the context of India-Pakistan relations or due to the Soviet war in the context of the war against the Soviets in Afghanistan or in the context of the war against terrorism. It's about time that the US paid attention to Pakistan in its own right, a nation of 160 million people with a very strong army and nuclear weapons, with the potential for being a moderate, democratic, tolerant, pluralist state while at the same time having the threat of terrorism and militancy. Senator Joseph Biden is the author of a bill called the Biden-Luger Bill, which expects to triple civilian economic aid to Pakistan to $1.5 billion every year for five years and possibly for 10 years as a long-term engagement with Pakistan so that Pakistanis know that the United States is a friend of Pakistan. I think it's time for Pakistan and the United States to move away from their short-term, quid pro quo engagements, and develop a strategic partnership for peace in that region and for consolidation of Pakistani democracy and strengthening of Pakistani democracy. And, I think that while there will be disagreements between candidates on how to do that, I think that the important thing is that both presidential candidates in the United States understand the importance of Pakistan and they also understand that for stability in Pakistan, there must be democracy, and that Pakistan's stability is important to American security.

Chanda: With that, Ambassador Haqqani, thank you very much.

Haqqani: Pleasure talking to you.

Pakistan's New Generation of Terrorists

JAYSHREE BAJORIA

Introduction

Pakistani authorities have long had ties to militant groups based on their soil. They have supported some organizations fighting Indian forces in Kashmir and played a pivotal role in supporting the Afghan resistance against the Soviets throughout the 1980s. In the 1990s, Pakistan's government supported the Taliban's rise in Afghanistan in the hope of having a friendly government in Kabul. But with Pakistan joining the United States as an ally in its war against Islamic extremists since 9/11, experts say Islamabad has seen harsh blowback on its policy of backing militants operating abroad. Leadership elements of al-Qaeda and the Afghan Taliban, along with other terrorist groups, have made Pakistan's tribal areas (the semi-autonomous region along the Afghan border) their home. Pakistan's deployment of troops in the tribal areas has generated resentment among tribal leaders and others who sympathized with the Taliban. In recent years, many new terrorist groups have emerged in Pakistan, several existing groups have reconstituted themselves, and a new crop of militants have taken control, more violent and less conducive to political solutions than their predecessors.

Terrorist Groups

Many experts say it is difficult to determine how many terrorist groups are operating out of Pakistan. Most of these groups tend to fall into one of the five distinct categories laid out by Ashley J. Tellis, a senior associate at Carnegie Endowment for International Peace, in January 16, 2008, testimony (PDF) before a U.S. House Foreign Affairs subcommittee:

- **Sectarian:** Groups such as the Sunni Sipah-e-Sahaba and the Shia Tehrik-e-Jafria, which are engaged in violence within Pakistan;
- **Anti-Indian:** Terrorist groups that operate with the alleged support of the Pakistani military and the intelligence agency Inter-Services Intelligence (ISI), such as the Lashkar-e-Taiba (LeT), the Jaish-e-Muhammad (JeM), and the Harakat ul-Mujahedeen (HuM). This Backgrounder profiles these organizations which have been active in Kashmir;
- **Afghan Taliban:** The original Taliban movement and especially its Kandahari leadership centered around Mullah Mohammad Omar, believed to be now living in Quetta;
- **Al-Qaeda and its affiliates:** The organization led by Osama bin Laden and other non-South Asian terrorists believed to be ensconced in the Federally Administered Tribal Areas (FATA). Rohan Gunaratna of the International Centre for Political Violence and Terrorism Research in Singapore says other foreign militant groups such as the Islamic Movement of Uzbekistan, Islamic Jihad group, the Libyan Islamic Fighters Group and the Eastern Turkistan Islamic Movement are also located in FATA;
- **The Pakistani "Taliban":** Groups consisting of extremist outfits in the FATA, led by individuals such as Baitullah Mehsud, the chieftain of the Mehsud tribe in South Waziristan, Maulana Faqir Muhammad and Maulana Qazi Fazlullah of the Tehrik-e-Nafaz-e-Shariat-e-Mohammadi (TSNM), and Mangal Bagh Afridi of the Lashkar-e-Islami in the Khyber Agency.

The Pakistani Taliban

Supporters of the Afghan Taliban in the tribal areas transitioned into a mainstream Taliban force of their own as a reaction to the Pakistani army's incursion into the tribal areas, which began in 2002, to hunt down the militants. This Pakistani Taliban is organizationally distinct from the Afghan Taliban. Gunaratna says it is clear that Afghan Taliban only fights in Afghanistan, emphasizing it is the Pakistani Taliban that is operating in Pakistan against the state. Analysts say it is this arrangement with the Pakistani authorities that keeps members of the Afghan Taliban safe from arrest or transfer to U.S. or NATO forces based in Afghanistan. But Pakistani authorities have repeatedly denied any involvement with the Taliban and have often said the problem lies within Afghanistan, saying Taliban sympathizers from Afghanistan slip across the border to recruit in refugee camps in Pakistan.

Experts say most adult men in Pakistan's tribal areas grew up carrying arms but it is only in the last few years that they have begun to organize themselves around a Taliban-style Islamic ideology pursuing an agenda much similar to that of the Afghan Taliban in Afghanistan. The people of Pakistan's North West Frontier Province (NWFP) and FATA, as well as the adjacent eastern regions of Afghanistan, are overwhelmingly Pashtun and share ethnic and linguistic links. Hassan Abbas, a research fellow at Harvard University's Kennedy School of Government, writes (PDF) in a January 2008 paper that the Pakistani Taliban have effectively established themselves as an alternative to the traditional tribal elders. Abbas adds that the Taliban killed approximately 200 of the tribal leaders and these indigenous Taliban groups coalesced in December 2007 under the umbrella of Tehrik-i-Taliban Pakistan (TTP). He writes that a *shura* (consultative council) of more than 40 senior Taliban leaders established the TTP under the militant commander Baitullah Mehsud from South Waziristan.

TTP not only has representation from all of FATA's seven agencies (please refer to this interactive map of the area) but also from several settled districts of the NWFP. According to some estimates, the Pakistani Taliban collectively have around 30,000 to 35,000 members. Among their other objectives, the TTP has announced a defensive jihad against the Pakistani army, enforcement of sharia, and a plan to unite against NATO forces in Afghanistan. Pakistani authorities accused the group's leader, Mehsud, of assassinating former Prime Minister Benazir Bhutto in December 2007.

Analysts say it may be too early to say how successful the TTP will be in unifying the disparate militant groups across diverse tribal regions, or how loyal the tribes will be to Mehsud's leadership.

Changing Face of Terrorism

The new Taliban are fiercer, younger and impatient for results, say experts. Steve Coll, president of the New America Foundation, a Washington-based think tank, tells CFR.org the Afghan-oriented Taliban of the 1990s had a sort of a political cover in Pakistan. But what's happening now, he says, is that those traditional intermediaries between the Taliban and the establishment are being displaced by "a younger generation of more violent radical leaders who are in a hurry and have no patience with compromise with the state." Coll adds: "These are like hard-core breakaway children militias of the sort you encounter in failed states in Africa and elsewhere," running roadblocks, moving around in bands on highways in the tribal areas, and operating under some notion of political control under this Tehrik-i-Taliban set-up. "But they are the law and that is real change."

> **"Pakistani Taliban are a younger generation of more violent radical leaders who are in a hurry and have no patience with compromise with the state."**
>
> —Steve Coll

This new generation of terrorists is also more willing to engage in suicide attacks; there were more than fifty in 2007, compared to no more than twenty between 2001 and 2007. Gunaratna attributes this to the influence of al-Qaeda. He says

bin Laden's group is training most of the terrorist groups in FATA. "Al-Qaeda considers itself as the vanguard of the Islamic movement," Gunaratna says, and has introduced its practice of suicide bombings to both the Afghan and the Pakistani Taliban.

Pakistan's tribal areas are also experiencing growing extremism. Like their Taliban predecessors in Afghanistan, the younger militants consider music, TV, and luxuries like massage parlors un-Islamic and wage war against them. Local Taliban leaders in the tribal agencies tell men to keep beards and women to wear the veil. In a January 2008 article in the *New York Times* magazine, writer Nicholas Schmidle quotes Maulana Fazlur Rehman, chief of Jamiat Ulema-e-Islam (F), a pro-Taliban religious party: "When the jihad in Afghanistan started, the maliks [tribal leaders] and the old tribal system in Afghanistan ended; a new leadership arose, based on jihad. Similar is the case here in the tribal areas."

Terrorist Breeding Ground

Pakistan's tribal areas, which have long been torn by ethnic and tribal rivalries, became radicalized during the 1980s when the Pakistani state supported the Afghan jihad against the Soviets. To escape the post-9/11 U.S.-led war in Afghanistan, most militants, including those in al-Qaeda, fled eastwards into western Pakistan, further destabilizing the tribal areas. Having served as the logistical route for weapons to the mujahideen, experts say, the area is awash with small weapons and the current population of more than a million men under the age of twenty-five grew up carrying weapons. As this backgrounder on the troubled Pakistan-Afghanistan border explains, the tribal areas also became critical to the illicit drug trade and criminalized economies of the region. Counter-terrorism experts say these traditional smuggling and criminal activities continue to fund the militants.

Pakistan's tribal region is governed under the colonial-era Frontier Crimes Regulations (FCR) Act by a political agent in each of the seven tribal agencies. Experts say the tribes have long struggled with each other over economic or territorial issues. Coll says what has happened in FATA during the last twenty years is "almost like painting a coat of Islamist radicalization over this complicated structure of smuggling and competition" among the tribes. He says "by painting this coat of Islamist ideology over certain areas of FATA, it's changed the dynamic of competition in ways that are really complicated and very hard for us to understand on the outside."

Counterterrorism Challenges

Pakistani authorities are struggling to confront the changing dynamics in the region. There is growing criticism both within and outside Pakistan that the army does not have the capacity to fight insurgency within its borders. Militants increasingly target the army with suicide attacks and in August 2007, the kidnapping of around 250 soldiers by Baitullah Mehsud in FATA's South Waziristan posed a huge embarrassment for Pakistan. These soldiers were only released when the government released twenty-five militants associated with Mehsud. The army faces a tough fight not only in the tribal areas but increasingly the settled areas of NWFP, which are being targeted by militants. In 2007, the militant group TSNM led by Maulana Fazlullah took control of large areas in the Swat valley, previously a tourist destination. The army, after a long fight, reclaimed it but experts say hundreds of militants continue to operate there.

Coll questions the will of the Pakistani military to confront the new Taliban groups. He writes in the *New Yorker* that there was evidence to suggest that "some current and former Pakistani military and intelligence officers sympathize with the Islamist insurgents with whom they are notionally at war." U.S. officials have made similar allegations but Pakistani officials have pointed to the death of about a thousand Pakistani soldiers fighting the war on terror and several attempts made by the militants on President Musharraf's life as proof that such allegations are not true.

One approach taken by Islamabad is to deploy the Frontier Corps, Pakistan's paramilitary organization that operates in the FATA and has played an important part because of their local language skills and familiarity with the local terrain. But numerous defections and refusals to fight and follow orders have taken place within the Frontier Corps. Rand Corporation expert Christine C. Fair, in January 2008 testimony to a U.S. House Foreign Affairs subcommittee, says while its officers are seconded from the Pakistan army, its cadres are drawn from the local Pashtun population. According to Fair, the Corps is "inadequately trained and equipped and has been ill-prepared for counter-insurgency operations in FATA." Fair also says the Corps "was used to train the Taliban in the 1990s and many are suspected of having ties to that organization." Yet many experts believe that Frontier Corps has a much better chance than the Pakistani army in securing the tribal areas. Washington plans a significant increase in current military assistance to the Frontier Corps. Its effort to secure the tribal belt includes a proposal by U.S. Special Operations Command to train and arm tribal leaders to fight al-Qaeda and Taliban and a $750 million aid package for the border area over the next five years.

Another approach taken by the Pakistani government in the tribal areas was to sign some peace agreements with the tribal leaders but most of them have failed so far and critics, including many in Washington, said they only ended up strengthening the militants. In January 2008, news reports saying the United States was considering sending U.S. troops to Pakistan's tribal areas drew angry reactions from Pakistani authorities and analysts said it would further destabilize the country. Imran Khan, chairman of the opposition party Tehreek-e-Insaf in Pakistan, says political negotiations are the only way to deal with terrorism.

Gunaratna, too, says a military solution is not the answer. A "strategy to manage the threat of terrorism is to co-opt the groups that are in the margins, in the periphery," he says, "and draw them to mainstream politics to create opportunities for them."

Pakistan Reborn?

Confounding all predictions, the Pakistani people have clearly demonstrated that they want to choose their own rulers and decide their own future. There is a consensus from Lahore to Karachi.

WILLIAM DALRYMPLE

It has not been a good year for Pakistan. President Musharraf's sacking of the chief justice last spring, the lawyers' protests that rumbled on throughout the summer and the bloody storming of the Red Mosque in June, followed by a wave of hideous suicide bombings, all gave the impression of a country stumbling from bloody crisis to bloody crisis. By the autumn it had grown even worse. The military defeats suffered by the Pakistani army at the hands of pro-Taliban rebels in Waziristan, the declaration of a state of emergency and, finally, the assassination of Benazir Bhutto led many to predict that Pakistan was stumbling towards full-scale civil war and possibly even disintegration.

All this has of course been grist for the mill for the Pakistan-bashers. Martin Amis, typical of the current rash of instant experts on Islam, wrote recently: "We may wonder how the Islamists feel when they compare India to Pakistan, one a burgeoning democratic superpower, the other barely distinguishable from a failed state." In the run-up to the elections, the *Washington Post,* among many other commentators, was predicting that the poll would lead to a major international crisis.

That the election went ahead with no more violence and ballot-rigging than is considered customary in south Asian polls, and that a new government will apparently come to power peacefully, unopposed by Musharraf or the army, should now give pause for thought and a calmer reassessment of the country that many have long written off as a basket case.

Certainly, there is no question that during the past few years, and more pressingly since the death of Benazir Bhutto on 27 December last year, Pakistan has been struggling with an existential crisis. At the heart of this lay the central question: what sort of country did Pakistanis want? Did they want a western-style liberal democracy, as envisaged by Pakistan's founder, Muhammad Ali Jinnah? An Islamic republic like Mullah Omar's Afghanistan? Or a military-ruled junta of the sort created by Generals Ayub Khan, Zia and Musharraf, and which has ruled Pakistan for 34 of its 60 years of existence?

That question now seems to have been resolved, at least temporarily. Like most other people given the option, Pakistanis clearly want the ability to choose their own rulers, and to determine their own future. The country I saw over the past few days on a long road trip from Lahore in the Punjab down through rural Sindh to Karachi was not a failed state, nor anything even approaching the "most dangerous country in the world".

It is true that frequent shortages of electricity made the country feel a bit like Britain during the winter of discontent, and I was told at one point that I should not continue along certain roads near the Bhutto stronghold of Larkana as there were dacoits (highwaymen) ambushing people after dark. But by and large, the countryside I passed through was calm, and not obviously less prosperous-looking than its subcontinental neighbour. It was certainly a far cry from the terminal lawlessness and instability of post-occupation Iraq or Afghanistan.

The infrastructure of the country is still in many ways better than that of India, and Pakistan still has the best airports and road network in the region. As for the economy, it may be in difficulties, with fast-rising inflation and shortages of gas, electricity and flour; but over the past few years the Pakistani economy has been growing almost as strongly as that of India. You can see the effects everywhere: in 2003 the country had fewer than three million cellphone users; today there are almost 50 million. Car ownership has been increasing at roughly 40 per cent a year since 2001; foreign direct investment has risen from $322m in 2001 to $3.5bn in 2006.

Pakistan is clearly not a country on the verge of civil war. Certainly it is a country at the crossroads, with huge economic and educational problems, hideous inequalities and serious unresolved questions about its future. There is much confusion and disillusion. There is also serious civil unrest, suicide bombings and an insurgency spilling out of the tribal areas on the Afghan border. But judging by the conversations I had, it is also a resilient country that now appears to recognise democracy as its best hope. On my recent travels I found an almost unanimous consensus that the mullahs should keep to their mosques and the military should return to their barracks, like their Indian counterpart. Much violence and unrest no doubt lie ahead. But Pakistan is not about to fall apart.

Elections in south Asia are treated by the people of the region as operating on a quite different basis from those in the west. In Pakistan, as in India, elections are not primarily about ideology or manifesto promises; instead, they are really about power and patronage.

For most voters, elections are about choosing candidates who can outbid their rivals by making a string of local promises that the electors hope they will honour once they get into office. Typically, a parliamentary candidate will go to a village and make promises or give money to one of the village elders, who will then distribute it among his *bradari,* or clan, which will then vote for the candidate en bloc. To win an election, the most important thing is to win over the elder of the most powerful clan in each village. As well as money, the elder might ask for various favours: a new tarmac road to the village or gas connections for his cousins. All this costs the candidate a considerable sum of money, which it is understood he must then recoup through corruption when he gets into office; this is why corruption is rarely an important election issue in Pakistan: instead, it is believed to be be an indispensable part of the system.

According to the conventional wisdom in Pakistan, only one thing can overrule loyalty to a clan, and that is loyalty to a *zamindar* (feudal landowner). Democracy has never thrived in Pakistan in part because landowning has historically been the social base from which politicians emerge, especially in rural areas. Benazir Bhutto was from a feudal family in Sindh; so is Asif Zardari, her husband and current co-chairman of the Pakistan People's Party (PPP), as also is Makhdoom Amin Fahim, the most likely candidate for prime minister. The educated middle class—which in India gained control in 1947—and even more so the rural peasantry, are still largely excluded from Pakistan's political process. There are no Pakistani equivalents of Indian peasant leaders such as Laloo Prasad Yadav, the village cowherd-turned-former chief minister of Bihar, or Mayawati, the Dalit (untouchable) leader and current chief minister of Uttar Pradesh.

Instead, in many of the more backward parts of Pakistan, the local feudal landowner could usually expect his people to vote for his chosen candidate. As the writer Ahmed Rashid put it, "In some constituencies if the feudals put up their dog as a candidate, that dog would get elected with 99 per cent of the vote."

Such loyalty could be enforced. Many of the biggest *zamindars* are said to have private prisons, and most of them have private armies. In the more remote and lawless areas there is also the possibility that the *zamindars* and their thugs will bribe or threaten polling agents, then simply stuff the ballot boxes with thousands of votes for themselves.

Yet this is now clearly beginning to change, and this change has been give huge impetus by the national polls. The election results show that the old stranglehold on Pakistani politics that used to reduce national polls to a kind of elective feudalism may finally be beginning to break down. In Jhang district of the rural Punjab, for example, as many as ten of the 11 winning candidates are from middle-class backgrounds: sons of revenue officers, senior policemen, functionaries in the civil bureaucracy and so on, rather than the usual *zamindars.*

The Punjab is the richest and most developed part of rural Pakistan; but even in backward Sindh there are signs of change, too. Khairpur, on the banks of the Indus, is the heartland of exactly the sort of unreformed local landowners who epitomise the stereotype painted by metropolitan Pakistani sophisticates when they roll their eyes and talk about "the feudals". Yet even here, members of the local middle class have just stood successfully for election against the local *zamindars.*

Nafisa Shah is the impeccably middle-class daughter of a local lawyer promoted in the PPP by Zulfiqar Ali Bhutto in the 1970s; she is currently at Oxford doing a PhD in honour killings. She was standing in the same constituency as Sadruddin Shah, who is often held up as the epitome of feudal excess, and who went electioneering with five pick-up trucks full of his private militia, armed with pump-action shotguns.

As you drive along the bypass his face, complete with Dick Dastardly moustache, sneers down from hoardings placed every 50 yards along the road. In the past week the local press had been full of stories of his men shooting at crowds of little boys shouting pro-Benazir slogans. Shah was standing, as usual, for no fewer than three different seats; this time, however, to the amazement of locals, the PhD student and her PPP allies have all but wiped out Shah and his fellow candidates of the PML-Functional, so that Shah himself won only in his own home town.

Even the most benign feudal lords suffered astonishing reverses. Mian Najibuddin Owaisi was not just the popular feudal lord of the village of Khanqah Sharif in the southern Punjab, he was also the *sajjada nasheen,* the descendant of the local Sufi saint, and so regarded as a holy man as well as the local landowner. But recently Najibuddin made the ill-timed switch from supporting Nawaz Sharif's PML-N to the proMusharraf Q-league. Talking to the people in the bazaar before the election, his followers announced that they did not like Musharraf, but they would still vote for their landlord:

"Prices are rising," said Haji Sadiq, the cloth salesman, sitting amid bolts of textiles. "There is less and less electricity and gas."

"And what was done to Benazir was quite wrong," agreed his friend Salman.

"But Najib Sahib is our protector," said the haji. "Whatever party he chooses, we will vote for him. Even the Q-league."

"Why?" I asked.

"Because with him in power we have someone we can call if we are in trouble with the police, or need someone to speak to the adminstration," he said.

"When we really need him he looks after us."

"We vote according to local issues only. Who cares about parties?"

Because of Najibuddin's personal popularity, his vote stood up better than many other proMusharraf feudals and he polled 38,000 votes. But he still lost, to an independent candidate from a non-feudal, middle-class background named Amir Waran, who took 59,000 votes and ousted the Owaisi family from control of the constituency for the first time since they entered politics in the elections of 1975.

If the power of Pakistan's feudals is beginning to be whittled away, in the aftermath of these unexpectedly peaceful elections there remain two armed forces that can still affect the future of democracy in the country.

Though the religious parties were routed in the election, especially in the North-West Frontier where the ruling religious MMA alliance was wiped out by the secular ANP, their gun-wielding brothers in Waziristan are not in retreat. In recent months these militants have won a series of notable military victories over the Pakistani army, and spread their revolt within the settled areas of Pakistan proper.

The two assassination attempts on Benazir—the second one horribly successful—and the three recent attacks on Musharraf are just the tip of the iceberg. Every bit as alarming is the degree to which the jihadis now control much of the north-west of Pakistan, and the Swat Valley is still smouldering as government troops and jihadis loyal to the insurgent leader Maulana Fazllullah—aka "Mullah Radio" vie for control. At the moment, the government seems to have won back the area, but the insurgent leaders have all escaped and it remains to be seen how far the new government can stem this growing rebellion.

The second force that has shown a remarkable ability to ignore, or even reverse, the democratic decisions of the Pakistani people is of course the army. Even though Musharraf's political ally the PML-Q has been heavily defeated, leaving him vulnerable to impeachment by the new parliament, the Pakistani army is still formidably powerful. Normally countries have an army; in Pakistan, as in Burma, the army has a country. In her recent book *Military, Inc,* the political scientist Ayesha Siddiqa attempted to put figures on the degree to which the army controls Pakistan irrespective of who is in power.

Siddiqa estimated, for example, that the army now controls business assets of roughly $20bn and a third of all heavy manufacturing in the country; it also owns 12 million acres of public land and up to 7 per cent of Pakistan's private assets. Five giant conglomerates, known as "welfare foundations", run thousands of businesses, ranging from street-corner petrol pumps and sprawling industrial plants to cement and dredging to the manufacture of cornflakes.

As one human rights activist put it to me, "The army is into every business in this country. Except hairdressing." The army has administrative assets, too. According to Siddiqa, military personnel have "taken over all and every department in the bureaucracy—even the civil service academy is now headed by a major general, while the National School of Public Policy is run by a lieutenant general. The military have completely taken over not just the bureaucracy but every arm of the executive."

But, for all this power, Musharraf has now comprehensively lost the support of his people—a dramatic change from the situation even three years ago when a surprisingly wide cross-section of the country seemed prepared to tolerate military rule. The new army chief, General Ashfaq Kayani, who took over when Musharraf stepped down from his military role last year, seems to recognise this and has issued statements about his wish to pull the army back from civilian life, ordering his soldiers to stay out of politics and give up jobs in the bureaucracy.

Though turnout in the election was low, partly due to fear of suicide bombings, almost everyone I talked to was sure that democracy was the best answer to Pakistan's problems, and believed that neither an Islamic state nor a military junta would serve their needs so well. The disintegration of the country, something being discussed widely only a week ago, now seems a distant prospect. Rumours of Pakistan's demise, it seems, have been much exaggerated.

Sri Lanka: Calming Moves

Sri Lanka's assurance on the humanitarian situation in the country's North and East defuses tensions, for the present.

B. MURALIDHAR REDDY

Good news is a rare commodity in Sri Lanka these days. With a war raging between the security forces and the Liberation Tigers of Tamil Eelam (LTTE), an estimated three lakh internally displaced persons (IDPs) are suffering untold miseries; with inflation at close to 30 per cent, ordinary citizens are experiencing one of the worst periods in the country's post-independence history. So Colombo's assurance on October 26 to India on civilian safety in the districts of the North and East came as a huge relief to Sri Lanka watchers. The public outcry in Tamil Nadu over the plight of the people caught in the war zone and the pressure that the South Indian State mounted on New Delhi to spur Colombo into action were threatening to snowball into a crisis. However, the deft handling of the situation by Colombo, New Delhi and Chennai has defused the threat. It now remains to be seen how Colombo implements the commitments it has made.

That the concerns of India, particularly Tamil Nadu, were not misplaced was vindicated by the report of the Inter-Agency Standing Committee Sri Lanka Country Team, a consortium of the United Nations and international non-governmental agencies engaged in emergency relief operations in troubled zones. Its report for the period from October 16 to 23 shows that the districts of Kilinochchi and Mullaithivu, where military and the LTTE have been engaged in fierce battles for several weeks now, are the worst affected. The number of IDPs in the two districts is close to three lakh. These people have no escape route, and the sheer logistics of providing minimum comfort to them is mind-boggling, particularly after the Sri Lankan government, in early September, ordered the U.N. and other relief agencies to move out of the LTTE-controlled areas. The report lists the number of families and individuals displaced in the three districts of the North and five districts of the East.

On the Jaffna peninsula, the report noted, the general security situation remained tense during the week, especially in the areas around the Forward Defence Lines. "Checks on vehicles and personnel in the mainland and islets have increased. Cordon-and-search operations, especially in the Thenmarachchi area, have increased. Roads continue to be blocked regularly to allow military convoy movements," the report said.

"The general situation in Vavuniya and Mannar district remains tense and potentially volatile. Security forces remain on high alert and regularly carry out cordon-and-search operations," it said.

"Restrictive procedures at Medawachchiya and at checkpoints along the A-14 road continue. Small numbers of IDPs continue to arrive in Mannar by sea from LTTE-controlled areas. The population at the Sirukkandal IDP site now stands at 142 families (323 individuals), whereas 217 families (497 individuals) are accommodated at the Kallimoddai site. The WFP [World Food Programme] transported 755 MT [metric tonnes] of mixed food commodities, including 403 MT of rice, 250 MT of wheat flour, 71.4 MT of lentils and 30.8 MT of vegetable oil to provide a week's ration for approximately 210,000 beneficiaries in the Wanni."

It is against this backdrop that diplomatic manoeuvres commenced in Colombo and New Delhi. The outcome of the discussions, articulated in the form of a joint statement and a joint press statement on October 26, is significant. The statements were the result of frenzied behind-the-scenes negotiations, spread over 10 days, between New Delhi and Chennai, on one hand, and New Delhi and Colombo, on the other. Sri Lankan President Mahinda Rajapaksa dispatched Basil Rajapaksa, his brother and Senior Adviser, for the clinching round in New Delhi. The results of his mission were indeed pleasing for both sides. The joint statement on fishing arrangements is an important breakthrough. If implemented in letter and spirit, it will go a long way in tackling a problem that has been a source of constant friction between India and Sri Lanka for years.

It involves the livelihood of hundreds of thousands of fisherfolk on both sides of the Palk Straits and has evaded a satisfactory answer, especially since the current phase of hostilities in Sri Lanka began in June 2006. The dimension of the problem could be gauged from the fact that on an average an estimated 200 fishing boats/trawlers stray into the territorial waters of the other side every day. The Sri Lanka Navy has been walking a tightrope in taking care of the safety of the fisherfolk while ensuring that the LTTE does not take advantage of the situation. For the first time since the 1974 agreement under which India conceded the Katchatheevu island to Sri Lanka, Colombo has made significant concessions in favour of the fisherfolk. The understanding was made public in the form of a joint statement under the title "India-Sri Lanka Joint Statement on Fishing Arrangements".

It reads: "Keeping in mind the humanitarian and livelihood dimensions of the fishermen issue, India and Sri Lanka have agreed to put in place practical arrangements to deal with *bona fide* Indian and Sri Lankan fishermen crossing the International Maritime Boundary Line (IMBL). This was agreed to during the visit to New Delhi on 26th October 2008 of Honourable Basil Rajapaksa, Member of Parliament and Senior Adviser to the President of Sri Lanka.

"As part of these practical arrangements, following the designation by the Government of Sri Lanka of sensitive areas along the Sri Lankan coastline and their intimation to the Government of India, Indian fishing vessels will not venture into these identified sensitive areas. Further, there will be no firing on Indian fishing vessels. It was agreed that Indian fishing vessels would carry valid registration/permit and the fishermen would have on person valid identity cards issued by the Government of Tamil Nadu. India and Sri Lanka have agreed to continue with their discussions, initiated in 2005, on the proposed Memorandum of Understanding on development and cooperation in the field of fisheries."

It remains to be seen what kind of mechanisms will be put in place to implement the statement with a certain degree of transparency.

In contrast, the concerns expressed by India over the humanitarian crisis were outlined in a press release. New Delhi made it known right from the day an "all-party conference" presided over by Tamil Nadu Chief Minister M. Karunanidhi on October 16 urged the Government of India to counsel Colombo to cease fire, that the war being waged by the Sri Lankan forces against the LTTE was an internal matter of the island nation and New Delhi had no jurisdiction over the issue. It sought to make a difference between the war against the LTTE, an organisation banned in India in the aftermath of the assassination of former Prime Minister Rajiv Gandhi in May 1991, and the sufferings of innocent citizens caught in the crossfire.

The operative portions of the joint press release are self-explanatory. It reads: "India conveyed its concern at the humanitarian situation in the northern part of Sri Lanka, especially of the civilians and internally displaced persons caught in the hostilities, and emphasised the need for unhindered essential relief supplies. Mr. Rajapaksa briefed the Indian authorities of the efforts by the Sri Lanka Government to afford relief and ensure the welfare of the civilian population in the North. He assured that the safety and well-being of the Tamil community in Sri Lanka is being taken care of.

"As a gesture of goodwill, India has decided to send around 800 tonnes of relief material to Sri Lanka for the affected civilians in the North. The Government of Sri Lanka will facilitate the delivery. Both sides agreed to consult and cooperate with each other in addressing these humanitarian issues. Both sides

discussed the need to move towards a peacefully negotiated political settlement in the island, including in the North. Both sides agreed that terrorism should be countered with resolve. The Indian side called for implementation of the 13th Amendment [to the Constitution] and greater devolution of powers to the provinces. Mr. Basil Rajapaksa emphasised that the President of Sri Lanka and his government were firmly committed to a political process that would lead to a sustainable solution. Both sides agreed to further nurture the democratic process in the Eastern Province. Mr. Rajapaksa briefed the Indian side of the large development effort under way in the Eastern Province."

The President's Assurance

In his interview to the Editor-in-Chief of *The Hindu*, N. Ram, on the evening of October 27, a day after the two statements were released, Mahinda Rajapaksa elaborated on various elements of the understanding between New Delhi and Colombo and made use of the opportunity to address matters of concern to the leaders and people of Tamil Nadu in particular and India in general. "Let me reiterate that my government is firmly committed to a negotiated political solution—based on devolution of power and ensuring the democratic, political, including linguistic, rights of all our Tamil brethren within an undivided Sri Lanka," he told Ram, allaying apprehensions that his government was for a military rather than a political solution to redress the grievances of minorities in the island nation.

"I am absolutely clear that there is, and can be, no military solution to political questions. I have always maintained this. A military solution is for the terrorists; a political solution is for the people living in this country," he emphasised. Conceding the slow progress of the All Party Representative Committee (APRC), which was constituted by him to evolve a consensus on the resolution of the ethnic conflict, in coming up with its final proposals, he asserted: "I myself will take charge of the political process and see it through politically."

Emphasising that "our military operations are directed exclusively at the Liberation Tigers of Tamil Eelam"—a terrorist and secessionist organisation banned or designated as terrorist in more than 30 countries—he renewed his call to the LTTE even at this late stage to "lay down its arms, surrender, and enter the democratic political process". He further argued that the military operations directed against the LTTE were not intended to harass Tamil civilians or cause any harm or hardship to them. His government was doing, and would do, everything in its power "to mitigate and resolve the plight of the civilians displaced or affected by the conflict". In addition to ensuring that food, medicines and other essential commodities were "within the reach of every one of our Tamil brethren affected by the conflict", it would rehabilitate "every civilian affected by the conflict in a fair and transparent manner".

On the contours of the political solution he had in mind, Rajapaksa explained his four 'Ds' approach—demilitarisation, democratisation, development and devolution.

Glossary of Terms and Abbreviations

Adivasi Literally, "first dweller"; members of India's tribal population, officially recognized in the Constitution as Scheduled Tribes eligible for placement up to a designated percentage in schools and government jobs.

Al-Qaeda "the Base"; a loose collection of Islamic terrorist cells held together by their fundamentalist zeal to resist the encroachment of Western secularist power and values on the Muslim community (Ummah), and by financial support from contributions to Salafiyyah mosques throughout the world and from patrons like Osama bin Laden.

Asoka A Mauryan emperor in northern India from 268 to 232 B.C. Overcome with remorse about deaths caused by his military conquests, he abandoned warfare as an instrument of imperial power and adopted the Buddhist Dharma as the standard for his rule. He enforced this expectation in a series of edicts carved into stones and pillars throughout his kingdom. His example is recognized today in the adoption of the lion capital on one of his pillars as the insignia of the Republic of India.

Ayodhya, Uttar Pradesh A small city in the eastern part of India's largest state which became a national pilgrimage center as the birthplace of Lord Ram with the rise of Hindu religious nationalism in the 1980s. The destruction of the Babri Mosque there by Hindu pilgrims in 1992 led to communal riots throughout India and abroad. *See* Babur.

Babur The first of the Moghul emperors, who engaged in a military conquest of northern India from 1526 to 1529. It was during his brief reign that the Babri Mosque was built in Ayodhya, purportedly on the site of an earlier Hindu temple, the destruction of which, in December 1992, led to communal riots across India. Akbar, the greatest of the Moghul monarchs, who ruled from 1556 to 1605 and completed the Moghul conquest of northern India, was Babur's grandson.

Bharatiya Janata Party (BJP) "Indian Peoples Party" grew as a Hindu nationalist party out of the heartland of the Gangetic plain to become the only party to challenge Congress Party hegemony on a national level. Led by Atal Behari Vajpayee, it attained leadership in Parliament with the support of a 19-party coalition in 1998, and with a 24-party coalition in 1999. Riding high on a platform of Hindu nationalism and economic reform, it lost to the Congress Party in the elections in 2004.

Brahmin The priestly community, ranked highest on the varna caste scale.

Buddhism A religious faith that started in India in the sixth century B.C. by Siddhartha Gautama, who renounced his royal heritage to seek enlightenment for the salvation of all humankind. The attainment of Nirvana (his death) is placed at 483 B.C. This faith extended throughout Asia in two major traditions: Theravada ("Teaching of the Elders") to Sri Lanka and Southeast Asia; and Mahayana ("Great Vehicle") to China and Japan. Tibetan Buddhism is a subset of the Mahayana tradition. Theravada has been called Hinayana ("Lesser Vehicle") by Mahayana Buddhists to distinguish that tradition from their own.

Chola A Tamil dynasty centered in the Tanjavur District of the current state of Tamil Nadu, which dominated that part of south India from A.D. 880 to 1279. The temples built and the bronzes cast under the patronage of the Chola kings remain some of the most beautiful and cherished works of Indian art.

Congress Party As the successor of the Indian National Congress in 1935, under the leadership of Jawaharlal Nehru, it led to the independence of India in 1947, and to the Republic of India in 1950. The party remained in power in Parliament for 45 years, led by Nehru's daughter, Indira Gandhi, after his death in 1964, and by his grandson Ranjiv Gandhi, after her death in 1984. Narasimha Rao became prime minister after the death of Ranjiv Gandhi in 1991, until 1996. Nehru's granddaughter-in-law, Sonia Gandhi, elected president of the party in 1998, led it to victory in the parliamentary elections in 2004.

Dalits The "broken" or "oppressed"; this is the name preferred by those traditionally known as scheduled castes, outcastes, or untouchables, members of the lowest-rank communities in the classical caste system, below the four ranks of priests, rulers, citizens, and laborers on the varna social scale. Mahatma Gandhi, deeply concerned about removing their oppression, called them *Harijans*, "children of God."

Deccan Literally, "southern"; refers to the plateau between the eastern and western mountains (ghats) and south of the Vindhya Mountains in peninsular India.

Dharma Translated as "law, justice, duty, cosmic order," the moral standard by which society and an individual's life are ordered and given meaning.

Godhra, Gujarat A small city in a growing industrial state in which Mahatma Gandhi was born, where a gang of slum dwelling Muslims set fire to a railway car full of pilgrims returning from Ayodhya on February 27, 2002. The death of 59, including women and children, led to violent reprisals against Muslims in the city, which killed more than 1,000 Muslims, and left many more homeless.

Green Revolution An upsurge in agricultural production that followed the introduction of high-yielding hybrids of rice and grains, developed by the Rockefeller Foundation in Mexico and the Philippines, into South Asia during the 1950s and 1960s.

Harappa and Mohenjo Daro The two largest cities excavated during the 1930s in the Indus River Valley to reveal an ancient urban culture that began around 3000 B.C. It flourished for 1,000 years and then inexplicably disappeared.

Herat A 5000-year-old city along the silk route to China, in a fertile valley in the northwestern corner of Afghanistan. Long a center of Afghan Sufi religious life, art and poetry, it was decimated by Genghis Khan in 1222, damaged by the British in 1885, and heavily bombed and mined by the Soviets in 1979. Ismael Khan led the city's insurrection against the Soviets in 1979, and served as governor of Herat Province from 1993–1998 and 2001–2004.

Hindi The prevalent language and literature of northern India.

Hindu One who follows the faith of Hinduism.

Hinduism The dominant religion of India, emphasizing Dharma, with its ritual and social observances and often mystical contemplation and ascetic practices.

Hindutva "Hindu-ness"; a political platform of the Hindu nationalist Bharatiya Janata Party, which aspires to rule India according to the classical norms of Great Tradition, i.e., pre-Islamic, India.

Hurriyat Conference The consolidation of some 23 Kashmiri Muslim insurgent groups in 1993 to seek an end to Indian military occupation and an independent Islamic Kashmiri homeland. Many in these groups are committed to finding a peaceful resolution and are in dialogue with the government of India. Others have received monetary support, arms, and training from Pakistan as well as the support of *jihadis* from all over the Islamic world.

Indian National Congress An association of educated Indians and sympathetic Europeans who gathered in Bengal in 1885 to seek admission for qualified Indians into the British Indian Civil Service. In the early twentieth century, this association became the bearer of the independence movement of the subcontinent from British colonial rule. Following the establishment of a provisional government in 1935, it evolved into the Congress Party.

Islam A religious faith started in Arabia during the seventh century A.D. by the prophet Mohammad.

Islamization A policy adopted by General Mohammad Zia-al-Haq of Pakistan in the late 1970s to win political support for his martial rule from a growing Islamic fundamentalist movement in his country, spurred by the Soviet military incursion into neighboring Afghanistan.

Jain A religious faith started in India by Mahavira in the sixth century B.C. Its primary teachings include the eternal transmigration of souls and the practice of nonviolence toward all living creatures.

Jajmani A barter system of economic activity in the village, in which villagers provide their services on a regular basis to particular land owners—their patrons—in exchange for fixed portions of the annual harvest.

Jati An extended kinship group, usually identified with a traditional occupation, that defines the parameters of accepted marriage relationships. It is the unit that is ranked in the hierarchical social (caste) structure of a village and that moves within that structure.

Jihad "Struggle"; the quest to become part of a pure Muslim community (*Ummah*) by practicing an exemplary religious life in submission to Allah and by protecting it from all that would deny or destroy it. In the twentieth century, it took on the obligation among fundamentalist Muslims to become religious warriors, *jihadis,* on behalf of the faith.

Khalistan An independent state in the South Asian subcontinent for Sikhs.

Koran The sacred scripture of the Islamic faith, the teachings of Allah (God) as revealed to His prophet Mohammad in the seventh century A.D.

Ladakh The easternmost and highest region of the state of Kashmir-Jammu, inhabited mostly by Buddhists.

Lama A leader of a Tibetan Buddhist monastic community (sangha).

Lashkar-e-Taiba (Militia of the Righteous) is a militant wing of a large Pakistan Sunni religiously fundamentalist organization, Markaz-ud-Dawa-wal-Irshad. Committed to restoring Islamic rule over all of India, it has been actively supporting the insurgency in Kashmir to free Muslims from Indian military occupation since 1993. It was declared a terrorist organization by the United States in 2001, and banned by the Pakistan Government in 2002. Identified with many terrorist acts in India, including the bombing of commuter trains in Mumbai on July 11, 2006, it played a major role in fund raising and relief work following the massive earthquake in Pakistan in October 2005. It is also known as Jamaat ud-Dawa (Party of the Calling).

Liberation Tigers of the Tamil Nation (LTTE) The militant separatist organization of Tamil-speaking Hindus in northern Sri Lanka. This insurgency sprang up in the 1980s under the leadership of V. Pirapaharan to seek by force a homeland independent of Sinhalese domination. Its violent ravaging, including suicide bombings, continued until it declared a cease-fire in December 2001 and entered into peace negotiations under Norwegian auspices with the Sri Lankan government in September 2002.

Lok Sabha and Rajya Sabha The two houses of Parliament in the Republic of India: "The House of the People" has 545 members elected directly by voters on the district level; "The Council of States" has 250 members, 12 appointed by the president and 238 elected by state legislatures.

Loya Jirga A council of Afghan chieftains and clan leaders called by claimants to regional power to recognize their authority to rule. Such a council was convened in June 2002 under United Nations auspices in Kabul to create a provisional government to restore civil order to the war-ravaged country of Afghanistan.

Mahabharata The Great Epic of India, with more than 90,000 stanzas, composed around the third century B.C. The longest poem in the world, it is the story of five brothers' struggle to wrest their father's kingdom from their cousins. This epic contains the *Bhagavad Gita,* a discourse between one of the brothers, Arjuna, and his charioteer, Krishna, on the eve of the culminating battle with their cousins, when Arjuna is overcome by concerns about appropriate behavior and quality of life.

Mahar A depressed (untouchable) community in the state of Maharashtra, which converted to Buddhism in October 1956 as an initiative to free themselves as a community from the social burden of untouchability, under the leadership of Dr. B. R. Ambedkar.

Mahatma Literally "great souled one"; a title given to Mohandas Gandhi by Rabindranath Tagore in 1921 and adopted by the people of India to express their belief in Gandhi's saintliness.

Mandal Commission Established by the government in India in 1979 to identify backward communities eligible for reserved access for placement in schools and government jobs and to recommend quotas for reservation.

Mandala An intricate visual symbol developed in the Tibetan Buddhist tradition, revealing elaborate patterns of many shapes and colors, intended to lead its creator and observer into supranormal levels of consciousness.

Moghuls Islamic invaders of Turkish descent who established the longest dynastic imperial rule in the Great Central Plain of South Asia, from A.D. 1526 to 1857.

Mohajirs "Immigrants"; those Muslims who moved from their homelands in India at the time of partition in 1947 to settle in Pakistan. Because they have retained many of the customs as well as the language (Urdu) of their former homes, even today they remain a distinctive community and political force, as the Mohajir Quami Movement (MQM) in Pakistan.

MMA (Muttahida Majlis-e-amal) A coalition of 5 Islamist political parties which won control of the North-West Frontier Province

Glossary of Terms and Abbreviations

of Pakistan in the 2002 elections. It used this base to push its fundamentalist, anti-American agenda nationally until its defeat by the Awami National Party in the 2008 elections.

Monsoon An annual torrential rainfall, which normally begins during the month of June, when the prevailing winds shift to the west, gather clouds with water from the Arabian Sea, and deluge the subcontinent with rain as the clouds rise over the Himalayan Mountains. The dramatic shift from the torrid dry heat of late spring to this stormy wet season and the lush growth that it provides has an immense impact on the economies, the literature, and the consciousness of South Asian peoples. Raja Rao gives a brief, gripping description of the coming of the monsoon on page 50 of his novel *Kanthapura* and in his notes, pages 215–216.

Mujahideen Militant tribal leaders in Afghanistan who joined in alliance to protect their authority from national and foreign (Soviet) incursion.

Muslim One who submits to the supreme will of Allah (God), as revealed to the prophet Mohammad; one who practices Islam. Sometimes spelled Moslem.

NATO (North Atlantic Treaty Organization) established in 1949 as an alliance of now 26 North American and European countries "to unite their efforts for collective defense and for the preservation of peace and security."

Naxalites A loose collection of militant groups in central India inspired by the Maoist revolution in China, who attack any element of the Indian establishment in the name of the landless and the tribal people of that region. Their name comes from an uprising of a tribal community in the village of Naxalbari in western Bengal in 1967. Though mostly active in the 1960's and 70's, now largely fragmented, small bands of the People's War Group or the Maoist Communist Centre still attack landlords and politicians sporadically in Chhattisgarh Andhra Pradesh, Jharkhand, Orissa and Bihar.

Nirvana Literally, "blowing out, extinguishing"; the ultimate enlightenment of Buddhism: departure from the relentless trans-migratory cycle of births and deaths into nothingness.

NREGS (National Rural Employment Guarantee Scheme) Proposed by the Congress Party-led United Progressive Alliance to respond to increasing unemployment among the rural poor in India, and enacted by the Lok Sabha in 2005. It guaranteed employment for one member of a landless family for 100 days per year in public works projects set up by district panchayats, paid 90 percent by the national government, 10 percent by state governments. First implemented in 2006 in 200 districts, it extended to all districts in India in 2008.

Pali One of many regional Indo-European languages (called Prakrits) spoken in the northern plains region of South Asia following the Aryan Invasion (ca. 1700 B.C.) and before the evolution of the subcontinent's modern languages, following the twelfth century A.D. It was the language in which the earliest documents of the Buddhist faith were composed in northern India.

Panchayat Literally, "council of five." This traditional leadership of elders in the jati kinship group was adopted in the Panchayat Acts in state legislatures during the 1950s as the appropriate form of democratically elected village government in the Republic of India.

Parsi A member of the Zoroastrian faith, the ancient religion of Persia. Most of the Parsis in South Asia live in Bombay (Mumbai) and Karachi.

Pathans Tribal peoples in the northwest corner of the subcontinent who speak the Pushtu language.

Punjab Translated as *panch* ("five") and *ap* ("water"), designates the land in the western portion of the Great Central Plain through which the five rivers forming the Indus River System flow. The province that had this name during the British Indian Empire was divided between India and Pakistan in 1947.

Purana "Tradition," a genre of Sanskrit religious texts of different sects of Hinduism from the Classical Period (A.D. 300 to 1200), setting forth their primary myths and teachings; also the accounts in local languages of the sacred significance of religious sites, temples, places of pilgrimage, etc.

Rabindranath Tagore An outstanding Bengali poet and educator (1861–1941), whose collection of poems, *Gitanjali,* published in English translation in 1912, won the Nobel Prize for Literature.

Raj Translated as "rule" or "king," a term that designates political sovereignty. (The word *reign* comes from the same Indo-European root.) "Raj" is used with "British" to identify the British colonial government in India; it is used with *maha* ("great") to identify rulers of the Indian princely states; and it is used with *swa* ("self") to mean self-rule or independence. Swaraj also has the connotation of self-discipline, which is an important aspect of Mahatma Gandhi's concept of independence.

Ramayana An epic Sanskrit poem, composed around the second century A.D. and attributed to Valmiki, describing the ordeals of the ideal prince Rama. Most of the text describes his ultimately successful quest for his faithful wife Sita, who was abducted by the demonic King Ravana.

Rashtriya Swayamsevak Sangh (RSS) An organization founded in 1925 to train Hindus to seek independence from the British Raj by whatever means necessary and to further Hindu nationalistic objectives. Recognized as a militant alternative to Mahatma Gandhi's nonviolent movement, it is today a significant political force within the Bharatiya Janata Party (BJP).

Rg Veda The first of the four Vedas, which are the earliest and most sacred of the writings of the Hindus. Around 1000 B.C., it was compiled into an anthology of 10 books containing 1,028 hymns.

Salafiya Movement to advocate a fundamentalist reform of Sunni Islam, began in the late Nineteenth century in Egypt to protest the imposition of Western secular thought. Based on a literal interpretation of the Koran, it espouses severe puritanical behavior and punishment for any apostasy from their rigid beliefs.

Salt March An act of nonviolent civil disobedience (*satyagraha*) led by Mahatma Gandhi in 1930. He and his followers marched from his *ashram* at Sabarmati 241 miles to Dandi on the coast to evaporate salt from the sea, in order to protest the British tax on salt.

Sangha A Buddhist community of holy men and women who follow the Buddha's path called Dharma. The Buddha, Dharma, and Sangha are called the "three jewels of the Buddhist faith."

Sanskrit Translated as "made together, formed, perfected," as descriptive of the classical language of India as structurally perfected.

Satyagraha Literally, "holding the truth," the name that Mahatma Gandhi adopted while in South Africa to describe his nonviolent civil protest against the South African government's oppression of the people from India. Gandhi's translation of this term as "soul force" affirms that, even early in his public career, he understood such action to be primarily religious and only secondarily political.

SEWA (Self-Employed Women's Association) Began as a union of textile workers by Anasuya Sarabhai in Ahmedabad in 1920, following upon Mahatma Gandhi's successful strike of textile workers in 1917. It became registered as a trade union in 1972. Under SEWA's General Secretary, Ela Bhatt, it has grown to seven hundred thousand members, the largest member-based organization of poor working women in India.

Shariah "The Path to the Water Hole"; Islamic sacred laws, based upon the Koran as revealed to Mohammad and the *Sunnah,* the record of his exemplary life. These laws are affirmed by the Sunni followers of Islam to be divinely inspired and immutable guides for Muslims' everyday life.

Sherpa Literally "eastern people"; an ethnic group in Nepal who live in the high Himalayan region, but also a name applied to any Nepali who is skilled in climbing and navigating the mountain peaks.

Shia Followers of Islam (approximately 15 percent of Muslims) who differ from the Sunnis in their belief that the traditions of Islam are sustained by a divinely inspired succession of Imams (religious leaders) who are descended from Ali ibn Abi Talib, the cousin and son-in-law of the Prophet Mohammad. He was elected the fourth Caliph in the Sunni succession and was assassinated in A.D. 661. Especially sacred to this tradition is the 10th day of the Arab month of Muhurram (Ramadan), on which Ali's son, Husain, the third Shia Imam, was killed on the plain of Kerbala. This community developed with the rise of the Safavid Empire in Persia in the sixteenth century. Today Shia live mostly in Iran and southern Iraq.

Shiva Literally, "auspicious"; the name of God in one of the two main sects of Hinduism: Shaivism (from Shiva) and Vaishnavism ("followers of Vishnu").

Sufi A person of the Islamic faith who affirms through religious discipline and mystical experience the spiritual union of self with God.

Sunnah "Custom"; practices of the Prophet Mohammad remembered by his early followers as the guide for an ideal Islamic life.

Sunni The tradition of the majority of Muslims, based on strict adherence to the Sunnah of the Prophet Mohammad.

Taliban "Seekers of religious knowledge"; members of a militant and exceptionally conservative freedom force named after the Pathan students of Islam from Kandahar who started a fundamentalist crusade to free Afghanistan from foreign and modern corruptions of their faith and traditional way of life.

Tsunami An enormous ocean wave created by an earthquake on an ocean floor. Occurring with some frequency in the Pacific Ocean, the Indian Ocean tsunami on December 26, 2004, was the result of a totally unexpected earthquake that measured 9.0 on the richter scale along the Sunda trench west of Sumatra in Indonesia. The worst tsunami in history, it extended across the entire Indian Ocean to the coast of Africa, causing death and damage in 13 countries. Indonesia reported a death toll of over 110,000. On the eastern shore of Sri Lanka it killed 38,000; along the coast of Tamil Nadu, in India, 7,968 and the Indian Andaman and Nicobar Islands, 1,837, with 5,625 missing; and in Thailand, an estimated 11,000 deaths.

Upanishads A collection of profound religious teachings that form the last stage in the development of Vedic literature, beginning with the *Rg Veda* and continuing with the *Brahamanas,* which are manuals for the performance of Vedic sacrifices.

Varna Originally translated as "class," later as "color"; the fourfold division of classical Indian society, ranked on a purity—pollution scale: priests, rulers, citizens, and laborers. The untouchables and tribals are a fifth group, known as outcastes, ranked below the laborers.

Vellalas Among Tamil-speaking peoples, the dominant landholding and cultivating communities, similar to the Jat communities in the Hindi-speaking regions of the subcontinent.

Vishnu Receiving somewhat minor attention as a solar deity in the *Rg Veda,* Vishnu became recognized as Supreme Lord of the universe, its creator and preserver during the classical period (A.D. 300–1200). He is worshipped widely throughout Hinduism through His incarnations (*avatars*), of whom Rama and Krishna are the most prevalent.

WAHABISM A fundamentalist tradition of Islam initiated by Muhammad ibn Abd-al-Wahhab in the Eighteenth century, adopted as the national religion of Saudi Arabia after the collapse of the Ottoman Empire in the early Twenteeth century.

Yoga A highly disciplined set of exercises to identify, nurture, and develop different parts of one's natural body, breathing, nervous system, and consciousness. Practice of this discipline leads to the integration of one's total self—physical, mental, and spiritual, the unconscious as well as the conscious.

Bibliography

SOURCES FOR STATISTICAL REPORTS

U.S. State Department *Background Notes* (2008–2009).
C.I.A. *World Factbook* (2008–2009).
World Bank *World Development Reports* (1978–2009).
UN *Population and Vital Statistics Reports* (2007).
SIPRI (Stockholm International Peace Research Institute) military expenditure database (2008).
The Statesman's Yearbook (2009).
Population Reference Bureau (2009).
The World Almanac (2009).
The Economist Intelligence Unit (2009).

GENERAL

A. L. Basham, *Wonder That Was India,* (Picador, 2005).
Sumit Ganguly, *Conflict Unending, India-Pakistan Tensions since 1947,* (Columbia University Press, 2002).
Sumit Ganguly and Devin T. Hagerty, *Fearful Symmetry: India Pakistan Crises in the Shadow of Nuclear Weapons,* (Oxford University Press, 2006).
Ayesha Jalal, *Partisans of Allah: Jihad in South Asia,* (Harvard University Press, 2008).
Jonathan M. Kenoyer, *Ancient Cities of the Indus Valley Civilization,* (Oxford University Press, Islamabad: American Institute of Pakistan Studies, 1998).
Todd Lewis and Theodore Riccardi, *The Himalayas: A Syllabus of the Region's History, Anthropology, and Religion,* (Association of Asian Studies, 1995).
Ann Leonard, *Seeds: Supporting Women's Work in the Third World,* (Feminist Press, 1989), Chapters on Credit Organization in Madras, India; Non-craft Employment in Bangladesh; and Forest Conservation in Nepal.
Jane McIntosh, *A Peaceful Realm: The Rise and Fall of the Indus Civilization,* (Westview Press, 2001).
Francis Robinson, (ed), *The Cambridge Encyclopedia of India, Pakistan, Bangladesh, Sri Lanka, Nepal, Bhutan, and the Maldives,* (Cambridge University Press, 1989).
Francis Robinson, *Islam and Modern History in South Asia,* (Oxford University Press, 2001).
Joseph Schwartzberg, *A Historical Atlas of South Asia,* (Oxford University Press, 1993).
Stanley J. Tambiah, *Leveling Crowds, Ethno-Nationalist Conflicts and Collective Violence in South Asia,* (University of California Press, 1997).
David Gordon White, *Kiss of the Yogini: "Tantric Sex" in its South Asian Contexts,* (University of Chicago Press, 2006).

INDIA

Joan Bondurant, *Conquest of Violence,* (Princeton: Princeton University Press, 1988).
William Dalrymple, *The Last Mughal: The Fall of a Dynasty, Delhi, 1857,* (Knopf, 2007).
Dennis Dalton, *Mahatma Gandhi, Nonviolent Power in Action,* (Columbia University Press, 1995).
Nicholas Dirks, *Castes of Mind: Colonialism and the Making of Modern India,* (Princeton University Press, 2001).
Diana Eck, *Darshan—Seeing the Divine Image in India,* (Columbia University Press, 1985).
Ainslie, Embree, *Utopias in Conflict, Religion and Nationalism in Modern India,* (University of California Press, 1990).
Bill Emmott, *Rivals: How the Power Struggle Between China, India, and Japan Will Shape Our Next Decade,* (Harcourt, 2008).
Eric Ericson, *Gandhi's Truth,* (Norton, 1970).
Mohandas K. Gandhi, *An Autobiography: The Story of My Experiments With Truth,* (Beacon, 1957).
Rajmohan Gandhi, *Gandhi: The Man, His People, and the Empire,* (2008).
Sumit Ganguly (ed), *India as an Emerging Power,* (Frank Caso, 2003).
Sumit Ganguly, Larry Diamond, and Marc F. Plattner, *The State of India's Democracy,* (Johns Hopkins University Press, 2007).
Ramachandra Guha, *India After Gandhi: The History of the World's Largest Democracy,* (Harper Perennial; Reprint edition, 2008).
Arthur Herman, *Gandhi and Churchill,* (New York: Bantam Books, 2008).
Thomas Hopkins, *The Hindu Religious Tradition,* (Belmont, CA: Dickenson, 1971).
Tarun Khanna. *Billions of Entrepreneurs: How China and India Are Reshaping Their Futures—and Yours,* (Harvard Business School Press, 2008).
David Knipe, *Hinduism, Experiments in the Sacred,* (Harper, 1990).
Edward Luce, *In Spite of the Gods: The Rise of Modern India,* (Anchor, 2008).
Suketu Mehta, *Maximum City: Bombay Lost and Found,* (Alfred A. Knopf, 2004).
Maria Misra, *Vishnu's Crowded Temple: India Since the Great Rebellion,* (Yale University Press, 2008).
Aditya Mukherjee, Mridula Mukherjee, and Sucheta Mahajan, *RSS, School Texts and the Murder of Mahatma Gandhi: The Hindu Communal Project* (([Response Books]), Sage Publications Pvt. Ltd, 2008).
V. S. Naipal, *India: A Million Mutinies Now,* (Viking, 1992).
Jawaharlal Nehru, *The Discovery of India,* (John Day, 1946).
Martha C. Nussbaum, *The Clash Within: Democracy, Religious Violence, and India's Future,* (Harvard University Press, 2007).
Arvind Panagariya, *India: The Emerging Giant,* (Oxford University Press, 2008).
Raja Rao, *Kanthapura,* (New Directions, 1963). A novel describing the impact of Mahatma Gandhi on a South Indian village.
Lloyd and Suzanne Rudolph, *The Modernity of Tradition,* (University of Chicago Press, 1984).
Srirupa Roy, *Beyond Belief: India and the Politics of Postcolonial Nationalism,* (Duke University Press, 2007).
Amartya Sen, *The Argumentative Indian: Writings on Indian History, Culture, and Identity,* (Allen Lane, 2005, Farrar, Straus & Giroux, 2005).
Vikram Seth, *A Suitable Boy,* (Perennial, 1994). A monumental novel about pursuing the choice of a husband in 1950s north India.

Spear & Thapar, *A History of India, 2 vols.* (Penguin, 1965).

M. N. Srinivas, *Social Change in Modern India,* (University of California Press, 1969).

Alex Von Tunzelmann, *Indian Summer: The Secret History of the End of an Empire,* (Henry Holt, 2007).

Asutosh Varshney, *Ethnic Conflict and Civic Life: Hindus and Muslims in India,* (Yale University Press, 1993).

William Wiser, Charlotte Wiser, and Susan Wadley, *Behind Mud Walls,* (University of California Press, 2001). A classic description of an Indian village in 1930 and 1960, with a new chapter on 2000.

Stanley Wolpert, *Nehru, A Tryst with Destiny,* (Oxford University Press, 1996).

R. C. Zaehner, *Hinduism,* (Oxford University Press, 1970).

Heinreich Zimmer, *Myths and Symbols in Indian Art and Civilization,* (Harper, 1946).

AFGHANISTAN

Steve Coll, *Ghost Wars: The Secret History of the CIA, Afghanistan, and Bin Laden, from the Soviet Invasion to September 10, 2001,* (Penguin ([Non-Classics]) 2004).

Sarah Chayes, *The Punishment of Virtue: Inside Afghanistan After the Taliban,* (Penguin ([Non-Classics]) 2007).

Robert D. Crews (ed) and Amin Tarzi (ed), *The Taliban and the Crisis of Afghanistan,* (Harvard University Press, 2008).

James F. Dobbins, *After the Taliban: Nation-Building in Afghanistan,* (Potomac Books Inc., 2008).

Martin Ewans, *Afghanistan: A Short History of Its People and Politics,* (Harper Perennial, 2002).

Khaled Hosseini, *The Kite Runner,* (Riverhead Books, 2003) A novel of an emigrant's childhood in Kabul and his return during Taliban rule.

Robert D. Kaplan, *Soldiers of God, With Islamic Warriors in Afghanistan and Pakistan,* (Vintage, 2001).

David Macdonald, *Drugs in Afghanistan: Opium, Outlaws and Scorpion Tales,* (Pluto Press, 2007).

Ahmed Raashid, *Taliban: Militant Islam, Oil and Fundamentalism in Central Asia,* (Yale University Press, 2001).

Barnett R. Rubin, *Afghanistan's Uncertain Transition from Turmoil to Normalcy,* (Council on Foreign Relations, 2007).

Barnett R. Rubin, *The Fragmentation of Afghanistan: State Formation and Collapse in the International System,* (Yale University Press, 2002).

Rosemarie Skaine, *The Women of Afghanistan Under the Taliban,* (McFarland, 2001).

Mohammad Yousaf, *Battle for Afghanistan,* (Pen and Sword Books, 2007).

BANGLADESH

David Bornstein, *The Price of a Dream: The Story of the Grameen Bank,* (Oxford University Press, USA, 2005).

Hanifa Deen, *The Crescent and the Pen: The Strange Journey of Taslima Nasreen,* (Praeger Publishers, 2006).

Katy Gardner, *Global Migrants, Local Lives: Travel and Transformation in Rural Bangladesh*

Katy Gardner, *Songs at the River's Edge: Stories from a Bangladeshi Village,* (Pluto Press, 1997).

Amitav Ghosh, *The Hungry Tide: A Novel,* (Mariner Books, 2006).

Maneeza Hossain, *Broken Pendulum: Bangladesh's Swing to Radicalism,* (Hudson Institute; 1st edition, 2007).

Rokeya Sakhawat Hossain, *Sultana's Dream,* (The Feminist Press, 1988) Bengali Muslim writer on purdah and a dream of its reversal.

Taslima Nasrin, *Meyebela: My Bengali Girlhood,* (Steerforth, 1998).

Sufia M. Uddin, *Constructing Bangladesh: Religion, Ethnicity, and Language in an Islamic Nation,* (The University of North Carolina Press, 2006).

Muhammad Yunus, *Banker To The Poor: Micro-Lending and the Battle Against World Poverty,* (PublicAffairs; 2003. Corr. 2nd edition, 2003).

BHUTAN

John Berthold, *Bhutan: Land of the Thunder Dragon,* (Wisdom Publications, 2005).

Russ and Blyth Carpenter, *Blessings of Bhutan,* (University of Hawaii Press, 2002).

Britta Das, *Buttertea at Sunrise: A Year in the Bhutan Himalaya,* (Summersdale Publishers, 2006).

Michael Hutt, *Unbecoming Citizens: Culture, Nationhood, and the Flight of Refugees from Bhutan,* (Oxford University Press, USA, 2005).

John Wehrheim, *Bhutan: Hidden Lands of Happiness; Texts and Photographs,* (Serindia Publications, 2008).

Richard Whitecross, *Bhutan,* (Lonely Planet; 3rd edition, 2007).

Jamie Zeppa, *Beyond the Sky and the Earth: A Journey into Bhutan,* (Riverhead Trade, 2000).

MALDIVES

Asian Centre for Human Rights, *Maldives: The Dark of the Life,* (2006).

Maumoon Abdul, Gayoon, *The Maldives: A Nation in Peril* (Ministry of Planning Human Resources and Environment, Republic of Maldives, 1998).

NEPAL

Monica Connell, *Against a Peacock Sky,* (Viking Press, 1991).

John N. Gray, *Domestic Mandala: Architecture of Lifeworlds in Nepal,* (Ashgate Publishing, 2006).

Jonathan Gregson, *Massacre at the Palace. The Doomed Royal Dynasty of Nepal,* (Miramax Books, 2002).

Mahendra Lawoti, *The Maoist Insurgency in Nepal: Dynamics and Growth in the Twenty-first Century,* (Routledge, 2009).

PAKISTAN

Stephen Cohen, *The Idea of Pakistan,* (Brookings Institution Press; 2nd edition, 2006).

Husain Haqqani, *Pakistan: Between Mosque And Military,* (Carnegie Endowment for International Peace, 2005).

Arif Jamal, *Shadow War: The Untold Story of Jihad in Kashmir,* (Melville House, 2009).

Adrian Levy, *Deception: Pakistan, the United States, and the Secret Trade in Nuclear Weapons,* (Walker & Company, 2007).

Bibliography

Greg Mortenson, *Three Cups of Tea,* (Penguin ([Non-Classics]), 2007).

Ahmed Rashid, *Descent into Chaos: The United States and the Failure of Nation Building in Pakistan, Afghanistan, and Central Asia,* (Viking Adult, 2008).

Mary Anne Weaver, *Pakistan, In the Shadow of Jihad and Afghanistan,* (Farrar, Straus and Giroux, 2003).

SRI LANKA

William Clarance, *Ethnic Warfare in Sri Lanka and the U.N. Crisis,* (Pluto Press, 2007).

R. B. Herath, *Sri Lankan Ethnic Crisis: Towards a Resolution,* (Trafford Publishing, 2006).

Pradeep Jeganathan, *At the Water's Edge,* (South Focus Press, 2004).

Michael Ondaatje, *Anil's Ghost: A Novel,* (Vintage, 2001).

John Richardson, *Paradise Poisoned: Learning About Conflict, Terrorism and Development from Sri Lanka's Civil Wars,* (International Centre for Ethnic Studies, 2005).

Stanley Jeyaraja Tambiah, *Sri Lanka—Ethnic Fratricide and the Dismantling of Democracy,* (University of Chicago Press, 1991).

Margaret Trawick, *Enemy Lines: Warfare, Childhood, and Play in Batticaloa,* (University of California Press, 2007).

Mark P. Whitaker, *Learning Politics From Sivaram: The Life and Death of a Revolutionary Tamil Journalist in Sri Lanka,* (Pluto Press, 2007).

Deborah Winslow and Michael D. Woost (eds.), *Economy, Culture, and Civil War in Sri Lanka,* (Indiana University Press, 2004).

Index

Index

Index